Boko Haram

Boko Haram

THE PAST OF THE PRESENT UPHEAVAL

Moses E. Ochonu

UNIVERSITY OF CALIFORNIA PRESS

University of California Press
Oakland, California

© 2026 by Moses E. Ochonu

All rights reserved.

Library of Congress Cataloging-in-Publication Data

Names: Ochonu, Moses E. author
Title: Boko Haram : the past of the present upheaval / Moses E. Ochonu.
Description: Oakland, California : University of California Press, [2026] |
   Includes bibliographical references and index.
Identifiers: LCCN 2025027937 (print) | LCCN 2025027938 (ebook) |
   ISBN 9780520417687 cloth | ISBN 9780520417694 paperback |
   ISBN 9780520417700 ebook
Subjects: LCSH: Boko Haram—History | Terrorism—Nigeria,
   Northern—Religious aspects | Jihad—History | Religious
   militants—Nigeria, Northern | Islam and politics—Nigeria, Northern
Classification: LCC HV6433.N62 B64 2026 (print) | LCC HV6433.N62
   (ebook) | DDC 363.32509669/5—dc23/eng/20250922
LC record available at https://lccn.loc.gov/2025027937
LC ebook record available at https://lccn.loc.gov/2025027938

GPSR Authorized Representative: Easy Access System Europe,
Mustamäe tee 50, 10621 Tallinn, Estonia, gpsr.requests@easproject
.com

35 34 33 32 31 30 29 28 27 26
10 9 8 7 6 5 4 3 2 1

Contents

Acknowledgments		vii
	Introduction: Boko Haram Beyond the Spectacle of Violence	1
1.	Before Boko Haram: Contexts and Catalysts	33
2.	Reform and Rejection	71
3.	Boko Haram's Antimodernism Historicized	109
4.	Combat, Captives, and Coping	154
	Epilogue: Historical Speculations on Boko Haram's Future	199
Notes		219
Bibliography		247
Index		269

Acknowledgments

This book has zig-zagged its way to publication. Along the way, it mutated, expanded, and shrank. It was also enriched by many conversations and archives.

One colleague who contributed the most to the conversations that shaped aspects of this book is Abdulbasit Kassim. When I recruited him into the project as a coauthor, he was deeply committed to its realization. Over several years, in several conversations, he engaged me on different aspects of the Boko Haram insurgency. Unfortunately, he had to withdraw as coauthor for personal reasons. As I drafted and redrafted the chapters of this book, our conversations replayed in my head, and his published works on Boko Haram provided a rich intellectual reference for my analyses and explorations.

The book took almost a decade to conceptualize, write, revise, and bring to publication. During that time, I accumulated a lot of intellectual debt. Farooq Kperogi, Toyin Falola, and many other Nigerianist colleagues expanded my perspectives and horizons.

The works of Elisha Renne, Ebenezar Obadare, Olufemi Vaughan, Alexander Thurston, Mohammed Sani Umar, Jennifer Lofkrantz, Andrea Brigaglia, Murray Last, and Abiodun Alao on religious experiences in

Nigeria and on aspects of Northern Nigerian Islamicate culture helped me to think more critically about the place of Boko Haram in Nigerian and Northern Nigerian religious history.

Jack Fidelis was a productive research assistant. He used his vast network in the Nigerian Northeast to facilitate interviews with Nigerian Army soldiers and "rehabilitated" Boko Haram fighters.

The book benefited from the feedback of colleagues and students at the University of Pittsburgh, who were my audience as I presented the earliest iteration of the paper that burgeoned into this book. I thank Yolanda Covington for giving me the opportunity to preview several of the points in this book to an engaged audience at that institution.

I am grateful to Douglas Anthony for inviting me to give a presentation to students and faculty at Franklin and Marshall College on Boko Haram. The feedback from him, his students, and faculty helped me, at an early stage of this project, to sharpen my thoughts and explore new angles.

I presented a third version of the nucleus of this book as a public lecture in Vanderbilt University in 2017. Students and faculty offered perceptive and probing comments and questions that caused me to expand and deepen my analysis.

My colleagues in the History Department at Vanderbilt University, especially Tasha Rijke-Esptein, Samuel Dolbie, David Wasserstein, and Leor Halevi, provided collegial intellectual support that kept me going and the project on track.

Finally, the patience and nurturing love of my family gave me the energy to see to the completion of this book. They deserve much of the credit for this book being in print.

Introduction

BOKO HARAM BEYOND THE SPECTACLE OF VIOLENCE

On the night of April 14, 2014, militants of the Nigerian Salafi–Jihadi group Boko Haram kidnapped 276 female students from Government Secondary School, Chibok, Borno State, northeastern Nigeria, as the girls prepared for their secondary school exit exams in their dormitory. Hardened nomadic bush fighters, the militants knew the lay of the land and struck with the knowledge that the school was unprotected, isolated, and hemmed in by the Borno wilderness. A few girls managed to escape by scaling fences, hiding in the dark, and running into the surrounding bush undetected, but most were abducted by the militants. Later, a few more girls, taking advantage of the chaotic journey that followed and consciously risking their lives, jumped off the vehicles of the militants and raced away, managing to escape the hail of bullets the insurgents unleashed on them. The abduction shocked the world. For many people outside Nigeria, it was the event that acquainted them with Boko Haram or alerted them to the group's existence. For Nigerians, the act served to calcify a growing perception of Boko Haram as a group of militants committed to irrational and unrestrained violence. The resulting national and global outrage focused new attention on Boko Haram and its ideology.

For its part, Boko Haram remained defiant and defended the abduction in the face of global condemnation. In one of his bombastic video messages, Abubakar Shekau, the group's leader at the time, pronounced that the girls should not have been attending a secular school and would now be married off to Boko Haram suitors. Boko Haram's rejection of the near-universal denunciation of the girls' kidnapping intensified global indignation and further amplified the #BringBackOurGirls movement, which sprouted spontaneously to help secure the girls' release.

Boko Haram's explanation of the kidnapping as a legitimate undertaking in the context of jihad against a secular, un-Islamic Nigerian state left many confused and drew unequivocal rebuke, including from some Islamic authorities. For many observers, the action of Boko Haram was a mystery, an unsettling occurrence in the present with no discernible linkage to history and no precedent in the past. For those who had limited or no knowledge of the group and the history of jihadist militancy in Northern Nigeria, this was a phenomenon both new and foreign. Boko Haram's vigorous defense of the abduction triggered questions in the minds of local and international observers regarding the genealogy and ideology of the group. For many Nigerians the predation of Boko Haram, unsparing and venal in its manifestation, was shocking precisely because it seemed to lack a local historical frame of reference, a precedent that could render it legible and historically foreground the outrage against it. For others, however, Boko Haram's self-declared jihad resonated into a long, local, contested historical memory of religious militancy dating back to the nineteenth century.

This book makes sense of these two seemingly contradictory perceptions of Boko Haram. It analyzes Boko Haram's simultaneous connection to and disconnection from a complex history of religious dissidence and militancy in Northern Nigeria. In the weeks and months after Chibok, and as Boko Haram held on to the girls and declared them captives of war to be enslaved according to Islamic rules of war, it dawned on Nigerians that this was no ordinary kidnapping for ransom but an ideological act, prompting several questions: Where did these militants come from, and what motivated them? Who or what inspired such a ruthless group of militants? Was there a history of militancy that could both illuminate and challenge Boko Haram's self-proclaimed violent jihad? How can we explain Boko Haram within and against the contested and contentious religious pasts of the geographical site of its operation? These questions are still with us fifteen years after the insurgency began, and cannot be properly addressed without historicizing Boko Haram, framing the militant movement in a longer history, and posing historical questions about it.

First, as a militant reformist movement, Boko Haram is motivated by some of the same moral revulsion against the religious, political, and socioeconomic status quo, and by the same professed political end goal, as the nineteenth-century jihad led by Usman Dan Fodio. Both movements are ideologically anchored in rejectionist angst toward the perceived evils of bad governance, syncretism, injustice, corruption, and poverty. Both share a desire to cure those evils by installing a new moral order of "pure" Islam underwritten by Sharia legal principles.[1] Second, Boko Haram was seeking to revive a "deeply rooted historical precedent and resonance for a caliphate in Nigeria and neighboring countries,"[2] of which the Dan Fodio–led jihad was, in some ways, a practical culmination in the nineteenth century.[3] Third, by its own proclamation, Boko Haram sought to create a replica of the defunct Sokoto Caliphate, albeit largely on territory previously controlled by the older Kanem-Bornu Muslim state. Lastly, Boko Haram has consciously appropriated the living legacy of that caliphate since it "seeks legitimacy and inspiration from Dan Fodio, the Fulani founder of [that] caliphate."[4]

For Boko Haram, the Dan Fodio jihad was a model of a jihad that succeeded not only in overthrowing a political order of unbelief but also in forging Muslim unity in a single caliphate while engineering a new moral system grounded in the Sharia:

> In those days, it was the *Shari'a* that was the practice in this country. Dan Fodio and other Islamic scholars carried out the *jihad* and ensured that Qur'anic law was implemented. Allah did not interfere with this situation until when our Muslim leaders accepted . . . the Europeans' secular constitution. Since that time, Allah took away the comfort and peace Muslims used to enjoy, [and] replaced it with suffering and poverty.[5]

In this passage Boko Haram's founder, Muhammad Yusuf, expresses a nostalgia for what he posits as an era of caliphal peace and prosperity brought on by the Sokoto jihad. He anchors this narrative of nostalgia on the statecraft of the Sokoto Caliphate, the largest polity assembled in nineteenth-century Africa.[6] The establishment of a caliphate, Yusuf argues, attracted providential blessings, which Allah withdrew from the Muslim community when colonization destroyed the caliphate and, along with it, infrastructures of the Sharia. For Yusuf, the beginning of the caliphate and its end in the crucible of colonial conquest were bookending events that signaled both the revival of a lost ideal of an Islamic society and the loss of that revived society.

This veneration of the Sokoto Caliphate tradition by Boko Haram contains two related claims: first, that secularity, Western education, and European modernity were responsible for the ascendancy of injustice in Muslim Northern Nigeria, and second, that Islamic practice in the region since the British colonial conquest had become polluted, recreating the conditions that necessitated the Dan Fodio–led jihad. This is a cyclical historical logic that, for Yusuf, pointed to the necessity, once again, of an armed Islamic revolution. The colonial destruction of the caliphate and the advent of a "secular constitution" inaugurated "suffering and poverty" and other vices. According to Yusuf, these events, taken together, significantly de-Islamized the polity, including Islamic leadership. Yusuf was strategically signaling and reinforcing the popular perception that the Sokoto Caliphate is the baseline of Islamic statecraft in this part of the world, and that its erasure by colonialism marked the beginning of the current troubles plaguing Muslim-majority Northern Nigeria.

Boko Haram would extend this critique of the postcolonial Islamic status quo in Northern Nigeria to the current sultan of Sokoto, Sa'adu Abubakar, a direct descendant of Dan Fodio. Yusuf claimed that the sultan "does not follow the Islamic system of government, and therefore should not use the title *Sarkin Musulmi* [leader of the Muslim faithful] but should simply be called *Sarkin Sokoto* [king of Sokoto]."[7] This critique was as bold as it was revealing of Boko Haram's rhetorical maneuver within a local tradition of reform and revival.

Boko Haram stripped the current sultan and other Muslim leaders of their legitimizing symbolic connections to the Sokoto Caliphate, and positioned itself as the legitimate heir to the Sokoto jihad reform tradition. The group was trying to revive the lost caliphate, something that Muslim leaders in the region had, in Yusuf's assessment, failed to do in colonial times and in the decades since the end of colonization. This was, of course, an intellectual and political play for legitimacy and popular support on

Yusuf's part. However, it also demonstrates Boko Haram's keen awareness of the enduring politico-religious resonance of the Sokoto Caliphate tradition in Northern Nigeria, and the fact that subsequent reformers are inevitably compared to and judged against that tradition in the region's Muslim popular consciousness.

Boko Haram's self-positioning within the regional reformist history that the Sokoto jihad emblematizes is complicated. This complexity points to significant differences between the two reformist movements, which are separated by two centuries. While Boko Haram shares or professes the same moral rejection of forms of politics, governance, and religious conduct that the leaders of the Sokoto jihad invoked as the justifications for their reformist movement in the nineteenth century, the group's reformist agenda is more expansive than that of the Fodiawa.[8] As will be demonstrated in this book, Boko Haram's implacable opposition to Western education, secular ideas and ideology, the material and symbolic signifiers of Euro-American modernity, and the pragmatic moral complexities of governance in a politically diverse and multiethnic polity directly contradicts major aspects of the Fodiawa reformist creed and statecraft.

This book explores this complicated history of connection and divergence. This history clarifies Boko Haram's flourishing, from its preaching phase to its jihad phase, as part of a long, nonlinear history, as well as its jarring divergence from precedents of Muslim reformism and dissidence in Northern Nigeria. It moves between critical analysis of Boko Haram's self-narration within existing traditions and analysis of parallels and contradictions, convergences and divergences, and similarities and differences between the movement and previous dissidents in the region. The analysis examines the historical backgrounds to present-day jihadism represented most visibly by Boko Haram. The chapters unravel the past of the present upheaval, working from the hypothesis that the current Islamist rebellion connects circumstantially to a long history of Islamic reform and dissidence in Northern Nigeria.[9]

Boko Haram did not emerge in a historical vacuum. For this reason, the complex religious, political, and socioeconomic processes that birthed the movement should be examined within the long trajectory of Islamic reform and counterreform in Northern Nigeria. This explanatory imperative is what drives this book. It is important to consider the historical backdrops to and precedents for today's jihadism. Doing so does not entail positing causality or linear connections, but it demands that continuities and ruptures be reconstructed, as well as the interplay between them. It calls for discerning historical tropes and delineating enduring rhetorical patterns that enable present-day reformers to thrive and plausibly formulate their agenda. Such an analysis must consider the ways in which past reform efforts—armed and unarmed—and the ideational norms they established created conditions that present reformers can leverage, exploit, or rhetorically mine to support their projects.

The following chapters connect the dots between the present and the past. This analytical endeavor of historicizing Boko Haram and situating it in a more extended regional history of peaceful and militant Islamic reform is structured into three main categories: modernity and contestations around it; warfare and the ethos of religious war-making; and related processes of captivity in the context of religious warfare. In examining these three aspects of Boko Haram's twenty-first-century jihadism, the book considers the ways in which the present militants' engagement with and deployment of these three practices and rhetorical modes both recall and challenge how previous reformers approached these same phenomena.

Much of the current scholarly and popular literature on Boko Haram caters to two overlapping impulses, reflecting either the understandably emotive perspective of a majority of the Muslim population of Northern Nigeria or a "security and terrorism studies" outlook. In both of these frames Boko Haram is presented solely as a problem to be solved. While these approaches are reductive, since they equate the violent aspect of Boko Haram with its complex whole, the focus in this book is not so much a critique of these perspectives as it is rooted in concerns that transcend them. Here Boko Haram is viewed as a legitimate phenomenon of religious dissidence and as one of the corporate actors in a long-running drama of religious reform and dissidence in Northern Nigeria.

A PRIMED RELIGIOUS MARKETPLACE?

In illustrating the point that Boko Haram emerged from a tense religious landscape defined by a sense of diminishing Muslim piety and a hunger for reform, societal change, and Muslim political ascendance, a few interrelated vignettes are advanced. The first occurred in Kano in the aftermath of the 9/11 attacks. In the months and years that followed, many families named their newborn male children Osama to demonstrate their reverence for bin Laden, whom they lionized as a hero of Islam in the face of Western neocolonial maneuvers in the Muslim world.[10] On October 19, 2001, the *Weekly Trust* newspaper, a Northern Nigerian publication, published a news report titled "Price of bin Laden's Portraits Hikes in Kano." The gist of the report, as the headline suggests, was that "as a result of the increasing popularity of Osama bin Laden in Kano, especially among the youth, portraits of the man the United States government alleges is the prime suspect in the September 11 bombings of the World Trade Center and the Pentagon have now become so sought after to the extent that people who trade in them have hiked the prices."[11]

What do we make of these events? In and of itself, no single story or set of stories demonstrates or indicates the existence of an ideological landscape conducive to the rise of Boko Haram or any other militant religious group, but two things are worth noting. These events coincided with a growing aspirational longing for jihad, capaciously defined, and a caliphate. They occurred in the context of disenchantment with the secular Nigerian state and the growth of revivalist strains of political Islam that had already been mainstreamed in Northern Nigeria in the previous two decades. These related currents created conditions in which the 9/11 attacks resonated with particular emotional appeal since Northern Nigerian Muslims felt that, locally and internationally, their faith community was under assault from Western imperialist and secular pressures.

The ensuing proliferation of what one could call jihad discourse and consciousness was boosted by the American military action in Afghanistan and Iraq. This further inflamed passions throughout the Islamic world and seemed to confirm the narratives of Muslim victimhood in which Muslims in Kano articulated their understanding of the 9/11 attack and its alleged protagonist. However, there were earlier signifiers of jihad discourse and its normalization as a language of Muslim revivalism and grievance. One example can be found in the anthem of the Muslim Students' Society of Nigeria (MSSN), widely recited by Muslim youths in secondary and tertiary institutions across Nigeria:

> I pledge to Islam, my religion
> To be faithful, loyal, and honest
> To serve Islam with all my power
> And I pray for Allah's assistance
> I have testified that there is no God (x2)
> There is no God except Allah and His prophet Rasul Allah.
> I have promised to be a Muslim
> I have promised to work for Islam
> I have the promise to serve Islam
> So that we may get eternal bliss
> We want Quran as the constitution
> We want Hadith as the constitution
> We want Quran as the constitution
> We will no more accept theories
> Human theories are barbarisms
> Human theories are barbarisms
> Human theories aimless theories
> We will no more accept theories
> Oh, you brothers, jihad is coming
> Oh, you brothers, jihad is coming
> Oh you sisters, jihad is coming
> We will no more accept theories
> In sha Allah

Today memories of neojihad popular Muslim discourse and the ideological crystallization that enabled it have been largely erased from the official histories of modern Northern Nigerian Islamic revivalism.[12] The projihad antecedents of some clerics have also been largely excised from ongoing debates on extremism, radicalism, and jihadism in Northern Nigeria, in part because the clerics later took a stand against Boko Haram, some of them paying a heavy price for doing so.[13] Jihad discourse was variegated because the word meant different things to different Northern Nigerian Muslims at different times. Its work as a signifier, a rhetorical instrument of sociopolitical mobilization to fight injustice, and an idiom for religious revival and purification was as ubiquitous as its signaling of reformist militancy, if not more so.

The road from the religious environment that praised bin Laden for standing up to defend Muslims against Western imperialist military maneuvers to Boko Haram was thus convoluted and nonlinear. Yet broad connections are discernible if one follows the actors who moved specifically between the worlds of Salafi reformism and that of jihadi-Salafism, rhetorically exiting one and entering or reentering the other as personal circumstances and local and global ideological currents evolved. Furthermore, these examples raise some important questions about the ideological milieu in which Boko Haram emerged, and the theater in which its ideologues spoke and wrote their creed. These events and episodes collectively demonstrate that the Northern Nigerian Muslim public sphere had already developed proclivities toward the ideational aspirations of Muslim revivalism by the early 2000s, even if the question of armed jihad as a legitimate instrument of reform remained contested. Why did Northern Nigeria become an epicenter of political Islam and reformist Salafism in the late 1990s and early 2000s? Why did some Muslims there develop what one might call a jihad consciousness and a concomitant discourse of jihad as one instrumental option of local and international sociopolitical redress?

This analysis explains the historical processes by which this religious landscape evolved and created a receptive environment for the populist Salafi jihadism of Boko Haram. Boko Haram's success in capitalizing on this religious environment and further steering it toward the incubation of armed and unarmed jihadism at the grassroots level explains one side of the picture. On the other side, it should be pointed out that the existence of this Muslim public sphere that was saturated by proreform sympathies, whether these sympathies were expressed in the context of local or global events and confrontations, points to a more profound history of ideological, theological, and reformist evolutions in Northern Nigeria, one that needs to be understood as a condition for fully situating the emergence of Boko Haram. This volume explains this history in all its convoluted, confusing, and complicated unfolding.

The purpose is to ask why Northern Nigeria arrived at the juncture that made the above-mentioned neojihad public spectacles and commemorations possible. The working premise is that this religious public sphere in the early 2000s connects, however tenuously, forward to Boko Haram's full emergence as a jihadist movement, and backward to a long history of the gradual but discernible reformist transformation of Northern Nigerian Islam. The starting point for providing answers to the question of connection and divergence between old and new reformist projects is in exploring the histories of three ideas and practices that feature prominently in Boko Haram's repertoire and that of earlier Muslim reformers in the region: antimodernist discourse; the philosophy of warfare and military organization; and processes of war-related captivity.

THE CASE FOR HISTORICAL CONNECTION

"Quietist" Salafi clerics were no doubt instrumental in the recent processes that established a new revivalist Islamic culture in Northern Nigeria.[14] At the same time, the theological creeds of the Salafi clerics and the religious activists who embraced political Islam did not emerge from a historical void, nor were they a product of a swift infusion of foreign ideologies into Northern Nigerian Islam. There is a discernible Northern Nigerian reformist tradition with its own complex history. This reformist history is a precursor to more recent Salafi-ization of the Northern Nigerian milieu. The first two chapters of this book outline this history and its convoluted connections to the present insurgency. While the analysis of this historical tapestry is not intended to be read as a linear progression, I argue that the ideational transformations resulting from successive reformist projects made the Boko Haram moment, if not Boko Haram itself, possible.

Boko Haram maps onto the regional history of reform in several respects but also rejects and deviates from it in marked ways. This fraught history of connection and tension makes it impossible to analyze Boko Haram outside this overarching historical universe. In some ways, Boko Haram is the violent, twenty-first-century iteration of a long intra-Islamic struggle for space, power, and reformist legitimacy in Northern Nigeria. After the Fodiawa jihad of the early nineteenth century, this struggle had been largely nonviolent, exegetical, theological, polemical, and political until jihadi-Salafism interjected itself into the contested space and reshaped the terrain of debate and the stakes involved. The analysis below demonstrates the ways in which Boko Haram, even while being rooted in this history of reform and rejection, represents both a tactical and theological shift in the long tapestry of Islamic revival in Northern Nigeria.

This book explores a generational reformist critique of what purists and reformers regarded as betrayal within the Northern Nigerian Islamic tradition, a critique inspired by both local and external political and theological currents. The nexus of theological innovation and generational reformist impulses illuminates Boko Haram's emergence and evolution. In this long history, successive reformers critiqued the existing orthodoxy on two main grounds: *shirk* (polytheism and idolatry) and betrayal of the faith. The writings of Usman Dan Fodio, considered the intellectual and theological standard that subsequent reformers tried to replicate and emulate, pioneered the tradition of promoting a fuller conformity to the prophetic tradition (*Sunna*) while condemning *bid'a* (sinful innovation) and critiquing syncretism. His writings, some of which are analyzed in the chapters of this book, are rife with cautions against innovation and admonishment to the faithful to uphold the *Sunna* in its most complete and purest form.[15]

Dan Fodio posited a critique of hypocrisy as a central part of his teachings, making it the subject of an entire treatise. His pioneering theological critique of syncretism and *bid'a* established the textual and ideational basis for considering some Muslims inadequately committed to the revealed canon and the *Sunna*, thereby qualifying them for anathematization and excommunication (*takfīr*). In fact, as Dan Fodio's jihad progressed, he extended the designation of takfir to established and even reformist Muslim scholars and scholar-merchants who opposed his movement on religious grounds, assigning them to the same category as the Hausa rulers he had named as relapsed Muslims.[16] This foundational and paradigmatic intellectual precedent made it possible for a vast array of reformers spanning several generations, as well as political opportunists claiming the mantle of reform, to discredit and then attack Muslims representing an established form of Islamic practice that reform-minded purists considered corrupted. Boko Haram's theological and ideological evolution and claims advertise the movement's complicated relationship with this historical precedent and its inspirational and oppositional emergence in relation to the longue durée of jihad in Northern Nigeria.

THE FODIAWA JIHAD AND ITS LEGACIES

In the first decade of the nineteenth century a group of clerics of Fulani origin, led by Usman Dan Fodio, relied on the support of Fulani nomads and poor Hausa farmers to overthrow the Hausa Muslim dynasties of Northern Nigeria. This jihad birthed the Sokoto Caliphate, the largest West African polity since the Songhai Empire. The Fodiawa jihad was one in a long line of jihads inspired by the Qadiriyya Sufi brotherhood and intended to establish an Islamic orthodoxy defined in terms of untrammeled piety and a just political and social order modeled on Sharia.[17]

If the jihad itself did not supply an example for Boko Haram, the instructional writings of Dan Fodio and his family members established seminal theological precedents that future reformers could invoke. In *Wathīqa (ila jamī') ahl al-Sūdān*, Dan Fodio issued a set of clerical decrees that laid out both the guidelines for the jihad and the political and juridical hierarchy of the caliphate that was emerging from it. The document prescribed attacking a ruler "who has not abandoned the religion of Islam" but "who mingles the observances of Islam with the observances of heathenism, like the kings of Hausaland for the most part."[18] Dan Fodio declared that it was lawful to make war against Muslims who attacked the reformist militants, but that it was unlawful to enslave such Muslims. This issue would become the basis of justificatory rhetoric and contestations within Boko Haram, as discussed later.

The most important textual precedent in the Fodiawa corpus for latter-day reformist movements looking to authenticate themselves through an appeal to locally resonant jihadi examples and histories is the *Bayān wujūb al-hijra 'alā 'l-'ibād*,[19] a voluminous, multichapter treatise Dan Fodio penned as a comprehensive guide to jihad. This text contains detailed guidelines for contemporary and future jihadis, instructions so detailed that a would-be dissident in the Northern Nigerian environment in any era could plausibly adopt them and secure instant credibility, given the scholarly and popular lionization of Dan Fodio's jihad, the reluctance to criticize his prescriptions, and the tendency to blame abuses and uncomfortable excesses of the jihad on deviants, opportunists, and hypocrites. This manual on jihad contains guidelines that are adaptable to many jihad epochs, contexts, and purposes. Much of the text is didactic and prescriptive, and there is hardly any logistical, military, or theological detail regarding the waging of militant jihad that the book does not cover. The chapters in the treatise focus on topics such as "who should be fought in jihad," "the methods of battle, the rule of fighting the infidels if they take their children or Muslims as shields," "kinds of spoils," "methods for distributing spoils," "the planning of war and its stratagem in jihad," "the rule of jihad," and "the rule of waxing proud when shooting, and chanting, mentioning one's name and yelling during jihad." These topics run the gamut of the militant jihad enterprise, and Dan Fodio's exegeses on them were intended as timeless prescriptive treatises whose validity was not restricted to the time of the Fodiawa jihad.

There is no evidence that Boko Haram or latter-day reformist and dissident movements, regardless of their methods, were directly inspired by or studiously followed the prescriptions laid out in Dan Fodio's jihad manifesto. However, manifestos and the *aqīda* (creed) that underpins them are malleable utilitarian ideational constructs that take on their own transhistorical lives. In the case of Dan Fodio's manifesto, the evidence is clear that the paradigms of responsible jihad conduct he espoused outlived his reform movement and remained useful to multiple generations of reformers and revivalists. The evidence for Boko Haram is overwhelming. Boko Haram leaders sporadically make ideational gestures to the Dan Fodio jihad, invoking and acknowledging it in video propaganda as an example, inspiration, and local precedent for their reformist commitments. In one particularly searing video treatise, Boko Haram propagandists located their own jihad within the historical practice of revival and reform pioneered by Dan Fodio's revolution and its culmination in the establishment of the Sokoto Caliphate.[20]

Similarly, Abubakar Shekau, Boko Haram's second leader, not only invoked the glories of the Sokoto Caliphate in a nostalgic recollection of an ideal Islamic society, he sought to rekindle Muslim angst regarding the British colonial defeat of the caliphate. Shekau suggested that the current Boko Haram rebellion not only continues and revives that truncated caliphal tradition of reform, but promises to avenge the humiliating defeat and restore the lost caliphate.[21] Strategic references to the Fodiawa creed indicate that the Boko Haram ideologues making them have read the Fodiawa jihad manifesto and other texts in the Fodiawa corpus. The ideologues of Boko Haram were explicit in their attempt to present themselves as heirs of the jihadist reformism of the Fodiawa jihad, while rejecting or being indifferent to historical religious figures deemed undesirable or whose images are disputed in the region's public religious imagination.

WHY NOT BORNU?

Why do Boko Haram ideologues appropriate the historiography and theology of the Fodiawa jihad to cultivate legitimacy despite the existence of competing narratives and other institutionalized discourses of jihad in their northeastern Nigerian region of provenance? What utility does the revival of the Fodiawa jihad offer to their understanding of political and religious struggles in Northern Nigeria that is lacking in the historiography of Kanem-Bornu? Why do Boko Haram radicals shun the proximate, older Islamic history of Bornu while actively and self-consciously attaching their dissident project to the Fodiawa reformist legacy? A careful exploration of Bornu's history, the history of religious warfare in northeastern Nigeria, and contemporary debates on the comparative Islamic stature of Bornu reveals some clues.

The region of Kanem-Bornu has a long history of religion-tinged internal and external rebellions that predated the nineteenth-century jihad of the Fodiawa. As part of their documentation of the religious history of Kanem-Bornu, prominent members of the Bornu 'ulamā,' including Ahmad Ibn Furtuwa, Muhammad Yanbu b. Ali b. al-Hajj Dunama, and Muhammad Salih b. Ishaq, wrote chronicles that are replete with dynastic feuds, civil wars, and the monomyth of iconic figures who consolidated political power and merged the two capitals of Kanem and Bornu through religious and quasi-religious warfare directed at those who were deemed to be outside the religious community of Bornu.

In *Ta'rīkh Mai Idris wa-Ghazāwatihī*, Ahmad Ibn Furtuwa documents the five expeditions of Mai Idris Alooma and his wars against the sultan of Bulala, Abdullahi b. Abduljalil b. Kadai, over the dominion of Kanem.[22] In *Ta'rīkh Birni Gazargamu*, written in 1658, Muhammad Salih b. Ishaq documents the life of Mai Ali b. al-Hajj Umar and his defense of the people of Gazargamu against the sultanate of Ahir. By several accounts, Bornu was a well-established Islamic polity and a political arena of religious warfare and reformist political projects. Ali Arkwayami's poem "Waqu'i al-Rābih" is a treatise on an important instance of rebellion and dissidence in Kanem-Bornu. The poem chronicles the activities of the neo-Mahdist and Sudanese warlord Rabih az-Zubayr ibn Fadl Allah who invaded and occupied Bornu. In eighty-eight verses, Ali Arkwayami provides a firsthand account of the campaign of Rabih in Wadai, Bagirmi, Kukawa, Dikwa, and Bornu. He narrates the prevailing moral breakdown in the region among the ruling class and their followers. This moral decadence, according to Ali Arkwayami, was the reason God unleashed Rabih as divine punishment.

Muhammad Yusuf, Shekau, and other leaders of Boko Haram were obviously familiar with this deep history of Islamic state-building and rebellion in the Bornu area. They were also acquainted with documented historical sources authored by prominent *ulamā* from Kanem-Bornu. Yet, Boko Haram leaders have rarely cited these references. On the few occasions that they have, they refrained from the political and religious appropriation of the centuries-old histories of Kanem-Bornu as a model for their armed jihad. The only exception is Mai Idris Alooma, whom Boko Haram celebrated for expanding the frontiers of Islam in the Lake Chad region. Most revealingly, Boko Haram's founding ideologues condemned Muhammad al-Amin al-Kanemi and other iconic figures in Kanem-Bornu for their alleged desecration of Islam. Boko Haram's attack on the Islamic bona fides of al-Kanemi, who was regarded—at least in Bornu aristocratic circles—as the great restorer of the Bornu Islamic heritage, is as significant as it is iconoclastically blunt.[23]

In his 2007 sermon "Tarihin Muslumai," Boko Haram's founder, Muhammad Yusuf, made several mutually complementary points. First, he sought to discredit the main nineteenth-century reformist figure in Borno's religious history—a contemporary of the Fodiawa. Instead of Borno Muslims' view of al-Kanemi as a pious, reformist Islamic empire builder, Yusuf, in a strategic piece of revisionist history, recast him as a marauding, slave-raiding usurper with no commitment to Islam and no clear reformist agenda. Stripping al-Kanemi of a reformer's garb justified Boko Haram's preference for a Sokoto inspirational reformist reference. It also aligned Boko Haram with the dominant perceptual index of reformist credibility in Northern Nigeria. Second, by highlighting al-Kanemi's alleged un-Islamic acts, Boko Haram hollowed out existing narratives of al-Kanemi as a promoter of Islam and Islamic statecraft. Third, Yusuf sought to rehabilitate the pre–al Kanemi Borno leadership as possessing more authentic Islamic credentials than al-Kanemi, who is widely regarded as a reformer who improved the Islamic state that the Mais, or rulers, of Kanem-Bornu had established and managed for centuries. In doing this, Muhammad Yusuf radically went against the grain of reputational perceptions of the two Borno dynasties. He rejected the conventional wisdom that the Mais represented a traditional, complacent, and, in some ways, syncretistic Islam while al-Kanemi reformed Bornu Islam into the modern age of revival and restoration. Yusuf was disavowing an unwritten analogy in Northern Nigerian Islamic discourse: that the Mais were to al-Kanemi what the prejihad Hausa rulers were to the Fodiawa.

Yusuf's pronouncement may have been a preemptive response to what he would have anticipated as the likely response of his Borno audience to his movement's veneration of the Sokoto tradition—questions about preferring a "foreign" Hausa-Fulani reformist tradition to a local Kanuri/Bornu one. One other factor may have played a role in Boko Haram's strong denunciation of the al-Kanemi tradition of reformist Islam and jihad. Pieri and Zenn, relying on the field notes of Ronald Cohen, a historian of Bornu, highlight the persistence of "non-Islamic" practices such as the use of charms and belief in magic in Muslim Borno.[24] Such practices are not unique to Bornu; they were prevalent in prejihad Hausaland and survived into the postjihad period. The difference was that the hegemony of the Fodiawa tradition in Muslim-majority Northern Nigeria canceled out any claims that such practices defined Hausaland after the jihad.

Two reasons are responsible for the wide acceptance of the claim that the jihad erased non-Islamic practices in Hausaland. First, the Fodiawa's own prolific scribal establishment of a hard moral binary between pre- and postjihad society in Hausaland. This discursive claim that the jihad stamped out non-Islamic practices in Hausaland, which had been a justification for the reform movement, is of course debatable, but it soon assumed a paradigmatic position in how the jihad and its impact on Hausaland were perceived. The second point is that the narrative of a morally and politically superior postjihad society in Hausaland, one that supplanted a decadent prejihad society and presented a glorious example for Muslim political organization and governance in the region, became a useful idiom in colonial and postcolonial Northern Nigerian regional politics dominated by the scions of the Sokoto Caliphate.

Yet another reason Boko Haram settled on the Fodiawa tradition as its historical frame of inspiration and reference is that, for centuries, Bornu has been in a struggle to demonstrate its Islamic authenticity to both internal and external actors, seeking recognition and acceptance as a Muslim polity. The prompt for these gestures of self-authentication and external credentialing is the skepticism that abounded outside Bornu about the kingdom's true Islamic status and the internal reputational insecurities that this perception fostered among Bornu's ruling elite. It was this same skepticism that had caused the rulers of the Sokoto Caliphate to attack parts of Bornu in their jihad, sparking textual recriminations between the two states (see chapter 1).

This baggage of perceptual inauthenticity has continued to plague the Bornu sphere even in the twenty-first century, as is evidenced by a widely read exchange between Kyari Tijanni and Sanusi Lamido Sanusi in *Daily Trust* in April 2003.[25] Aside from the wider contemporary resonance of the Fodiawa caliphate legacy in Northern Nigeria, which made it more appealing to Boko Haram ideologues, the histories of Islamic militancy, warfare, rebellion, and state-building in Bornu do not readily lend themselves to the contemporary jihadism of Boko Haram. For one thing, those Kanem-Bornu struggles were as political as they were religious, and could thus not be written neatly into the reformist rhetorical corpus of Boko Haram. For another, the rulers of Bornu neither proclaimed their statecraft nor the expansionist warfare of multiple rulers in explicitly religious terms as acts designed to purify the faith. For this reason, Bornu is rarely associated with explicit religious revivalism in the way the Fodiawa and the caliphate they built are.

For Boko Haram the Fodiawa reformist genealogy, with its overtly reformist creed, thus provided a perfect model while the credibility of the Bornu tradition was questionable.

One important caveat is in order here. As noted in chapter 4, and as Scott MacEachern argues, Boko Haram's violence maps onto a long history of predation, raiding, and nonstate violence in the Lake Chad and Mandara Mountains regions of northeastern Nigeria. Some of Boko Haram's military repertoire subconsciously extends and revives this history.[26] Because Boko Haram founders harbored the ambition of extending their reformist project to all of Northern Nigeria and eventually all of Nigeria, the Fodiawa/Sokoto reformist tradition was compatible with their ambition, and Bornu's was not. The Sokoto tradition and its enduring resonance in the present offered an inspirational template for Boko Haram's territorially ambitious reformist aspiration. Bornu's territorially limited reform would not have been effective as a historical and inspirational anchor for Boko Haram's expansive reformist agenda.

ARGUMENTS AND SCHOLARLY ENGAGEMENTS

Scholarly and popular writings on Boko Haram have documented the decade-and-a-half-old evolution of the movement and its transition from a dissident Salafi movement propounding the abstract virtues of jihad to one that deploys jihadism as its primary method for achieving its objectives.[27] My analysis builds on this body of knowledge by highlighting the historical dimensions of Boko Haram's rhetorical and practical jihad. This book presents answers to the question of how Boko Haram fits into and diverges from a long and muddled history of Islamic reform and dissidence in the region. The analysis establishes a convoluted, nonlinear road map to Boko Haram that includes a regional intellectual history of contestations, ideational developments, debates, reform, and militancy. It traces the histories of three major ideational rubrics central to Boko Haram's legitimization of its contemporary jihad, analyzing the continuities and ruptures in these three projects from the precolonial to the contemporary period.

Historian and anthropologist Murray Last is perhaps the first scholar to situate Boko Haram in the region's history of Islamic dissidence, and to identify parallels between the current insurgency and that of the Fodiawa jihad. For Last, dissent and dissidence, even of the violent type, is not unique to Boko Haram or other contemporary insurgent movements.[28] Rather, radical rebellions against existing religious orders have been a constant, evolving feature of Northern Nigerian Islamic history and of global Islamic history. According to Last, three factors make Muslim polities prone to cycles of rebellion and convulsions. The first is the existence of multiple perspectives on how the guiding, canonized revelation, sayings, knowledge, and traditions, collectively called the Sunna, should be interpreted and applied; how much, if any, innovations in technology and practices should be pragmatically permitted to accommodate evolving situations and circumstances; and debates about how to best replicate the example of the Muslim pioneers of the seventh century in contemporary Muslims' daily lives.

The second factor, Last explains, is the presence in every historical epoch of Islamic history of Muslim groups who self-designate as *Ahl al-sunna*, people committed to upholding, defending, and practicing the prescriptive and exemplary contents of the Sunna by "rejecting some key dimensions of contemporary life—whether technologies or ideas," including modern secular government, by refusing to adapt to modernity, and by steadfastly proclaiming that "any compromise is a denial of the Sunna."[29]

The third factor is the historical determination of secular and theocratic governments to "use their security forces to eliminate any *ahl al-sunnah* that resorts to violence," with "that counter-violence then escalat[ing] the confrontation" since the insurgents could plausibly designate the government as *kufr* or *Taghut* (a non-Muslim, idolatrous entity persecuting Muslims), legitimizing the killing of anyone associated with the government and the destruction of all government-allied institutions and infrastructures.[30] For successful jihads such as the Fodiawa reform movement, this counteroffensive became even more imperative in the caliphate phase as several disillusioned, disappointed, and ambitious internal rebels, *'yan tawaye* in the language of postjihad rulers, emerged to oppose the policies and suzerainty of caliphate and emirate rulers.

On the foregoing premise, Last proposes that we understand Boko Haram in historical context as connected to the Fodiawa legacy, not in terms of doctrinal inspiration but in the context of the persistence of dissidence and the escalatory violent response of the state. In particular, Last situates Boko Haram in the history of the second or secondary phase of the Fodiawa jihad after the death of Dan Fodio. In that period several commanders fought the caliphate rulers for independence, violently rejected the suzerainty of the caliphate rulers, and defied or defeated efforts to bring them back to the caliphal fold, while several heterodox, insurgent theological and sectarian tendencies asserted themselves against the caliphate doctrinal orthodoxy.[31]

The approach here, which highlights circumstantial and opportunistic inspiration and parallels, complements Last's explanation of the dissent and disagreements that led to the constitution and reconstitution of the Fodiawa and postjihad *ahl al-sunna* and other insurgent tendencies that often occurred at the doctrinal level before manifesting in the political and sometimes military realms. Similarly, the violent counterinsurgency of state entities, which, as Last rightly posits, exacerbated or prolonged Muslim dissidence in the past, sometimes stemmed from the states' refusal to acknowledge, let alone engage, alternative doctrinal and ideological formations. Such refusal to accord legitimacy to the doctrinal positions of rivals and insurgents, as was the case in the caliphate in several instances, often rested on commitments to established, canonized caliphal doctrines of appropriate Muslim political and moral conduct.

Historicizing Boko Haram entails exploring two interrelated phenomena. The first is the ways in which jihads by their nature provoke violent state repressions that unwittingly vindicate the rhetoric of insurgents. They also incite internal dissidence that sometimes triggers offshoot jihads against such internal disruptors or *'yan tawaye*. The second phenomenon is the fact that most religious rebellions stem from doctrinal and ideological disputes, which in turn elicit retaliatory state violence. It is worth analyzing the parallels between the doctrinal claims of the Fodiawa jihad against the Hausa rulers and its subsequent violent responses to internal rebels, and the jihad of Boko Haram against the Nigerian state and its ruthless response to internal dissidence.

In the case of Boko Haram, the relevance of Last's secondary jihad thesis is borne out by the internal rebellions that have provoked a parallel internal jihad, even as the jihad was directed outward against the state, non-Muslims, and so-called bad Muslims. The Nigerian state's violent response to Boko Haram's early, largely nonviolent expressions is also clearly reminiscent of the way that the reaction of Hausa rulers to Dan Fodio's *Ahl al-sunna* community exacerbated the conflict. These two factors clearly connect Boko Haram to the Fodiawa jihad and its history. An additional factor to consider in analyzing the parallels between Boko Haram and the Fodiawa jihad is the fact that the contemporary militant group actively connects itself both ideologically and tactically to the Fodiawa jihad and the caliphate that resulted from it.

Although this is the first book-length discussion of the historical context of Boko Haram, the work complements three recent works that have also explored the issue of Boko Haram's connection and divergence from the history of Islamic insurgency in the region.[32] This analysis joins these works to explain the historical factors and processes that enabled Boko Haram to emerge, and on which the movement continues to draw inspiration and legitimation wittingly and unwittingly. The ways in which Boko Haram is both a new and different Islamist rebellion are explored. The approach is grounded in a conscious decision to engage Boko Haram on its own terms, using its own proclamations, statements, rhetoric, preachings, and actions as points of departure rather than relying on nonmembers' perspectives and perceptions of the movement.

The movement is considered a legitimate actor in the theological and ideological contestations of a fast-evolving Northern Nigerian Islamic landscape, with a long history that should be understood alongside today's schisms. Accordingly, Boko Haram is discussed as part of a long historical and ideological process of Islamic reform and revolution in Northern Nigeria. In this process, a common conventional wisdom about Boko Haram is challenged—the belief that its militancy is an entirely new phenomenon in Northern Nigeria. The overarching argument here is that Boko Haram emerged from and is a participant in long-running historical and ideological processes and ruptures within the Muslim community in Northern Nigeria, but at the same time Boko Haram's ideological and military repertoires extend and complicate old traditions.

Outside of Nigeria, Boko Haram remains a largely unknown entity, shrouded in mystery and understood through familiar caricatures and stereotypes of jihadists as irrational nihilists and sometimes through Islamophobic tropes. Because of the relative geostrategic unimportance of the Nigerian Northeast, the operational epicenter of Boko Haram, very few epistemological and logistical resources in the United States and other countries of the West have been devoted to understanding the Islamist insurgency in the region. The result has been a thirst for informed perspectives on a movement that, by some grisly indices, is the world's deadliest jihadist group. In the quest to understand Boko Haram and its motives, fantastical tales have emerged, concocted to provide comforting explanations.

The widespread curiosity about Boko Haram only adds new layers to the mysteries surrounding the movement as fabrications, exaggerations, and embellishments have become ways through which many people in and outside Nigeria make sense of the movement's atrocities. When a movement is as violent as Boko Haram and its various factions and offshoots, every exaggeration or fabrication concerning them seems plausible. Plausibility only incentivizes more exaggerations and sensationalizing, producing a continuous loop of misunderstanding. The task of explaining the movement's origins and locations in particular ideologies and histories is magnified by the lingering misconceptions and sensational theories surrounding it.

Boko Haram is not inscrutable; it is a rather garrulous movement. It announces every step it takes and every attack it carries out, and advances ample theological, historical, and ideological explanations, rationalizations, and polemics as clues to why it does what it does. Boko Haram produces and releases videos, audiotapes, and print pamphlets, and engages in public theological disputations, records of which exist in a dynamic but accessible multimedia archive. Sometimes pronouncements are made in advance of attacks and seminal actions in the insurgency. Many of these clues, signs, and messages are missed because many observers are preoccupied with the movement's spectacular atrocities or are victims of them. Others are so outraged that they dismiss any suggestion that the movement is a rational, calculating, and savvy actor with any connection to or origins in local religious histories and contestations.

Many Nigerians reject outright Boko Haram's claim that they are Muslim. Many Nigerian Muslims understandably reject the notion that Abubakar Shekau, the eccentric and unpredictable ideologue who led one faction of Boko Haram until his death in 2021, was a coreligionist or that a movement that seems to celebrate violence against other Muslims could be characterized as Muslim. Once Boko Haram's claim to a higher, purer form of Islamic devotion is rejected, many observers simply refuse to take the movement's theological and ideological claims seriously, preferring to regard it as a sinister internal enemy of Islam at best, and an externally unleashed monster mandated to destroy Islam and Muslims at worst. Even non-Muslim Nigerians, long accustomed to a different expression of Islam in the local milieu and groaning under the nondiscriminating violence of Boko Haram, hesitate to accord the movement serious, engaged attention. To study the movement, its motivations, goals, and aspirations is considered a dignifying gesture that confers credibility on its violent insurgency, or at least takes its claims seriously. These claims are seen to be incompatible with the realities of a modern secular Nigerian state struggling to manage the volatile religious diversity of its peoples.

The moral premise of this perspective is understandable, but I take a slightly different approach in this study. Rather than dismiss Boko Haram's claim to the mantle of Islamic reform, their claim is scrutinized in relation to claims made by previous generations of Muslim rebels, and in the context of a long history of Muslim reform, dissidence, and radical change in Northern Nigeria. The popular refusal to accord Boko Haram serious attention as a group comprised of rational actors produces an ignorance that is at once willful and incidental. It is willful because not knowing the depth and historical roots of such a violent movement provides comfort and establishes a belief that it is just a passing phase, a fad of dissidence that will unravel on its own, and a temporary burst of misguided apocalyptic religiosity rather than a deep-seated, well-entrenched ideological tendency. It is incidental because in refusing to consider Boko Haram a legitimate subject of inquiry many Nigerians have unwittingly developed blind spots regarding the movement, even as they grapple with its atrocities and reverberations across the country.

Whatever its basis and origins, ignorance of Boko Haram becomes, in a region largely unfamiliar with scorched-earth jihadist violence in contemporary times, a comforting framework that separates peoples and communities in Northern Nigeria from Boko Haram and repositions the movement as an external phenomenon, whether this separation is real or simply imagined for convenience. Willful popular ignorance becomes a way to cast Boko Haram jihadists as outsiders, people unconnected to the historical evolution of Northern Nigerian Islam, which was characterized by several phases of rebellion and heterodoxy that were similar in some respects to the ongoing Boko Haram insurgency. As soothing as claims and constructs that dehistoricize and decontextualize Boko Haram may be, this book shows that they are largely inaccurate, and that Boko Haram lends itself to historical comparison.

PHASES AND MODELS OF MUSLIM DISSIDENCE IN POSTCOLONIAL NIGERIA

In the effort to understand Boko Haram as part of a historical matrix of Islamic dissidence in Northern Nigeria and to situate the group in a broader analytical context, I have, for analytical convenience and for reading ease, created an intellectual historical map of four main phases of dissidence and reform in Northern Nigerian postcolonial Islam.

In the first model, Sheikh Abubakar Gumi and his Izala sect disrupted the Northern Nigerian Islamic scene not just with an anti-Sufi reformist message that sought to stamp out what they considered the rampant normalization of *bid'a* (sinful innovations), but also by employing politics in the service of Islam and vice versa. In the 1970s and 1980s Gumi sought to explore the symbiotic possibilities that existed between Nigerian secular politics and governance on the one hand, and his commitment to expanding the *Ummah* and protecting its interest within the wider adversarial power configurations of Nigeria on the other.

Under the slogan of *a shiga a gyara* (enter to reform), Gumi's Izala promoted Muslim participation in secular politics and encouraged Muslims to support their coreligionists in political contests. Izala scholars themselves rarely vied for political positions, but they backed Muslims they believed would support their goals of societal religious reform and the enthronement of Islamic values in governance. Much of this advocacy for reform was anchored on Gumi's strategic moderation of his anti-Sufism and a concomitant commitment to a unified Muslim political ascendancy as a means to accomplish Islamic societal reform (see chapters 2 and 3).

The second phase of postcolonial Islamic dissidence in Northern Nigeria was characterized by its overarching "Islam only" slogan and message. Several notable Northern Nigerian Islamic figures did not support Sheikh Abubakar Gumi's position regarding Muslim participation in secular politics. Under the campaign of "Islam Only," some of these figures, notably the academic Mallam Ibraheem Suleiman, argued that the political goals of Islam could not be accomplished under political structures inherited from colonialism. Muslims, they contended, had to establish parallel political structures and systems of governance to realize the ideal Islamic society in Nigeria. Throughout the 1980s this position defined the opinion articles Mallam Ibraheem Suleiman published in widely read Northern Nigerian newspapers such as *The New Nigerian*, *The Triumph*, and *Weekly Trust*, and in *Radiance*, the official magazine of the Muslim Students Society of Nigeria (MSSN).

In this phase of revivalist ferment, reform-minded Muslim youth who emerged from youth-led Islamic organizations such as MSSN and the Muslim Student Organization (MSO) studied and proselytized the literature of reformist Muslim scholars such as Hassan al-Banna, Sayyid Qutb, Zainab Ghazali, Hassan al-Hudaybi, Saeed Hawa, and other figures of Ikhwan in Egypt, Jamaat-e-Islami of Abū al-Aʿlā al-Mawdūdī in Pakistan, and the Ruhollah Khomeini of the Iranian revolution. In these wide-ranging engagements with the literatures and politics of international Muslim reform and revolution, the reformist youths, educated in both secular and Islamic modes of learning, began to explicitly articulate radical change as a nonnegotiable baseline of Islamic revival, positing this agenda in contrast to the "reform from the inside" engagement agenda of Sheikh Gumi and the Izala.[33]

The search for change and a revolutionary model to effect the desired change was a product of disillusionment. Reform-minded Muslim activists were searching for models of Islamic revolution they could draw from to inspire their own imagined Muslim futures in Nigeria. This search for a method and strategy took the conveners beyond the local Muslim milieu. They listened to speakers from diverse international Islamic contexts "on model Islamic movements like the Prophet's Model, the Khomeini's model, the Mahdiyya Model and the Sokoto (Shehu Usman's) model."[34] Unencumbered by sectarian divisions, reformist Muslim youth under the auspices of MSSN were influential in the activist Muslim grassroots. They sought to replicate, appropriate, and domesticate existing models of Islamic reform.

The Iranian revolution sparked uncommon revivalist zeal in Northern Nigerian Muslim youth. To satiate this zeal and fortify themselves intellectually, they traversed the sectarian and creedal divides of Islam to explore, consume, and internalize Islamic models of change and revival, and the modalities for building imagined ideal Islamic societies. A spokesperson of the Iranian revolution attended the 1980 Kano MSSN Conference. The Iranian ambassador to Nigeria at the time had already given speeches to Muslim groups to advertise the success of the Iranian revolution. Soon after, the Iranian outreach included scholarships that funded the study and immersive experience in Iran of several members of the MSSN and similar groups of educated Nigerian Muslim youth. One of those young men, Ibraheem El Zakzaky, an official of the Ahmadu Bello University MSSN and later its national executive, returned from Iran to consolidate the Islamic Movement of Nigeria (IMN). Zakzaky and other students at Ahmadu Bello University had founded the IMN shortly after the Iranian revolution in 1979 to use it as a platform for the propagation of Shia Islam in Nigeria, and for replicating the ideals of the Iranian revolution.

The international Islamic revolutionary vocabulary exported from the Iranian revolution to Muslim societies around the world proved a particularly potent lexical instrument as Muslim Northern Nigerian youths developed their "Islam Only" script of dissidence. However, they also openly claimed that, in urging Muslims to completely abstain from participating in the secular political structures of Nigeria and to engineer parallel ones, they were influenced by the Fodiawa political thought paradigm. The "Islam only" curriculum was an iteration of Muslim dissidence with the end goal of radical societal reconfiguration, but it stopped short of advocating armed revolutionary change. Although it never acquired hegemonic sway in the wider Muslim community, the "Islam Only" project endured in the rhetoric of Muslim reform activists, and the Islamic revolutionary imaginary it sparked remained in various forms in the Muslim community as it navigated the Nigerian present and imagined a new future of ascendant Islamic values and politics.

The third model of dissidence and reform was a complex one. In the 1990s and early 2000s Nigeria was undergoing a transition from military rule to electoral democracy, and popular sovereignty and participatory engagement were widely accepted political phenomena even in Muslim-majority Northern Nigeria. This placed Salafi clerics in the region in a difficult position regarding the question of accepting and participating in democratic institutions. Most of the Salafi figures in Saudi Arabia and Yemen whom the Nigerian Salafi clerics revered and considered authorities on the Salafi canon, notably Sheikh Muqbil bin Hādī, held the position that democracy, elections, and participation in secular politics were *Kufr al-Akbar*, nullifiers of Islamic identity.

It was easy for Salafi figures to endorse this view in Saudi Arabia, which has a monarchical system. However, Nigeria, with its ethnic and religious pluralism and its unfolding democratic practice, a result of a decade-long agitation for civilian democratic leadership, was not Saudi Arabia. Unlike their Salafi teachers in Saudi Arabia, the Salafi clerics in Nigeria could not openly call for a complete abstention from democracy, elections, or secular politics. Nor could Nigeria's Salafi clerics label these political processes as *Kufr al-Akbar* without legitimizing the theological position of Muhammad Yusuf and his emergent Boko Haram fringe reformist elements, who had become outlaws of sorts from mainstream Nigerian Salafism by the mid-2000s. Yusuf and his cohort of Salafi renegades openly challenged Nigerian Salafi clerics to take a clear stance on democracy, elections, and Muslim participation in secular politics. Yusuf had sufficient knowledge of the fatwa of the Salafi clerics in Saudi Arabia regarding secular electoral democracy. He challenged his Salafi teachers and mentors to express similar positions in Nigeria, a difficult pronouncement for the scholars to make because they were trying to reconcile their own Salafi reformist convictions and impulses with the pragmatic reality of secular democratic practice in Nigeria.

Understandably, but to Muhammad Yusuf's disappointment, the Salafi clerics opted for a middle position. They endorsed a stance that urged temporary support of Muslim coreligionists vying for political positions, a partial nod to Gumi's *a shiga a gyara* or "participate to reform" advocacy. However, unlike Abubakar Gumi, the Salafi clerics added an important caveat to their fatwa. Democracy, they argued, was un-Islamic, but for now Muslims lacked the power to establish a parallel political system reflective of the prescriptions of Sharia. Their fatwa was a product of pragmatic necessity. Its rationale was therefore the logic of *Maṣlaḥan* and *Ḍarūra*, the doctrines of temporary existential necessity in Islam. The clerics declared that Muslims should continue to participate in secular democracy in Nigeria until they attained the power to establish the ideal Islamic political system. The time frame for this conditional participation was not specified, but the ambiguity left the matter open-ended in addition to serving to demarcate mainstream Salafism from Boko Haram's hardline creed and praxis of total separation from and attacks on secular politics and statecraft.

This brings us to the phase of full-blown dissidence, the Boko Haram phase. In this model those Muslim dissidents who grew impatient with what they regarded as the failures of the previous models and were dissatisfied with the results of previous reformist dissidence opted for jihad against Nigeria's secular political system, envisioning a resuscitation of the *Khilafa*.

Yusuf and his cohort grew disillusioned about the capacity of decades-old models of Islamic reform to secure the political sovereignty of the Muslim community and the resuscitation of the defunct caliphate. For them the final straw was what they saw as the fence-sitting and prevarication of Salafi scholars. Their mantra of dissidence and rebellion was as simple as it was novel: Muslims had to wage jihad, an armed revolution, against the secular state and dismantle the secular political structures inherited from colonial times. This model of change, violent and implacable, has produced fratricidal killings, displacement, and the rupturing of previously stable communities in large swaths of Northern Nigeria.

SOURCES, ARCHIVES, AND SPECULATIVE COMPARATIVE HISTORY

For several years Abdulbasit Kassim, a scholar of West African Islamic history, has been collating and translating Boko Haram's multimedia archive from multiple avenues and sources. This archival corpus includes texts of speeches, audios of sermons, videos of teaching sessions, videos filmed in the aftermath of major attacks or in response to major developments globally or in Nigeria, photographs released as propaganda, and letters and correspondence between Boko Haram operatives and between them and Islamic State jihadists. This archive is growing, and new materials will need to be added. The product of this project is the seminal sourcebook *The Boko Haram Reader: From Nigerian Preachers to the Islamic State*, which he and Michael Nwankpa compiled and annotated. The sourcebook contains over eighty Boko Haram sermons and broadcasts transcribed and translated for the first time. These documents have informed some of the analysis in this book. I build on the sourcebook by grounding the transcribed and translated texts in a rich analytical fabric that explores the intellectual, religious, and social contexts of the topics discussed in the documents and audiovisual sources.

These translated sources provide new insights and understandings into Boko Haram's inner workings and ideological claims. They have also transformed the ways that researchers engage with the movement's history and evolution. Like this book, *The Boko Haram Reader* is an intervention designed to redirect scholarly focus to the texts produced by Boko Haram itself as a point of analytical departure. In order to understand what is driving Boko Haram and to grasp why it conducts itself in the way that it does, it is crucial not only to recognize as important the texts that the movement produces, but also to analyze them seriously and draw out salient insights that contribute to ongoing efforts to demystify the movement. In this respect, what the movement says about itself, how it says it, and how it invokes and manipulates theological polemics and historical traditions to legitimize its actions and discredit or confound its critics is an important analytical starting point.

This book builds on the important contribution of *The Boko Haram Reader*. I have translated and deployed other vernacular sources and English-language newspaper sources, and interpreted and mediated these sources to offer inferences and insights to those seeking a greater illumination of the Boko Haram phenomenon in relation to the broader history of Northern Nigerian Islamic reform, dissidence, and religious rebellion. In addition to this core Boko Haram archive, the analytical explorations here rely on a trove of Arabic sources, Hausa-language fatwas, transcribed oral interviews, written interviews, and many informal conversations from a diverse array of interlocutors. A growing body of secondary sources on the Boko Haram insurgency and its related issues provide the historiographic backdrop and foil for the analysis, arguments, and narratives in this book.

These sources offer a snapshot of Boko Haram's multiple self-conscious and accidental entanglements with past and present ideologies of dissent, dissidence, and rebellion. However, the comparative historical approach of this book required a deeper and more creative analytical intervention in the sources than a simple historical interpretation of sources entails. Although the analysis is grounded in an evidentiary quilt of diverse sources, interpretations have also benefited from informed speculations on the patterns, forms, and depths of connections and divergences between multiple waves of religious militancy in Northern Nigeria. Traditional source criticism and discourse analysis are supplemented, where necessary, with authorial analytical interventions to track and signal continuities, changes, through lines, and disruptions to those through lines. The analytical approach of speculative history is sporadically employed in this book. This analytical method is used to mitigate some obvious methodological challenges: deliberate silence on the part of militants about aspects of their insurgency, strategic exaggerations or understatements of outcomes, and propagandistic vilifications of adversaries and disagreeable interlocutors.[35]

The militants and dissident movements analyzed in this book were prolific producers of textual and nontextual narratives, but these sources are necessarily fragmentary, incomplete, and full of strategic silences and self-interested biases. They are also contextually grounded in specific periods and in the prevailing ideologies and sentiments of those periods. Thus I make sense of these sources by intelligently extrapolating their meanings beyond the contexts of their production and by highlighting biases, implications, and larger insights when considering available evidence from other sources. On that note, in the book's conclusion I take the liberty of "speculating about the history of the future,"[36] projecting from historical analysis and evidence to make observations about Boko Haram's possible future trajectories.

SYNOPTIC MAPPING

The chapters of this book are thematically ordered and are, for the most part, chronology-sensitive, even if the analytical emphasis on forward and backward historical comparison occasionally disrupts the chapters' chronological consistency. Chapter 1 looks back to locate precedents, precursors, contexts, and prompts to Boko Haram within and against three seminal developments in Northern Nigerian religious history: one precolonial, the other two postcolonial. I first discuss the ways in which the contradictions and evolutions of what scholars call the Fodiawa tradition in Northern Nigerian Islam illuminate the novel aspects of Boko Haram. Parallels and differences between the discourses and contingent practices of nineteenth-century jihadists and those of Boko Haram are highlighted. Second, the chapter examines the emergence of a volatile postcolonial terrain of interreligious contestations and conflicts in Northern Nigeria, and the ways in which Boko Haram was partly a reaction to this history and maps onto it. Lastly, the debate and crises precipitated by the implementation of Sharia legal codes in Northern Nigeria in the early 2000s are analyzed, as well as how the sharia controversy further inflamed the interreligious landscape while emboldening new groups such as Boko Haram and reifying their rhetoric of militant religious reform.

Chapter 2 provides a historical overview of the long history of Islamic reform and jihad in Northern Nigeria. I argue that it culminated in and in some respects primed Northern Nigeria for the militant dissidence of Boko Haram. The different phases, periods, and movements of reform and dissidence in the Sokoto Caliphate are surveyed. Reform discourses and practices during British colonization and in several postcolonial phases are also dissected. The chapter analyzes the different ideological, theological, organizational, and tactical signatures of these reformist movements in relation to those of the current Boko Haram insurgency. I also outline the ways in which this history of reform and dissidence both anticipated the current rebellion and points away from it to alternative modes of religious reform.

One of the identification marks of Boko Haram is its opposition to Western education and, more broadly, to the ideas, influences, technologies, material culture, forms of entertainment, and symbols it considers conveyors of Western modernity. Chapter 3 provides a historically grounded analysis of this aspect of Boko Haram's ideology. It inserts Boko Haram's antimodernist activism into a long-running, broader history of antimodernism in Northern Nigeria. I argue that this history of suspicion and theological delegitimization of Western things and thoughts dates back, in part, to the Sokoto jihad, even if some aspects of it contradict the complex engagement of the Fodiawa with the accouterments of European modernity. Northern Nigerian Muslim antimodernism was crystallized during the colonial period when anticolonial fervor meshed with and was expressed through popular quasi-theological critiques of Western modernity. The postcolonial continuation of this sacralized antimodernist ferment made the antimodernist reformist claims of Boko Haram plausible, and established a receptive religious marketplace that the Boko Haram's antimodernist creed mapped onto.

Chapter 4 analyzes Boko Haram's war-making and its military strategies in the context of a regional history of Islamic warfare. It also examines the movement's complicated efforts to reconcile Islamic combat prescriptions and prophetic examples with the exigencies and imperatives of contemporary warfare, a struggle eerily similar to that of previous regional religious militants. This comparative transhistorical exploration produces a number of discernible differences and similarities between past and present. The single event that brought global attention to Boko Haram was the abduction and subsequent "enslavement" of hundreds of schoolgirls in Chibok in northeastern Nigeria. This chapter takes this event, along with Boko Haram's vast infrastructure of warfare and captivity, as its point of reference for exploring the movement's attempt to revive and expand old practices of Islamic warfare and its associated forms of captivity. The chapter explores the extent to which Boko Haram's robust practice and discursive justifications of its appropriation of humans and material goods from designated enemy communities recall, expand, and deviate from the practice of and prescriptive discourses on loot and human war captives in previous militant reformist movements and periods. Finally, the analysis moves beyond the violence to discuss the multiple historical and contemporary strategies for forging resilience and coping with crisis that communities in the insurgency's epicenters have implemented, revived, and repurposed to enable them to not only survive the predation of Boko Haram but also recover.

The epilogue is a provisional reflection on the future of reformist insurgency in Northern Nigeria, with extrapolations that are informed by analysis of its past and present. This section looks at the current trajectory of the decade-and-a-half-long Boko Haram insurgency and offers a tentative prognosis of its future. In drafting this provisional prognosis, I take into account historical contingency, the inevitable atrophying of reformist fervor, fragmentation and schism within the ranks of the jihadists, fatigue, the changing local and international dynamics of jihad, the transformation of the local Islamic scene, and the persistence of a volatile Sahelian political economy that encourages and rewards nonstate militant actors. I contend that all of these factors suggest an insurgency that may wane and mutate over the next decade, but one that will also fragment into many semiautonomous pieces and continue in multiple forms across Nigeria, Niger, Chad, and northern Cameroon.

1 Before Boko Haram

CONTEXTS AND CATALYSTS

The primary Islamic reformist tradition of reference and record in Hausaland and Borno, the Islamic epicenters of modern Northern Nigeria, is the Sokoto jihad, which birthed the Sokoto Caliphate. Our analysis of the convergence and divergence between Boko Haram and existing reformist histories in the region thus focuses primarily on the Sokoto jihad and its aftermath, and secondarily on Bornu's older but less paradigmatic Islamic tradition. Accordingly, the first half of this chapter explores the question of how Boko Haram's project of armed reformist dissidence may be partly explained by looking back to how nineteenth-century reformists pursued their agenda and the challenges they faced in doing so. The chapter also analyzes the various ways in which Boko Haram departs from the Sokoto jihad tradition, represents something new, and is a movement that both challenges our understanding of the precolonial religious politics of Northern Nigeria and illuminates the region's postcolonial religious crises.

The second section of the chapter argues that Boko Haram can be explained in part as a cumulative and violent response to and a beneficiary of Christian adversarial politics in Northern Nigeria and its tentacles in Western hegemonic discourses and practices. This reactive and increasingly bellicose political Christianity is rooted in Judeo-Christian expansionist idioms with which Muslims in Northern Nigeria contended, perceiving them as an existential threat to their piety and majoritarian political position. Violence between Christians and Muslims produced a charged religious environment in Northern Nigeria. This conflict legitimized fringe groups such as Boko Haram, enabling them to reposition as mainstream defenders of Islam and Muslims' rights.

The last section discusses the role of the Sharia implementation controversy of the early 2000s in reshaping the intra- and interreligious landscapes of Northern Nigeria, catalyzing more religious violence, and opening the door to the violent reformist disruption that Boko Haram represents.

The chapter begins with an extensive discussion of the Sokoto jihad tradition. It is also known as the Fodiawa tradition because of the central role of the Fodio family in establishing the intellectual and programmatic basis of that jihad movement, which most Muslims in Northern Nigeria consider the archetype of reformism in West Africa. This discussion makes copious comparative references to Boko Haram, contrasting the past and the present. It then places Boko Haram against the Fodiawa tradition to tease out the ways in which present-day jihadists have invoked the Fodiawa tradition even while inventing a new, more expansive jihad ideology.

THE FODIAWA TRADITION AND BOKO HARAM ALTERITY

It is no accident that Boko Haram ideologues, despite the fact that most of them identify ethnically as Kanuri and are thus situated within the ethnocultural orbit of Borno, draw self-consciously on the Sokoto Caliphate tradition. This both legitimizes their jihadist project and answers fellow Muslims who criticize them by strategically referencing the Sokoto jihad and its leaders. No exploration of Boko Haram's parallels to and deviation from the existing traditions of reformism and armed jihad in the region would be complete without a closer look at the fraught processes that produced both the Sokoto jihad and the caliphate that resulted from it. Such an exploration can provide a backdrop for analyzing the rebellion of Boko Haram while highlighting parallel and diverging trajectories for jihad projects separated by two hundred years. Before attempting to locate Boko Haram both along and against the Sokoto reformist tradition, it is important to examine the extent to which the Sokoto tradition exists as a coherent body of theological consensus on jihad, reform, and postjihad consolidation and governance. How much coherence and consistent ideological unity existed among the three main leaders of the jihad—Usman dan Fodio, his brother Abdullahi, and his son and successor as sultan, Muhammad Bello? The answer to this question provides one important caveat in discussions of the Sokoto reformist tradition and Boko Haram: the internal ideological fragmentation in both jihads makes comparison necessarily provisional. A related point is the mediating role of events and contingency on the evolution of the positions and decisions of the triumvirate leadership of the Sokoto jihad. If the jihad, along with the theological and political positions of the trio, changed over time, then any discussion of an old caliphate tradition functioning as an inspiration, a challenge, and a basis of critical engagement for twenty-first-century jihadists in the region must be qualified.

On both of these points, an important new book by Paul Naylor, *From Rebels to Rulers*, gives us unprecedented insight into the intellectual and tactical fragmentation within the Sokoto Jihad and the shifts in the theological and political discourses and positions that attended the jihad's multiple phases. Naylor questions the long-held historiographical position on the Sokoto Caliphate as a cohesive political and intellectual project founded on a shared, stable set of theological consensuses.[1] He identifies four phases in the evolution of what we call the Sokoto reformist tradition. Discerned from their writings, the positions and discourses of the triumvirate leadership changed and evolved, Naylor argues, sometimes radically. These evolutions became evident as the trio sought to establish Usman's legitimacy prior to the jihad, use that legitimacy to discredit and apostatize the preexisting Hausa states and their rulers, consolidate and protect the gains of the Jihad from internal dissenters and rebels, and prevent but also respond to discordant discourses and critiques.[2] Some of the phases overlapped, while others did not.

The shifts were the products of the unforeseen and at times messy unfolding of the jihad, internal power struggles, and tension between idealism and pragmatism among the jihad leadership. The most important through line in this evolution of the jihad was what Naylor calls "discursive flexibility." As the triumvirate and other leaders of the jihad navigated the vagaries and challenges of religious warfare, territorial expansion, and political governance, and as they struggled to reconcile theocratic idealism with the exigencies of managing a complex and fluid Muslim political community, they explored and maneuvered into several, sometimes contradictory, intellectual terrains.[3]

Naylor's framing is useful as a conceptual anchor for the present analysis of how the Fodiawa's intellectual and practical legacies fragmented into several different noncoherent strands, making talk of a single caliphate or Fodiawa tradition inherited by or available to present jihadists problematic. As an analytic construct, the Fodiawa tradition is thus only a convenient heuristic for making legible the strategically homogenizing ways present-day jihadists are using that complex legacy for their own ends.

As the jihad progressed between 1804 and roughly 1811, some of Usman's earlier discourses that were used to establish the basis for the movement ran into trouble, necessitating clarifications and modifications that at times contradicted earlier positions. These contradictions manifested within and between the works of the three individual members of the triumvirate, complicating any historiographical notion of a unified and stable caliphate tradition that was preserved as a discrete ideology for future rebels and insurgents to use.

RADICAL EVOLUTIONS IN THE FODIAWA JIHAD

The shift between prejihad, jihad, and postjihad discourses of the triumvirate is sometimes quite jarring. As part of the stage setting for jihad, Usman had declared *takfir* on the Hausa states whose leaders were adjudged to be steeped in non-Islamic practices and to be practitioners of *takhlit* (syncretism). Usman did not distinguish between the rulers and their subjects, stating only that if the subjects did not endorse the non-Islamic practices of their rulers and wished to avoid the violent jihad that was the leaders' fate, the subjects must emigrate from these states to territory that Usman and his supporters controlled. Usman pronounced further that Muslims who maintained *muwalat* (friendly relations) with unbelievers were legitimate targets of jihad and their wives, children, and property subject to enslavement and legitimate appropriation.[4] This clear, absolutist position of distinction between the *dar al-harb* and *dar al-Islam* was not only used as the basis of delegitimizing the Hausa rulers and their subjects who remained loyal to them; Usman invoked it in 1810 to justify the jihad on Muslim Kanem-Bornu. When challenged by Muhammad al-Amin al-Kanemi, the Bornu leader, to legally justify his attack on Kanem-Bornu, Muhammad Bello accused Bornu rulers of sinful conduct and referenced the foundational *takfir* of Usman.[5]

Two points are worth stressing here. One is that as the jihad progressed, the leaders resorted to improvisational theological arguments to justify the political project of expanding the emerging caliphate. The second is that such theological flexibility risked contradicting earlier rulings and creating disagreement and dissent in the jihadists' ranks. For instance, in invoking Usman's *fikh* rulings to justify attacking Bornu, Bello had ignored a caveat in Usman's *takfir* that sinful conduct by the rulers of a state, in and of itself, did not justify waging war on their territory. There is similarity between the contingent dynamism of jihad discourse and its costly contradictions in this jihad, and Boko Haram's ideological evolutions and the internal crises these changes provoked.

Usman's son, Bello, appears to have been trapped in, and his position complicated by, his father's earlier writings. He sought ways to advance the political and territorial aims of the jihad without appearing to disregard or contradict his father's foundational *takfir*, the raison d'être of the jihad. The other complicating factor was not an intellectual one—it was the political imperative of the jihad, which grew as the military battles continued and as the jihad made territorial gains and morphed into a territorial political community to be expanded, preserved, and protected. This political imperative came to overshadow the ambiguity or purism of the original authorizing *takfir*. In regard to Boko Haram, *takfir* similarly became malleable and dispensable in the fast-paced political vagaries of jihad. The question of why Boko Haram attacks Muslim communities and has killed more Muslims than non-Muslims is answered in part by this dissonance between the theological and political pressures of jihad.

One example of this tension between the textual and the political in the nineteenth-century jihad was the jihadists' raiding and destruction of the famed Yandoto clerical community, a vibrant town founded and populated by prolific Islamic scholars, some of whom traced their ancestry to the Wangara scholar-proselytizers who had helped spread Islam in Hausaland in the fifteenth and sixteenth centuries. Contemporaries of the Fodiawa, the Yandoto scholars had been preaching actively in the Katsina area since about 1774. It can be plausibly assumed that the Fodiawa in fact consulted some of the works that the Yandoto scholars produced. Their scholarly fecundity was second only to Bornu's in this part of West Africa. The projects of the Fodiawa and the Yandoto scholars overlapped, and ought to have been complementary. However, instead of cultivating the alliance and cooperation of the Yandoto community of scholar-preachers, the Fodiawa took a rather adversarial position regarding them, viewing them as political and theological rivals rather than potential allies. Because of the Fodiawa's destruction of the centuries-old library of the Yandoto scholars during the siege and conquest of Yandoto, our only contemporaneous source for what transpired and why is the *Infaq al-Maysur fi ta rich bilad al-Takrur* of Muhammad Bello, who ordered the attack.

In the *Infaq al-Maysur*, Bello justifies the attack on the Muslim scholarly community of Yandoto not by invoking *takfir*, new or old, but by arguing that the Yandoto scholars had declined the Fodiawa's offer to debate. The crux of the Fodiawa's complaint against the Yandoto scholars was the latter's refusal to submit to the clerical and political authority of the caliphate. Bello could not declare *takfir* on them even within the parameters of Usman's broad *takfir* declaration in Hausaland. Yandoto was ruled by scholars, and its affairs were steeped in the strict observance of Islamic obligations. The city could not have been said to be in alliance with Hausa rulers who had been declared infidels, yet the community was attacked and destroyed.

At the core of the Fodiawa's hostility toward Yandoto was an imperative that came to supplant legalistic considerations: political loyalty. As the jihad progressed, the Fodiawa became more concerned with political incorporation and vanquishing those who stood in the way of that goal than about legalistic minutiae and anxieties regarding observing the pedantic nuances of *takfir*. Usman himself had set the stage for this kind of maneuver when he declared that only those in Hausaland who joined the *jama'a* (supporters and foot soldiers) or pledged alliance to Fodiawa authority could be legitimately regarded as Muslims and protected from raids. This was a pragmatic political decision more than a theological one. A political pledge of alliance to the caliphate was the overarching signifier of legitimate Muslim status, not the nuances of Sharia legalism on *takfir* and *tawalli* (alliance with nonbelievers). Muhammad Bello was thus extending a Fodiawa precedent of flexibility and pragmatism.

It was not only Bello who deviated from the abstract and pedantic theological rulings that Usman advanced to guide the jihad; many of those who had joined the ranks of the *jama'a* were raiding, killing, and looting indiscriminately, disregarding Usman's carefully laid-out conditions, restrictions, and terms of jihad. As evidence of indiscriminate opportunistic killing, enslavement, and the looting of the property of Muslims became undeniably clear, a discursive shift was inevitable, although this shift would not be unanimous and would lead to disagreement between Usman and his brother Abdullahi. As opportunistic raiding proliferated and abuse of the ideals of jihad became widespread, the leaders, some more than others, not only were disappointed but attempted to restate the principles of the jihad. Abdullahi expressed contempt for the undisciplined and self-serving conduct of his own troops, and Bello is said to have said in indignation about his own men, "If I could find another people, I would wage jihad with them against you."[6]

PRAGMATISM AND IMPROVISATION

The most significant outcome of the disappointing conduct of the troops was an internal discursive reckoning among the leaders and a marked shift to a less absolutist and less totalizing rhetoric of reform and rejection. Usman's prejihad pronouncements were unambiguous, rigid, and categorical about the juridical tenets of jihad and the laws and terms governing the *mujahid*'s conduct in battle. He was precise in his rulings on the repercussions of cooperation and friendship with entities designated as *kufr* (unbelievers), the obligations of Muslims to desert nonbelieving political entities to escape the fate that would befall such polities, and the terms for enslaving and appropriating relatives and possessions of nonbelievers.

However, as the jihadists gained ground and the territorial, political, and juridical outlines of a caliphate emerged, Usman's discourses, as conveyed in his postjihad works, shifted to a more compromising and moderate mode. For instance, while his 1803 writing on the eve of the jihad declaration stated that the property of Muslims living among nonbelievers and polytheists could be legally appropriated, in 1811 he cautioned his followers against it because the matter was "in dispute among the scholars."[7] Gone was the cocksure absolutism of his earlier pronouncement, which was now replaced by ambiguity and tentativeness.

Similarly, as the conduct of the troops increasingly contradicted some of the foundational discourses of dissent and legitimation of the jihad, Usman modified his position to avoid explicitly condemning his fighters, which would discredit the pious foundations of the jihad. In 1803 he had ruled that the men of apostate communities could not be enslaved and that their women could not be taken as concubines. In 1811, however, he moved away from this position, stating that "we do not outlaw categorically their enslavement and that of their children and their families . . . since this is a subject that is in dispute among the scholars."[8] His new ruling seemed calculated to accommodate the ongoing conduct of his militant supporters and to provide legal justification for what was already happening in the grind of battle, which he was helpless to stop.

Increasingly confronted with the contradictions and confusion created by his absolutist *takfir* rulings, and with the most active phase of the jihad over, Usman modulated and clarified his positions. On the declaration of *takfir* and jihad on Bornu, he stated in November 1811 that his position was predicated on his own judgment and not on a preponderance of scholarly rulings or consensus.[9] Furthermore, Usman credited his jihad with having transformed both Hausaland and Bornu from their status as lands led by nonbelieving rulers and thus subject to jihad, to lands of Islam, *Dar al-Islam*.[10] In this way Usman was able to discursively maneuver changes in his position by attributing the changes to the success of his jihad. The two territories, Hausaland and Bornu, had now been transformed by his jihad to *Dar al-Islam* and freed from the judgment of *takfir*, thereby nullifying his earlier *takfir* on Bornu.

DISSENT FROM WITHIN

The multiple and multistage evolutions in the discourses of the jihad leaders can modulate assertions of a coherent caliphate reformist tradition and legacy that can be accessed, appropriated, or challenged by subsequent generations of dissenters and rebels. Another such factor is the existence of intense disagreements among the leaders of the Fodiawa jihad. At the center of many of these internal ideological and political schisms was Abdullahi, Usman's brother and ally. This dispute had probably been present from the preaching phase of the reform movement and grew as the jihad unfolded, revealing the different orientations of each man.

The disagreements also fed on the frustrations of seeing their pious and idealistic endeavor polluted by the secular pecuniary pursuits of their fighters and being helpless to stop it. Each man reacted to the military and territorial successes and the moral disappointments of the jihad differently. From the writings of the brothers during the last phase of the first jihad between 1808 and 1811, it is clear that while Usman moderated his positions to maintain the credibility of the jihad, accommodate the imperfections of his supporters, discourage rebellion against the new caliphate, and project an image of Muslim unity and competent Islamic governance, Abdullahi's discourses evolved in the direction of dogmatic literalism and orthodoxy.[11]

Abdullahi and Usman disagreed on the ideals of Islamic governance and the attributes of a good Muslim leader.[12] They also diverged on the contentious issue of *takfir*. In 1811 Usman wrote to justify his original *takfir* on the Muslim rulers of Hausaland, whom he accused of not observing the tenets of Islam and of performing non-Islamic acts and rituals.[13] Abdullahi disagreed with the unqualified broadness of the ruling because he had seen firsthand, and with dismay, how this blanket pronouncement had authorized troops to unleash unbridled violence on Muslims accused of apostasy, nonbelief, and *shirk* (idolatry). Abdullahi was more forgiving of non-Islamic rituals as an automatic condition for the declaration of *takfir* than his brother, distinguishing between harmless cultural rituals and idolatrous conduct.[14] Abdullahi went so far as to argue that merely being friendly with "infidels" was not enough grounds for *takfir* to be declared on a state, sharply contradicting the very basis of the jihad as Usman had laid out in earlier years.

The disagreements between the brothers expanded into several new theological and topical territories as the jihad entered its concluding phase and the conduct of rank-and-file militants and commanders came under scrutiny.[15] The biggest disagreement in the leadership of the jihad came after Usman's death in 1817 and Muhammed Bello's succession to the sultanate. In his earlier treatises on ideal Islamic leadership, Abdullahi had criticized hereditary succession as a manifestation of pagan kingship.[16] He revived this critique in the wake of Usman's death. Drawing on leadership succession rulings and invoking problems of succession in early Islamic history, Abdullahi returned to his position that upon the death of its leader, a Muslim community was required to constitute an electoral council, or *shura*, to choose a worthy successor, and that the *shura* could consider the preferred successor that the deceased ruler had designated only if the designated successor was not the son of the former leader.[17] Bello defended his succession to the sultanate vigorously, penning a lengthy treatise, *al-Insaf*, to defend his succession. He relied for his defense on the texts Abdullahi had referenced in his critique to argue that, regardless of method of succession, the successor, as leader of the *ummah*, should be accepted, obeyed, and supported.[18] This disagreement between Abdullahi and his nephew marked the culmination of many episodes of internal dissent, fragmentation, and divergence on the vision, values, and aftermaths of the jihad.

These fissures illustrate the ways in which puritan visions of religious change, especially those supported by military force, can generate their own contradictions, leading to multiple complementary and conflictual trajectories. Some of this schism emanates from the strain and stress of jihadist warfare, while other parts of it are caused by personal grievances and differences. Yet others are the inevitable outcomes of the struggle to maintain the original idealism of a jihad project in a territorial space inhabited by people with various levels of devotion to Islam and various approaches to promoting the Islamic community.

BOKO HARAM IN THE SHADOW OF THE FODIAWA TRADITION

In examining how Boko Haram's jihadist project parallels and diverges from this fractious history of the Sokoto jihad and its many mutations and contradictions, one needs to investigate the absence or presence of the factors mentioned earlier in respect to the Sokoto jihad. Such comparative analysis also must reckon with another reality that the jihadists of the nineteenth century did not have to contend with: the overarching presence of secular, multireligious states in territories that present-day jihadists claim as the site of their religious community. This reality of suffocating political and religious pluralism manifests today in the ubiquitous presence of competing discourses, knowledges, practices, and commodities associated with Euro-American and Judeo-Christian modernity in Northern Nigeria.

Since there was no singular Fodiawa legacy for future generations to draw on or engage, Boko Haram's invocation of and engagement with the old caliphate project has been strategically selective, based on a fragmentary and self-serving reading of the texts produced and bequeathed by the Fodiawa, a reading that ignores the diffuse and pluralistic character of the Fodiawa legacy. This also means that there is no linear connection between the nineteenth-century jihad of the Fodiawa and the jihad of Boko Haram. What remains is to explain Boko Haram's strategic appropriation of a complicated and variegated Fodiawa legacy for its own ends, and to highlight the differences—and coincidental parallels—between the jihad projects separated by two centuries.

How do we situate Boko Haram in relation to this history of Muslim reformist rebellion in Northern Nigeria? Boko Haram evolved and struggled through the same phases that the Sokoto jihad did, and was wracked by internal leadership dissent, disagreements, and fracture similar to the Fodiawa's. Like the jihadists of old, Boko Haram lost control of its own *takfir* discourse. As was the case in the nineteenth century, the *takfir* of Boko Haram proved useful in the early days of the insurgency when the militants sought to sharply delineate the boundaries of their rebellion and define their enemies. However, similar to the evolution and elasticity of the *takfir* narrative in the Sokoto jihad, Boko Haram's *takfir* discourse became unwieldy, expansive, and subject to abuse, leading to internecine military confrontations and Muslim-on-Muslim atrocities that threatened the very legitimacy of the insurgency and horrified some of its leaders.

Much like the Sokoto jihad, Boko Haram started from a preaching phase in which the leading scholars of the movement—Muhammad Yusuf, Abubakar Shekau, and others—sought to establish the legitimacy of the movement's reformist mission in relation to existing secular and rival Muslim orders and tendencies. This phase witnessed the anticipatory production of broad ideas and rulings to guide and direct a future jihad that the leaders considered inevitable. Like the Sokoto jihadists, the militants of Boko Haram saw their textual and intellectual prescriptions on jihad tested during the military phase. In this phase decisions had to be made as unforeseen situations arose, threats to the jihad threatened to deal it a fatal blow, fighters with diverse motivations and interests joined the ranks, and abuses of earlier declared guiding principles of jihad surfaced in the expanding crucible of insurgent warfare.

Boko Haram dealt with the surprises and complications resulting from a dynamic battlefield and the fluctuating fortunes of the project somewhat differently than the Fodiawa did. Beset on multiple sides by modern national armies, and confronted sporadically by local vigilantes and communities resentful of its seemingly indiscriminate violence, Boko Haram reacted impulsively and out of a desperate instinct of self-preservation. In the early stages of the military phase there was a siege mentality that dictated how the group related to the many communities in the Mandara Mountains and Lake Chad regions where it operated. The reactions were driven more by paranoia than by a calculated assessment of threats. The result was that Boko Haram leaders increased the tempo and scale of violence, and removed guardrails and restrictions on fighters. This was a marked departure from the Sokoto jihadists' self-critical reaction to the vagaries of an evolving battlefield. Furthermore, unlike in the Sokoto example, there were no early voices of moderation in the movement to try to discipline the violence, modulate it with legal constraints, or redirect the righteous angst of the fighters away from Muslims and toward non-Muslim enemies. Internal dissent only emerged when Boko Haram's violence had taken a significant toll on Muslim communities, creating a narrative among local Muslims that Boko Haram was a nihilistic, bloodthirsty band of insurgents unmoored from the tenets of Islam and the prescriptions of the Sharia on reformist warfare. This image would continue to haunt Boko Haram.

In the Sokoto jihad, the messy by-products of a fast-changing battlefield and of expanding warfare were relatively contained. This containment was achieved through the balance of pragmatic adjustment, represented by

Usman and Muhammad Bello, and doctrinaire dogmatism, represented by Abdullahi. As a result of this internal equilibrium, the reputation of the jihad as a reformist movement of Islamic state-building did not suffer much and outlived the moment. Unlike Boko Haram, the Fodiawa did not see the jihad as an open-ended struggle of infinite and continuous purification of the *Ummah*. The Sokoto jihad was envisioned as a finite endeavor culminating in the establishment of a theocratic state governed according to Islamic prescriptions on statecraft. Therefore, once the outline of this state began to emerge, the Fodiawa transitioned to a governing mode in their discourses and actions, concerned with how to secure the state created, how to do justice in conformity with the Sharia, and how to establish a model of Islamic governance. Boko Haram never made this transition even when it declared the territories it captured to be a *Dawla* (state). One possible explanation is that pressures from the Nigerian, Nigerien, Cameroonian, and Chadian militaries made it impossible for Boko Haram to consolidate and properly govern the state it declared, a coordinated military pressure that the jihadists of the nineteenth century did not face. Moreover, the territorial span of Boko Haram's declared caliphate shrank with every military offensive of the national armies.

Boko Haram's leader in its violent jihad phase, Abubakar Shekau, differed in temperament, depth of learning, organizational acumen, and leadership skill from Usman. While the latter was reflexive, self-critical, and humble, the former was impulsive, self-absorbed, and incorrigible. While Usman grounded himself in theological justifications of his actions and devoted himself to creating the intellectual space for sound, Islamic statecraft, Shekau had no patience for the intellectual and organizational dimensions of leadership and was impulsive, reactive, and bombastic. That was another reason that under his leadership Boko Haram failed to craft or implement a plan of governance and consolidation after it captured significant territory and declared it to be a state.

Boko Haram grappled with some of the same challenges that the Sokoto jihadists faced, and debated the issues involved as fiercely as the debate of the Fodiawa. In the nineteenth century the Fodiawa argued about how, when, and on whom *takfir* should be declared. They disagreed on whether or when alliance or friendly relations with nonbelievers made a state a legitimate target of jihad. They argued about how to distinguish between people who were "infidel by origin" and those who could be regarded as apostates. They sparred intellectually on the question of who could be lawfully enslaved in the course of jihad.

The same set of debates raged among Boko Haram's leadership, and particularly between Shekau and Mamman Nur, debates that ultimately caused the first major split in Boko Haram in 2016. At the core of the debate between the two Boko Haram leaders was the controversy caused by the *takfir* Shekau declared on the people of Chibok, a predominantly non-Muslim town, and the people of Baga, a historically Muslim town. While Nur and Shekau agreed on the verdict regarding the people of Chibok, who were deemed to be "infidels by origin," Nur disagreed with Shekau's *takfir* on the people of Baga, whom Shekau accused of engaging in *Tawalli*, which made them apostates. Shekau's specific accusation regarding Baga was that the residents were cooperating with Nigerian army troops and had spurned the jihadists' self-declared caliphate to remain in the orbit of the Nigerian state. Echoing some of the logic used by Abdullahi in his disquisition against Usman's *takfir* in the nineteenth century, Nur argued that even if the people of Baga were guilty of apostasy they could not be given the same treatment as the people of Chibok, and should, as prescribed by the Sharia, be given an opportunity to repent before military action could be taken against them.[19]

The similarities in the challenges and schisms faced by jihadists of old and Boko Haram are at times striking, but the differences in how they responded to the practical and unpredictable problems and complications of jihad are equally, if not more, remarkable. One sees traces of the past in Boko Haram's intellectual and political project, but one also sees significant divergence. One reason for this divergence is the fact that Boko Haram has had to contend with the ubiquitous presence of a plethora of signs, phenomena, commodities, modes of thought, and actions that can be described under the rubric of Euro-American modernity, which threatens its project but also legitimizes some of its rhetoric of rejection. Boko Haram has not just had to fight off threats and carve out an autonomous territorial space for its project of Islamist state-making; it has also had to combat what it regards as the encroaching and polluting influence of modernity (see chapter 3). Boko Haram thus has had to develop much broader terms of intellectual and programmatic engagement than earlier

Muslim insurgents, and compile a longer list of enemies and abominable anathemas than the one the Sokoto jihadists maintained.

The toll of internal schism on Boko Haram has been significantly higher than it was on the Sokoto jihad. As of the time of writing this book, Boko Haram had split further into multiple competing factions in the wake of the death of Abubakar Shekau, and the issues in contention had multiplied, as had the stakes in them. Unlike the Sokoto jihadists who managed to paper over their differences or found ways to live with them in the interest of their project, Boko Haram ideologues of different factions have dug in to protect their turfs and damage other factions in a scorched-earth, zero-sum jihad within the fracturing broader jihadist project.

BOKO HARAM AND THE FODIAWA EXAMPLE

In discussing the aspects of the Fodiawa's multivalent ideology that are eerily similar to Boko Haram's operative ideologies, this book seeks to underscore the obvious historical connections as well as the ways in which Boko Haram itself makes occasional appeals to the Fodiawa tradition of jihad, whether as opportunistic invocation or in genuine reverence for what came before. The claim here is not that there is a direct instructional value in this preexisting jihad template for Boko Haram; rather, the point is to highlight the fact that Boko Haram and other jihadi-Salafi movements operating in Northern Nigeria today see themselves as continuing in the Dan Fodio jihad tradition and routinely rebuff criticisms of their methods and pronouncements by referencing the deeds and jihad instructions of Usman Dan Fodio as paradigmatic precedents and examples.

In this respect, the Fodiawa jihad traditions and their elaborate textual legacies and prescriptions provide current jihadis a culturally resonant set of idioms and symbols with which to justify their acts and, when critiqued by other Muslims, defend their deeds. This history and tradition of reform, dissidence, and jihad have collectively become an all-purpose alibi to draw on. This is not what Dan Fodio intended, since his jihad postulations were meant as a one-off, time- and space-specific ideological and practical guide. However, the Sufi Islamic orthodoxy that resulted from the jihad canonized the Fodiawa corpus of writings and made them available for both inspiration and reference. It should thus be no surprise that there are some uncanny similarities between the rhetoric of Usman Dan Fodio and those of present-day Boko Haram ideologies.

In *Bayān wujūb al-hijra ʿalā ʾl-ʿibād*, Usman Dan Fodio defines the target of jihad as robustly as today's jihadi-Salafi movements do. On the question of who should be fought in jihad, Usman Dan Fodio offers this answer: "They are three kinds: infidels [unbelievers], transgressors, and rebels."[20] This is a much more expansive jihad target group than the narrow, restricted one that is asserted in some popular and scholarly representations of the Fodiawa jihad. It is also quite similar to Boko Haram's capacious definition of who constitutes legitimate targets in its jihad enterprise. That non-Muslims are legitimate targets in jihad requires no explanation or debate. However, the categories of "rebels" and "transgressors" are broad and are subject to the interpretive whims of subsequent jihadists and reformers.

The extension of jihad to these categories is analogous to Boko Haram's controversial extension of *takfīr* (excommunication) to a broad array of Muslims whom they consider insufficiently committed to the revealed canon and the *Sunna*. It appears that Dan Fodio unwittingly created an elastic textual template that gave permission to jihadists on the battlefield to attack not just non-Muslims but also a great number of Muslims who could be characterized, even if subjectively and opportunistically, as rebels and transgressors. Like Boko Haram's justification of its targeting of Muslims today, the Fodiawa's legitimization of attacks on Muslim rebels and transgressors gave his jihad allies the power to declare some Muslims or Muslim societies rebels or transgressors against the law of Allah—the authority to judge and render fellow Muslims legitimate targets of reformers' military action.

The parallel between this old jihad template and the current jihadi-Salafi one is discernibly clear. It is unlikely that Boko Haram insurgents take conscious notes from and adhere to the Fodiawa jihad model. They probably would not consciously and doctrinally emulate Usman Dan Fodio's jihad template, considering that Usman was a Sufi. However, the Fodiawa jihad casts a long shadow on all subsequent reformist jihad movements. It provides such a broad, open-ended operational platform for reformist jihad that it would have been surprising had Boko Haram not tried to connect to it as a way of gaining acceptance and support among Muslims in Northern Nigeria.

Perhaps the most telling ideological connection between the Fodiawa jihad tradition and Boko Haram's jihadi-Salafi militancy can be located in chapter 38 of *Bayān wujūb al-hijra 'alā 'l-'ibād*, which deals with the question of "the law concerning giving freedom to slaves of unbelieving belligerents if they flee to us, and the permissibility of taking as concubines the women who have been captured from them after waiting for the passing of one menstruation (*Istibra'*) even if they have husbands in the non-Muslim territory."[21] Ruling on the contentious issue, Dan Fodio approvingly quotes *Lubāb al-ta'wīl fī ma 'ānī 'l-tanzīl*, the *tafsīr* of 'Alī b. Muḥammad b. Ibrāhīm b. Khāzin al-Baghdādi (d. 1340), as interpreting Qur'an 4:24, which states, "Also [prohibited are] women already married except those whom your right hand possesses."

Instructively, as discussed in chapter 4, Boko Haram invokes similar theological and jurisprudential logic to justify enslavement generally and the enslavement of non-Muslim women, including young, unmarried girls such as those kidnapped from the secondary school in Chibok. If the Boko Haram theological defense of its forms of gendered captivity echoes the Fodiawa prescription outlined above, it is because these latter-day dissidents are reading both consciously and subconsciously from similar reformist scripts, or at least relying on the power of local jihad discursive communities and the polemics that circulate within them.

RUPTURE AS CONNECTION

There are notable differences between the Usman Dan Fodio jihadi corpus and Boko Haram's indiscriminate, scorched-earth jihadi warfare ideology. While legitimizing the appropriation of the property of *Kuffār* (non-Muslims), Dan Fodio declared as unlawful the seizure of the property of apostate Muslims. This is a departure from the twenty-first-century jihadi-Salafi formula of Boko Haram, which delegitimizes so-called apostates and makes little distinction between them and non-Muslims. Another striking difference between the Fodiawa reform tradition and the jihad rhetoric of Boko Haram and other twenty-first-century jihadi-Salafi movements is that Dan Fodio forbade declaring *takfīr* (excommunication) of Muslims on the "pretext of heretical observances" or "disobedience."[22] This seems like a direct repudiation of Boko Haram's capacious and seemingly capricious *takfīr* practice.

These differences are as striking as the similarities between the guidelines of the nineteenth-century Fodiawa jihad and Boko Haram's elaborate justifications and guidelines for its own jihad. What this analysis demonstrates is that when Boko Haram invokes the nineteenth-century jihad, as it has sometimes done,[23] it is keenly aware that Northern Nigerian Muslims view that jihad as the sacralized standard of reform, the right way to purify Islamic practice and seek the establishment of an Islamic society. The Fodiawa jihad continues to be regarded as an enduring social construction that informs how other forms of militant Islamic dissidence are judged. Boko Haram wants to be taken as seriously as the nineteenth-century jihad and to be accorded the reformist credibility that is extended to Dan Fodio's jihad. Thus, much of its reference to the Fodiawa jihad tradition is propagandistic and opportunistic, but that propaganda is possible because there is a field of play and a compatibility, no matter how tenuous, between the old and new jihad.

The legacy of the caliphate is one context against which Boko Haram can be analyzed, a history that both Boko Haram and Muslims who oppose and fight against them draw on to make their cases. However, the Fodiawa tradition is not the only factor that has shaped or complicated the emergence of Boko Haram. A second, perhaps more important, reality that has both catalyzed and made Boko Haram more intractable is postcolonial religious violence in Nigeria. The next section of this chapter analyzes how interreligious violence and its adversarial legacies opened the door to fringe groups such as Boko Haram to attempt to mainstream their agenda.

BOKO HARAM AND INTERRELIGIOUS VIOLENCE IN
NORTHERN NIGERIA

In some ways, Boko Haram represents an extreme Muslim reactionary expression of a long-seething Muslim sense of insecurity in an evolving universe of Judeo-Christian and modernist transformation in Northern

Nigeria. This is the second context and catalytic phenomenon within which Boko Haram can be understood. Historically, this social change has caused various degrees of discomfort and resentment among a Muslim community upended by British colonial incursion at the turn of the twentieth century. Boko Haram does not represent the totality of the Muslim reaction to this long colonial and postcolonial encroachment of cultures, beliefs, and ideas associated with Judeo-Christian colonizers and their perceived present-day Christian inheritors. However, it is a religious movement that cannot be separated from or explained outside the broader history of interreligious tension and violence in Northern Nigeria.[24]

In Northern Nigeria violence in the name of religion has been a significant feature of the region's postcolonial history. This conflict maps onto preexisting and new politics of religious differentiation, ethnic rivalry, land disputes, and ruthless, zero-sum competition for resources. In addition to these factors, postcolonial Northern Nigeria has become a battleground for new, expansionist strains of militant Christianity and Islam. Both of these radical religious tendencies are connected to and embedded in geopolitical struggles that are increasingly defined or understood in the idiom of religious difference, primarily between a dominant, hegemonic Judeo-Christian world and a marginalized but resurgent Islamic world.

Northern Nigeria, the scene of Boko Haram's incubation and activities, has historically been a crossroads of several religious currents. Beginning in colonial times, the region experienced several waves of Christian missionary activity. In addition, colonialism brought several tangible and intangible symbols of European modernity that Muslims consider a threat to their way of life and to centuries-old investments in pietistic cultures (see chapter 3). The entry into Northern Nigeria of Christian and European cultures and ideas triggered a backlash that, while not leading to violence in colonial times, prepared the stage for the eruption of violence in the postcolonial period. Among the Muslim population of Northern Nigeria there was a fear that their faith was being overwhelmed by Judeo-Christian cultural resources, ideas, and modes of thought, and that colonial power and colonization undergirded these new cultural waves. The well-documented Muslim opposition to missionary education and to the establishment of missionary schools in certain emirate spaces was one manifestation of this fear.[25] Whether it was true or not, Muslims in the region believed that Christianity and colonization were part of a single package, the latter a vehicle to propagate the former. Despite the British colonial government outlawing Christian missionary proselytizing in predominantly Muslim provinces of Northern Nigeria,[26] there remained an antipathy in the Muslim-majority parts of the region toward the establishment of Christian institutions, including mission schools. There was a sense that Muslims were under siege and needed to defend their religion against a Christian evangelical enterprise that became more aggressive and ambitious as the colonial era unfolded.

Another dimension to this entry of Christian and Judeo-Christian ideology into the Northern Nigerian colonial body politic was the subsequent, overt politicization of Christianity for purposes of non-Muslim ethnic minority struggles and agitations. As Niels Kastfelt, Chunun Logams, Yusufu Turaki, and other scholars have documented in their various works, Christian missionaries not only converted non-Muslim ethnic minorities, they also encouraged them to instrumentalize their new Christian identity in the political arena under the rubric of a nascent Middle Belt or non-Muslim political identity.[27] This new identity was explicitly articulated and understood in opposition to the dominant Muslim caliphate identity in the region. An insurgent Christian political identity benefiting from foreign Christian missionary support was understood in Northern Nigerian Muslim political circles in conspiratorial terms as a threat to the Muslim-majority identity.

After independence this identity narrative, along with its adversarial idioms, fears, and militant posturing, caused further aggressive religious responses in the predominantly Muslim areas of the region. It also seemed to vindicate earlier discourses and suspicions regarding a colonial and neocolonial plot to destabilize the Muslim community in Northern Nigeria or to divide the region along religious lines to the advantage of the competing eastern and western regions of Nigeria. The effort of Ahmadu Bello, the premier of the region after independence, to promote Islam and religious homogeneity in the region through state-funded conversion campaigns and through the cultivation of political, cultural, educational, and diplomatic ties to the Muslim World was partly informed by the fear of the North being weakened by religious strife.[28] This postcolonial policy of Islamic propagation and the deliberate substitution of Muslim world diplomatic outreach for Western ties alarmed Christians in the region, heightening interreligious tension and driving Christians farther into militant and adversarial forms of religious expression and mobilization.

This history of ethnoreligious tensions and contestations between and within both sides of the Muslim-Christian regional divide demonstrates that religious competition stood in legitimately for contestations in the political and economic spheres, and that this competition had a profound effect on the polity. Religion became the primary instrument of political mobilization in postcolonial Northern Nigeria. In the same period, religion remained the central idiom of identification in the region—a contrast to Southern Nigeria, where ethnicity largely trumped and still eclipses religion as the central factor of political identification.

Furthermore, religion became a charged and volatile site of intense contestations in the postcolonial period in Northern Nigeria. Sometimes these religious contests assumed nihilistic dimensions and antagonists passionately invoked the rhetoric of scorched-earth violence. It was not always clear whether religion itself was the primary passion driving postcolonial relational fissures between Muslims and Christians or was merely a convenient, emotive, and resonant platform for expressing socioeconomic and political anxieties and fears of the ethnoreligious Other. A crisis that began in a nonreligious context often morphed into a full-blown religious conflict. Conversely, religious contests in Northern Nigeria often concealed underlying nonreligious factors. Because of the fraught status of religion in the region, religious rhetoric has, more often than not, shaped conflicts between groups that are predominantly Muslim and Christian, further widening the chasm between the Muslim majority and the Christian minority.

In the same period Christian Northern Nigerians, fearing that a postcolonial regional government dominated by Muslims and Muslim-run institutions would further marginalize them, cultivated a more militant ethnoreligious imaginary. Christians also began to cultivate independent ties to Euro-American Evangelical and Pentecostal organizations and actors to empower themselves against what they saw as their marginalization in postcolonial Northern Nigerian politics. Foreign Evangelical and Pentecostal partners provided funds, platforms, and pipelines, as Ruth Marshall and other scholars have noted.[29] However, they also exported a more impactful resource: the rhetoric and lexicon for producing and engaging the religious Other, primarily Muslims in the Nigerian context. The foreign patrons were often invested in a vision of religious combat and zero-sum competition for global religious supremacy. As they established roots in Christian communities in Northern Nigeria, this vision of religious competition began to permeate the Christian communities and institutions in which they worked. Over time, this drove some Northern Nigerian Christians deeper into a stronger, implacable resentment of what they regarded as the political and economic domination of Muslims and state bias in favor of Muslims. Challenging Muslims and Muslim-superintended institutions for rights morphed into Christian rebellion and militant self-assertion that cared little for the rights of Muslim minorities in Christian-majority areas. Needless to say, it drove adherents of the two contending religions in Northern Nigeria further apart, setting the stage for violent confrontations in multiple places and periods.

INTERRELIGIOUS VIOLENCE IN NORTHERN NIGERIA

The history of interreligious violence in Nigeria began with simmering tensions and mutual suspicions and antagonisms that seemed primed to erupt into violence. Many scholars of the phenomenon date the first of many conflagrations to the Kafanchan religious uprising of 1987, which spread from its epicenter in Kafanchan town in Southern Kaduna to other parts of Kaduna State with mixed populations of Christians and Muslims. Most academic and journalistic analyses of religious violence in Northern Nigeria begin with the Kafanchan crisis. However, it was not the first violent religious conflict between Christians and Muslims in Northern Nigeria. That grisly position belongs to a little-known crisis that engulfed Sabon Gari quarters in Kano in 1982. That year a group of Muslim zealots, protesting the decision of the Anglican Church Hausa Section in Fagge quarters to build a bigger sanctuary within the walled compound of the church, rioted and burned several churches in Sobon Gari, an enclave in Kano that housed Southern Nigerians and included churches and hotels.[30]

The Kano attacks had occurred in the context of long-simmering interreligious tensions resulting from what scholars have come to refer to as the Sharia debate in Nigeria. The Sharia debate began during the constitution-drafting process of the transition from military rule to civilian democratic rule between 1976 and 1978.[31] When the text of the draft constitution was released by the Constitution Drafting Committee in 1976, it not only provided for a federal Sharia Court of Appeal but also mentioned the proposed court forty-six times. Christian delegates vehemently protested what they variously criticized as a stealthy Islamization campaign and as an attempt to subject Christians to Islamic law.[32] The rancorous and feisty constitutional debates subsequently traveled from the elite political circles of the constitutional assembly to the Northern Nigerian streets as both Christian and Muslim politicians and clerics fired up their bases and dug in.

Some Christians insisted that this was a new jihad, a way for Muslims to assert their superiority over Christians. Muslim clerics and politicians cast the Sharia provision as justice for Muslims, whose rights to live under the juridical authority of Sharia law had been curtailed by the Judeo-Christian orientation of colonial and postcolonial administration and judicial bureaucratization. For these Muslims, their coreligionists merely wanted the right of judicial appeal in a system founded on and mandated by the jurisprudential corpus of their religion. The ensuing exchange of incendiary rhetoric and recriminations not only threatened the transition to democratic rule, it also poisoned the Northern Nigerian interreligious relational landscape and deepened burgeoning suspicions.

The provision for a federal Sharia Court of Appeal was eventually dropped from the final draft of the 1979 constitution, but the religious fabric of Northern Nigeria, where religion is the preeminent associational and identity factor, had been frayed. The reverberations continued in the form of sporadic debates on the issue in the 1980s as Muslims sought to revive bureaucratized Sharia as a necessity for Muslims and contrast it with the secular legal system, while insisting that the two could coexist to cater to different legal issues and different religious communities in Nigeria.[33] Philip Ostein calls the failure to reach a compromise on the Federal Sharia Court of Appeal "the 1979 debacle," and argues that it was the result of Christians' paranoia and shortsighted recalcitrance. This failure enraged Muslims, pushing Muslim resentment to the margins where it waited to erupt.[34]

In the decades to come, Boko Haram would thrive on two mutually reinforcing maneuvers. It would exploit the long-simmering grievances and sense of injustice that Muslims in Northern Nigeria harbored against secular political and judicial institutions in Nigeria. It would also position itself as an avenger of Muslims, a fighter against the allegedly Islamophobic residue of British colonization, and a restorer of a precolonial Muslim sovereignty. Boko Haram succeeded in this maneuver because there actually was an existing groundswell of Muslim resentment that it would opportunistically appropriate for its own end. This preexisting Muslim grievance had a postcolonial history bound up with the familiar primordial contestations that plagued Nigerian nation-building from independence and assumed a volatile character in the 1970s and 1980s.

The Sharia constitutional debate was an offshoot of the Muslim struggle to reorder and rework the Nigerian state toward a direction that Muslim reform activists believed was an existential necessity. They believed that British colonizers and postcolonial Nigerian institutions and constitutions had subordinated Muslims' religious obligations and values to secular and Judeo-Christian institutions. This effort to "re-Islamize" the polity through political and constitutional reengineering outlived the Sharia constitutional debate and was constantly reenergized since the outcome of that debate was, from the perspective of Muslim reformist scholars and intellectuals, inconclusive and incomplete and therefore unsatisfactory. This struggle to return the Nigerian state to a condition that Muslim reformists preferred shaped the reformists' attitude toward nation-building and influenced their positions on national political debates in several periods.

In the mid-1980s when the military regime of General Ibrahim Babangida announced a plan to transition the country to civilian democratic rule, Northern Nigerian reformist intellectuals and a few Southern Nigerian Muslim allies such as Ishaq Oloyede saw both opportunity and concerns in the transition program. Political alliances and cleavages coalesced around the country. Civilian political actors in both Northern and Southern Nigeria strategized on how to position themselves in relation to the announced democratic transition. Prodemocracy and human rights NGOs and civic society organizations began work to ensure that the promised transition occurred as announced. All these groups, whatever their differences, converged on their desire for a state organized around liberal democratic and secular political principles. Their political imagination was decidedly secular and liberal democratic in orientation. This emerging national consensus was a source of concern and anxiety for Muslim reformers. They saw not just an impending transition to democracy but also an attempt by a pan-Nigerian coalition of secular forces to capture and consolidate the secular and liberal foundations of the Nigerian state and revictimize Muslims, whom they believed the postcolonial Nigerian state had already marginalized. The struggle over the political future of Nigeria was underway and was increasingly cast in religious terms.

The response of these concerned Muslim reformist scholars, intellectuals, and activists was to articulate an alternative vision for the future of Nigeria, one that sought to recalibrate the state to give more visibility and institutional representation to Muslims and also to radically transform the foundation of the Nigerian state to accommodate Sharia and other priorities the reform activists deemed integral to Muslims' dignity and sovereignty within the nation-space of Nigeria. In 1988 they published *On the Political Future of Nigeria* to announce their political vision for Nigeria's future as it prepared to transition from military to democratic rule.[35] That book was a manifesto and blueprint for the imagined re-Islamization of the polity, which they believed could only happen when the secular, liberal, and Judeo-Christian foundations of the Nigerian state were reformed. It was a text that proclaimed the authors' intention to accomplish what they regarded as a long-overdue rebalancing of the Nigerian state to achieve equity and justice for Muslims. The Muslim reform activists positioned themselves in parallel and in opposition to the secular prodemocracy coalition, leading to the emergence of a bifurcated vision of the future Nigerian state.

A survey of the chapters in that book, the topics covered, and the caliber of contributors indicates the heft of the Muslim reclamation project that it documents. It also reveals that the grievances, concerns, and aspirations that Muhammad Yusuf would crudely and angrily articulate in his sermons two decades later were not entirely new. Some of them were already percolating and circulating in the reformist ideational circuits of Muslim Northern Nigeria, albeit in refined, civil, and intellectual forms. Reformers saw minefields for Muslims in transitioning to democracy on the basis of the existing Nigerian state structure and advocated for serious institutional and legal reforms to prepare for and enrich that transition with their semitheocratic agenda. Boko Haram repatented the grievances and yearnings of many Muslims and turned them into an implacable rhetoric of violent revolution. Boko Haram would later view democracy itself and the Nigerian state and its institutions as enemies of Muslims that needed to be physically confronted and dismantled.

Boko Haram's more revolutionary agenda initially resonated because it benefited from prior developments in the 1980s and 1990s: violent quotidian and intergroup conflicts between Muslims and Christians. The Sharia constitutional debate broke relational trust between Christians and Muslims and heightened a seemingly irrational fear of Muslim domination in Northern Nigerian Christian communities. The road to more interreligious conflict and a hardening of the religious rhetoric of dissidents on both sides was laid. It seemed like it was only a matter of time before more interreligious conflicts erupted, and when they did in Kafanchan it was hardly a shock.

Why is the Kafanchan crisis often regarded as the watershed moment in Northern Nigeria's history of religious disharmony if it was not the first incident of religious violence? Why is it often treated as the first violent confrontation between Christians and Muslims in Northern Nigeria? One of the reasons the Kafanchan crisis remains a pivotal development in Northern Nigerian religious history is that it was the first time that Christians were seen as aggressors, proactively killing, destroying, and causing harm in the name of religion. Prior to this event, there was a fairly widespread stereotype in Northern Nigeria, if not in Nigeria as a whole, of Muslims as intolerant, prone to violence, domineering, and impossible to cohabit with. The Kafanchan religious conflict challenged that stereotype and demonstrated that Christian communities were also capable of all that had been attributed to Muslims, a perception of Muslims that developed in part because of their dominant demographic and political position in the region. Minority Christian status had been erroneously associated with docility, submission, tolerance, and nonviolence. In the Kafanchan conflict Christians were shown to be far from incapable of violence toward ethnoreligious Others. Christian minority violence was enacted for the first time in this volatile regional religious context, and it punctured the myth that only Muslims sought sociopolitical and economic dominance or expressed grievances through the rhetoric of religious supremacy.

There are several versions of how the conflict began and what triggered it, but the most generally accepted story is that a cavalier, combative Evangelical preacher spoke incendiary religious words into an already volatile interreligious situation. During the annual retreat, hosted by the College of Education, Kafanchan, of the Fellowship of Christian Students (FCS), an Evangelical student body of self-identified born-again Christians, the preacher reportedly antagonized Muslim students of the institution by copiously quoting from and commenting on the Qur'an.[36] This openly antagonistic sermon provoked protests from Muslim students at the religiously mixed institution. The original rioting occurred in Kafanchan and its environs, in a predominantly Christian town with a historic Muslim Hausa-Fulani minority that was targeted. This then led to rioting that quickly spread to the towns of Kaduna and Zaria, with many lives lost. Kafanchan demonstrated the capacity of Christian minority ethnic groups to inflict harm on Muslims where the latter were in the minority. Christian Northern Nigerians, who historically organized politically around their asserted common victimhood of and resistance to perceived caliphate and Muslim domination, inflicted violence on members of the Hausa-Fulani Muslim community.

KAFANCHAN AND THE PRELUDE TO BOKO HARAM

Because it was precipitated, whether intentionally or not, by provocative minority Christian activity, Kafanchan was a rallying cry among Muslims for the defense of Muslim lives and property, and Islam itself. Many Muslims, alarmed by the carnage, changed their attitude toward the Northern Nigerian Christian community and became more receptive to the rhetoric of Muslim hardliners who had been espousing a more confrontational religious politics for decades and saw Kafanchan as a vindication of their advocacy of aggressive Muslim defense against what they saw as the global and local expansionism of Christianity. Kafanchan seemed to alert mainstream Muslims to the threat of Christian radicalism and violence, and many Muslims came to view their Christian neighbors, colleagues, and interlocutors in a different light—as competitors and antagonists. The feeling was mutual since in the Kafanchan violence, which spread to other towns and cities, Christians also lost their lives, property, and sense of security.

After Kafanchan the two main religious communities retreated further into their insular communal spaces, consuming an ever-growing collection of messages that amplified the threat that the other religious community allegedly posed. In both Christian and Muslim communities some post-Kafanchan religious sermons explicitly promoted a sense of supremacy and the propriety of violence in defense or propagation of the faith. Subsequent Muslim mobilization, and even the growth of rejectionist and insurgent sects with explicitly anti-Christian doctrines, benefited from the legacy of Kafanchan and its spillover religious violence. Christian radicalism and violence provoked a reaction in kind, creating what would become a cycle of nihilistic religious violence that all but guaranteed groups such as Boko Haram a favorable reception. Many Muslims came to believe that protection against the contaminating influence and threats of Nigerian Christians and their global Judeo-Christian allies lay in a more militant pietistic practice that did not rule out violence when necessary to defend the faith.

Another reason that Kafanchan proved to be so seminal in the postcolonial religious history of Northern Nigeria and in the emergence of radical Muslim reaction is that it was followed by the Zangon Kataf ethnoreligious conflict that killed hundreds of people, mostly Hausa-Fulani Muslims. In January 1992 a new chairman of the Zangon Kataf Local Government, Jury Babank Ayok, a Christian ethnic Atyap, proposed moving a market located in section of the town populated by Muslim Hausa-Fulani to a neutral site. The purported rationale for the move was to enable the Christian Atyap people, who made up the majority of the local government and whose settlements ringed the market and the Zango area inhabited by Hausa-Fulani Muslims, to trade in the market. However, it soon emerged that the Christian Atyap had nurtured a historic resentment against the Hausa-Fulani Muslims, who, allegedly with the support of the government, had prohibited the Atyap from trading beer and pork—items forbidden in Islam—in the market. While the Atyap saw the chairman as correcting a historic injustice by relocating the market to a location in which they could freely trade in any product, the Hausa-Fulani community, who dominated the market in its current location, saw the move as an assault on their economic livelihood and their religion.

In the ensuing ethnoreligious standoff, each group prepared for violence and accused the other of attacking it. Each group also received the backing of coreligionists in other Kaduna State cities and Northern Nigerian cities and states. It was only a matter of time before violence broke out. The first wave of violence occurred in February 1992 and resulted in the death of ninety-five people. Property, farms, and places of worship were destroyed. Further violence erupted in May, reportedly coordinated by Atyap leaders who claimed that the Hausa-Fulani Muslims had killed many Atyap in the February crisis and had continued to attack Atyap people on their farms. They further claimed that the Hausa-Fulani Muslims were interloping strangers whom the Emir of Zaria had imposed on the community in colonial times. They vowed to uproot them and reclaim the Zango area. In the Atyap-led violence that followed, hundreds of Hausa-Fulani Muslims were killed. Homes and property were burned, and many of the Hausa Muslim survivors, violently removed from their homes, fled and became displaced. When news of these tragic events reached Kaduna metropolis, Zaria, and Ikara, all cities with large Hausa-Fulani Muslim populations, reprisal killings and destruction of property ensued. Hundreds of people, most of them Christians of different ethnicities, including Southern Nigerians, were killed.

The spiraling violence further inflamed religious animosities in an already religiously flammable region of Nigeria. It also vindicated Muslim groups, both mainstream and fringe, that had been articulating and advocating a more radical posture toward Christians, Christianity, and the commodities, ideas, beliefs, cultures, and practices allegedly associated with local and global Christian hegemonic projects. At this very time in the late 1980s and early 1990s, increased access to satellite broadcasting had exposed Muslim youth in the region to foreign-produced radical messages of Muslim revolutionary resistance against Western and Judeo-Christian global dominance and their local manifestations. Radical Muslim precursors of Boko Haram had not yet emerged, but the sentiments they would later espouse and embody incubated in some Muslims in the region as radical Christian vigilantism turned increasingly violent.

INTERRELIGIOUS CONFLICT AND THE EMERGENCE OF BOKO HARAM

The two incidents of Christian minority violence in the same Southern Kaduna zone of Northern Nigeria occurred in an area with a Christian majority and a Muslim minority. In that area, Muslims saw themselves as victims of Christian aggression. That narrative of Muslim victimhood resonated widely among Muslims in Northern Nigeria and became the basis for political mobilization and helped to legitimize groups that mainstream Muslims in the region had previously considered too extreme.

The possibility of further Christian violence, no longer in the theoretical realm, renewed the discourses that emphasized the necessity of Muslim defensive and offensive violence in defense of the Muslim faith and its propagation. This is one remote postcolonial context for understanding the emergence of Boko Haram and its violent creed of anti-Christian, antisecular, and antimodernity insurgency. In this articulation Christianity, local and foreign, was conflated with the ascendancy of *boko* (Western education), along with its ideational, cultural, and commodified signs and materiality. As Abdulbasit Kassim and Michael Nwankpa demonstrate, many of the Boko Haram leaders' fiery sermons were aimed against the alleged threat that radical Christianity and expansionist Christian ideas and things posed to the Ummah. Many of these sermons copiously referenced incidents of religious conflict in which Christians killed Muslims, making the case for Muslim retaliatory and counterbalancing violence.[37]

In the 2000s a series of overlapping events and trends further frayed the religious fabric of Northern Nigeria, fracturing intergroup religious relations, igniting more religious violence, and enabling extremist groups such as Boko Haram to emerge from the fringe into the mainstream of Muslim discourse. The 2000s were a period of recurring Christian vigilantism and proactive and defensive violence. This intensifying Christian militancy further radicalized Muslim youth already prone to the rising influence of media-borne radicalism in the age of information democratization and connectivity. The resulting cauldron not only caused much religious strife but it also emboldened groups such as Boko Haram, who were now assured of an even larger pool from which to recruit and radicalize.

One of the developments that inflamed the volatile religious terrain of Northern Nigeria was the extension of Sharia law from the civil to the criminal domain by several Northern Nigerian states, beginning with Zamfara in October 1999. Between 2000 and 2001 several states in the region followed the example of Zamfara, many reluctantly caving to popular grassroots pressure.[38] It is important to note that Sharia penal codes were written into and implemented in a context of another tragically resonant development: the Al-Qaeda attack on the World Trade Center and the Pentagon on September 11, 2001, the ensuing U.S. "War on Terror" in Afghanistan and Iraq, and the unprecedented increase in Islamophobia in the West and in local Christian circles. The incendiary politics of the September 11 attack and its geopolitical consequences coincided with and further complicated the controversy and crisis that followed the implementation of Sharia criminal law in about a dozen states in Northern Nigeria. The violent religious conflicts that occurred in the 2000s were thus traceable, to varying degrees, to these two crosscutting events.

SHARIA AS AN INFLECTION POINT

In the Muslim community of Northern Nigeria, the implementation of Sharia criminal codes had a seminal discursive and practical effect. It triggered a contestation, once again, about which reformist outcome could be accepted as sufficient or satisfactory. Many clerics and scholars who had advocated for reform and even invoked the idiom of jihad in that advocacy considered the Sharia declaration in Zamfara State a seminal moment of triumph and embraced the Sharia project of then governor Ahmed Sani Yerima. For them this marked the triumphant endpoint of their decades-long struggle, the realization of a struggle pursued under a variety of rubrics.[39] Most of the scholars and intellectuals who had participated actively in the activist circuits of the Muslim Students' Society of Nigeria (MSSN) had now come of age. They had continued to struggle in the social, political, professional, academic, and intellectual arenas for the reform of the Nigerian state away from a secular constitutional and governmental order they regarded as colonial and Judeo-Christian in origin, toward a state form and a bureaucratic system they believed to be more aligned with Islamic principles and precepts. For them, the Sharia criminal code implementation was a victory. These intellectuals not only supported and celebrated the Zamfara declaration, they owned it as the fruit of their long struggle to rebalance the postcolonial Nigerian state from what they believed was its inequality in favor of Christian values that British colonizers had instituted.[40]

However, other Muslim intellectuals were skeptical of the Sharia moment and critiqued it in real time as both the euphoria and controversy surrounding it raged. For instance, the leader of the Shiite Islamic Movement of Nigeria, Sheikh Ibrahim Zakzaky, criticized the governor of Zamfara State and supporters of his Sharia project for assuming, erroneously in his opinion, that they could graft Sharia onto an overarching un-Islamic state system founded on secular democracy and the supremacy of a secular constitution. His verdict was that Sharia would only serve the interest of the Muslim ruling elite, who would use it to further oppress the masses.[41] Zakzaky also critiqued what he regarded as the contradiction of leaders elected under and sworn to uphold a liberal secular constitution implementing Sharia. Zakzaky was not the only one who considered Sharia implementation a half measure and an incomplete effort to restore the idealized precolonial Islamic system of Muslim Northern Nigeria. Many holdouts remained, yearning for what they considered the moment of true reform and revolution to restore Sharia and Muslim values as the supreme governing and judicial systems of Nigeria. One of those who followed the debate between the supporters of Sharia criminal code implementation and its critics was the future Boko Haram founder, Muhammad Yusuf.

Yusuf, like most clerics and Muslims of Salafi persuasion, at first enthusiastically welcomed the Sharia project, regarding it as a culmination of a long struggle for Muslims to live under God's law. Yusuf went on to participate in Sharia implementation in Borno State, negotiating a deal with then governorship candidate Ali Modu Sheriff for Yusuf's support of the candidate in exchange for full Sharia implementation. Yusuf, as many scholars have noted, subsequently nominated his father in-law, Buji Foi, to serve as a commissioner for religious affairs in Sheriff's cabinet before Yusuf and Sheriff had a falling-out over what Yusuf interpreted as Sheriff's half-hearted commitment to Sharia.[42]

It is well known that Yusuf and many other clerical figures soured on the Sharia project as it became clear that political leaders had merely used it to secure political support and legitimacy and had no intention of fully implementing Sharia. By late 2001 Sharia implementation had fizzled out, compromised by contradictions, controversies over the morality and constitutionality of some of the verdicts and punishments, and the weight and supremacy of Nigeria's constitution. For radical reformers like Yusuf, this was one more evidence that the Nigerian state system was irredeemable, that all previous peaceful reform efforts had failed, and that an alternative path of action was necessary.

The belief that the latest effort to re-Islamize the polity through Sharia had failed was shared by many Muslims, and the content of Northern Nigeria's most read newspapers reflected this sentiment of disillusionment.[43] Nor was Yusuf the only one to reject a pragmatic compromise with Nigeria's secular state. One commentator in a widely read 2003 essay lamented how the "re-Islamisation" Muslims yearned for remained "uncompleted," and argued that it was "wishful thinking" for Muslims to think that "Islamic salvation" would come through "the secular political machinery."[44] The difference between Yusuf and others such as this commentator was that Yusuf seemed to be drifting into a revolutionary frame of action while others remained in the realm of dissidence and discontentment. Yusuf's attitude evolved into rejection and jihad; others remained in the rhetorical frame of dissent.

CHRISTIAN REACTION AND THE SHARIA CRISIS

Sharia implementation was fraught with trouble in part because Northern Nigerian Christian minorities responded to it in violent ways and thenceforth built a framework of violent retaliation and retribution that would outlast the Sharia controversy and provide a justificatory frame of reference for radical Muslim groups such as Boko Haram. In his book *Rage and Carnage in the Name of God: Religious Violence in Nigeria*, Abiodun Alao identifies at least five strains of Christian violence in postcolonial Northern Nigeria, with most of these manifesting in the 2000s and beyond.[45]

The first of these reactionary episodes of Christian violence occurred in response to the implementation of Sharia criminal law and was driven by Christians' widely expressed fear that the laws would be imposed on them and that they would be subjected to criminal punitive and corrective measures prescribed in the Sharia. In February 2000 Christian youths rampaged in Kaduna metropolis, burning a mosque and harassing people in traffic. Retaliation by Muslim youths escalated the crisis, forcing the governor at the time, Ahmad Makarfi, to impose a curfew. In 2001 Christian youths protested against the implementation of Sharia in Bauchi metropolis. In Tafawa Balewa Local Government the protest turned violent when Christian youths reacted to a rumor that the state government was planning to impose Sharia law on the predominantly Christian Kutaru community. They protested, destroying property and disrupting activities until security forces intervened.

In some cases Christian youths took the law into their own hands to protest allegations that Muslims had abducted and forcefully converted young Christian girls in order to marry them.[46] In other cases Christian youth violently protested the construction of mosques in areas they considered Christian zones or too close to their traditional institutions. In July 2010 Christian youths destroyed the walls and windows of a mosque that had just been built by a police area commander, Mohammed Mustafa, in the town of Wukari in Taraba State. Muslim youths retaliated by burning a church, and fighting broke out between the two groups, leading to the loss of five lives and the destruction of homes and property.[47]

Around 2006, gunmen of Fulani ethnicity, known in Nigerian popular discourse as "armed herdsmen" and "Fulani herdsmen," began deadly sporadic attacks on Christian-majority communities in Northern Nigeria. When these assumed a more destructive dimension, Christian youths began to respond by attacking innocent Muslims in their midst. Because the Fulani invaders were Muslim, even if only nominally so, and often destroyed churches along with homes, the Christian youths interpreted it as a religious war on their communities and responded in kind, targeting Muslims who had nothing to do with the attacks. These incidents exacerbated violent religious conflict in Northern Nigeria, incubating and provoking anti-Christian rhetoric and reprisals.

When Boko Haram transformed into a violent insurgency in the wake of the police killing of Muhammad Yusuf in 2009, Christian youths recalibrated to engage in defensive violence in the face of a group avowedly dedicated to killing, enslaving, and cleansing their claimed territories of Christians. Violent Christian responses to Boko Haram took at least three forms. When Boko Haram began attacking churches and Christian communities in Borno, Yobe, and Adamawa States, Christian youths mobilized themselves as part of the vigilante Joint Task Force (JTF) that used violence to protect communities and deal with alleged Boko Haram members and spies in those communities. When Boko Haram began bombing churches around 2011, Christian youths formed protective cordons around churches and established church-backed vigilante groups to patrol the churches' perimeters. In some cases, when these measures failed to prevent the bombing of a church, Christian youths went on rampages against Muslims.[48]

These violent Christian acts, reactive as some of them may have been, did little to reduce interreligious conflicts. Instead, they fed into the rhetoric of Boko Haram and other radical Islamist groups, who seized on these actions to justify and reinforce their "religious war" rhetoric. On the Christian side, as Boko Haram attacks intensified and coincided with attacks on Christian communities by armed Fulani herdsmen, Christian leaders such as David Oyedepo, Apostle Johnson Suleiman, and former president of the Christian Association of Nigeria (CAN), Pastor Ayo Oritsejafor, began making increasingly bellicose statements endorsing and authorizing Christian defensive violence against Muslims.[49]

The transformation of Boko Haram into a violent jihadist organization intent on forcefully establishing an Islamic state and cleansing their claimed territories of Christians and Muslims who disagreed with their ideology exacerbated an already existing Christian militancy and provoked new incidents. Some of this Christian militancy quickly morphed from being a response to Boko Haram into platforms for a radical anti-Muslim agenda. This is clear when their stated intensions are scrutinized. In 2011 Northern Nigeria saw the emergence of a radical Christian group calling itself Akhwat Akwop. Through a series of statements, the group proclaimed itself ready not only to defend Christians against Boko Haram attacks but to cleanse Muslims from Christian-majority spaces in Northern Nigeria.[50]

These instances of Christian radicalism and the Islamophobic statements of some Christian preachers helped deepen the interreligious fissures in Northern Nigeria, a region where religion was already a charged arena of conflict, competition, suspicion, and conspiratorial discourses. It was into this charged but opportune space that Boko Haram ideologues wrote their rejectionist and violent jihadist creed. This postcolonial interreligious environment provided a fecund ground for groups such as Boko Haram to thrive. There were global and local examples of Muslim persecution, Islamophobia, and anti-Muslim violence for the ideologues of Boko Haram to draw on to make their case for violent jihad, and to criticize the pacifist counterpoints of their Muslim interlocutors.

SEIZING THE MANTLE OF JIHAD

When Muhammad Yusuf transitioned from dissidence to violent rejection, it was not an impulsive or instinctive move on his part. Yusuf had participated in the debate within Muslim reformist circles about the direction Muslims should go to reclaim their precolonial glory as they saw it. When he did not participate directly, he became deeply acquainted with events and discourses that fed his sense of righteous grievance. His lectures—long, detailed, and full of historical references—illustrate this gradual accumulation of grievances he harbored on behalf of the Muslim community of Nigeria.[51] He saw Nigerian Muslims as serial victims of the violence of colonial and postcolonial secular politics and policies, and as a persecuted religious community denied the right to live under the laws and values that their religion prescribed.

In his sermons, Yusuf copiously referenced interreligious violence in which Muslims were killed. He invoked the Nigerian government's imposition of a state of emergency on Zamfara State in the wake of the Sharia declaration as evidence of a federal secular assault on Islam and Muslims, and as a demonstration that Sharia and Islamic values could not thrive if the secular Nigerian state remained in place. Yusuf cited the Miss World blasphemy incident in 2002 as yet another instance of the indignities and disrespect Muslims had suffered, which were enabled, in his opinion, by a secular state structure founded on values diametrically opposed to Islamic principles.[52]

For Yusuf the events that grieved Muslims and Islam were not isolated: they were connected in a pattern of secular Nigerian state assaults on Islam. When individual Christians and Muslims did things that were insulting to Islam or stood in the way of the quest for longed-for reform and re-Islamization, they were, in Yusuf's mind, enabled by the secular state and its constitutional values of individual freedom and democracy. For Yusuf the enemy of Islam was thus the Nigerian state and its un-Islamic institutions and foundational principles and texts. In terms of methodology, his argument for transitioning from a rhetorical and intellectual struggle to a practical one of jihad and revolution was simple: previous efforts at reforming the Nigerian state to assuage Muslims' grievances and make it compatible with Muslims' aspirations for Sharia had failed, and so there was a need for a new praxis, a new paradigm of action.

Having positioned himself as the avatar of a radical alternative to existing approaches to reform and re-Islamization, and having separated himself from Salafi and non-Salafi clerics who espoused the existing paradigms of struggle, Yusuf proceeded to try to establish his credibility by debating and critiquing the approaches of these clerics. When those clerics questioned what they characterized as his extreme positions on democracy, secularity, and the Nigerian state institutions, Yusuf was able to answer their criticism on two grounds. He challenged them to point to how their approach had restored dignity and sovereignty to Muslims. He then affirmed his credibility on the claim that he was the only one brave enough and committed enough to the re-Islamization cause to move from rhetoric to action. Perhaps this was the reason that the efforts of his Salafi clerical critics and mentors to correct and temper his creedal "extremism" failed to gain purchase with his followers, and only served to make his Yusufiyya movement, as it was known in Maiduguri before the name of Boko Haram was applied, more popular in its early days.

CONCLUSION

This chapter argues that Boko Haram's emergence and rapid rise to prominence as a platform of violent jihad cannot be understood without explicating the ways in which the group diverges from and, in some cases, recalls the legacy of the Fodiawa jihad movement of the nineteenth century. The latter remains a paradigmatic point of departure for discourses and practices of reformism and religious dissidence in Muslim Northern Nigerian to date. The chapter also asserts that Boko Haram is in part a product of more recent postcolonial interreligious conflict, specifically that produced by the unresolved questions of Nigerian postcolonial nationhood, local and global shifts in religious politics, and the sparsely acknowledged phenomenon of Christian radicalism and violence. Boko Haram, a group self-consciously committed to fighting against what it regards as the aftereffects and accoutrements of Judeo-Christian colonization and neocolonialism—secular education, modernity, democracy, and westernization—feeds off Christian radical attitudes toward Muslims in Northern Nigeria to sustain its legitimizing claim of being a militant defender and avenger of Muslims and Islam. The implementation of Sharia legal codes by many Muslim-majority Northern Nigerian states in the 2000s not only exacerbated interreligious violence but also intensified intrareligious debate on the trajectory of reform, with the result that new, insurgent militant groups were able to revive the jihad option as both a solution to Christian violence against Muslims and a response to the disappointment of "failed" Sharia implementation.

2   Reform and Rejection

This chapter illuminates the long history that led from a predominantly Sufi Muslim consensus, with its own story of fissures and dissent, to a Salafi-dominated orthodoxy in Northern Nigerian Islam. The chapter transitions from this foundational analysis to a discussion of the ruptures, creedal reconfigurations, and ideological realignments that mainstreamed a reformist ethos, which generated its own contradictions, controversies, and rebellions. Beginning with the Sokoto Caliphate, the major contours of the history of heterodoxy and dissidence in Northern Nigeria are discussed chronologically from the precolonial to the postcolonial period as a way of story-mapping the waves of reform and dissidence that help explain the rise of Boko Haram.

The connective through line in this analysis is the persistence of discontent and the moral claim that piety and the "correct path" would assuage and satisfy sociopolitical and spiritual anxieties and yearnings, enabling a return to an idealized past of superior Islamic devotion. This yearning for the lost caliphate is the crux of the Boko Haram insurgency even if it is expressed in a more absolutist and bellicose language in Boko Haram's rhetorical repertoire than it was in preceding iterations of it. The historical analysis of the ideological roots of Boko Haram highlights the recurring baseline of dissatisfaction with the status quo and the attendant transhistorical search for an ideal society governed by God's law. The transition from Sufi to Salafi preeminence convulsed the Northern Nigerian Islamic social fabric with sectarian tensions, but it did little to undermine the longing for reform and the idealized Islamic society that reform is believed to birth. The road from Salafi ascendancy to Boko Haram was convoluted, messy, and riddled with detours, but the multiphase transitions are discernible.

DISCURSIVE CONTESTATIONS REGARDING BOKO HARAM'S ORIGIN STORY

In his article "The Metamorphosis of Boko Haram: A Local's Perspective," Shaykh Abdulfathi acknowledges other factors that contributed to the emergence and metamorphosis of Boko Haram, including the Nigerian military's extrajudicial killings of its founder, Muhammad Yusuf, and many of his followers, the elite's manipulation of Boko Haram members for their political ambitions, the Kanuri community's ethnic protection of Boko Haram members, and poverty. He also stresses the need to pay attention to "the roles played by Malam Ja'far Mahmud Adam in association with Alhaji Mohammed Indimi in radicalizing the Wahhabi ideology of the community," which he argues "produced the likes of Mohammed Yusuf who took the ideology to the utmost extreme." Building on this thesis, Shaykh Abdulfathi proposes that the defeat of Boko Haram would be incomplete without tackling the ideological roots of Wahhabism and regulating the activities of Salafi scholars who "propagate their ideology of segregation and apostatizing of Muslims who do not tag along with them."[1]

Although Shaykh Abdulfathi's postulations regarding the contemporary ideological origins of Boko Haram seem plausible, they are likely driven by the author's own ideological and creedal leanings. As Andrea Brigaglia rightly notes, scholars of different sectarian formations who articulate positions on Boko Haram's roots are entering "the debate about the origins of Boko Haram with a baggage of theological, political and emotional commitments."[2] Shaykh Abdulfathi is no exception. Abdulfathi's diagnostic analysis of Boko Haram's ideological origins can be situated within the "Sufi/Good Muslims vs. Wahhabi/Bad Muslims" narrative that developed within the "War on Terror" paradigm,[3] which treats Boko Haram solely as a problem of religious extremism to be solved rather than as one of many actors in a historical and contemporary religious marketplace accustomed to disruption and contestation.

While reproaching Ja'afar for spearheading an exclusivist, literalist, and rigid Wahhabi variant of Salafism that birthed "Bad Muslims," Shaykh Abdulfathi positions himself and his Sufi followers as "Good Muslims" who preach tolerance and accommodate Muslims, Christians, northerners, southerners, Nigerians, and non-Nigerians in their mosque complex in Maiduguri without resorting to abuse, apostatizing, or violence. The most controversial feature of this school of thought lies in the attempt to frame a linear process of mentorship that connects Salafi clerics to the leaders of Boko Haram. Abdulfathi ignores the nuances and divergences that differentiate Salafi clerics and the leaders of Boko Haram, particularly on the issues of Western education, Muslims' participation in democracy and secular politics, and the advocacy of immediate jihad in the local milieu. This school of thought also elides the range of religious philosophies that may have influenced the careers and trajectories of Boko Haram leaders, who are known to have drawn inspiration and influence from an eclectic and divergent body of Islamic thought in their preaching and ideological exploration phase.

Since Boko Haram commenced its active phase of insurgency in 2009, the relationship between the mainstream Salafi clerics and the leaders of Boko Haram has come under academic and public scrutiny. Besides Shaykh Abdulfathi's school of thought, three additional paradigms are discernible in the corpus of writings that have attempted to dissect the relationship between Salafi clerics such as Ja'far and the leaders of Boko Haram, particularly Muhammad Yusuf.[4] The first of these analytical modes is mainly represented by the students, followers, and close associates of Ja'far. They accentuate the burgeoning position that the religious thought of the Iranian-influenced Islamic Movement of Nigeria led by Shaykh Ibraheem Zakzaky was the core influence on the political theology of Muhammad Yusuf and the leaders of Boko Haram.[5] Yusuf is portrayed reductively as a religious zealot who smuggled the jihadi thought he acquired from his "non-Salafi Nigerian mentors" into a quietist Salafi community with no palpable ideational leanings toward jihadism.

A second explanatory school sees Muhammad Yusuf as the architect of a reincarnated Boko Haram ideology, the inheritor of a rebellious tradition and opposition toward Western education and secular government that can be traced to the 1980s "Islam-only" activism led by Shaykh Ibraheem Zakzaky. In an attempt to defend Salafism and Salafi clerics from charges of extremism and radicalism, the proponents of this paradigm also focus their theological examination of Boko Haram's origins on intra-Salafi debates over the permissibility and impermissibility of Western education, while dismissing the electronic and textual archives of Salafi clerics who had openly preached messages in support of global jihad movements that espoused positions similar to Boko Haram's. The polemical undercurrent of this hypothesis in a predominantly Sunni Muslim society is to deflect arguments about Boko Haram's connection to Salafism and to do so by discrediting the movement through associating it with Shiism.

A third thesis on the emergence of Boko Haram views the group as an offshoot of intra-Salafi conflict, a conflict that was itself precipitated by the geopolitical entanglements of a "War on Terror" that reshaped the spectrums of global and local Salafism. This theory examines the stage-by-stage ideational convergence and divergence between the so-called "quietist Salafism" and the "jihadi-Salafism," with particular emphasis on the progressive deradicalization of the public discourses of the former, starting with a shift from endorsement to avoidance to rejection of global jihad movements.[6] Proponents of this approach recognize the non-Salafi associative religious philosophies that may have influenced the careers and trajectories of Boko Haram leaders. However, they contend that these non-Salafi religious philosophies had a minor ideational influence on Boko Haram compared to the Salafi canons the movement deploys, however simplistically, to legitimize its religious philosophies and theological beliefs.

Although not yet formalized or codified in scholarship, a fourth view on Boko Haram's ideological origins traces its rise to the continuities and changes in the centuries-old intellectual history of Islamic thought and reform in Northern Nigeria. This school of thought employs a historical approach that seeks to place Boko Haram within the continuum of millenarian movements of dissent and rebellion that emerged at different periods in the precolonial, colonial, and postcolonial histories of Northern Nigeria.[7]

The central arguments of the present volume are situated within the fourth approach and, to a lesser extent, the third. The analysis that follows fleshes out the long historical process from the Sufi-led jihad of the early nineteenth century to the resistance against colonialism in the early twentieth century, to Salafi reformism, and, finally, to the evolution of jihadi-Salafism in the late twentieth and early twenty-first centuries. Mainstream Salafi clerics and religious activists who embraced political Islam, a literalist creed, and a revivalist and reformist agenda were central to the profound transformation of the Northern Nigerian Islamic landscape in the last two decades of the twentieth century and the first decade of the twenty-first, a transformation that, while not directly connected to the emergence of Boko Haram, created conditions that enabled it to thrive. The analysis begins with the role that some mainstream Salafi clerics played in creating this transformed Muslim public.

NIGERIAN SALAFISM, GLOBAL JIHADISM, AND BOKO HARAM

In April 2021 a scandal erupted on Nigeria's social media and in Nigeria's vibrant traditional media. Tapes and excerpts of the past preaching and jihad advocacy of Sheikh Dr. Isa Ali Pantami, then Nigeria's minister of Communications and Digital Economy, came to light. The *Daily Independent* newspaper published a story alleging that the minister was on a U.S. terrorism watch list due to his jihadist sympathies and past pro-jihad preaching. The minister denied this and furiously threatened a libel lawsuit if the newspaper did not retract the allegation and apologize to him, which the newspaper did. In the meantime, a debate over Pantami's preaching dating back to the mid- to late 2000s ignited. Journalists investigating Pantami's past unearthed a video of a 2004 twenty-minute sermon in which Pantami combined advocacy for global jihad with volunteering to lead jihad in defense of Muslims locally.[8] In the sermon he declared that jihad was a *fardh ayn*—an obligation for every Muslim. He urged Muslims to shun clerical and political figures who were calling for peaceful coexistence between Christians and Muslims, and volunteered to lead a squad of Hisbah (Sharia paramilitary enforcers in Muslim-majority states of Northern Nigeria) to defend Muslims against Christian attacks in Yelwan Shendam, a town in Central Nigeria where clashes between Muslims and Christians had led to many deaths. In the same sermon Pantami tearfully prayed for the success of Taliban and al-Qaeda Islamic militants, connecting the local to the global in one homiletic gesture of jihad advocacy. Pantami's documented past preaching resonated negatively across Nigeria's ethnoreligious and sectarian spectrums, and polarized public opinion because of his visibility in the Nigerian government at the time. Many Nigerians called for his firing while some defended him.

Two years later, on September 12, 2006, Pantami had delivered a fifty-four-minute sermon at a mosque in Bauchi, followed by a question-and-answer session. The tape of this Hausa-language sermon is publicly available on a Nigerian Islamic website, DawahNigeria.com.[9] Titled "Su waye Yan Taliban" (Who Are the Taliban?), the sermon eulogized, lionized, and humanized visible figures in the global jihadist community. He offered condolences on the death of Abu Musab Alzarqawi, leader of al-Qaeda in Iraq. Pantami described Alzarqawi as a martyr who, along with Taliban leader Mullah Omar and other "incredible people of faith . . . who follow the Sunnah," had ensured that "the enemies of Allah are unable to find rest in this world." The translation of the sermon by Andrea Brigaglia, a religion scholar and expert on Islam in Northern Nigeria, is accurate and captures Pantami's rhetorical fervor. Pantami praised the emergence of the Taliban as a necessary and timely initiative that promised not only to end the civil war in Afghanistan but also to banish "infidels" who invaded the country, and to establish "a Caliphate and the Sharia, as every Muslim is commanded to." Pantami described the Taliban as a group committed to the "purest Sunni doctrine."

For Pantami the Taliban modeled several virtues for Nigerian Muslims and should be emulated.[10] According to Pantami, Nigerian Muslims should emulate the Taliban's destruction of "the idols of Buddha" by pushing for the erasure of "idolatrous images" from the Nigerian currency, international passports, electoral materials, and other documents since, in his view, the production and dissemination of images contradicted the Sharia. Another Taliban example Pantami considered worthy of emulation was the imposition of a dress code dictated by the Sunnah, such as full-face veiling for women and long beards and ankle-length trousers for men.

After offering prayers for Sheikh Nasiruddin Albani and Ibn al-Uthayimin, Pantami told his followers to replicate the Taliban experience by studying "medicine and engineering" as they prepared for the emergence of a leader of the stature of Mullah Omar, who would lead the jihad in Nigeria when the time was right. Here Pantami hinted at his inclination toward what some scholars call jihadi gradualism. He was rhetorically gesturing toward a position that was somewhere between the jihadist urgency and immediacy advocated by Boko Haram leader Muhammad Yusuf and the gradualist Salafi reformist path of influential Salafi theologian Nasiruddin al-Albani, who advocated for preparing and purifying the Muslim *Ummah* while the faithful waited for Allah to bring about change at a time of his choosing.[11]

During the question-and-answer session Pantami was asked if armed jihad was possible in Nigeria given the absence of a central legitimate leader such as Mullah Omar of Afghanistan. This question gave Pantami an opportunity to elaborate on his position on preparation and leadership as prerequisites for jihad. Pantami emphasized jihad as an imperative and inevitability, but he stressed the need for a legitimate leader to emerge before Muslims could proceed to the next step of launching a jihad. He reiterated that this was a time for *gyara* (correction) and *isti'dad* (preparation), a transitional period preceding jihad. Pantami invited his audience to understand the importance of purification and the establishment of the Sunnah before jihad could be launched: "How can you start a jihad when your father is still going around without a beard [and] when your mother is still going around with a mere transparent veil [*gyale*] rather than with a full hijab?" Pantami stated that "any effort to start a jihad without having established the correct Islamic practices is doomed to failure." He again recommended the Taliban example, whose success he attributed to the group's "unwavering attachment to the Sunnah" and prior preparation.[12]

Pantami claimed that he had opposed the ill-fated jihad declaration of the Nigerian Taliban group, which had retreated to Kanama, Yobe State, and had later launched a small, contained Islamic uprising, "because it was not led by scholars and there was no understanding of the Sunnah." Pantami was previewing his famous debate with Boko Haram founder Muhammad Yusuf, with whom he agreed on the necessity for jihad in Nigeria but disagreed on its timing.[13] Like other mainstream Salafi scholars, Pantami extolled the external jihad of the Taliban and Al-Qaeda but stopped short of calling for a jihad in Nigeria, arguing that the condition and timing were not yet right.

Another questioner wanted to know if it was appropriate for *Ahlus-Sunnah* (Salafis) to disavow Osama bin Laden because of his killing of innocent nonbelievers. Pantami answered by arguing that Bin Laden might be guilty of some errors but that "I still consider him a better Muslim than myself" and that "we are all happy whenever nonbelievers are being killed, only that the Sharia stipulates that there must be a reason for killing them."[14]

As revelations of his previous projihad pronouncements circulated in Nigeria's traditional and social media ecosystems, Pantami declared that he no longer held these positions and that he had allowed his youthful exuberance to lead him to an error he now regretted. Nonetheless, the unearthed tapes revealed his and other Salafist clerics' past rhetorical excesses in support of violent jihad, statements made at a time when these sentiments were commonly expressed in mainstream Muslim circles as the *Ummah* faced domestic and external pressures. Pantami's nuanced commentary on jihad was a familiar script among Salafi clerics who considered Boko Haram's declaration of jihad in Nigeria premature, even while broadly endorsing violent jihad as a legitimate corrective religious, sociopolitical, and state-building instrument.

Beyond Pantami, the scandal opened a window into the little-scrutinized jihadist dispositions of and radical views expressed by several Northern Nigerian clerics in the 2000s. In the aftermath of the scandal, many commentators began to rhetorically compare these previous pronouncements with similar statements made by Boko Haram. Extrapolations, some riddled with Islamophobic prejudice but others specific and legitimate, were made between the neojihad ideology revealed in Pantami's preaching and popular neojihad sentiments circulating at different times and for different purposes in the Northern Nigerian Islamic public sphere.

BOKO HARAM AND QUIETIST SALAFIS

Pantami was hardly alone among mainstream Salafis in amplifying the ideology of global jihad and suggesting the imperative of future jihad in

Nigeria. As Andrea Brigaglia states, several Salafi scholars were echoing and pandering to the prevailing projihad sentiments among Salafi Muslims in Northern Nigeria: "It was ordinary for Nigeria's mainstream Salafis to endorse Al-Qaeda publicly in their speeches and lectures." The scholars contend that in this open, widespread display of affection and support for global jihadists, "Nigeria was probably a unique case in the Muslim world."[15]

Such was the depth of the projihad ferment in post-9/11 Nigeria that Islamic scholars found themselves establishing and retaining their legitimacy by reinforcing the existing popular Muslim narratives in support of jihad as a correction against oppression and injustice, and as a way to reform and purify Islam and enthrone the Sharia in Nigeria. The popularity of the iconography of global jihad in Northern Nigeria was overwhelming. Many families in Kano and across Northern Nigeria were naming their male newborns Osama in honor of Osama bin Laden, whom many Northern Nigerian Muslims, including some Sufis, viewed as a hero of Islam for defending the dignity of Muslims against Western imperial violence.[16] Additionally, bin Laden posters could be found on vehicles and homes all over Kano and other parts of the Nigerian Northwest and Northeast. Islamic singers composed songs in praise of bin Laden and the Taliban, and these performances lionized global jihadists. Radio stations broadcast messages and programs in support of bin Laden. Many Northern Nigerian Muslim youths yearned to join the jihad in Iraq and Afghanistan.[17]

Salafi clerics such as Pantami, Ja'afar Adam, Aminu Daurawa, Auwal Albani Zaria, and Sani Rijiyar Lemo raised the consciousness of jihad in their sermons, but these sermons also drew on projihad idioms and narratives that were already in popular, vernacularized circulation in the Northern Nigerian Muslim public sphere. These Salafi clerics expressed support for the jihad of al-Qaeda and the Taliban. Auwal Albanin Zaria even went so far as to invoke a personal association with Osama bin Laden to underscore his support for the global jihad of al-Qaeda. Aminu Daurawa took his support for global jihad even further by issuing a fatwa to justify suicide bombing,[18] stating in a moment of rhetorical flourish that God himself was a suicide bomber, a position he publicly renounced in a December 2020 video in which he announced that he had read the books of an unnamed Saudi scholar that caused him to change his position.[19] This was a symbiotic dynamic and a feedback loop in which scholars both fed the neojihad narratives of the post-9/11 global Muslim struggle and enriched their homiletic repertoires by invoking themes popular with their followers.

Despite the existence of some evidence that appears to associate some Salafi clerics, early in their careers, with the same projihad ideological creed as Boko Haram, the relationship of so-called quietist Salafi clerics with Boko Haram and its founding clerics such as Yusuf was ambivalent. Yusuf and the other Salafi clerics came from the same tradition that extolled reform, a strict adherence to the Sunnah, and the establishment and enforcement of the Sharia. In that regard, the influence of the ideas and ideologies that the mainstream Salafi preachers propagated helped build the momentum toward the reformist consensus that Boko Haram exploited. Through their preaching and theological pronouncements, the Salafi clerics also unwittingly but quite plausibly provided Boko Haram with a pool of pliable, receptive, and ideologically primed youths from which to recruit for its jihad project.

However, while the mainstream Salafi clerics converged with Boko Haram on the imperative and legitimacy of waging local and global jihad, they differed from the group on the timing of such a jihad in Nigeria, and most of them disassociated themselves from Boko Haram when the latter's violent confrontation with the Nigerian state began in 2009. Other doctrinal differences between mainstream Salafi scholars and Muhammad Yusuf were hashed out in debates and articulated in the former's homiletic criticisms of the latter. Pantami's well-known debate with Yusuf, a six-hour affair, encapsulates this ambivalent ideological kinship of convergence and divergence between Boko Haram and quietist Salafi scholars.[20] Like other Salafi clerics, Pantami disagreed with Yusuf on the impermissibility of working within the secular Nigerian state and enrolling in Western education. Mainstream Salafi clerics saw Western education as a tool they could use to prepare for and further jihad if it became necessary, taking their cue in this respect from global Salafi-Jihadi movements. Boko Haram's creed took a more absolutist view on Western education.

While Boko Haram was implacably opposed to engagement with or participation in the institutions of the secular state, mainstream Salafi clerics adopted the pragmatic if equally reformist philosophy of entering the state and using its levers to reform it from within. Failing that, their plan was to undermine and destroy it, making the establishment of Sharia easier. Their Hausa slogan *A shiga a gyara* (enter the state to reform it) was inherited from the earlier reformist enterprise of Sheikh Mahmud Abubakar Gumi, which is discussed extensively later in this book. The slogan succinctly captured their conviction about participating in Nigeria's secular government to leverage the power of participation to realize their goal of establishing a Sharia-governed state in the future, with or without formal jihad.

In opposing Boko Haram, Salafi clerics made sure to observe the delicate protocol of highlighting granular doctrinal differences without altogether condemning the creed of Boko Haram or disavowing the group's members' Islamic identity. They tried to distinguish between their criticism of Boko Haram's method and totalizing absolutes of exclusions and prohibitions, and their own support for the underlying reformist and rejectionist motivations at the heart of Boko Haram's insurgency. They viewed Boko Haram as well-intentioned but misguided and unlearned reformers. One example of this solidarity with Boko Haram as a group of "misguided" coreligionists is a sermon Pantami preached sometime between 2010 and 2015, in which he tearfully lamented that Nigerian soldiers fighting against Boko Haram were killing "our fellow Muslim brothers."[21]

Given this ambivalent history and interlocution between Boko Haram and quietist Salafi clerics, the popular sentiment that Boko Haram's atrocities against Muslims and Muslim communities, more than its doctrine and creed, caused what is now clearly an acrimonious rift between the former and the latter is at best only partially credible. The preexisting disagreement over the timing of jihad and Nigeria's readiness for radical re-Islamization was real and caused mainstream Salafi clerics to begin distancing themselves from Boko Haram. Boko Haram's seemingly indiscriminate violence against Muslims and its suspected assassination of prominent Salafi clerics Sheikh Ja'afar Adam and Sheikh Auwal Albani Zaria deepened the rift and compelled the mainstream Salafi scholars to withdraw into what Thomas Hegghammer calls pietism enforced through moral vigilantism.[22]

In explaining Boko Haram, Alexander Thurston argues that the movement is a product of circumstances.[23] He is right that an existing and deepening state dysfunction opened the door to nonstate entities to demonstrate their claimed capacity to spiritually ameliorate the dysfunction while growing their influence and success. However, a fuller account of the emergence of Boko Haram must recognize another important factor. Boko Haram blossomed out of the fluctuating, unstable, and at times conflictual symbiosis between the group's founders and a precursor reformist movement, namely the existing Salafi establishment of the late 1990s and 2000s. More importantly, the group emerged out of a radical reformist ferment nurtured and sustained by the vibrant circulation of revivalist ideologies that quietist Salafi scholars and their followers helped to propagate and normalize.

Belief in the legitimacy of armed jihad, either as a first or last resort, became the contested terrain of Northern Nigerian Salafi discourse. By the time Boko Haram emerged in the early 2000s and its transformation into an armed jihad entity in 2009, the ideology, if not the practice, of jihad as a legitimate methodology for effecting societal change, challenging unjust governmental authority, and purifying the *Ummah* already had purchase in Northern Nigeria, some but not all of it attributable to Boko Haram's preaching. The origin story of the acceptance of jihad as an option of reform and redress in Northern Nigeria harkens back to the Sokoto jihad movement. The acceptance of righteous insurgence as a method of ameliorating perceived religious betrayal and egregious violations of faith is not the isolated accomplishment of twentieth- and twenty-first-century Islamic dissidents. As discussed in the previous chapter, the Sokoto jihad set the tone and primed the polity to be receptive to a righteous discourse of revival and the accompanying language of reformist critique that today's reformers, armed and unarmed, have seized on.

THE FODIAWA JIHAD AND THE CONTINUUM OF REFORMIST CRITIQUE

The nineteenth-century Islamic reform movement established an important baseline of Islamic piety in Northern Nigeria. In the ensuing history of reform and revival, the jihad made it possible to use the language of purification and reform to designate whole groups of people as bad Muslims and apostates, and to legitimize physical and textual attacks on them. It also established a tradition of reformist Islam whose endpoint is a seemingly elusive ideal Islamic community. It is precisely because this imagined ideal Muslim community is elusive and impractical in a dynamic and plural society that it creates both disappointment and disenchantment among committed reformers. In other words, the ironic legacy of the Fodiawa jihad is that it birthed a recurring discourse of disappointment that was later expressed through a critique of heretical betrayal and through new, countercaliphate reformist insurgencies.

Even during the heyday of the caliphate, critical narratives of betrayal proliferated, articulated by those who either took the reformers' ameliorative promises literally or considered the rebels' claims inadequate as a blueprint of reform. This narrative of elusive redemption came from two main sources in the nineteenth century. The first was an apocalyptic vision rooted in Ashari theology, the second an expectation of radical political departure from the preexisting political order. Dan Fodio's reformist movement legitimated itself in part by appealing to and amplifying the millenarian image of the Mahdi. In this tradition time is understood as a linear but regressive force that culminates inexorably in the end of days, a triumph of divine justice, and the final overthrow of a political order of unbelief. Given this theological backdrop, the failure of the Mahdi to arrive in the spectacular way Muslim folk millenarianism anticipated, Dan Fodio's postjihad disavowal of the Mahdi label, and the subsequent unraveling of Mahdist rebellions against British colonial invasions in Anglo-Egyptian Sudan and Northern Nigeria roiled Muslims in the region and deepened both their despair and their desire for a new era of God's just reign.[24]

Furthermore, in strategically exaggerating the misdeeds and allegedly un-Islamic ways of the Hausa Muslim rulers while overstating their own redemptive mission, the Sokoto jihadists inadvertently sowed the seeds of disappointment and disillusionment, opening the door to dissidence and rebellion when former reformist rebels became rulers (emirs and ruling aristocrats) and were unable to translate highfalutin idealism and elevated moral claims to egalitarian governance and practical social justice. This original caliphal condition of constant disillusionment and dissidence endured into the subsequent colonial and postcolonial periods.

Thus, our somewhat Hegelian argument is that, by its very nature, a reformist movement generates its own contradiction because the elusiveness of the hoped-for outcome makes disappointment and the emergence of new reformist movements inevitable. Once victorious, insurgent movements then become orthodoxies to be challenged by new ideological dissidents. The logic of reform and purification requires new generations of reformers to designate older, more established ones as failed reformers or, worse, apostates and infidels. Reform movements also become inevitable incubators of hierarchy and zones of elitist exclusivity, shutting out younger, more radical, zealous upstarts. Such was the case of Boko Haram founder Yusuf, who struggled for visible operative space within an established, older, and better-educated Salafi hierarchy and only got attention and followers when he challenged that Salafi establishment and its "quietist" creed. Boko Haram fits perfectly into this pattern and, in some ways, embodies and extends this logic of infinite, self-reproducing reform. At the same time, Boko Haram departs from this trajectory and represents a violent rejection and disruption of an old reformist tradition that only occasionally and finitely employed violence as a method to achieve the goal of enthroning the rule of Allah.

FROM SUFI JIHAD TO REFORM AND REJECTION

The critique of existing orthodoxy and the longing for a romanticized past of untrammeled piety is a staple of reformist vernacular in Northern Nigerian Islam. Boko Haram appropriated and deployed it to win popular support, but its origins lay in the past. There is a long tradition of generational reformist critiques that are framed in this rubric, most of them benign internal ferments, some rejectionist and even sporadically violent. For instance, after the Sokoto Caliphate was established, many subsequent Islamic discourses critiqued the mundane, secularized preoccupations of the emirs who ruled its various territorial units. Some of these discourses even went so far as to proclaim that reformist jihad had simply removed one set of nominally Muslim rulers and replaced them with another. The narrative of lost reform and betrayal persisted and thrived as the caliphate became, in the opinion of dissidents, little more than a secular political entity profiting from the reputational cachet of religious reform.

Since the nineteenth-century jihad, Northern Nigeria has been a hotbed of several waves of Islamic reformist movements, some violent and ideologically insular, others peaceful and pragmatic. Some were more directly inspired by the Fodiawa jihad tradition than others, but all of them operated in the spirit and example established by that seminal jihad. These post-Fodiawa reformist movements posited the fundamental argument that present rulers were corrupt and oppressive and "should be overthrown on religious grounds," and that strict and total adherence to the sayings and deeds of the Prophet and the teachings of the Qur'an was the only acceptable form of life for a Muslim. There were several movements in the mold of *Ahl al-Sunna wa 'l-Jama'a*, dissident Islamic communities. These groups argued that Muslims in any era ought to consciously "behave exactly as did the earliest Muslims" (*al-salaf al-ṣāliḥ*), strictly emulating the details of the Prophet's life gathered from the Qur'an, the *ḥadīth* (sayings of the Prophet), and the *Sunna* (deeds and examples of the Prophet), and rejecting the corrupting technologies and accouterments of modern life.[25] Others preached unconventional, heterodox doctrines outside the mainline interpretive and jurisprudential schools in Islam.

In the Sokoto Caliphate Tijaniyya networks secretly formed in opposition to the dominant caliphal Qadiriyya *tariqa*. These attracted several scholars in Gwandu, Adamawa, and elsewhere, some of whom had to relocate to remote corners of the caliphate away from the eastern and western headquarters of Sokoto and Gwandu in order to escape the scrutiny of the Qadiriyya clerical establishment. Several millenarian Sufi sects emerged that led followers on long migratory marches through the rural countryside to evade the authority of established emirates. In the 1850s one such group was led by Liman Yamusa in Dutse. Its growing membership was violently disbanded by state forces on the eastern flank of Kano emirate.[26] Some communities were inchoate, finding momentary territorial solidarity in their status as maroons and refugees established deep in the hinterland. Such groups attracted runaway slaves who asserted their freedom by converting to Islam and pledging allegiance to the sectarian heterodoxy of the community.

Millenarian groups such as the Digawa, Salihawa, Isawa, and other sects with diverse doctrines considered contrary to mainstream Islamic tenets emerged. Their adherents were insurgents who sporadically employed violence to advance their goals. The Isawa in particular ran egregiously afoul of the existing theological consensus of the caliphate by recognizing the messianic status of Jesus and integrating that belief into their Muslim devotion. The violent persecution of the Isawa culminated in the beheading of their leader in Kano,[27] but their story demonstrates the depth and breadth of the landscape of dissidence in the caliphate, provides a window into anticaliphate rebellions and heterodoxies and their legacies, and historicizes contemporary heterodox rebellions.

THE ISAWA-NINGAWA HETERODOX REBELLION

The rise of the Isawa entailed the intermeshing of two simultaneously occurring events. One was the emergence of a heterodox Islamic doctrine that challenged the doctrinal consensus not only of the Sokoto Caliphate but also of all mainstream Islamic exegetical traditions. The other was a history of grassroots peasant resentment and revolt against excessive taxation and other perceived exploitative practices of an established caliphate aristocracy. Rulers of the Sokoto Caliphate and its emirates considered the Isawa (lit. disciples of Isa/Jesus) sect a particularly potent countercaliphate insurgent movement because the group, an eclectic Islamic sect with unorthodox beliefs, posed a doctrinal threat as well as a socioeconomic one to some of the caliphate's emirates. The Isawa *mallams* (Isawa clerics) not only led a doctrinal rebellion against the established Sunni teachings of the caliphate but also fused their dissidence with and took on the identity of a rural, grassroots uprising against the exacting demands of caliphate rulers. This convergence of secular socioeconomic grievance and heterodox, syncretistic, and, from the perspective of caliphate Islam, heretical practices and creeds presented both an ideological and existential challenge that the caliphate and some of its federated emirates would struggle to contain.

Who were the Isawa, and what were their beliefs? The historical records date the emergence of the sect to the 1850s. The sect began in Kano metropolis as an urban clerical dissent, but it quickly spread in the rural fringes of Kano, becoming at first a dissident group that aroused more derision and curiosity than hostility. Persecution followed when the group's teachings became more well known and more apocalyptically opposed to some foundational teachings of Islam. The group held beliefs that contradicted some tenets of Islam. While subscribing to *tawhid*, the Muslim creed of monotheism and the absolute oneness of God, the Isawa rejected the special prophetic status assigned to Muhammad, audaciously refusing to verbalize the second part of the Kalimat Shahada, "Muhammad is the messenger of Allah."[28] The Isawa repudiated all the established Muslim traditions and instead preached that the Qur'an alone and the Christian scriptures should be the foundations of a Muslim's faith. The Isawa clerics declared that Jesus (Prophet Isa) was the "word" and "spirit" of Allah as declared in the Qur'an. For that reason they accorded him a higher status than Muhammad, whom they claimed the Qur'an never proclaimed as the "word" and "spirit" of God. The Isawa refused to perform basic Muslim rituals, including the *qibla* (facing in the direction of the Ka'aba in Mecca when praying), and modified the Ramadan fast, declaring that fasting could be done at any time of the year and should be observed discreetly rather than announced.[29] The group prohibited the use of tobacco and kola nuts. Unlike other Muslims, they believed in the resurrection of Jesus, whose biblical miracle of raising the dead they emphasized.

Between 1913 and 1922 missionaries Rev. G. P. Bargery and Rev. Walter Miller of the Church Mission Society (CMS) collected several testimonies from members or former members of the Isawa group, some of whom had converted to Christianity by this time. These collected accounts give us a synopsis of the group's beginning. Another set of testimonies collected or obtained by historian Ian Linden in the 1960s and 1970s contains accounts passed down to descendants of the original Isawa sect members. These oral sources are unanimous in their core elements about the beginning of the sect. They recount that the founder, Mallam Ibrahim, had been a court adviser to the emir of Kano Abdullahi in the early to mid-1850s. By some accounts, Mallam Ibrahim returned from a pilgrimage to the Mecca with a new doctrine venerating Isa (Jesus) and deemphasizing the primacy and special prophetic status accorded Muhammad.[30] Other accounts do not reference a return from the pilgrimage and its insinuation of a possible exposure to Christianity along the way, and instead claim that Ibrahim had realized through his own *tafsir* (contemplative exegesis) that Jesus/Isa was accorded great honor in the Qur'an, which refers to him as "Word of God" and "spirit and breath from God." The accounts diverge in their subsequent details, but Mallam Ibrahim is said to have confronted Emir Abdullahi and senior Islamic scholars, accusing them of hiding the esoteric truth (*asir*) of the Qur'an's references to Isa.[31]

Linden argues that some of these details may have been contaminated by their transmission through missionary mediums and by the fact that some of the informants were now Christians or secret Isawa and may have thus embellished some elements of the story. What we do know is that, far from satisfying the inquiries inspired by his new exegetical trajectory, whatever clarification and correction Ibrahim got from the senior court clerics he consulted escalated his doctrinal rebellion. Many accounts state that Mallam Ibrahim began to openly proclaim his rejection of some of the tenets of Islam. For instance, he began to say that he and his followers no longer considered Muhammad a prophet of God and instead proclaimed the messianic status of Isa/Jesus. He also began to articulate an eschatological, quasi-Mahdist claim of Jesus's return. Some of the recorded oral accounts claim that the Isawa were persecuted and their members imprisoned, and associate their membership in the sect with a life of great suffering.[32] This persecution seemed to have only served to fuel the counter-caliphate zeal of Ibrahim and his followers, who continued their heterodox activities and open challenges to established tenets of Islam.

It is not clear what triggered the official decision to extirpate the group and its doctrine, but the doctrinal rebellion of the group seems to have reached a point considered both implacably heretical and potentially politically disruptive. What happened next is supported not just by the oral accounts of the original Isawa or their descendants but also by Islamic scholars in Kano, who confirmed the rebellion of Ibrahim and the Kano court's reaction to it to British colonial officials when, in 1914, the colonial officers solicited their version of the Isawa story.[33] The Kano court and other Islamic scholars treated Ibrahim's new creed as heresy. Ibrahim was brought to the market in Kano's walled city around Dala hill and asked to recite the *shahada*, "There is no God but Allah, and Muhammad is his messenger." When he refused, he was impaled in the market square, an exemplary punishment that sent his followers scampering in several directions away from Kano.

Many of the Isawa refugees ended up settling in Zaria and Kano emirate frontier towns such as Turawa, Daba, Burum Burum, Rano, Kankanri, Tsakuwa, and Kawuri, a migration that shielded most of them from the wrath of the Kano caliphate Islamic establishment.[34] Oral testimony states that the Isawa clerics who inherited the mantle of their executed leader continued to conduct itinerant preaching, visiting followers and touring villages and towns in the Kano-Zaria frontier zones where members had quietly congregated to continue to practice their creed. Among these Isawa clerics, one Mallam Yahaya clearly stood out as the inheritor of the clerical authority of the martyred Ibrahim.

By all accounts, after the scattering of the Isawa, Malam Yahaya continued to proselytize in the dissident group's underground networks, leading the largest of such networks in Tsakuwa, his hometown. It was at this time that the story of the Isawa's religious insurgency intersected with a brewing rural peasant revolt against the alleged oppressive rule of Kano rulers. In the mid-nineteenth century, a group of fifteen Islamic scholars operating in the Tsakuwa frontier zone of Southeast Kano, led by a certain Mallam Hamza, had revolted against the imposition and collection of *kudin kasa* (land tax) by the Kano emirate authorities.[35] They refused to pay the tax and defied the Kano rulers' attempts to collect it from their followers. In the late 1840s and 1850s this Hamza-led defiance of Kano continued.

Tsakuwa was the geographical node of intersection between Hamza's anti-Kano revolt and the Isawa's underground dissidence. Whether and how Mallam Hamza interacted with Yahaya is not clear from the available sources, but Linden suggests that it is possible that Hamza was a clerical contemporary and peer of the Isawa founder Ibrahim, and that both men may have been acquainted through their advisory roles to Kano aristocrats before each man revolted against caliphate political and religious orthodoxies respectively. Tsakuwa's reputation as an anticaliphate rebel town fenced off from Kano's dreaded burden of peasant taxes and as a refuge for insurgent scholars was well established by the 1850s. This was probably why, when Hadejia revolted against the authority of the caliphate from 1848 to 1855, the rebels camped out in Tsakuwa.[36] Clearly, Tsakuwa was attractive to the displaced Isawa sect members because they knew its reputation as a hotbed of anticaliphate mobilization, a town that would not only empathize with their status as persecuted dissidents but would also be receptive to their unorthodox and insurgent attitude toward the caliphate.

Pressure from Kano's caliphate rulers eventually forced both Hamza's group of rebels and the Isawa out of Tsakuwa, with one tradition stating that Hamza and the rebels of Tsakuwa fled when the emir of Kano, Abdullahi, "ordered that [Hamza and his fellow insurgents] should be brought to Kano willingly or by force."[37] Fleeing further southeast, the anticaliphate rebels settled in the village of Umbuta, in Ningi territory, inhabited by several noncentralized non-Muslim ethnic groups such as the Butawa, Warjawa, Chamawa, Basawa, Pa'awa, Sirawa, Kalok, Zeda, Tiffi, Wushi, and Burra. Whether the Isawa and Hamza's followers journeyed to Umbuta/Ningi together or separately is not clear, but they forged an alliance when both groups arrived.

Furthermore, Hamza, himself credited by procaliphate traditions with unorthodox Islamic practices such as magical demonstrations of spiritual powers and what caliphate rulers regarded as *tsafi* (rituals associated with traditional African religion),[38] clearly embraced or at least tolerated the unorthodox beliefs of the Isawa because the latter too practiced an eclectic heterodox Islam that one source described as "embodying in it many pagan beliefs and habits."[39] Together the two dissident groups formed the nucleus of the Isawa–Ningawa–Umbutawa community that would align itself with many of the non-Muslim peoples of the Ningi hills and valleys to attack and harass Kano, Bauchi, and other caliphate polities. Once settled in Ningi, the Isawa–Ningawa–Umbutawa insurgents and their non-Muslim allies intensified their anticaliphate activities. This was a diverse ethnic, religious, and sectarian community of insurgents. The glue in the rebellion appears to have been resentment against various forms of caliphate orthodoxies, practices, exactions, and enforcement of ideological consensus.

Aside from his knowledge of Islamic talismanic arts and his knack for dazzling feats of magic that won him reverence and legitimacy among his Muslim and non-Muslim allies in Ningi, Hamza rallied his anticaliphate rebels by appealing to their secular quotidian grievances against caliphate rulers. As the *Tarikh 'Umara Bauchi* claims, Hamza's rallying cry was "follow me and I will save you from the service of these tyrant Fulanis who use you and ask of you what you cannot do."[40] Here we see how secular socioeconomic grievance was framed in religious idioms and vice versa to produce a potent cocktail of anticaliphate ideology that united Hamza's allies and legitimized his popular Islam. As indicated earlier, this folk, insurgent Islam aligned with the Isawa's intensely syncretistic creed.

Over the next several decades, beginning in the 1850s, the Isawa–Hamza–Ningi rebels led by Hamza and his successors repeatedly attacked the frontier territories of Kano and Bauchi, taking slaves and booty and violating the sovereignty of the caliphate. Despite repeated military campaigns against the rebels and some victories, the fearsome army of the Bauchi Emirate never fully defeated the rebels, who continued to regroup and attack caliphate territories and caliphate-protected non-Muslim *aman* (trust/tributary) polities until the British colonial military occupation in the first decade of the twentieth century.[41]

The Isawa creed and its diffusion in emergent anticaliphate social rebellion and discourses presented a uniquely potent challenge to caliphate ideological orthodoxy. As Linden puts it, the Isawa–Ningi rebels "threatened the emirates and led a peasant revolt legitimated by the very syncretistic religious practice the leaders [of the Sokoto jihad] had set out to combat in the Hausa States" earlier in that century.[42] This threat caused emirate sources and chronicles such as the *Tarikh ʿUmara Bauchi* to allege that the Isawa–Ningi rebels were similar to Kharijites, the recalcitrant and implacable rebels of early Islamic history.[43]

The Isawa were one of many dissident religious movements that undermined, at different moments, the ideological cohesion of the caliphate Islamic realm. Some of these groups were urban dissidents; others were syncretistic, rural, and populist in character; and yet others were militant in orientation. In combining elements of a popular antiestablishment revolt with heterodox and eschatological elements, the Isawa were a rough composite of the types of religious insurgencies the caliphate had to contend with throughout the nineteenth century as it sought to maintain a cohesive religious orthodoxy in a vast, diverse theocratic empire. A shared creedal affiliation was crucial to consolidating a religious community founded on the foundational teachings of the Sokoto jihad leaders. It was useful for isolating dissenters and dissidents and meting out decisive and exemplary punishment on them. The caliphate's religious orthodoxy, underpinned by the consensus of its religious scholars in the dominant Maliki jurisprudential tradition, was fragile and contested, as chapter 1 demonstrated. However, its brittle underbelly was revealed by insurgencies and by the radical doctrinal dissidence of groups such as the Isawa.

Several similar movements emerged and fizzled out with various degrees of success throughout the life of the caliphate, but the Fodiawa orthodox tradition endured. More crucially, the status of the Fodiawa theological corpus as a prescribed guide for reform and revival in all ages and for all times remained, available to be invoked directly or indirectly by future militants claiming the reformist mantle for themselves. At the same time, previous rebellions against the caliphate remained referents for future dissidents who would challenge the settled ideological and doctrinal orthodoxies of their time and seek to show that no established orthodoxy was beyond reproach and critique. In this way both the Fodiawa tradition and rebellions against it in the nineteenth century remained available for both inspiration and invocation to future generations of dissident militants such as Boko Haram.

THE FODIAWA REFORMIST LEGACY IN COLONIAL AND POSTCOLONIAL TIMES

Boko Haram's antimodernism, analyzed in detail later in this book, is often discussed as a stand-alone, but it should be understood in part as a continuation of a long-established tradition of reaction to colonial and foreign influences, systems of knowledge, and material goods deemed threats to Muslims' piety. This tradition derives some its elements from the Sokoto jihad, but it also represents a departure from the disposition of the leaders of that jihad to modernity, a divergence occasioned by the new reality of British colonial cultural violence.

The persistence of what Mervyn Hiskett calls the legacy of "Islamic conservatism," which was inaugurated by the jihad of Usman dan Fodio, never dissipated and in fact enjoyed a renaissance during the colonial period as Muslims' cultural and intellectual opposition to westernization intensified. Even among establishment clerics and scholars, the effort to cleanse the polity of unbelief, heterodoxy, and "foreign" ideas considered capable of diluting the faith remained and increased during the colonial period. Clerics and scholars continued to act as "the guardians of reform" and as "custodians of orthodoxy," just as reformers emerged to challenge established orthodoxies. As spiritual brokers during caliphate times, Muslim clerics modulated and mediated the relationships of Muslims to the Islamic canon and its prescriptions. During the colonial period (1900–1960) their role remained intact, rendered even more important by the invasion of the caliphal space by nonbelievers and their institutions and practices. Although publicly compliant with British colonial dictates, religious scholars remained intensely suspicious of the new cultural order of westernization. With colonial cultural invasions occurring at a rapid pace, this suspicion morphed into hostility, discomfort, and unease.[44]

Clerics upheld orthodoxies by trying to divest them of practices deemed exogenous and harmful. Opposition to practices, ideas, and goods considered foreign to Islam and thus sacrilegious began in the nineteenth-century reformist jihad, but the story of caliphate antimodernism is not so straightforward and contains several mitigating caveats. For one thing, neither Dan Fodio nor Abdullahi ever made a complete denunciation of modern goods, practices, and ideas. Their primary concerns were the capacity of innovation and change to pollute the devotion of Muslims, whether the innovation was expressed through material goods, practices, or ideas. For another, Nana Asmau, Dan Fodio's daughter and a prolific scholar in her own right, organized the famous Yan Taru movement that promoted the education and empowerment of rural women and girls, a radical modernist initiative in a conservative patriarchal caliphal society.[45]

Muhammad Bello was an eager, adventurous coveter of modernist goods and ideas. When English envoy Captain Hugh Clapperton visited him in 1823, Sultan Bello, as was the custom of the time, requested and received a watch, a telescope, and a thermometer from the traveler.[46] When Clapperton visited Bello for the second time in 1825, the sultan specifically requested and received a copy of Euclid's *The Elements* from the king of England.[47] When Clapperton negotiated a treaty with the sultan on behalf of the king, Bello's demands in exchange were European arms, ammunition, gunpowder, muskets, cloth, and other European goods. Bello also requested that the King of England send him a physician who would set up a clinic in the caliphate, as well as merchants who would ensure the flow of European goods to his domain.[48] Dan Fodio had also been receptive to modernist influences from the Mediterranean and beyond, seeking recognition from the Ottoman Caliphate and Alouite Morocco, two regional and global Islamic states enmeshed in the modernist cultural and political currents of the nineteenth century.

The Fodiawa were thus avid consumers of cultural resources from multiple contemporaneous worlds in their time and did not shy away from a strategic engagement with modernity. Nonetheless, their legacy came to be understood as an antimodernist one, a popular perception that, while not entirely faithful to their writings about and engagements with modern influences, indicates the trepidation and self-conscious ambivalence with which they treated and related to European modernity and its cognates. Some of the writings of both Abdullahi and Muhammad Bello emphasize the dangerous potential of goods, practices, and ideas from the non-Islamic world, even those that had been mediated and domesticated in Islamic societies, to lead Muslims into the serious infraction of *bid'a*. This belief in an ever-present risk of *bid'a* infused the Fodiawa's attitude toward European modernity and other secular innovations with ambivalence. It caused them to counsel a scrutinizing self-awareness on the part of Muslims who encountered innovative ideas and goods of foreign provenance.

This original ambivalence regarding Western things and ideas established a baseline for evaluating and reacting to subsequent external influences associated with nonbelievers. During the colonial period, this narrative anxiety of piety and threats to it crystallized in the form of opposition to multiple modernist innovations and institutions that came with the array of colonial cultural influences. Purity, this narrative went, could only be obtained through dewesternization and demodernization.

Confronted by a changing world marked by the erosion of traditional ways of life and by a dizzying cocktail of modern goods and practices associated with neo-Christian British colonizers (*nasara*), Muslims in Northern Nigeria responded by adopting a new form of piety marked by a "general re-Islamization of the Muslim Ummah [that] would please Allah [so that] He would then get rid of the Christians (and their [Muslim] collaborators)."[49] Subsequent Islamic militant and reformist movements in Northern Nigeria tried to align their ideologies with this vision of piety and the concomitant suspicion of modernity as a force capable of threatening Muslim devotion. Successive reform movements, most notably Boko Haram, have sustained this suspicion and ambivalence regarding colonial modernity (*zamani*), which is perceived as a threat to the vision of a just, moral Islamic society, and against Christians who purportedly embody this modernity, as well as Muslims who allegedly imitate it or allow it to infect their religious obligations.

These revivalist movements benefited from the religious environment that the Fodiawa jihad of the nineteenth century created. They also followed the same model of rejecting the theological, socioeconomic, and political status quo and imagining a different, more pious, and just society as defined by their own particular doctrinal inclinations. The template was predictable in its simplicity. The reformers would accuse previous generations of reformers, now ensconced in orthodox institutions, of betraying the reformist path. The reformist movements also tended to emulate another feature of the Fodiawa jihad of the previous century—separating themselves from modern society by constructing alternative Islamic communities on the fringes of mainstream Muslim societies in Northern Nigeria.[50] These isolated communities, imagined to be free from the modernist and secularist contagion of the rest of society and from influences and tendencies deemed sacrilegious, would then become the staging ground for reformist rebellion. Boko Haram followed this same multiphased paradigm of antimodernist critique, reform, rejection, self-isolation, and revolution.

THE GUMI-IZALA REVOLUTION

Ubiquitous, anticolonial, and antimodernist discourses in Northern Nigeria did not fundamentally alter the theological consensus in Northern Nigerian Islam. Sufism, the central creedal practice that animated the nineteenth-century jihad and solidified in its wake, remained the dominant paradigm of Islamic practice in the region. It took a revolution, beginning in colonial times and concluding in the late postcolonial period, to produce a shift. That revolution was led by Shaykh Mahmud Abubakar Gumi (1922–92). More than any other single individual, Gumi was instrumental to the long process of Islamic dissidence that transformed the Northern Nigerian Muslim landscape from a predominantly Sufi one to one that came to be suffused in anti-Sufi reformist theologies and ideologies. This primed the religious environment for the ascendancy of Salafism, which in turn preceded the militant, violent jihadi-Salafist reform agenda of insurgent movements such as Boko Haram. Because of his centrality to this history of religious change, a change that led to the ongoing contestation between various strands of Salafism on one side and the remaining old Sufi orders on the other, it is important to explore aspects of his momentous life with particular attention to his long, successful ideological dissent against the old, post-Fodiawa jihad Sufi orthodoxy. This biographical analysis relies on his own words in his autobiography, *Where I Stand*.[51]

Gumi's life was marked by a restless quest for alternative theological and exegetical directions. However, it should be noted that his was only one of the most successful in a long genealogy of reformist theological traditions in Northern Nigeria, a tradition dating back to the Sokoto jihad. In moving away from the religious status quo, Gumi helped to deepen and extend the inherited reformist strain and its suspicion of modernity and modern practices deemed incompatible with Islamic devotion. Gumi's streak of contrarian theological and ideational positions stretches back several decades before the founding of Izala, the movement that he led and with which he is most prominently associated. Gumi began his challenge of the existing Islamic orthodoxy in his early clerical life in his native Sokoto Province, but it was in Kano that he sharpened his anti-Sufi teachings, explicitly instructing his students away from the "dangers" of Sufi texts and exegesis.[52] From Kano, Gumi traveled to Sudan for advanced studies on Sharia. In 1960 he was appointed deputy grand khadi (deputy chief judge of the Islamic court) of Northern Nigeria and relocated to Kaduna to assume the position.

His work in Kaduna, first as deputy grand khadi and then grand khadi after his promotion in 1962, gave him both visibility and a judicial and political platform to chip away at what he regarded as the pollution of Islam by pre-Islamic cultural beliefs, Sufi traditions not rooted in the canons of Islam, and a plethora of practices associated with colonial modernity. He continued to preach in Kaduna as grand khadi. This time Sufi shaykhs aligned with the *tariqa* brotherhoods paid more attention to him and his dissident teachings against their accommodationist creed since, as the preeminent judge in the Sharia judicial system, he had authority and credibility within the Muslim *Ummah*.

Gumi's work superintending the Sharia judicial sector provided an opportunity for him to launch the reform of Islamic practice in the region and rescue the religion from *jahilci* (ignorance) and practices he considered un-Islamic. In his biography he cites several instances in which, as the chief judicial officer of the Sharia court in Northern Nigeria and as a member of a panel of judges, he sought to affirm the supremacy of Sharia above all else and to root out customs that "had not been completely stopped even after centuries of Islam."[53] For Gumi, total adherence to the Sharia was every Muslim's obligation. He identified multiple institutions and practices that conflicted with that imperative, ranging from what he considered an inferior English common law, to Nigeria's secular constitution, to traditional cultural practices.[54] His judicial opinions and rulings reflected his tenacious reformist commitments and his rejection of the superiority of secularity and modernity, both of which he associated with foreign, Western, and colonial influences.

As grand khadi in the 1960s, Gumi was also a religious adviser to Ahmadu Bello, the premier of Northern Nigeria. With Bello, Gumi embarked on a tour of the Muslim world, visiting several Muslim-majority countries in Africa and the Middle East. In May 1961 Gumi visited Saudi Arabia with Bello. Gumi was subsequently a regular visitor to Saudi Arabia as head of the Northern Nigerian delegation to the *hajj*. Through the efforts of Gumi and Bello, the World Muslim League was launched in Mecca in 1962. When Bello was asked to take the position of vice president and member of the League's constitution council, he asked Gumi to represent him. Gumi then became a member of the council, a position that took him around the Muslim world and led him to visit Saudi Arabia even more frequently.

This Saudi connection, which would grow over the next few decades, had two profound impacts on Gumi and his reformist agenda. First, it gave him access to a vast apparatus of Wahhabi-Salafi Islamic knowledge that would affirm and solidify his reformist leanings. Second, his frequent visits to the kingdom to lead Northern Nigerian delegations on the *hajj* exposed him to and accentuated the differences between Islam as practiced and taught in Saudi Arabia, and Islam as practiced by Northern Nigerian Muslims. Gumi writes in his autobiography that during the *hajj* he witnessed Northern Nigerian pilgrims, out of ignorance, "throwing huge pieces of rock, shoes or whatever they could find around in the name of stoning the devil." He contrasted this with the prescribed throwing of seven pieces of rock at the *jamarāt* (three pillars at Mina), directed symbolically at the devil.[55]

The Saudi connection blossomed even further, supplying Gumi with the logistical and financial support to fulfill his vision of expanding and reforming Islam in Northern Nigeria. When Gumi joined other Muslims in establishing the Jama'atu Nasril Islam (JNI) to, in the words of the founders, promote Islam through education and training, the Saudis were the first foreign government to support the effort, donating $50,000 to build a primary school in Kaduna, where the JNI was headquartered. The Saudi government subsequently supported the organization with the same amount "every year for many years."[56] With continued Saudi financial support and theological inspiration, in the 1980s and 1990s the Gumi-led Izala movement reached the peak of its influence, became mainstream, and effectively supplanted the existing Sufi order. As is analyzed in chapter 3, the ascendancy of Izala wrought a profound change in the culture of Islam in Northern Nigeria. It reinforced a historical critique of Western modernity while advancing a new, appealing Islamic modernity that stressed an Islamic moral ethos and the pursuit of political influence.

PREFIGURING BOKO HARAM IN THE POSTCOLONIAL REFORMIST LANDSCAPE

The Northern Nigerian Muslim public sphere experienced a new wave of reformist intervention in the late 1990s and early 2000s as the Izala movement consolidated its position and the harder-edged messages of returnees from the Islamic University of Medina resonated among the Muslim populace, producing new understandings of appropriate Muslim behavior and expectations of pietistic expressions. The region's newspapers tracked this new reformist energy and the ways in which it was expressed to curb what reform agents believed to be un-Islamic habits and influences. Moral discourses authorized a praxis of vigilantism that was rooted in the Muslim idea of *al-amr bi al-ma'rūf wa al-nahy 'an al-munkar* (commanding what is right and forbidding what is wrong).[57]

Several reform-minded Muslim actors staked out moral territories to critique the behavior and conduct of Muslims and societal practices deemed inimical to Islamic moral standards. Not surprisingly, many controversies and debates between reformist and liberal voices dominated the Muslim public sphere in this period, debates that, whatever their outcome and tenor, provided a public platform for and accorded unprecedented visibility to reformers and purists who wanted the Muslim *Ummah* sanitized of influences and practices they considered sinful. This was a precursor to and in some cases was contemporaneous with the radical reformist ideologies of the predecessors of Boko Haram.

One such debate was the Sarkin Karuwai controversy in Kano. In September 1998, a seemingly insignificant controversy erupted in Kano. As reported by *Weekly Trust*, the district head of Tudun Wada, Kano metropolis, conferred the title of *Sarkin Karuwai* (overseer of prostitutes) on a twenty-seven-year-old man named Magaji Ali.[58] The conferment was done in a public ceremony where Ali's mandate was spelled out to the hearing of witnesses. He was given the task of protecting sex workers located in the district from harassment, and settling disputes among them and between them and their clients. Ali went to work immediately, occupying an office located in the red-light district, where he received delegations of sex workers and mediated between parties in disputes.

There was nothing remarkable about this event, and it would have passed unnoticed in a previous time. However, the Northern Nigerian Islamic public sphere was evolving rapidly in a more reformist direction, making the very idea of creating the office of *Sarkin Karuwai*, which endorses sex work and confers on it the credibility of Kano's emirate traditional institution, out of step with the emerging Islamic moral consensus. Weeks after the appointment of the new *Sarkin Karuwai*, word of the development got out and citywide public outrage erupted. This caused embarrassment to the Kano emirate council, which called an emergency meeting of all the *Hakimai* (district heads) to discuss the matter and warn them against conferring traditional titles without seeking approval from the council.[59]

When religious clerics waded into the controversy, their intervention magnified it into a full-blown moral panic. The district head who appointed the official, Alhaji Ibrahim Mohammed Dankadai, was compelled to deny his action. In the face of escalating religious outrage, Dankadai stated that he had appointed Magaji as overseer of the district's outskirts, or *Sarkin Banki*, and that the titleholder's mandate was to help coordinate the effort against crime and vice on the wild fringes of the district. Further defending himself, the district head argued that as a devout Muslim and a guardian of Islamic morality in the district, he would not have tacitly approved prostitution by appointing a titleholder to oversee it.

The *Sarkin Karuwai* scandal was a seminal event, but it preceded and foreshadowed more contestations over morality and culture as Northern Nigerian Islam moved in a reformist trajectory at the end of the twentieth century. In 1999, as the Nigerian home video industry, Nollywood, was growing in reach, a Hausa-language offshoot was emerging with Kano as its hub. Christened Kannywood, it had an organic linkage with Hausa traditions of television drama (*wasan kwaikwayo*) and the new technologies and techniques of filmmaking circulating in Nigeria. Hausa-language films had been made and released on various themes without controversy. However, in the late 1990s the films emerged as another site of moral intervention by a rising class of reform-minded Islamic groups seeking to purify society and build a new order governed by the strict moral codes of Sharia. Filmmakers found themselves in the crosshairs of the new reformers, who viewed films with secular themes and plots as antithetical to their goal of building a new society cleansed of influences they deemed capable of threatening Islamic moral standards.

One of the most prominent targets of this new censorship campaign was Yakubu Lere El-Saeed, producer of the film *Saliha*, which was released in 1999.[60] Saliha is the story of a Muslim woman who led her would-be husband to believe that she was a virgin, but after marriage is revealed to have already had sexual experiences. Reformist Muslim commentators and clerics were enraged. They questioned why a Muslim girl wearing a hijab would be portrayed as a woman of deceit and sexual impurity. In the outrage that followed the release of the film, clerics and regular Muslims weighed in to condemn the film as an attack on Islam itself, a charge that the producer denied.[61] Some of the enraged moral vigilantes threatened to harm El-Saeed and the film director unless they withdrew the tapes from circulation.

Producers of secular cultural materials seemed oblivious to the fact that Northern Nigerian Islam was changing in a more conservative direction, making such materials increasingly anomalous. The implementation of Sharia criminal codes complete with *ḥudūd* punishments for moral vices and violations was one hallmark of this transformed religious scene. Some of the same Salafi groups who campaigned successfully for Sharia implementation in the early 2000s saw social vice as a threat to the new moral order and were determined to eradicate it. This emerging order was less tolerant toward secular and westernized institutions, laws, education, and modes of recreation. By the year 2000, articles were appearing in the *Weekly Trust*, Northern Nigeria's most widely read weekly newspaper, with headlines such as "Hausa Films and Moral Degeneration," which criticized the making of Hausa-language films for entertainment purposes as injurious to the region's moral aspirations.[62] The critics of Hausa films increasingly invoked Islamic moral registers to decry what they alleged was the films' "corrupting, polluting, and bastardizing" impact on the *Ummah*, as well as their "modernized, . . . westernized, Europeanized, [and] Americanized" artistic output.[63]

In August 2001, a new controversy exploded regarding Hausa musical performances in celebratory contexts. The debate turned on the question of whether such music conformed to or violated the new Sharia law passed in the state of Katsina. On July 17, 2001, youths associated with and mobilized by the association of performing artists marched on the streets of Katsina shouting, "Down with Yakubu and *sharīʿa* courts."[64] They were protesting the effort of Shaykh Yakubu Musa,[65] an Izala preacher who, along with like-minded clerics, had mounted pressure on the government to outlaw public musical performances as un-Islamic and a violation of the new Sharia legal codes of the state. The protesters attacked the mosque where the cleric preached, then marched to a court that was hearing arguments in a case brought by the Da'wa group, a coalition of Sharia implementation advocates and watchdogs, to force stricter enforcement of Sharia in the state.[66] The new moral vigilantism and the expanding reach of reformist activism that underpinned it found vice in several realms of cultural and social expression. The catchall label of *bidʿa* (innovation) became commonplace between the late 1990s and early 2000s as the reformist ascendance became fully realized, and as more expansive Salafist reformist doctrinal consensuses gradually replaced the Izala reformist tendency as the most vocal and visible reformist paradigm in the Northern Nigerian Islamic public sphere.

Other cultural domains became sites of debate as they were reimagined as threats to the new reformist moral consensus. In the 1980s a new genre of Hausa literature emerged in Northern Nigeria. Its hub was Kano, the region's largest metropolitan area. By the 1990s it had progressed from a trickle to a flood, with many titles appearing every year. Pioneered by women writers, *Soyayya* (love) novels circulated widely, read mostly by women and adolescent girls and boys. The novels focused on the themes of romantic love, heartbreak, divorce, difficult in-laws, polygamy, arranged marriage, purdah (Islamic seclusion of married women), and female education.[67] The backlash against this new literary genre and its growing popularity was swift and harsh. It was not just Salafi clerics who criticized the novels and their themes. By this time a critical mass of Muslims, most of them influenced by the ubiquitous proselytization of Izala and new Salafi clerics, agreed with the depiction of several old and new secular and aesthetic expressions as *bid'a* (innovation) and *shirk* (polytheism). It was within this charged, morally protectionist religious environment that the *Soyayya* authors wrote. As literary scholar Novian Whitsitt states, the "general public opinion harshly criticize[d] the literature for allegedly corrupting the minds of the youth, especially young women," for promoting "moral decay," for encouraging sexual promiscuity and youthful disobedience, and for propagating "Western notions of love" that contradicted Hausa Muslim traditions.[68]

Opinion editorials published in *The New Nigerian*, one of Northern Nigeria's most widely read newspapers, condemned the genre and connected it to a litany of vices in the region's Muslim societies. One Danjuma Katsina published an op-ed in *New Nigerian Weekly* titled "Death to the *Soyayya* Novel," in which he argued that "nothing beneficial will come out of [the *Soyayya* novels] but foolishness, lack of direction, and immorality."[69] Another interlocutor, Ahmed Mansur, contended that "most novelists are irrevocably damaging the attitudinal and ideological perceptions of readers towards the marriage institution, thereby throwing the youths, particularly girls, into the devil's arms." Mansur curtly concluded that "it is high time we did away with the junk."[70]

While critics articulated their positions, defenders of the *Soyayya* genre such as the literary scholar Abdallah Uba Adamu of Bayero University came to theirs from a secular premise. Adamu stressed the artistic integrity of the novels and argued that, like most literary works, the *Soyayya* novels largely reflected the prevailing anxieties and issues of the society from which they emanated.[71] By the time Adamu joined in the debate, the Kano branch of the Association of Nigerian Authors had been pressured into banning some of the titles in the *Soyayya* genre that were deemed offensive to the tenets of the Sharia or too explicit in their romantic and sexual explorations.[72] In addition, the Kano State government had set up a committee to censor the prolific offerings of novels and novellas in the genre. Adamu called the banning and censorship unnecessary, actions that, in his view, would only "stifle further [literary] creativity."[73] The unnamed referent in the treatises of Adamu and other Muslim *Soyayya* defenders was the reformist transformation of the Northern Nigerian Islamic sphere, which brought new prohibitions and disapprovals of practices, cultural expressions, and secular artistic materials deemed potentially corrupting of Muslim morality in the region.

These 1990s and early 2000s antisecular and antimodern critiques were a far cry from the absolutist antimodernist prohibition of Boko Haram, but they served to prime the religious marketplace of Northern Nigeria for its development. The moral vigilantism of this period created a space in which new reformist imaginations could thrive and in which alternative religious futures could be conceived and made plausible. This evolving religious landscape was animated by discourses and claims of harams and prohibitions before the emergence of Boko Haram and its formal articulation of a coherent, discrete ideology around a set of wide-ranging prohibitions. Once broached, the new narrative of moral and theological prohibitions, along with the quotidian praxis that gave it practical expression, not only expanded but also became unwieldy and far more expansive than the original actors had envisioned. Boko Haram would, in a few years, help crystallize seemingly sporadic and spontaneous manifestations of reformist fervor in Northern Nigeria into a formal program of change that it argued could either be accomplished peacefully or through armed jihad.

POSTCOLONIAL REFORMERS, THE FODIAWA LEGACY, AND NEW MUSLIM CONCERNS

The instances of rising moral enforcement in postcolonial Northern Nigeria were connected ideologically to the paradigmatic residues of the old Fodiawa orthodoxy, but they were also sparked by the rise of new concerns as new socioeconomic spaces and demographic configurations emerged and as old, comforting, homogeneous Muslim spaces appeared threatened by migration, modernization, westernization, and socioeconomic mobility. The impetus for new, militant reformism was an Islamic revivalism catalyzed by the rise of Izala reformism, but Izala itself harkened back to the Fodiawa legacy of reform. Similarly, Izala's revivalism may have inspired the new moral vigilantism that in turn provoked the backlash and contestation discussed above. However, the rise of Izala in the 1990s should be understood in the context of the accelerated spread of Western modernist trends as Western education, and intranational mobility and codependence transformed previously insular Muslim spaces and cultures into hybrid, cosmopolitan ones. The visible signs of this cultural cosmopolitanism, represented by new tastes, social practices, demographics, forms of entertainment and leisure, and tendencies toward theological pragmatism provoked anxiety among doctrinaire reformists, who lamented the stealthy but steady encroachment of Western modernist trends on the inherited Muslim cultures and spaces of Northern Nigeria.

Gumi's Izala creed of revivalism was rooted in the residual memories and textual bequests of the Fodiawa reformist movement. Gumi himself realized the continued centrality of the Fodiawa reformist paradigm, and as a result self-consciously situated his revivalist movement in the Fodiawa tradition, even though the latter was doctrinally Sufi. In Gumi's most important creedal writing, *Al-Akidatus Sahihat Bi Muwafakatus Shariah*, in which he outlined the manifesto of his reformist, anti-Sufi theological postulations, he copiously invokes Usman dan Fodio's canonical reformist writings to buttress and legitimize his own critiques of the existing Sufi devotional and moral order, as well as his prescriptions for a new way.[74]

In condemning the beating of drums, dancing, and singing in Muslims' devotional practice or as forms of leisure and celebration, Gumi quotes dan Fodio's text *Ihya 'us Sunnah Wa Ikhamadul Bid'ah*. Gumi posits that the use of dundufa and tambari traditional drums in Sufi devotions amounted to turning Islam into a form of leisure, a joke. Gumi then summons Dan Fodio's statement that "joking with religion is an innovation" to argue that Sufi orders were reducing Islamic devotion to the level of casual pastimes. Additionally, Gumi advances Dan Fodio's statement that if dancing and listening to music were permitted instruments of devotion, "Allah would have directed the prophets to practice them and even order[ed] their followers to do same."[75]

Gumi's harkening back to the preceding Fodiawa reformist consensus was not accidental; it was an homage to the persistent power of that reformist precedent in the late twentieth century. More crucially, apart from establishing his reformist project within the long history of reform and revival in the region, Gumi was signaling that moral and devotional reforms were not new, nor were the alleged innovations reformers intended to correct. Gumi framed his reformist enterprise as part of a regional history of revival and moral renewal. He was placing himself and his reformist agenda in the lineage of Dan Fodio, and in the continuum of corrective reform and rebellion that birthed the prevailing doctrinal orthodoxies and traditional Muslim rulership of twentieth-century Northern Nigeria. By invoking the reformist creed of Northern Nigeria's foundational Muslim reformist figure, Gumi was making an overarching point: that the struggle to purify the Muslim polity was a continuous, ongoing one, and that his reformist movement was aligned with the dominant historical ideology of religious devotion in the region.

The moral and devotional revolution of the early 2000s was both historically animated and rooted in the earlier reformist project of Izala. The nexus of the two was apparent to actors and observers alike. Following several scholars, I argue that the Izala revivalist project was possible because Muslims were already troubled by the moral and existential fears of disappearing Muslim urban spaces engulfed by the forces of modernization, the rapid spread of cosmopolitan influences, and the transformation of urban demographics. Geographer Michael Watts inaugurated scholarly commentary on the notion of Muslim insecurity and existential anxiety. In the context of rural, colonial agrarian transformation, Watts contends that the colonial capitalist agricultural economy stripped away an old, protective moral economy and established a new, routinized regime of vulnerability that normalized precarity and an accompanying sense of peasant grievance.[76]

Paul Lubeck expands this important notion of precarity to the urban Muslim spaces of Northern Nigeria, where "colonial-mercantile" pressures in colonial times and the "petroleum boom" of the postcolonial period decimated old Qur'anic student networks (*gardawa*) and their social dynamics of labor and learning. In precolonial times these networks connected the rural to the urban, and the world of learning to that of earning, while providing safe if marginal urban spaces for Muslim students to subsist, learn their faith, and mature into responsible adults with families.[77] Although Lubeck argues that Muslim nationalism and consciousness intermeshed and accommodated the class affinities of industrialization and the postcolonial petroleum economy of Nigeria,[78] he points to the "contradictory outcomes" of the interactions between "precapitalist communities" and postcolonial socioeconomic transformation. Traditional urban networks and logics, Lubeck argues, "were modified by, and in turn react[ed] to capitalist development during the contemporary period."[79]

These developments predisposed the increasingly marginalized and anxious urban Muslim populations of Northern Nigeria to antimodernist, antiestablishment, and more insular ideologies.[80] Reformist antimodernist ideological ferments, more recently that of Boko Haram, found a receptive audience in this evolving Muslim polity. This embrace of unorthodox theologies stemmed in part from the emergence of moral and cultural panic, and formulations about the unpredictable dangers and religious pollution that "foreign" ideas, strangers, and unfamiliar modern practices allegedly embodied. At the root of this phenomenon is, as Murray Last contends, the disruption of an insular, orderly society characterized and sustained by circles of trust, and a familiar, comforting Muslim sense of community.[81]

The heightened Muslim suspicion of strange people and things corresponded to the transformation of previously homogeneous urban Muslim spaces as non-Muslim and Muslim migrants arrived from Southern Nigeria, and as nominally Muslim Hausa folk arrived from the countryside. The resulting explosion of urban populations and new cultural interactions undermined the familiarity, kinship, sense of safety, and comfort that urban communal cohesion had provided. As urban diversity and cosmopolitanism increased, so did suspicions, rumors, speculations, and even conspiratorial explanations for new, rational fears of the cultural, ethnic, and religious Other.[82]

The sense that familiar cultural and even physical protections against modernist pollutants were collapsing under the weight of rapid population growth and demographic change called for new explanations for both what was allegedly being lost and how it could be retrieved.[83] This Muslim anxiety was expressed in moral terms, as a critique of an unsettlingly fluid social order and as a rhetorical blueprint for moral and religious reform. The subjects of such moral critiques, as the debates and controversies analyzed earlier in this chapter demonstrate, tended to be practices, commodities, and people deemed alien to the religious body politic and to the cultural fabric, both of which were being redefined in narrower terms to conform to an idealized past of moral certitude. This anxiety was, Last contends, both rational and historically grounded since it was consistent with notions of Muslim millenarianism and of the necessity of periodic revival of the Muslim polity.[84] The quest for a lost past founded on an allegedly superior moral consensus and the efforts to reclaim and reconstitute spaces and ways of life deemed endangered by unfamiliar cultural and religious tendencies made Northern Nigerian Muslims more receptive to new reformist creeds. Such reformist ideologies promised a return to a lost caliphal and precaliphal period of Muslim purity and community as a counterpoint to the moral regression and cosmopolitan accommodations of contemporary times.

CONCLUSION

To fully grasp the emergence of Boko Haram as both a creed and a corpus of ideational claims about appropriate behavior, forms of expression, and ways of engaging with or disengaging from modernity and secularism, the ways in which the Northern Nigerian Islamic public sphere shifted radically in a reformist direction—the debates and disputations profiled here being empirical evidence of that shift—need to be explained and understood. The theological terrain on which these debates were conducted, the declared and undeclared historical and contemporary premises, and new anxieties about unsettling change helped inspire the promulgation of new pietistic strictures and their ideological underpinnings. The implementation of Sharia criminal codes was one expression of this pivot. Instructively, it was the belief on the part of reformist scholars and activists that political leaders were not sufficiently committed to Sharia that produced Salafi critique and rejectionism, the renegade strands of which culminated in the emergence of Boko Haram.

3   Boko Haram's Antimodernism Historicized

This chapter analyzes seminal moments and transitions in the history of antimodernist ideologies in Northern Nigeria, a history that prefigured, contradicted, and, in some ways, established a receptive but also dissenting audience for Boko Haram's well-known antimodernist ideology. As in other chapters, I do not suggest a mechanical causal connection between the past and the present; rather, the argument is that, in order to understand the societal roots and resonances of Boko Haram's antimodernist creed, an intimate familiarity with several preceding and overlapping movements and episodes in Northern Nigerian history is necessary. These precedents preempted Boko Haram's antimodernism and can help to clarify it.

The first of these events is the jihad of the Fodiawa in the nineteenth century. While not explicitly antimodernist in their creedal productions, the Fodiawa established an influential example of agnostic engagements with innovations that they regarded as having an ambiguous and tense relationship with Islamic devotion. The second seminal event is the fraught engagement of Northern Nigerian Muslims with Western education during the British colonial era. In the analysis of foundational Muslims' suspicions regarding Western education and its technocultural cognates, the evolving perceptions of westernization and its relationship to folk Islamic obligations is discussed. The analysis then moves to examining the emergence and evolution of antimodernist critiques and how they meshed with and animated anticolonial resistance and postconquest militant uprisings against British rule. Anxieties about the colonial encounter birthed a strident antimodernist popular consciousness. The foundational Islamic rulings of the last precolonial Waziri of the Sokoto Caliphate, Muhammad Buhari, established a guiding template of suspicion and distrust regarding Western modernity. This attitude endured and morphed over decades in colonial and postcolonial Nigeria.

Connected to this foundational paradigm of Islamic reaction is the emergence of a new grammar and poetics of antimodernism that flourished in the Northern Nigerian public and artistic spheres. In this critical popular artistic enterprise, British colonization and the material cultures, practices, aesthetics, and ideas associated with it came under scrutiny in folk songs, poems, aesthetic public performances, and other religiously inspired popular cultures of the colonial period. This antimodernist corpus of ideas and texts endured in the Muslim body politic. The discourses were subsequently normalized as paradigms of appropriate Muslim engagement with Western cultural influences.

The chapter then discusses what can be called the Gumi religious revolution, the transformative theological and programmatic religious interventions of Sheikh Abubakar Gumi, who, over several decades, worked painstakingly and relentlessly to shift the fulcrum of Northern Nigerian Islam from an accommodationist Sufi Islamic consensus to one animated by rejectionist, conservative, and selectively antimodernist commitments. Although Gumi's reformist creed pragmatically accommodated certain elements of modernity, this moment of transition marked the intersection of reformist impulses with new gestures of antimodernism, which inaugurated a new era of ambivalence. The chapter then analyzes the antimodernist ideology of the 1980s sect Yantatsine/Maitatsine, its rural, unsophisticated, and theologically unorthodox opposition to modern goods, technologies, and ideas, and compares it to Boko Haram's well-known repertoire of antimodernism. Although Yantastine bears no theological resemblance to Boko Haram, there are clear parallels and differences between their respective campaigns against Western modernity. The historical antecedents and comparisons help insert Boko Haram into a deeper history of antimodernist ideologies in the region.

Finally, the chapter discusses a late twentieth- and early twenty-first-century history of Muslim debates and treatises regarding practices and objects under the rubric of Western modernity and claims about appropriate and inappropriate ways of relating to these symbols and materials of modernity. These debates, some of which overlapped with the emergence of Boko Haram's preaching and jihad phases and are analyzed in relation to them, illuminate the religious environment in which Boko Haram ideologues wrote and pronounced their robust antimodernist treatises. The chapter argues that Boko Haram's antimodernism, which is referenced and analyzed as a comparative foil throughout the chapter, is best understood in these broader historical contexts.

FROM CALIPHATE ANTIMODERNISM TO ANTICOLONIAL CULTURAL ANXIETY

In the nineteenth century Abdullahi Dan Fodio, the brother of Usman Dan Fodio and a leader in the Sokoto jihad, wrote the treatise *Diyā' al-sulṭān wa-ghayrihi min al-ikhwān fī ahamm mā yuṭlabu 'ilmuhu fī umūr al-zamān*, which echoed some of the antimodernist themes that are the staple of contemporary Muslim reformers and militants, including Boko Haram.[1] Notably, Abdullahi condemned the playing of musical instruments, describing it as distracting and polluting for a Muslim. Abdullahi made an exception for the tambourine, which is mentioned in a *ḥadīth*.[2] Abdullahi's treatise did not explicitly associate the practices and objects he condemned with Christian or European modernist influences. His pronouncement came in the context of a narrow, local, internal debate and was challenged by his older brother, Usman. Nonetheless, it is a remarkable, if dissenting, antimodernist opinion from a member of the caliphal triumvirate.

Abdullah also declared as *ḥarām* sick Muslims' consumption of any alcohol-laced medicinal substance.[3] Similarly, his nephew, Sultan Muhammad Bello, penned a treatise that reflected Muslims' concerns at the time about Judeo-Christian influence and culture. In *Talkhīs aṭ-ṭibb al-nabawī* he opposed the treatment of sick Muslims by Jewish physicians, even though in that milieu the likelihood of that happening was almost nonexistent.[4] The Fodiawa were not decidedly antimodernist, as noted elsewhere in this book. Nonetheless, they harbored an unease with modernity that was common among West African Muslims of their time and was rooted in an older theological curriculum, although the extent to which they self-consciously drew on that existing theological tradition is uncertain.

The most significant foundation of the Fodiawa's modernist agnosticism was their extensive writings and debates on *bid'a*, discussed in chapters 1 and 2, which conduced to a robust suspicion of and cautious engagement with modern things and ideas. However, the concept of *bid'a* was already fairly well diffused in the region by the beginning of the nineteenth century partly because of the circulation of writings by antimodernist, anti-*bid'a* Muslim scholars such as Ibn Abi Mahalli.[5] Change and innovation, especially when they involved secular ideas and materials of non-Islamic origins, were regarded with skepticism and sometimes rejected outright because of the fear that such innovations could lead Muslims into the sin of *bid'a*, which could then apostatize them.

Given these precolonial antecedents, the emergence and tenacity of colonial-era antimodernism is understandable. After the colonial conquest there was a semblance of order, but underneath the seemingly pragmatic détente with British modernity a suspicion of British goods and ideas as modernist pollutants of the piety of Muslims persisted. Much of this suspicion was rooted in the anxieties of precolonial times, as captured in the paradigmatic writings of the Sokoto Caliphate leadership. Many anticolonial Ajami texts circulated across Hausaphone West Africa and the Arabic-literature Islamic knowledge circuits of the greater West African Sahel region in the first decade of colonization, giving local critics of the cultures and influences of the new colonial order a regional intellectual framework for their own treatises. However, Northern Nigerian Muslim antimodernism also had its own distinct origins in the societal ruptures, apocalyptic anxieties, and radical disruptions of the British colonial conquest. Any serious analysis of Northern Nigerian antimodernism must thus start with the colonial conquest at the turn of the twentieth century, and with the resistance movements that attended and outlasted it.

THE NEXUS OF ANTICOLONIALISM, ANTIMODERNISM, AND REJECTIONISM

In colonial times (1900–1960) certain precolonial Islamic insurgent movements that had troubled the religious consensus of the Sokoto Caliphate in precolonial times persisted, some coalescing into movements of rebellion and resistance to both the British and the emirate system of traditional and religious leadership. Mahdist rebellions against colonial rule wracked several emirates in the newly declared British Protectorate of Northern Nigeria.[6] The Satiru revolt of 1906 and several other apocalyptic Islamic insurgencies sporadically rattled colonial Northern Nigeria during and after the colonial conquest.[7] Some of these movements began to articulate a clear message against Christian colonizers (*Nasara*) as a whole, a category embodied in the moment by British colonialists. Others railed against modernity, also represented by British systems of rule, colonial technologies, Western sartorial forms, Western goods, Western recreational practices, and Western education, and the Muslims who adopted them. This nascent antimodernist rejectionism prefigured rhetoric similar to that expressed by Boko Haram today.

Some Northern Nigerians accepted and made peace with British modernity as a necessary aspect of colonization in the aftermath of a brutal military conquest, while others continued to resist that modernity. As Muhammad Sani Umar argues, responses among the Muslim aristocracy to the British military invasion of the Sokoto Caliphate ranged from outright flight and hostility to pragmatic acceptance of the new colonial order.[8] The most dramatic act of hostile rejection of British rule and British ways was the flight of Sultan Muhammadu Attahiru I, who escaped from the caliphate headquarters of Sokoto with his followers as the British forces invaded the town and as initial military resistance collapsed under withering British firepower. After Attahiru's flight, the British force led by Frederick Lugard quickly organized a ceremony at which Muhammadu Buhari, the Waziri or chief adviser to the deposed sultan, led other caliphate officials to sign an article of surrender. Lugard then installed a successor sultan, Muhammadu Attahiru II.

The confrontation was not over, however. The deposed Sultan Attahiru I had made a strategic escape from his enemies, the British, in a move imitative of the *hijra*, the calculated flight of Prophet Muhammad from Mecca to Medina during the founding days of Islam.⁹ Attahiru I wanted to mobilize the caliphate's people, especially peasants in the countryside, to resist the colonizers and, failing that, flee east toward Mecca, the ultimate statement of rejection of the Christian invasion of his realm. He and his supporters subsequently marched eastward across the caliphate savannah to await the coming of the *Mahdi*, a messianic figure of Islam who, according to Islamic eschatological theology, would arrive to confront the unjust reign of nonbelievers—British colonizers, in this case. Attahiru's rural resistance had swelled with much of the countryside population joining his anticolonial movement. Attahiru amassed so much support and goodwill within the territorial space of the caliphate turned British colony that it alarmed British colonizers. In July 1903 the British colonial army traced him and his fleeing party, now numbering in the thousands, to the town of Burmi in present-day northeastern Nigeria and surrounded the town. The party now included the emir of Bida, the magaji of Keffi, Yamusa, and other unyielding notables of the defunct caliphate.

Burmi was a symbolic town because a few years earlier a cleric, Malam Jibrilla Gaini, had established his clerical mission there and declared himself the *Mahdi*. The British had quelled this Mahdist anticolonial revolt in 1902, capturing and exiling Malam Jibrilla to the central Nigerian town of Lokoja on the confluence of the River Benue and River Niger. Now in 1903, his successor, Imam Musa, made common cause with the deposed Sultan Attahiru and welcomed him and his supporters to the town. Together the large group of anticolonial resisters dug in and built fortifications against an anticipated British assault. As they prepared for war, they mobilized and motivated their followers with sermons, fiery speeches, and statements that criticized British rule, ways of life, education, goods, and culture as antithetical and threatening to Muslims' religious devotion. Herein lies the nexus of anticolonial resistance and early colonial-era antimodernism. This would be their last stand against the British army of conquest before they hoped to proceed east toward Mecca. In this moment a virulently antimodernist creed emerged, conflating an acceptance of British rule with an acceptance of Christian and Western cultural influences and goods, of which British colonizers were the conveyors.

The ensuing military confrontation was a lopsided massacre of thousands of the remnants of the deposed sultan's forces. The resisters had been convinced to believe that God, through the self-proclaimed *Mahdi* Mallam Musa, would deliver victory against the British. Motivated by this belief, the resistance fighters charged fruitlessly against the rapid-firing guns of the British colonial troops. Malam Musa and Sultan Attahiru were among the dead. Attahiru's son, Muhammad Bello bin Attahiru, escaped the siege with some supporters and marched away from Nigerian colonial territory in a symbolic *hijra*. They eventually settled in modern-day Sudan.[10]

FROM ANTICOLONIALISM TO ANTIMODERNISM

Confrontational rejection was not the only response of Northern Nigerian clerics, aristocrats, and peasants to the colonial invasion and its accompanying cultural and material impositions. In much of his book *Islam and Colonialism*, Umar covers a range of theological arguments that clerics and aristocrats marshaled in favor of surrender and submission.[11] Some clerics and aristocratic actors argued in favor of armed confrontation and resistance to British colonizers and their culture.[12] Others advocated strategic alliances with the colonizers and vigilant, careful engagements with their goods, ideas, and institutions—with modernity.[13] Thus both pragmatism and suspicion were expressed in these early Muslim debates on British influences.

Arguably, the most authoritative and enduring legal ruling regarding how Muslims should relate to British colonialism and by extension Western modernist institutions, practices, and goods is Waziri Muhammadu Buhari's 1903 treatise "Risālat al-wazīr ilā ahl al-'ilm wa al-tadabbur." In it Buhari sought to rationalize his submission to British authority but, more crucially, he defined the limit of that submission and outlined its terms. What emerges from his ruling are terms of strategic engagement with colonial modernity that he deemed imperative for Muslims who came under the rule of the British and the influence of European culture. Specifically, he urged Muslims to withhold their loyalty from the new regime. While outwardly obeying colonial ordinances in order to survive in the new order, Muslims were to reject the political and cultural accoutrements of British colonialism in their minds, and to strive and pray for their obliteration.

The referenced cultural and political aspects of colonialism are often coterminous with and synecdochical of the broader constellation of ideas, practices, and tangibles that are now colloquially called Western modernity. The obvious gist of Buhari's treatise is the explicitly political dimension wherein Muslims were warned against internalizing or legitimizing the new order. However, a holistic interpretation of this ruling, which has been operational in a paradigmatic way in Northern Nigeria since 1903, encompasses a denunciation of Muslims' acceptance of Western ideas, institutions, goods, and practices. Buhari's treatise did not translate into a uniformity of Muslim responses to colonization. Various degrees of reluctant but pragmatic submission to the might and influence of British colonizers eventually became the dominant pattern of engagement with British colonial culture and the colonizer's goods and practices. Quotidian reconciliation with the ubiquity of British goods and institutions became the norm. Colonial modernity, institutions, and ideas that reformist anticolonial clerics had condemned as sacrilegious found their way into the everyday existential repertoires of Northern Nigerian Muslims—aristocrats, commoners, and peasants. Inevitable mental and physical accommodations to colonialism ensued as Northern Nigerian Muslim subalterns found new ways to pursue piety in the midst of a suffocating British colonial institutional and cultural presence.

For reformers and reform-minded Muslims, the growing adaptation to and adoption of European modernist influences was a tragedy. For them, reluctant, self-preservationist acceptance of British modernity did not erase the theological imperative of rejecting objects and cultures that British Christian colonizers introduced. It did not nullify Waziri Buhari's famous proclamation. It did not mitigate enduring anxieties about colonial goods, practices, and influences. Moreover, the burgeoning conflation of anticolonialism and hostility to Western modernity remained. Antimodernist religio-political creeds continued to circulate and percolate at the Muslim grassroots level. This new ideology informed the consequential relationships many Muslims developed with imperial goods and cultures, as well as their engagement with Western modernity, represented by colonial and missionary secular education, forms of dress, musical entertainment, consumer commodities, and ideas about gender relations.

ANTIMODERNISM AND SECULAR EDUCATION

Boko Haram's most well-known antimodernist mantra is the one connected to its popular name, which means "Western education is forbidden." This critique of Western education as the conveyor of an allegedly polluting Western modernity is ironically traceable to the colonial history of secular educational restriction rather than to its expansion. Boko Haram's opposition to secular education and modernity broadly presents a contradiction. Although Boko Haram decries the expansion of Western education in its northeastern Nigerian stronghold and blames it for society's ills—corruption, maladministration, collapsing public and private morality, and poverty—many Nigerians believe that the manifestation of these ills in Northern Nigeria is more plausibly connected to the paucity of Western education in that part of the country than to its pervasive influence. The history of Western education in Northern Nigeria seems to support this contention, although the story is more complicated than proponents of the "poor education as culprit" thesis suggest.

Access to Western education for Northern Nigeria's youth has not kept pace with population growth. Boko Haram's complaint about the ubiquitous evils of Western education is thus somewhat ironic since large swaths of the region, notably the Northeast, have largely escaped the influence of Western education and the modernity associated with it. Preeminent in Boko Haram's leadership as well as their foot soldiers are men with little to no Western education. Given this reality, it is easy to see the source of the movement's ideological insularity and cultural parochialism that are at the heart of its opposition to Western education. They were driven to the insurgency in part because they lacked access to the secular economy in a postcolonial society where credentialed Western education and secular knowledge are requirements for upward socioeconomic mobility.

It is no coincidence that northeastern Nigeria, the region with the least Western education, is the epicenter of the current insurgency. The thin presence of Western education in the region makes it a receptive ground for the populist and nihilist messages of Boko Haram. Educational deficit and extremism are intricately correlated and reinforce each other. Contrary to the pronouncements of Boko Haram, then, it is difficult to sustain the claim that Western education is the problem. Rather, the problem is arguably Western education's uneven spread in the country, as many observers argue.

The dearth of Western education afflicts all Muslim-majority areas of Northern Nigeria. A combination of British colonial policy on education and a strong suspicion of both secular and Christian missionary education severely restricted the spread of secular schools, resulting in an educational lag in the region and a significant secular educational inequity between Northern and Southern Nigeria. Northern Nigeria became a British protectorate in 1900, and colonial control was consolidated between then and 1907. Unwilling to offend the Muslim populations of many provinces and wary of alienating Muslim elites whom the colonizers were cultivating as allies in their rule, British colonial authorities decreed a ban on Christian missionary activities in the Muslim emirates. This prohibition cut off these regions from the missionary educational enterprise, the major instrument for the spread of Western education in much of colonial Nigeria and Africa.

The British colonizers went even further, establishing a two-tiered educational system in the Muslim regions of Northern Nigeria that made colonial education an elitist affair reserved for a few privileged students, mostly sons of emirs and aristocrats. The first school system, exemplified by the prestigious Katsina College founded in 1921, catered exclusively to the sons of Muslim aristocratic allies of the British.[14] The declared aim of the school was to educate potential emirs and aristocrats who would succeed their parents and continue to help the British administer their constituencies while British officers supervised, a colonial system called *indirect rule*. The other branch of the colonial school system consisted of a few schools reserved almost exclusively for the sons of non-Muslim chiefs who also played a supporting role in colonization. This latter group of schools was designed to train teachers, clerks, and workers for the colonial civil service.[15] The vast majority of Muslims in Northern Nigeria remained without access to any form of Western education. Although there is no reason to believe that Northern Nigerian parents would not have enrolled their children and wards had schools been provided, the prevailing suspicious attitude toward Western education discouraged the establishment of schools even when putative educational institutions had no missionary affiliation and were thus not in violation of the colonial missionary prohibition.

The attitude toward missionary and government-funded colonial schools fluctuated, corresponding to events and the political moods and fortunes of emirs and aristocrats in relation to the colonial order, but a clear tone was set early on. For instance, Emir Aliyu of Kano emphatically rejected a missionary delegation that sought his permission to open a school and a hospital in Kano in 1899, making his position known with the following words: "Start a school? No. We have our own and our children are taught the Holy Qur'an. Medical work? No. Our medicine is in the Holy Qur'an and you can go. I give you three days to prepare—a hundred donkeys to carry your loads back to Zaria, and we never wish to see you here again."[16]

These were stern words that reflected the pervasive suspicion of Western religious and secular influences at that time, an attitude of hostility that was tempered by occasional pragmatic accommodations after the British conquest of Northern Nigeria between 1900 and 1903, but which never dissipated among the Muslim masses. It is said that even the decision of aristocrats to enroll their children in the schools designated for privileged aristocratic children took some persuasion and subtle blackmail. One story states that, in order to overcome the resistance of Northern Nigerian emirs and aristocrats enrolling their wards in Katsina College and the few other schools established as a pipeline for training the middle figures of colonial rule, colonial officials told the aristocrats that if they continued to refuse to enroll their children they would open the schools to the children of commoners, *talakawa*. The children of the *talakawa*, the aristocrats were told, would be given mediatory jobs in the colonial system and constitute themselves into a new colonial middle class that would rival and serve as a counterweight to the influence of the aristocracy. Upon hearing this, some relented and reluctantly enrolled their children in the schools.

The story is, of course, apocryphal, traceable to a lone British colonial official, Theodore Adams, the chief commissioner of the Northern Provinces from 1937 to 1943, who had made the statement to overcome the lingering opposition of some emirs to his proposal to establish a middle school exclusively for princes in Kaduna.[17] Its provenance aside, the encounter the story captures is consistent with the nature of the initial aristocratic suspicion of Western education and the British determination to overcome it for the sake of the stability of their colonial administration. This suspicion of Western education on the part of aristocratic and regular Muslims in Northern Nigeria is often presented in a "clash of civilizations" frame, as part of an allegedly visceral Muslim rejection of Christian-inflected institutions and cultures. However, this attitude toward Western education was not rooted in an impulsive or totalizing Muslim antipathy regarding the educational aspect of Western secular modernity.

There were Hausa Muslims who instinctively rejected any form of secular schooling that European Christians superintended. This attitude can be ascribed to the folk etymology and semiotic history of the word *boko* in precolonial Hausa society. Citing the preeminent historian of precolonial Hausaland, Professor Mahdi Adamu, blogger and syndicated columnist Aliyu Tilde posits a fascinating hypothesis about *boko* that might throw some light on the emergence of societal antipathy towards Western education.

> Before it was largely consigned to western education, boko was often used to connote the 'fake bride,' amaryar boko, who rode the horse in place of the real bride as the convoy of celebrants escorted her to her new home. The real bride would secretly be carried earlier by two or three women to her home. So when western education came to Hausaland, the learned rejected it and gave it a derogatory connotation, ilimin boko, 'fake education.' Sadly, this name has remained the standard translation of 'western education' among all Hausa speaking people of West Africa and I have never heard of any effort to change it ... To date, there is no alternative nomenclature for makarantar boko, 'fake school' that connotes modern schools for western education.[18]

If Tilde's rendering is faithful to Adamu's postulation, and if the hypothesis is credible, then one can surmise that *boko* was already saddled with nomenclatural and semiotic baggage, precisely the connotation of fakery, which was then transferred to Western education as a conscious sociolinguistic effort to mark it out, at its moment of entry into Northern Nigeria, as inauthentic and false.

Hostility to what was considered fake and connected to the British colonial conquest and its supplanting of the preexisting Islamic sovereignty would have been considered an honorable, principled, and perhaps obligatory reaction on the part of Muslims in the region. Even so, not all the skepticism about Western education in colonial times can be attributed to the preexisting cultural understanding of *boko* as a signifier of deception, subterfuge, and fakery. In fact, much of the Muslim skepticism regarding Western education stemmed from the way missionary education was envisioned as a tool of Christian evangelism, a fact clearly documented in internal missionary discourse and missionary sources.[19]

A cultural hostility founded on a transposed sociolinguistic construct was only one factor among several that produced a glaring lag in Western education in Muslim Northern Nigeria. Some emirs had expressed misgivings about the operations of missionary educators in their domain and had opposed the establishment of missionary schools because they took offense at what Peter Tibenderana argues was missionaries' demonizing of Fulani rulers as oppressors of poor traditionalists. This missionary propaganda made emirs hostile to missionaries and their educational enterprise because the missionaries posed both a political and religious risk in their domains.[20] Moreover, some missionaries sought to use their British affiliation and their connections to the colonial system to forcefully demand access and permission, or to punish emirs who resisted.[21] This attitude of entitled aggression on the part of missionary educators only hardened preexisting suspicions, and created further antipathy toward Western schools in some quarters, even as several emirs and members of the nobility recognized the instrumental potentials of secular education and embraced colonial schools with that pragmatic logic in mind.

Moreover, British colonizers were not keen on missionary education and placed restrictions on the spread of liberal Western education in Northern Nigeria, which they considered capable of radicalizing Africans in a conservative Muslim milieu. British colonizers placed these restrictions because they did not want to produce "disgruntled intellectuals," who were blamed for earlier anti-British rhetoric and actions in coastal West Africa, including Lagos. Due to a law established by Frederick Lugard, missionaries could not establish a religious or educational presence in the emirates without permission from the governor, and such permissions were rarely granted.[22] British colonizers did not want to antagonize emirs and the sensibilities of Muslims in the emirates. As a result, they frowned on the intrusions of missionary evangelists and educators who could undermine the evolving colonial administrative partnership.

The colonial failure to build more schools or allow missionaries to build them in Muslim regions of Northern Nigeria, as well as the enduring apprehension about the supposed anti-Muslim provenance of Romanized secular education, resulted in a palpable Western educational deficit in the Muslim regions. This educational backwardness, which triggered popular and political lamentation in both Northern and Southern Nigeria, stemmed from an additional factor. Until the reform of colonial education in Northern Nigeria that culminated in the 1948 Education Ordinance, much of the educational policy and the accompanying curricula at the elementary level focused exclusively on Romanized vernacular literacy,[23] specifically the teaching of basic reading and writing skills in Romanized Hausa.[24] English was not taught at the elementary school level prior to 1948. This diminished the instrumental incentives for acquiring Western education.

Northern Nigeria's educational disadvantage persisted until independence in 1960, when the region's leaders began to play catch-up. To this day, the educational gap between Southern Nigeria and Northern Nigeria is evident. This gap is captured in Nigerian policy parlance by the designation of many Northern Nigerian states as Educationally Less Developed States (ELDS) that require special consideration in federal secondary school and university admission decisions. This educational pedigree or lack thereof provides an important context for understanding the rise of Boko Haram, and especially the rise of antimodernist sentiments before and during Boko Haram's well-known campaign against Western education.

The word *boko*, which is now used as a stand-in for Western education, actually carries a more capacious meaning, and its contextual semiotics are expansive. *Ilimin boko* (Western education) is only one usage context in which *boko* clearly denotes "Western." This is a narrow sense of the word. Properly translated in its more expansive semiotic sense, *boko* is a prefix, qualifier, and modifier connoting "modern." It can thus be affixed to people, things, or phenomena to convey the sense, often negatively, that they are too modern or innovative to be compatible with or beneficial to traditional Northern Nigerian Muslims, and that the objects and subjects so designated could be harmful to Muslims' piety.

For instance, it is quite common in colonial and postcolonial Hausaphone Northern Nigeria for people to use the term *ginin boko* (modern architecture). Similarly, traditional clerics of the Sufi bent derisively refer to reformers, whether of Sufi or Salafi orientation, as *malaman boko* or *malaman zamani* (modern clerics/scholars/teachers).[25] Thus *boko* and *zamani*, connoting the allegedly corrosive and unsettling phenomenon of modern innovations underwritten by new secular trends and colonially mediated influences, became a multipurpose label used to separate, denigrate, and delegitimize interlocutors considered compromised by modern, secular things and influences. Before other Muslims named the group "Boko Haram," its founders were known for declaring repeatedly in their sermons that *boko* was *haram* (prohibited) in Islam. It was this obsession that *boko* or *karatun boko* (government-provided Western learning), in both its narrow and broad connotations, was *haram* that caused outsiders to name the group Boko Haram.

In contemporary reformist discourses in Northern Nigeria, the compound term *boko akida* (Western education as a creed) has become rhetorically useful for Muslims who have Western education and work in secular vocations in Nigeria's secular institutions but want to restate their reformist leanings while denigratingly designating Western-educated Muslims who allegedly operate by the logics of secularism. In this rhetoric *boko akida* refers to those for whom Western education and secular logics allegedly constitute a creed and a path that elevate secular knowledge above the logics of the Muslim canon.

Conversely, *boko sana'a* (Western education as a vocational instrument), a term that reform-minded Muslim professionals in Nigeria's secular economy and institutions claim for themselves, refers to the idea that they only use Western knowledge to earn a living and do not live by its logics. To invoke a Christian theological and idiomatic analogy, the rhetoric of *boko sana'a* claims that reform-inclined, Western-educated Muslims who label other Muslims as *y'an boko akida* (those who subscribe to the tenets of Western education as a creed of living) earn a living in Nigeria's modern, secular world but are not of that world. In contrast, those they label as *boko akida* are allegedly fully immersed in that world of modernity and secularism. Interestingly, these debates have precedence in popular folk discourses and debates about piety, secularism, and modernity in early colonial Northern Nigeria.

The *boko akida / boko sana'a* debate harkens back to the perennial struggle of Northern Nigerian Muslims to engage with Western education and modernity without compromising what they believe to be their inherited and obligatory commitment to a set of core Muslim epistemological and social ideals. "Mainstream Muslims" may "view western education as useful" and even "recognize western education as a body of knowledge to which Islamic culture has significantly contributed for centuries in the past," but as Tilde opines, that has not erased "the lingering suspicion" surrounding Western modernity, a rational engagement strategy that "has . . . hampered the domestication . . . and internalization [of Western knowledge] in the region." According to Tilde, Muslims in Northern Nigeria "go to school only [to] obtain a certificate that will earn us a job without imbibing the principles and fundamentals" of Western education and its associated technologies and systems of thought, which "are seen as alien, never to be imbibed."[26] What Tilde is signaling here is the mainstream prevalence of a *boko sana'a* ethos, in which Muslims engage with Western education primarily as a necessary personal investment in the secular instrument of socioeconomic mobility while continuing the internal struggle against its philosophical foundations. Ideologically speaking, this preexisting duality differs from Boko Haram's position that *boko* or Western education is forbidden only in terms of degree and scope since the latter stance also has its nuances and ambivalences.

By the time of Boko Haram's founding in the early 2000s, these unresolved questions, dilemmas, and debates were still raging, and Boko Haram's rather simplistic answers involving prohibitions, separations, and hard moral demarcations provided clarity for some Northern Nigerians who lacked an independent capacity to arrive at their own theological answers. Moreover, some controversial Boko Haram antimodernist ideas, such as the delegitimization of Nigeria's secular government, were articulated into a religious space in which such ideas were already familiar because "some learned traditional Islamic scholars" had already declared secular government to be haram while arguing that the origin of secular government and modernity is the same: Western education and thought, or boko.[27] The connection between past or preexisting antimodernisms and present ones, as the rest of the chapter demonstrates, may not be causal, but it is discernible.

INCIPIENT DISCOURSES OF ANTIMODERNISM

Early colonial Northern Nigeria was rife with antimodernist thought, but much of that discourse entered the consciousness of Muslims through popular vernacular arts as an underground theatre of anticolonial discourse developed away from the seemingly ubiquitous gaze of colonizers. Songs and poems articulating the antimodernist and anticolonial sentiments of the day were composed and circulated in this space, with a receptive audience spreading them and adapting them to their own anticolonial concerns. Quasi-religious opinions on prohibitions and allegedly anti-Islamic indulgencies involving modern colonial goods proliferated.

Imam Umar's "Zuwan Nasara" (Arrival of the Christians) appeared around 1906 as a long poem lamenting the threat that colonialism posed to existing political institutions and sovereignties, traditional Muslim ways of life, and the practice of Islam itself.[28] In the poem he attributes evil deeds and oppressive acts to the colonizers, accusing them of destroying indigenous cultural heritage and artifacts. He also underlines what he considers the helplessness of African Muslim resisters who were overwhelmed by the European invaders' superior military technology that gave them the ability to dominate and decimate existing cultures. Another important Hausa anticolonial text that circulated and primed the populace for the cultural critique of colonization's cultural domination was Malam Shi'itu's "Bakandamiya" (Hippo Hide Whip), with its transparent metaphor of the cultural violence of colonization.

These early popular poetic articulations of the political, cultural, and religious threat of colonization opened a wide vista for the outpouring of anticolonial and antimodernist folk literature, many of them expressed on a religious and quasi-didactic canvas. Hausa poems, widely recited away from the surveilling ears of British colonizers in the vernacular public sphere and in closed private spaces, continued to venerate the precolonial past and interpret the colonial present as a time of sin, deviance, and Allah's wrath. The current cultural decadence, as the poets saw it, was occasioned by Muslims' willingness to compromise their faith by embracing Christian colonizers and their cultural goods and practices. The first half of the twentieth century was defined by intellectual and artistic articulations of antimodernist and anti-Western themes that saturated the popular social and political imagination in Northern Nigeria's Hausaphone public sphere.

Several anticolonial discourses originated in the hostile emotions and crucible of colonial conquest. These ideas were provoked by an implacably adversarial interpretation of the conquest. The most prominent thread of this discourse is conveyed in a popular, anonymous poem of convoluted provenance, which praises flight and complete physical separation from British colonizers and the modern society they purportedly created in Northern Nigeria. It is titled "Wakar Nasara" (Poem on Christians) and circulated widely in both modified Arabic (*Ajami*) and Romanized Hausa scripts:

> Even if I have to leave Allah alone, I will not stay,
>   For, by Allah, I will not obey the Christians.
> Between two alternatives, one must be chosen:
>   Either *hijra*, or following the Christians.
> Even the Emirs have left their towns
>   So—if not *hijra*—what is there for a commoner
>   Other than to become Christian?
>   We are men, yet women have made it first before us
> Fear of death, and the love of life, we too have.
>   But to refuse the predestined is to follow the Christians.
> If you say it is difficult to leave,
>   The totality of *lahan* [injury, blemish] is with those who follow the
>   Christians,
> If you think you have power and refuse *hijra*,
>   What power reaches the power of the Christians?
> If they offer a gift, don't accept it.
>   It is poison they will give you; toxic is the gift of the Christians.
> They admonish us to stop oppression:
>   But they are themselves oppressors, these Christians.
> They have dark *fitna* and machination,
>   To spoil the religion of Islam—the Christians!
> It is obligatory on everyone to prepare for the *hijra*.
>   O Muslims! Let us not accept obedience to the Christians

Let us be in constant remembrance of Allah, and Supplication,
    With justice, we shall overthrow the Christians.
Commoners and rulers are the same to them;
    Contempt abounds with the Christians.
Rule has become impossible for those with authority.
    What do we do to overcome the Christians?
If Almighty Allah shows mercy on us,
    He will give us a *mujaddid* for us to overwhelm the Christians.[29]

Another popular, religion-themed poem rails against colonialism and modernity, both symbolized in the author's mind by Christian colonizers and their cultural and political work among Muslims in Northern Nigeria. Titled "Raʿiyya," the poem is in the collection of Muhammad Sani Umar and is analyzed in his book *Islam and Colonialism*. It is worth excerpting here:

We seek cover from the Almighty Allah
To protect us from the iniquity of the Christians
And from encounter with oppression and calumny,
And from the wretchedness of the Christians.
My dear brother, wherever you go,
Do not neglect to watch out for the Christians.
They are like the Devil in their habit.
Surely, the Christians are a *fitna* for humanity,
Their existence is a disaster.

The word "Christian" here (*Nasara* in Hausa) is an all-purpose semiotic device that appears in many similar poems and songs composed during the early colonial period.[31] In the semiosis of these anti-*Nasara* poems and songs, it is not just indulgence or participation in modernity that corrupts; associating, excusing, or tolerating modern and Western institutions is also corrupting.

Hausa songs and poems associated British and Western goods and bodily adornments with the acceptance of European colonizers' ways and lifestyles and an embrace of British-mediated Western modernity, which allegedly separated a Muslim from Allah and incurred his wrath. One such poem, "Yau Kufr" (Today Is Unbelief), was written in 1930 but the author remains unknown. This is not surprising since anonymity protected the authors of such subversive poems and songs from the colonizers' vengeful response. The poem is self-explanatory in its strident antimodernist critique:

> Today unbelief is established, and also innovation,
> Well, as for us, we have no use for this in our time,
> This is that I am about to say, there is no jesting in it,
> Now I am going to warn you, O people,
> Whoever heeds it, he will be happy,
> Whatever article of their clothing, if you wear it, I will tell you that you may understand.
>
> If you pray a thousand times, you will not be vindicated—
> And the same applies to the maker of hurricane lamp globes—
> Your short trousers together with your tight-fitting trousers,
> Whoever puts them on, his unbelief is wide.
>
> Whoever wears suits with buttons, he has apostatized,
> He has no religion at all, only pride,
> His state is the state of the makers of silver dollars,
> They are beyond our power to imitate,
> One should not wear shirts with collars,
> Whoever wears them, his unbelief is wide,
> Khaki and pajamas, whoever it is,
> Who wears them and prays in them, he has committed a crime.
>
> Here they are, three things, do not use them,
> All of them avoid them, without arguing,
> For to use them is not right, you have seen them,
> Towel and washing blue, and powder, whoever uses them,
> Certainly, on the Last Day, the fire is his dwelling."[32]

What is remarkable about this poem is not just that it polemically condemns engagement with Western goods as a form of apostasy; the poem is also insightful because it proves the persistence and prevalence of anticolonial and antimodernist discourses in the quasi-religious vocabulary of quotidian social relations in Northern Nigeria. Even in the mid-colonial period of the 1930s, Northern Nigerian Muslims continued to imagine a different world from the "modern" colonial world in which they lived, and associated the plethora of material, ideational, and cultural goods the British introduced to Northern Nigeria with sinful decadence, apostasy, and heresy.

It is not surprising that about a century later Muhammad Yusuf made multiple references in his lectures to this and similar poems in his attempts to legitimize and historicize his heterodox and antimodernist injunctions and exegesis.³³ Yusuf thus sought to underscore a preexisting vernacular Islamic culture of antimodernist discourse. In telling his audience that his critique of modernity, Western education, and Western secular political institutions mirrored those contained in popular folk songs and poems of the past, Yusuf wanted to show that there was nothing new or bizarre about his ideological positions, especially his acerbic critique of Western influences and secular institutions. He wanted to show a provenance, a genealogy.

As an antimodernist and anticolonial poem, "Yau Kufr" is proof of the existence of a long, constantly reinvented tradition of antimodernist popular discourses among Muslims in Northern Nigeria, a tradition Boko Haram tapped into and reactivated in the twenty-first century to legitimize and bolster its own antimodernist ideology. Because there are many such folk poems in circulation, and because they illustrate the nexus of antimodernist sentiments and folk Islam, Boko Haram ideologues could easily refer audience members who were shocked by their radically reformist and heterodox theological stances to this earlier, surviving culture of antimodernist discourse.

The rejection of Western modernity and all its components was central to one strand of the response to the colonial invasion and to colonial rule, events whose trauma and perceived damage to the Muslim order in Northern Nigeria were documented in poems and songs as adversarial and uncompromising as the one above. This discourse was not secular, it was largely theological and ideological, hence the pronouncing of apostasy, unbelief, and the eternal punishment of hell on Muslims who embraced the goods and modernity imposed and mediated by colonizers. This religious narrative of antimodernism predated the British conquest, and after the colonial occupation it remained in place and evolved in new directions in the underground vernacular space of religious intellection. In this vernacular sphere this ideology commingled with surviving caliphate discourses about unbelief, apostasy, excommunication, and about what was *ḥalāl* (lawful) and what was *ḥarām* (unlawful).

The iteration of this generational antimodernist anxiety captured in these poems owes its origins to the resistance and confrontation narratives that clerics and aristocrats articulated as religious idioms in the wake of the British invasion. This moral anticolonial struggle (or *gwagwarmaya* in Hausa) persisted as a theme in later forms of anticolonial and antimodernist popular arts. One Hausa poet, Mallam Labbo dan Mariya, was particularly explicit in his poetic musings, describing "the Europeans and Christians" as "enemies of Muhammadu."[34] He underlined the Muslim distrust of Europeans and their culture prevalent in Muslim Northern Nigeria at the time, describing the Christian European as a "white-skinned" person who was "charcoal-black" on the inside. The moral racial binary of good and evil stood in for the lingering hostility toward European colonial influences. Mallam Labbo claimed, "Whoever says they [European Christians] have anything good, should not be excluded from being one of the Christians." Labbo went even further to warn Muslims against cultivating friendly relations or exchanging material gifts with Christian Europeans.

In the 1940s a poet by the name of Abubakar Maikaratu captured the sentiments of many Hausa-speaking Muslims regarding the colonial cultural order with his acerbic poetic critique of Western modernity, Western culture, and the objects that he and many Muslims in the region believed were vectors of unlawful modern innovation (*bid'a*) in their faith. A popular writer whose poetic compositions enjoyed wide circulation,[35] Maikaratu gave expression to the growing resentment of seemingly ubiquitous modern goods, institutions, and practices in a Northern Nigerian colonial space saturated, to the consternation of many Muslims, with unfamiliar influences that arrived with European Christian colonizers. Like his fellow poets and singers who meshed popular anticolonial commentary with a theological disavowal of modernity, Maikaratu's poetic repertoire was consistently anticolonial, but rooted in anxieties about the ubiquitous material and symbolic signs of colonial modernity. Like Labbo, he described Muslims who imitated Christian Europeans in sartorial or other ways as non-Muslims, effectively equating the embrace of Western modernity and Western culture with apostasy.

Maikaratu's poetic niche in this period was the naming and shaming of specific objects and symbols of British colonial modernity as instruments of unbelief. In one poem he condemned the wearing of the short knicker, a sartorial symbol of the British colonial presence:

Whichever you wear, you should note that, if you
Pray a thousand times, it is ineffective; you remain
Like the manufacturer of a bulb. This short knicker
And tight pair of trousers; whoever wears them,
Unbelief has crept into him.[36]

Here the short knicker and pair of trousers function collectively as a sartorial symbol of modernity, the adoption of which, according to Maikaratu, amounted to accepting the Christian colonizer. In another poem Maikaratu railed against the P cap, which colonial officials and some Western-educated Africans wore. Maikaratu was convinced that "whoever wears the P cap would on the day of resurrection find himself at the punishment space in the hereafter."[37] Maikaratu's popular poems criticized Muslims who wore Western shirts, trousers, socks, shoes, handkerchiefs, and wristwatches. He also warned Muslims against adopting Western architectural styles. In Maikaratu's works antimodernism meshed with anticolonialism, with the category of *Nasara* or Christian working as a heuristic glue to hold them together.

In a prescription that seems to have foreshadowed Boko Haram's antimodernist pronouncements, Maikaratu advanced an expansive injunction condemning a plethora of activities as signs of unbelief: the riding of bicycles, which British colonizers had introduced; using British-manufactured walking canes; playing or watching sports and other recreational activities introduced by European Christians; learning English and other European languages; and acquiring Western education. Like many other Northern Nigerian Muslims who were uncomfortable with the influx of Western influences and the dizzying pace of what colonizers called modernization, but which many local Muslims understood as *kufr* culture (the culture of unbelief), Maikaratu used expressive art forms to recall and imagine a time before and without Western cultural, sartorial, and technological influences deemed capable of undermining Muslims' faith and devotion. Another poet from the period condemned the most recognizable symbols of Western education and the colonial bureaucracy—the fountain pen and the official paper used in schools and official correspondence.[38] He likened the pen to a shaft portending danger and the ink from it as "ceaselessly flowing," insinuating the permanence of the pollution he and other poetic commentators associated with Western culture and colonial modernity.

These antimodernist beliefs and critiques were rooted in a nostalgia for an increasingly romanticized premodern and precolonial cultural and religious environment devoid of these allegedly corrupting influences. Because these anxieties resided in the realm of everyday performances and quasi-religious folk art, they were widely diffused and subsequently informed the perception of Western-originated practices, knowledge, and objects. Antimodernist folk wisdom and artistic expressions became entrenched. They contained the ingredients for a robust, evolving ideological discourse on the imperative of protecting Muslims from the contagion of Western modernity and of reclaiming an Islamic cultural space purportedly desecrated by Western goods, practices, and institutions.

ENDURING ANTIMODERNIST CONCERNS

In the late colonial period of the 1950s, Muslim concerns about modern goods and technologies reemerged. They bubbled up to the surface when prominent leaders of the Sufi establishment began weighing in on the relationship of the Muslim canons and devotional practices on one side and Western technological innovations on the other. Debates in this period revolved around the extent to which Muslims could embrace Western-originated technologies and still maintain their piety. Like Muslims in many parts of the world contending with the ubiquity of modern goods and technology-enabled practices in a world of industrial capitalism superintended by Christian Europeans, Muslims in Northern Nigeria debated the appropriate relationship with modernity and its uncertain impact on their devotion. These debates pitted those who regarded technology and innovations as corruptors of Islam against those who saw nothing intrinsically corrupting in Western technology, and instead promoted an accommodative approach that harnessed the benefits of technological goods while being vigilant about their potentially harmful aspects.[39]

One of the most memorable debates on this topic occurred in 1954. In that year a heated conversation broke out among the *'ulamā'* on whether the Qur'an should be recited on the radio, a European "Christian" technological innovation. The debate took on more urgency when the sixteenth emir of Zazzau, Emir Ja'afaru Ishaq (1937–59), an adherent of the traditional Tijaniyya Sufi brotherhood, opposed the reading of the Qur'an on the Northern Nigerian radio service.[40] This position pitted him against Shaykh Ibrahim Niasse of the reformist Tijaniyya. Emir Ja'afaru Ishaq wrote a strongly worded letter of protest to the emir of Kano, Muhammadu Sanusi, the symbolic leader of Kano's reformist Tijaniyya brotherhood. The brotherhood had already begun leveraging radio technology and the colonial technology of loudspeakers and mobile public address systems for both Qur'an recitation and preaching.

Emir Ja'afaru Ishaq's letter, in which he challenged the emir of Kano to provide "specific references from the legal texts that contain proof that reading the Qur'an on the radio is legal," sparked the debate and prompted Emir Sanusi to appeal to the highest authority in the Tijaniyya brotherhood, Shaykh Ibrahim Niasse, for a ruling on the matter. Niasse's response, detailed and clear, appeared to settle the matter among the Tijaniyya:

> There has been a question directed to the people of Kano about whether it is legal for the Qur'an to be read over the radio. Innovation may be divided into five parts: necessary [*wajib*], recommended [*mandub*], permitted [*jaiz*], reprehensible [*makruh*], and forbidden [*haram*]. Whatever is an aid to Islam must be considered good, in the light of the Qur'an. If it would strengthen the law of Islam, then it must be considered a "necessary" innovation. An innovation that is not harmful to Islam is "possible." An innovation that weakens the traditions of the Prophet is to be "discouraged." An innovation that leads people away from Islam must be "forbidden." The innovation of the radio, if not "necessary," is at least a "recommended" innovation. Learned people also established printing presses for the spread of knowledge, and these presses may also be regarded as "necessary" or "recommended." In these modern times there are many innovations, for example loudspeakers and radios, and through them we may aid and help Islam. The number of pilgrims to Mecca increases each year because of the airplane. Praise to God. How can a large group of people follow their imam without a loudspeaker in the mosque? We have seen how ships and lorries and airplanes, and other means of communications such as the telephone, have played an important role in the development of Islam.[41]

Niasse's response anticipated and clarified the fraught relationship of Northern Nigerian Muslims with other modern technologies that, in his judgment, did not harm Islam and could in fact help in proselytizing the faith. Niasse's ruling became an iconic fatwa and carried a note of finality among the Tijaniyya brotherhood. It may have quieted the debate for the moment, but the clarity of his ruling did not carry over to the Qadiriyya Sufi brotherhood, let alone to the emerging reformist and, later, the Salafi movement. The result was that debates on modernity and on Western-manufactured goods and technologies continued to percolate in the region and would become even more intense during the Izala phase of reform in Northern Nigerian Islam.

Although Muhammadu Buhari's seminal "Risālat al-wazīr ilā ahl al-ʿilm wa al-tadabbur" urged a strategic, temporary, outward submission to the ways of British colonizers, the discourse of accommodation gained only little currency during the colonial period. The anticolonial, antimodernist texts circulating in the popular domain proved more durable. Antimodernism was legitimized by the uncompromising injunction on colonial cultural influences in this treatise. Although various forms of pragmatism ensued, the simultaneous existence of a paradigmatic fatwa urging an internal adversarial attitude toward colonial Western cultural influences ensured that rejection and antimodernist ideologies remained potent and legitimate Muslim responses to concerns about Western cultural imperialism. The entry of the Izala sect into the Northern Nigerian Islamic sphere in the late 1970s and 1980s not only revived the modernity debate but also brought new dimensions into it.

THE ANTIMODERNISM OF THE GUMI-IZALA REFORM

Chapter 2 outlined the long-lasting effect of the Abubakar Gumi-led Izala *ahlus Sunna* revolution on the Northern Nigerian Islamic landscape. The Izala ascendancy's primary impact was, of course, largely theological. Izala succeeded in drawing adherents away from the Sufi brotherhoods as it sought to establish itself as the reformist, true path. A less-emphasized impact of Gumi's revolution is the deft manner in which he posited a new idea of Islamic modernity, represented in his perspective by a "pure" Islamic creed that was forward-looking and empowered Muslims to thrive in a secular Nigerian society. This new idea of Islamic modernity was propounded as a counterpoint to and replacement for secular modernity, defined in colonial and Western terms.

In Kaduna, Gumi came into his own as an Islamic scholar, jurist, and preacher. Important members of the Muslim bureaucratic and business elite attended Gumi's *tafsīr* sessions regularly in the 1960s and 1970s. In this way, he succeeded in planting the seeds of his theological convictions in the minds of influential Muslim political actors in the region, and quietly mainstreamed his critiques of Sufi teachings, secularity, and modernity. The Kaduna phase of Gumi's preaching and clerical career unveiled this complex antimodernist agenda. For Gumi it was not simply enough to critique the modernity associated with Western material and symbolic cultures carried over from colonial times. Gumi was determined to give Muslims an alternate postcolonial modernity that was compliant with Sharia and compatible with the new literalist theological interventions associated with Izala's reformist creed. This alternative would enable Muslims to navigate the secular institutions of the Nigerian state without running afoul of the strict moral and quotidian prescriptions and restrictions of Sharia.

Gumi's effort to overthrow the Sufi clerical order turned on one strategy: he would use exegesis to delegitimize the Sufi brotherhoods. He would do so by delinking their beliefs from Islamic sources and locating them instead in non-Muslim religious and secular sources. Gumi pointed out to his audience that Sufism was a hodgepodge of Greek beliefs, Hindu mysticism, "Oriental philosophies," and "certain concepts in Islam."[42] By locating Sufism's origins in non-Muslim ideologies and by aligning its beliefs and teachings with secular and pre-Islamic ideas and in other religions, Gumi sought to present Sufism as a syncretistic creed.

Gumi's new Izala sect prescribed simpler, bare-bones ceremonies to mark the christening of newborns and other life events that had required elaborate and financially costly rituals and celebrations overseen by the Sufi hierarchy. This was a new modernity of simplicity and of ignoring age-old traditions deemed more secular than religious. Grassroots support predicated on the appeal of these simplified commemorations boosted Izala, which then consolidated this support by urging Muslims to embrace a literalist path of piety as dictated in the Qur'an and the Sunna.

Izala preachers who were followers of Gumi recommended this piety as liberation from the stranglehold of the Sufi clerical order and from the financial burdens and inconveniences it placed on them. The advancement of piety as a cure-all solution to life's travails dovetailed with notions of God as an omnipotent problem solver who would surely reward those who "return to the ways of God."[43]

Izala represented a bold, ironically modern face of Islam in a region in which a Sufi orthodoxy established by the Fodiawa jihad almost two centuries earlier held sway but had lost its revivalist luster. Izala thus positioned itself as a modernizer of Islam, a movement that brought Islamic practice in Northern Nigeria into alignment with current anti-Western and antimodernist anxieties of Muslims in the mid- to late twentieth century. This was a brazen claim: the Izala movement saw itself as a new kind of theocratic modernity that supplanted the allegedly secular modernity of colonial and neocolonial influences. At the same time, Izala encouraged Muslim secular empowerment as a counterpoint to the enduring and powerful influence of Western modernity in Nigerian society.

Izala's modernity also inhered in the fact that, unlike the Sufi clerical order whose relationship with secular education was at best ambivalent, Sheikh Gumi encouraged his followers to enroll in secular educational institutions, acquire degrees, and get into professions, the armed forces, and the civil service. He set the example by enrolling his own children, including female children, in secular universities to train as medical doctors, engineers, and army officers. Gumi even took the extraordinary step of legally registering his new organization with Nigeria's Corporate Affairs Commission, a radical move meant to demonstrate that reformers must engage with and eventually come to dominate the Nigerian secular state before reforming it or overthrowing it altogether.[44]

Gumi's philosophical engagement with modernity was complicated. He felt that work and secular accomplishments were important because they would give Muslims control over the instruments and institutions of the Nigerian state and eventually enable them to infuse Islamic principles into its workings. Gumi posited the dictum "Siyasa Tafi Sallah" (Politics is more important than acts of devotion). This counterintuitive reasoning encapsulated Gumi's idea of Muslim secular empowerment as a gateway to Muslim religious ascendancy in postcolonial Nigeria, a radically new conception of political Islam and Islamic modernity. This position caused some elements of Boko Haram to brand Gumi's Izala followers as "fake Muslims" in 2013 because his endorsement of Muslim participation in secular politics and institutions was antithetical to Boko Haram's creed.[45]

Gumi argued that Muslims should not simply obsess over theological and devotional commitments to the neglect of their position and status in Nigerian secular institutions because they would lose the state to Christians who would implement Western, modernist, secular, and anti-Muslim policies and ideas. This would then pollute Muslims' devotion and their compliance with Sharia. For him the ultimate goal of establishing a state governed by the tenets of Sharia would only be possible if Muslims did not shun secular and governmental endeavors but embraced them as part of their piety and complementary to their acts of devotion. Entering and thriving in the most consequential institutions of the Nigerian secular state would position Muslims to reform the state along an Islamic trajectory, Gumi argued.

Clearly this complex attitude toward Western modernity and secular institutions was at odds with the Boko Haram template. However, Boko Haram's relationship with modernity is similarly complicated and can sometimes raise questions about the rigidity of its antimodernist stance.[46] Like Gumi's Izala, Boko Haram has embraced a plethora of modern technologies, knowledge, and practices that it finds useful for disseminating and promoting its ideologies. Boko Haram's investment in modern instruments of mass communication—radio, television, and internet technology—and its management of this investment amount to an appropriation of Western knowledge, science, and technology for reformist ends. Although Boko Haram does not go so far as to state, as Gumi did, that an immersion in Western education and secular institutions and professions is necessary for Muslims' ascendance, its ideological repertoire suggests that its antimodernism is similarly circumscribed by the pragmatic challenges of promoting a reformist creed in a society suffused with the signs and materiality of modernity.

MAITATSINE'S ANTIMODERNISM—A PRECURSOR?

In the 1980s a religious upheaval wracked several states in Northern Nigeria. At the heart of it was the preaching and rebellion of Muhammadu

Marwa, whom detractors called Maitatsine.[47] The Y'antatsine movement of the 1980s, with its mix of antimetallurgical suspicions, heterodox theology, antimodernist ideology, antiestablishment populism, and reclusive practices, was a home-grown group of dissidents that drew on fringe apocalyptic Islamic doctrines to launch a bloody, widespread revolt against the state and society in general. However, its major target was a Sunni Islamic establishment that, in the eyes of Muhammadu Marwa and his followers, was too elitist and had been compromised by both a rigid, learned textual creed and secular technologies of knowledge and living.

The Y'antatsine, meaning "those who pronounce curses," were so named because the sermons of the group's leader were laced with curses—"Allah ya tsine" (may God curse you). He routinely cursed those he accused of departing from the true path. For Marwa, the Sunni Islamic establishment had become too modernized and thus too removed from the lives of Northern Nigerian Muslim peasants, who were unlettered in both classical Arabic and Romanized secular education. The Maitatsine sect rejected Western technology and modernity, living insular lives under their leader and his appointees in isolated rural and urban slum compounds located in a few cities and towns in northeastern and northwestern Nigeria. Syndicated columnist Aliyu Tilde asserts that Maitatsine's rejection of "the use of western technological products like watches, bicycles, radio and television" represented "an extreme variety" of an antimodernist creed that was already established to varying, fluctuating degrees in Northern Nigeria. He contrasts Maitatsine's expansive antimodernism with Boko Haram's limitedly strategic and nuanced antimodernist ideology, which allows "the use of even cameras, handsets and computers, as explained by its [founding] leader [Muhammad Yusuf] in his final moments."[48]

The first Maitatsine crisis erupted in Kano in 1980. The Y'antatsine (or Maitatsine) sect clashed with Nigerian security forces and the civilian, predominantly Muslim population of Kano. Thousands of Nigerians died in the conflict, including Marwa. In October 1982 members of the sect, now regrouped in Maiduguri, staged an uprising from their Bulumkutu base. Once again, the security forces were called in, and the ensuing conflict led to the destruction of the group's base and the loss of hundreds of lives. The scenes of destruction were eerily similar to the aftermath of the 2009 military raid on Boko Haram's headquarters in Maiduguri.

Reverberations of this clash were felt as far as Kaduna, where violence broke out as pockets of the sect's members attempted to stage their own uprising there. The last of the Maitatsine clashes occurred in 1984. Yola and Gombe, where members of the sect who had been displaced from Kano and Maiduguri had regrouped, experienced prolonged violence, loss of lives, and the destruction of property. It took the intervention of the Nigerian army to quell the violence.

Like much of the academic and popular commentary on Boko Haram, studies of the Maitatsine tend to privilege economic deprivation and political marginality as causative explanations and thus obscure the ideological and theological factors and claims that proved alluring to those who were attracted to the sect. This antimodernist, technology-skeptical ideology bears an obvious resemblance to Boko Haram's twenty-first-century antagonism toward an eclectic constellation of ideational and material instantiations of Western modernity. Scholarly perspectives on the Y'antatsine are marked by inattention to the group's heterodox religious exegesis and to the anti-intellectual and antimodernist folk Islam that this marginality produced.[49]

The followers of Maitatsine consisted of unlettered rural peasants and sections of the urban poor, many of them mobile or migrant populations who had integrated neither into the urban secular economy nor into the dominant urban Sunni religious environment.[50] Their resentment was thus as much against the prevailing religious orthodoxy of Northern Nigeria as it was against the political, social, and economic situation that the established clerics seemed at peace with. Whether they were new migrants to Northern Nigeria's urban centers or marginalized urban dwellers, their resentment had the same targets: modern objects, ideas, practices, and forms of leisure in cities and towns, which for them embodied the pollution of life by an irreligious quest for such aspects of modernity.

The fact that these people did not belong to or have a stake in the Sunni religious marketplace and were unable to access its literary and exegetical properties made them receptive to Maitatsine's heterodox, insurgent Qur'an exegesis. Like Boko Haram's Muhammad Yusuf, Muhammadu Marwa's appeal was his ability to combine a folksy preaching style with a knack for rendering the Qur'an and other texts in the Islamic canon relatable by adopting a simplified vernacular and an interpretive framework removed from the esoteric formality of classical Arabic and formalized Islamic learning. For Marwa, as it later became for Yusuf, a learned, sophisticated approach to Qur'an exegesis then became part of the problem, which each of them blamed on the modernization of Islam or the influence of modern intellectual and educational practices on Qur'an interpretation. In their thinking these influences and innovations were associated with Western education and with Western philosophical and scientific forms of knowledge.

It is a long-standing tradition in certain Islamic circles to subject the Qur'an to multiple inquiries in order to extract multiple layers of meanings from its verses. The process of going beyond the apparent or outward meaning to probe the inner or hidden meanings of a Qur'an verse is a particularly popular phenomenon among Sufi mystics, who postulate that a given verse of the Qur'an could be mined for an infinite number of meanings by a Muslim trained to engage with the hidden *tafsīr* (message) of the holy book. Theoretically, in this understanding the interpretive possibilities for any Qur'an verse are limitless. Combined with the principle that a verse could be abrogated or reinterpreted to suit the interests and circumstances of Muslims in a particular epoch, the interpretive elasticity of the Qur'an allowed some clerics to become inventive in their exegetical pronouncements.

Some ambitious and heterodox clerics, especially those without formal rigorous religious learning, tended to adopt a capacious interpretive frame that enabled them to offer novel, alluring, and experientially relevant doctrines. Muhamamdu Marwa was one such cleric. He adopted a Qur'an interpretive method that prefigured Muhammad Yusuf's own eclectically heterodox theology. Marwa developed a culture-bound exegesis of haram prohibitions that he creatively adapted to the sensibilities, illiteracy, and circumstances of his followers. According to Hiskett, Marwa "angled his interpretations to accommodate a largely non-literate congregation for whom the classical exegesis, based on classical Arabic, and a Middle Eastern frame of reference, was a closed book."[51] The result was an unconventional exegesis that resembled and preempted that of Boko Haram's Muhammad Yusuf in its certitude, heterodoxy, and fervor, and in its totalizing prohibitions.

For instance, Marwa found a way to reinterpret the word *tarakkuka* in Qur'an 62:11 to be a "hidden" reference to the Hausa word *kuka*, the baobab tree, whose leaves are widely used in Hausaphone Northern Nigeria to make a popular slimy sauce for a variety of starches. Marwa reinterpreted the verse to mean a divine injunction against the consumption of *kuka*. From this premise he pronounced the consumption of baobab leaves haram, a terrible infraction comparable to the sin of turning one's back on the Prophet.[52] Hiskett further argues that Marwa's audience, being largely non-Hausa Muslims, already avoided *kuka* as a condiment and thus enthusiastically received Marwa's proclamation as a divine affirmation. This is similar to what would happen several decades later when Muhammad Yusuf proclaimed to his largely non-Western-educated audience that modern secular education, or *boko*, was haram and was met with approving shouts and applause.

Similar to his *kuka* prohibition or haram, Marwa provided a strangely contrarian interpretation of Qur'an 19:60 and 25:70 in which the words *illa man taba* are used, meaning "except those who repent." Marwa plucked the word *taba* from its context and from its Arabic semiotic universe and rendered it into Hausa. In the Hausa language *taba* means cigarettes or tobacco in general. By thus appealing to the Hausa literacy of his Arabic-illiterate audience and invoking the logic of hidden meanings, Marwa reinterpreted the verse to mean that repentance was not complete unless a Muslim abandoned the use of tobacco products, most of them manufactured in the West or produced in mechanized, industrial settings in Nigeria by foreign multinationals. Here too, Marwa may have been pandering to his audience of poor urban and rural folk for whom cigarettes would already have been something of a luxury. Marwa's pronouncement was greeted with enthusiastic applause.[53]

Marwa's preaching repertoire contained an elaborate array of products and activities that he deemed to be haram. He railed against different objects, practices, and symbols of urbanity and modernity. He developed an expansive antimetallurgical ideology, condemning as haram most things made of metal (*karfe*), modern instruments of mobility, and other goods created through technological innovations and the metallurgical engineering profession of the modern age. For him *karfe* was a stand-in for modern technology, which he viewed as a corruptor of Muslims' morality. He cursed those who drove cars, rode on motorbikes, and lived a modern life.

This religious ideology led Hiskett to argue that Maitatsine was in part a revolt against the "activities characteristic of Hausa townspeople." Although that may be true, it seems that Marwa, like Muhammad Yusuf, simply sought to challenge the existing theological consensus by proposing interpretations that were as far from that consensus as possible in order to convince his impressionable followers that he was a revolutionary religious figure. Being theologically and ideologically different from the existing orthodoxy is the staple of reformers' claim to legitimacy and the basis of their appeal. Moreover, like Yusuf, Marwa had a gift of mockery and wit that he directed with fervor at critics who accused him of going too far in his critique of modernity and secular technologies. His conversational and almost comedic preaching style routinely set his audience "rocking with laughter and chanting with delight."[54] Several decades later, Yusuf would use a similarly folksy, mocking tone to attack his critics in the mainstream Salafi and larger Sunni establishments who accused him of being too extreme in his condemnation of Western education, secular institutions and practices, modern goods, democracy, secular governmental authorities, and modern vocational endeavors.

ANTI-*BOKO* AND ANTIMODERN

Boko Haram's antimodern *tasfir* (interpretation) turns on the group's position on Western education. It was not Western education per se that Yusuf considered antithetical to Muslim piety; rather, it was the elastic set of modern institutions, goods, and practices that he identified as the outcome of Western education. In his antimodernist proclamation, Western education comes across as a Trojan horse that in itself may not appear to be dangerous but the content of which could lead Muslims astray. At his most accommodative posture, he was agnostic toward *boko*. The implication is that the rhetoric of *boko* is just as important as its literal and connotative meanings. In Northern Nigerian history the term *boko* has come in handy for reformers and traditional clerics alike who desired to discredit people, goods, technologies, practices, and phenomena they considered potentially harmful to or at least incompatible with their idea of piety. *Boko* has functioned as an all-purpose idiom of critique, applied both to modernity as a temporal, chronological phenomenon depicting trends and more specifically to a set of phenomena associated with colonization and its aftermath.

In the case of Boko Haram, pronouncements on *boko* proceed from the narrow meaning of the word, Western education, to its broad connotations regarding Western modernist practices and phenomena. Much of Boko Haram's foundational theological positions on Western education came from Yusuf. However, Yusuf was not totally opposed to Western education, conceding in some sermons and debates that aspects of Western education that did not contradict the Qur'an, Sunna, and *ḥadīth* were permissible.⁵⁵ What he unequivocally opposed, which caused him to ultimately condemn Western education as a whole, was what he believed came with the literacy, education, practices, and socialization associated with a secular educational curriculum. For Yusuf it was difficult, if not impossible, to accept Western education and participate in its culture without embracing the associated practices that he claimed contradicted Islam.

For Yusuf *boko*, narrowly defined here as Western education, was constituted by curricula that promote secular law, Western classical philosophy, evolution, and even atheism, all of which he believed added up to a Western modernist worldview that could lead a Muslim away from Islam. He argued that other aspects of Western education, such as the veneration of secular national symbols, the use of English as a medium of educational instruction, and mixed-gender classrooms, contradicted Islamic prescriptions.⁵⁶ This ideology was not new, having been articulated to varying degrees in previous reformist contexts in the region.

Abubakar Shekau, Yusuf's successor as Boko Haram leader, produced a robust archive that expresses his rejection of Western education and, broadly, what he called "Western civilization" and its atheistic and "anti-Islam" orientation.⁵⁷ In a seminal sermon delivered in 2009, Shekau invoked the ambivalence of Northern Nigerian Muslims on Western education, recalling that after his and his friends' initial enrollment in secular schools, "our grandparents bemoaned, so they removed us." Elsewhere Shekau referenced apocryphal historical accounts of how "in the past . . . elders [were] fleeing with their children to the villages, in protest against Western education."⁵⁸ The elders' objection to Western education, Shekau posited, was wide-ranging. It included the fact that the school buildings were roofed with aluminum, which elders likened to a "fireplace," probably an allusion to the high temperatures of the classrooms and their metaphoric similarity to conditions in eternal hellfire.[59] Shekau was consciously, strategically, and selectively mining prior fraught histories of Northern Nigerian Muslims' suspicion of and engagements with Western education and modernity to legitimize and insert his own antimodernist narrative into a preexisting discourse of antimodernist dissidence.

Shekau's historical references were rhetorical strategies and were deliberately embellished with dramatic idioms of damnation and eternal punishment, but the references themselves, as invocations of the prevailing sentiment of an epoch and context, are not without evidentiary support. Shekau did not pull his stories out of thin air. Like many other young Northern Nigerian Muslim commoners in his generation, Shekau's parents, whether out of conviction or a lack of means, did not enthusiastically invest in the secular education of their children. Shekau would have heard stories, no doubt dramatized for effect and retrospective self-justification, from older family members about the evils of Western education and how parents and grandparents had steered children away from it.

The Northern Nigerian Muslim public sphere was inundated in colonial times with several anti-*boko* (anti–Western education) folk wisdoms, songs, poems, and proverbs (*Karin Magana*). Perhaps the most popular and encapsulating of these folk representations of the overarching sentiments against secular education was a song with a particularly searing theme of contempt for Western-educated Muslims:

> 'Yan makarantar bokoko (students of Western secular schools)
> ba karatu (you do not study [religious texts])
> ba Sallah (you do not pray)
> sai yawan zagin malam (all you do is insult the Islamic scholar/teacher)[60]

Young, Hausa-speaking Muslims in Northern Nigeria grew up singing and hearing this song, which remains a staple in the artistic mockery of Western education as an irreligious contaminant of piety and character. Songs that devalue and associate Western education with anti-Islamic secular indoctrination found companions in sayings and proverbs articulating the same sentiments. Take the popular Hausa adage "Boko sai arna, sai kuma dan musulmi da ya bar sallah" (Western education is for nonbelievers and Muslims who have apostatized). Like the song analyzed above, this saying underpins an anti-*boko* folk sentiment that constructed and sustained a seemingly irreconcilable dichotomy between Western education and modernity on one side, and Islamic devotion on the other. Such entrenched folk idioms discouraged those who wished to enroll in secular schools and rationalized the decision of those who had decided against doing so.

Furthermore, over time such popularly held binaries and beliefs produced structures and habits that hardened negative perceptions of Western education and its associated modernity since the perceptions emanated from and reinforced what Pierre Bourdieu, inspired by other scholars and thinkers, calls *habitus*, a collective social imaginary that supports and structures certain modes of seeing, perceptions, and moral economies while discrediting others.[61] In this case the habitus produced unquestioned understandings regarding the alleged capacity of Western education to pollute the minds of Muslims and move them away from the pure path of Islam. This antimodernist acculturation was especially profound among nonelites, who were outside the circle of those who were actively accessing the opportunities and socioeconomic benefits of secular learning in Nigeria's economic and political realms.

Autobiographies and personal stories from Northern Nigeria provide a window into the complex attitudes toward Western education in colonial and postcolonial times. Clearly, several emirs, district heads, and members of the nobility saw Western education as a way to perpetuate their influence and class privileges by transferring these to their children. As a result, they patronized the secular schools that the Northern Nigerian colonial authorities established for children of the nobility. Members of the nobility even embraced missionary schools in some instances where sufficient trust had been built, or as a way of receiving the more practical benefits of *boko*, understood here as Western modernity, such as clinics, schools, and infrastructures of mobility and convenience.[62] Several marginal groups, outcasts, traditionalist minorities, and stigmatized lepers flocked to missionary educational establishments, seeing Western education's capacity to elevate and rehabilitate them.[63]

However, this pragmatic attitude of strategically accepting the aspirational aspects of Western education always sat uneasily and in tension with more entrenched and organic grassroots Muslim beliefs about Western education's negative transformative effects.

No story illustrates this tension and complexity better than that narrated by Nuhu Bayero in his autobiography, *My Life*.[64] Bayero tells the story of how he grew up in penury despite his noble ancestry as a third-generation descendant of former emirs of Zazzau. Bayero writes that his father, determined to keep his son from the life of poverty he and his wife were accustomed to, made the decision to enroll him in Rev. Walter Miller's CMS Mission school in Zaria. His mother vehemently protested this decision, likening it to an initiation into an evil institution and calling the CMS school an "infidel school."[65] Bayero's parents embodied and vocalized the two positions and attitudinal paradigms regarding Western education. His father saw it as an avenue to give his son a life better than his own in a colonial order in which Western education, regardless of its source and religious foundation, was a ticket to upward socioeconomic mobility. The attitude of his mother, on the other hand, was rooted in and defined by the dominant view among Muslims in the region—that the acquisition of Western education effectively stripped one of Islamic identity.

The pragmatic sentiment of Bayero's father eventually grew as the quotidian and generational benefits of Western education became more apparent, but beliefs and suspicions at the grassroots level were difficult to change and persisted. The *talakawa* (the poor masses) and those unlettered in Roman, secular terms constituted the overwhelming majority in Northern Nigeria. It is therefore logical that, despite decades of postcolonial efforts to expand access to secular education in Northern Nigeria, popular anti-*boko* ideas and themes have continued along with their integration into the region's corpus of Islamic suspicions against Western influences. With the quest for piety and purity sometimes trumping socioeconomic aspiration in the lives of many Muslims, not only have the privileges conferred by Western education failed to erode the suspicions among Muslims in Northern Nigeria, but in some cases these privileges have stoked the belief that Western education is an instrument of corruption, a gateway to worldly, pecuniary benefits that are acquired at the expense of the possessor's Muslim devotion. When invoked by reformist clerical critics of Western education such as Boko Haram's Muhammad Yusuf and Abubakar Shekau, the benefits, advancements, and modern privileges associated with it became proof of the alleged anti-Muslim elements and repercussions of secular education and modernity. These reformist critics reinterpreted the benefits not as desirable aspirational objects but as religious burdens.

Reformist Salafi scholars held a creedal commitment to the idea that Western education, as a subfield of Western modernity, was riddled with risk and danger for Muslims and thus needed to be navigated carefully. Abubakar Shekau went further. For him, Western education contained "harmful knowledge" and compelled Muslims to "learn ... obnoxious behavior" that was internalized through mixed-gender socialization, secular extracurricular activities, and "ideological indoctrination." Such secular school rituals included reciting the Nigerian national pledge, singing the national anthem, and participating in annual school celebrations, all of which Shekau argued "are contrary to Allah's message." In the same aforementioned 2009 sermon Shekau blamed Western education for introducing the Gregorian calendar, whose month names he claimed "celebrate the idols of each month." He argued that in accepting the secular Nigerian state the *ummah* had ignorantly adopted this calendar and its association with idols. In Shekau's understanding, Western education fosters polytheism, which he argued is "worse than everything."[66] Shekau's analysis coupled polytheism and secularism as a two-sided evil—one side fostering "a godless world," the other a belief in multiple gods.

In another lecture in 2010, Shekau blamed an alliance of Europeans and Christians for damaging "the lives of our youth with football playing, watching films and illicit sexual relations."[67] Here Shekau de-Islamizes forms of recreation that British colonizers introduced and that were sustained by Western influence in postcolonial Nigeria. He posited Western recreational modernity as anti-Islamic, an ideological maneuver that replicates an older, totalizing antimodernist rhetoric articulated by anticolonial critics during the colonial period. Whether or not Shekau intended it, the antimodernist discourses of the past found new expression in his evolving rhetorical assault on Western modernity. He seemed to be subconsciously repurposing the preexisting antimodernist rhetoric of the region.

In understanding Western modernity to be the outcome of Western education, Boko Haram's ideologues were clearly operating within a historical trajectory of antimodernist ideological and polemical thought in

Northern Nigeria. In positing this modernity as injurious to Islamic devotion and piety, Boko Haram tapped, wittingly or unwittingly, into a historical vein in the region. That Yusuf went further than his clerical predecessors or contemporaries in denouncing Western education and its alleged complicity in Western modernity should not obscure this instructive connection between the past and the present.

THE AFTERLIVES OF ANTIMODERNISM

By 2009, when the armed jihad phase of Boko Haram began and almost fifty years after Nigeria's political independence, the debate on the use of modern Western goods, products of Western scientific and industrial processes, in Muslim religious settings was raging. This points to the ways in which the anxieties of Muslims regarding Western modernity endured and mutated over time, allowing new generations of clerics, reformers, and insurgents to stake out their own positions as part of their broader reformist claims. In that year, while preaching in Maiduguri, Boko Haram leader Abubakar Shekau was confronted by a questioner who asked him to pronounce on the permissibility of "using electrical appliances" such as "loudspeakers, mobile phones, and microphones," which Shekau and other Boko Haram leaders used in spreading their messages. The questioner wondered, "If Western education is impermissible, how would they invent all these appliances" that Boko Haram used to promote its teachings.[68]

In his response, Shekau surprisingly echoed some of the explanations of Sheikh Niasse in his response to the question of the emirs of Zazzau and Kano. He restated Boko Haram's theological position that "Western education is impermissible," but argued that "these electrical appliances are good" because they served a functional purpose that helped the *ummah* and the *'ulamā'* preach and spread Allah's message more effectively and conveniently. Shekau disassociated the inventions that Western education enabled from what he regarded as the unacceptable claims of Western science, such as the postulation that "the sun is stationary." "The sun is not the [loud]speakers," he retorted, adding, "If the same [unacceptable] view was said about the speakers, I can also abandon them."[69] Furthermore, Shekau rejected the notion that electrical appliances were synonymous with Western education, arguing that "even if there is no Western education, the people can learn how to create all these appliances."

Shekau contended that Western education was not a precondition for inventing machines and modern technologies because there were people who had not attended primary school but could dismantle and rebuild appliances, some of whom had simply taught themselves how to do so. Shekau then concluded his treatise on modern technological inventions and Western education with two arguments. One claim was that the West was hoarding technology and technological proprietorship while "repress[ing] the ability of people" in the non-Western world, especially Muslims, to invent their own technology. Shekau asked rhetorically, "If you can invent a gun, will they allow you?" He argued that if everyone were given a fair opportunity to express their inventive talent, they would produce useful technological goods even without Western education. Shekau's second point was that "these inventions do not emanate from [European Christians]" but that the technologies underlying them in fact "belong to Allah." Further, Shekau contended that the Western inventor "himself belongs to Allah."[70] Shekau effectively embraced the utilitarian value of modern technologies and goods while rejecting their association with the "harmful knowledge" of Western education and the alleged polytheism and secularism of Western civilization.

Shekau was, perhaps subconsciously, reproducing an older template of Muslim engagement with colonially mediated modernity in Northern Nigeria. Over the roughly six decades of the colonial period, the narratives of opposition to modernity persisted, sometimes marginally and other times ascendant, but always in pragmatic if tense coexistence with this same modernity and its usable quotidian technologies. British colonizers and the Muslim aristocrats who forged a political alliance with the colonizers in exchange for privileges and a share of colonial power managed this antimodernist underground and its mutations as best they could. The antimodernist strain remained strong nonetheless and was transmitted from one generation of reformers to another.

Even though accommodationist attitudes and rationalizations grew over time and competed with the adversarial and oppositional discourse of rejection in postcolonial Northern Nigeria, the former could not upstage the latter because it was not accompanied by, nor did it conduce to, a conscious, robust challenge directed at the antimodernist creed. Therefore, the established corpus of antimodernist narratives, theologies, and folk wisdom persisted unchallenged in many texts and popular songs and poems. This meant that these ideas were there—dormant in certain periods, resurgent in others, but always available to be invoked and appropriated by those who aimed to legitimize or historicize their militant opposition to Western modernity and its associated institutions such as secular Western education. This is what Boko Haram seems to have done in the twenty-first century. This line of inspiration, the ideological ferment that promoted a suspicion of modernity and Western technologies and practices, clearly influenced Boko Haram's antimodernist proclamations, or at least supplied a justificatory precedent for them.

ḤARĀM DEBATES AND BOKO HARAM ANTIMODERNISM

What has been mapped out here so far is a dynamic and evolving religious milieu fraught with Muslims' interactions with the goods and ideas emanating from Nigeria's historical and contemporary experience with colonial and Western cultural and technological influence. At issue is the question of whether Muslims could accept, domesticate, adapt, or appropriate Western ideas, phenomena, institutions, and goods without violating the Sharia or the pietistic expectations of settled theologies in the region.

Multiple generations of Nigerian reformers and dissidents staked out their positions on the issue, with each successive generation seemingly less compromising in its denunciation of Western modernity. The intervals between antimodernist movements and epochs were characterized by accommodation and acceptance, inspiring new dissidents to launch new reformist projects to cleanse the *ummah* of modernist pollution and sacrilegious innovations, a cycle of reform and dissidence that continues to this day and whose most recent face is Boko Haram and its robust antimodernist creed.

These debates and tensions around modernity prefigured and established the ideological antecedent for Boko Haram's obsessive declaration of haram on a number of modernist influences. In the late twentieth and early twenty-first centuries the fast-paced influx of westernization was aided in part by the new pressures and influences of neoliberal globalization. Globalization enabled the unbridled, unmediated, and unchallenged influx of Western cultural forms and ideas into the living spaces of Muslims as satellite television and communication technologies became increasingly democratized. In the late 1990s and early 2000s, mere years before the emergence of Boko Haram, Muslims in Northern Nigeria began to express new concerns about their engagement with a variety of modernist phenomena, seeking guidance from clerics but also initiating public debates on these issues. Public disputations among Muslim elites in the region's leading newspapers became quite common, and the topics of the debates were almost always Western goods, technologies, practices, and forms of entertainment, and their compatibility or otherwise with Muslim piety.

In Northern Nigeria, entertainment has long been a charged site of theological debates about modernity, and whether forms of leisure with provenance in the West were haram or halal. In these controversies music was a particularly contested art form, with reformist theological voices condemning both traditional and Western music as impermissible, and as innovations of pleasure that distracted Muslims from their devotional commitment. Along with music, dancing, partying, commemorative celebrations, and other forms of pageantry came under the scrutiny of Northern Nigeria's new Salafi theological insurgents of the 1990s and early 2000s. The ideological products of the Gumi Izala revolution, infused with new reformist energy through theological influences from Saudi Arabia, Sudan, and other Middle Eastern Salafi sources, began to attack music and leisure as sites of sin and compromise with modernity. At the same time, secular Muslims, increasingly out of favor in a rapidly changing religious environment, argued that these forms of entertainment were not in and of themselves impermissible. The debate about music in particular burst into the open in 2001, when *Daily Trust*, the region's best-known newspaper, featured Aliyu Tilde and Ahmad Dogorawa on opposite sides of the issue.[71]

Other topics of haram or halal newspaper debates included the secular industry of life and property insurance, in particular the question of whether Muslims could lawfully participate in the insurance industry. In a particularly notable intervention in the *Daily Trust*, Malam Usman

Muhammad Zunnaurain, an Islamic scholar, lawyer, and professor at Bayero University, declared that "conventional insurance is *ḥarām* in Islam."[72] He likened insurance to gambling, which the Qur'an forbids, equated monetized protection against risk and uncertainty with a disregard for divine predestination, and saw life insurance as a usurpation of God's predetermination of death. The president of the Nigerian Council of Registered Insurance Brokers (NCRIB), Alhaji Teslim Sanusi, argued the contrary point, contending that "insurance is not against Islam."[73] The modern Western capitalist provenance of financialized insurance proved to be a sticking point in this debate. Many similar topics attracted the scrutiny of Northern Nigeria's latest group of reformist *ulama*, who were increasingly able to define the debate about what aspects of modernity and secular socioeconomic practices could lawfully coexist with Islamic piety. In a religious marketplace that was rapidly evolving in the direction of Salafist revival, more accommodationist theological opinions on modernity were replaced by the increasingly reformist critique of secular and modernist institutions and practices as haram.

In addition to inveighing aggressively in the modernity debates of their time, some Boko Haram ideologues began their clerical lives studiously taking notes, biding their time, and preparing their own scripts for making their reformist interventions on the modernity question. The earlier debates about the unlawfulness of aspects of modernity opened the door to these ideologues, prepared their audience, and created a religious public sphere in which they could plausibly speak and write their antimodernist creed.

CONCLUSION

A long history of antimodernist reformist tendencies and theological paradigms connects the nineteenth-century reformist era to the twenty-first-century jihadi-Salafi era of armed dissidence, of which Boko Haram is the current face. The question of how Muslims in Northern Nigeria could lawfully engage with modern things and ideas dominated the discourse of several generations of reformers, who developed new critiques of modernity to respond to expanding westernization and as modern goods, phenomena, practices, and technologies proliferated and evolved from the colonial to the postcolonial period. I have argued that Boko Haram's antimodernist creed, which is steeped in the narrative of haram or impermissibility, benefited from an existing religious marketplace that, over a long period, became the hotbed of concerns over Muslims' relationship to Western, secular modernity, and of reformist attempts to define the parameters of Muslim engagement with and disengagement from Western modernity. Boko Haram's prohibitions, a subset of which is marked by the "haram" in its name, is only the latest manifestation of a long-running effort by Muslim reformers and dissidents in the region to demarcate the realm of piety from that of sinful modernity. To understand the genealogy, fervor, and reception of Boko Haram's antimodernist ideology one must understand earlier discourses, claims, and debates on modernity in Northern Nigeria.

4   Combat, Captives, and Coping

This chapter analyzes three interconnecting themes. First, we historicize, to the extent allowed by available sources, the military aspects of Boko Haram's long insurgency in relation to and in the context of earlier traditions of jihad and warfare in Northern Nigeria. Second, we explore one aspect of religious reformist warfare, the capture and confinement of people in raided or captured "enemy" territories. The comparison between Boko Haram and earlier traditions of captivity in jihad reveals both parallels and striking divergences. Finally, the chapter discusses the resilience and resistance of civilians and communities in the combat zones of the insurgency within the context and against the backdrop of a deep history of regional adaptations to earlier raiding, warring, disruptive violence, and brigandage.

Given the secrecy surrounding the movement's military operations, an important caveat is necessary from the outset: the analysis here is necessarily tentative and incomplete. We work with scattered pieces of information and narrative strands in different sources to construct an outline of the main features of Boko Haram's management of its war against the Nigerian military, allied regional armed forces, and civilian communities accused of supporting secular governmental institutions or opposing

Boko Haram's reformist agenda. From this source base, a rough outline can be sketched of the tactical, technological, and operational innovations of the insurgents, accounting, as much as possible, for evolutions that have occurred in the last fifteen years. The chapter advances a discussion of Boko Haram's war economy and how it compares to those of earlier insurgent groups in the region. Boko Haram's vast war economy, which comprises a massive arsenal of assorted varieties of imported and repurposed weapons, weapons smuggling pipelines, and multiple streams of revenue, funding, and money laundering demonstrates that it is a deeply entrenched movement. Additionally, the chapter outlines the ways in which Boko Haram has managed, against various odds, to resupply itself and sustain a jihad enterprise that has demonstrated remarkable staying power. Like previous religious rebels in the region, Boko Haram's mastery of the terrain and its members' natal connections to the sites of their militancy have given it the ability to build a war economy that is malleable and mutates in response to shifts in the dynamic of the insurgency and counterinsurgency.

As with the exploration of other themes in this book, the analytical exercise that follows is not meant to suggest that there is an ideological genealogy connecting leaders of older militant reform movements and Muhammad Yusuf or Abubakar Shekau in terms of military tactics, war management, and the capture and management of nonbelieving and apostatized humans and war spoils. The connections underscored and analyzed are merely historical, and the contention regarding these historical parallels is limited to the extent to which Boko Haram acknowledges and asserts them. The argument is circumscribed by the extent to which Boko Haram's own discourses reference the earlier traditions of jihad.

OLD AND NEW RAIDS

In highlighting similarities between Boko Haram and the earlier Fodiawa jihad warfare in the region, the present analysis attends to the vast differences and divergences between the military campaigns of the two groups, a topic that historian Murray Last has explored in great depth.[1] The most notable difference, aside from the divergent sectarian leanings of past and present jihadists, is weaponry. Connected to the weaponry factor is the scale of destruction and death, which is much greater in the current insurgency than in the nineteenth century.[2] However, there is an aspect of Boko Haram's military enterprise that recalls aspects of earlier religious militant campaigns in the region. Boko Haram's military tactic is defined by a recurring phenomenon: raids. The fighters of the group routinely raid communities, villages, schools, markets, and other institutions. These raids often appear indiscriminate but are calculated toward the achievement of a strategic goal or to satisfy the quotidian needs of fighters and the logistical needs of insurgent cells. Examples of such raids include attacks designed to replenish the movement's food supply, steal equipment from government institutions, replenish its weaponry from Nigerian Army camps, and kidnap people whom members can exchange for captured insurgents or a ransom. Other kinds of raids include those designed to acquire captives to perform nonmilitary tasks in the militants' bush camps. Boko Haram particularly desires females as captives because of their ability to perform a variety of domestic chores necessary for the daily functioning of the bush camps. Kidnapped females can also be forced to perform nurturing duties for insurgents. Some who are Muslim or who convert to Islam marry insurgents under duress or to cope with the stress of their captivity.

Boko Haram's elaborate economy of raiding similarly characterized the jihad of Usman Dan Fodio in the nineteenth century. Boko Haram's seemingly undisciplined military regime of raiding, which targets both Muslim and non-Muslim communities and sometimes resembles plunder and banditry more than it does a religiously inspired endeavor, recalls many aspects of the raiding practices of the Fodiawa jihad. Raids in that jihad also appeared to be indiscriminately targeting both Muslim and non-Muslim communities. Raiders, some of them associates of prominent jihad commanders and military leaders and a few of them aligned with Ali Jedo, the overall commander of the jihad and caliphate military forces, even targeted communities with whom the emerging caliphate had consummated an *aman* (truce).[3]

The prevalence of killing, enslavement, and plunder as "the sequel[s] to victory" in the Fodiawa jihad establishes it as one possible source of inspiration for contemporary jihadists.[4] Contemporary jihadists claim that they are fighting to establish their own caliphate among peasant and rural agrarian communities that, from the perspective of the jihadists, possess varying degrees of nonconformity with the standards of piety the militants expect of them. The old attacks on Muslim and *aman* communities violated the rules governing jihad as laid down by prophetic example, the Qur'an, and the Sunna. Such violations caused rifts between the trio of Dan Fodio, his son Muhammad Bello, and his brother Abdullahi on one side, and jihad leaders and field commanders on the other. Some disagreements resulted in field commanders threatening not only to strike out on their own, but also to turn their forces on the triumvirate leaders of the jihad if they tried to forcefully impose strict, scriptural rules and prophetic precedents on their military operations, or if they tried to micromanage quotidian military operations through an insistence on the strict observance of jihad rules regarding who could be raided and who could not.

Similarly, Boko Haram fighters and commanders often disregard the rules of jihad in their raiding activities. This flouting of the rules regarding combat and targeting, the prohibition of nonessential raiding, and fighters' relationship to booty accrued from raids has caused a rift among Boko Haram's principal actors, leading to the famous feud in 2016 between the Abu Musab Al-Barnawi faction, Islamic State in West Africa Province (ISWAP) and the Abubakar Shekau-led faction of Jamāʿat Ahl al-Sunna li-Daʿwa wa-l-Jihād (JAS). The former predicated its decision to split from the latter on Shekau's flagrant flouting of jihad rules, which it interpreted as a debasement of the jihad ideal.

The distinction between the tactics of Boko Haram's two factions is significant and has become the major touchstone of the ongoing scorched-earth clashes between the two groups that, according to former members of both factions, have claimed more fighters' lives than have the combined military efforts of the Lake Chad states' armies.[5] As the International Crisis Group explains in its March 2024 briefing, after Shekau's death in May 2021 the ideological and tactical disagreements intensified as ISWAP was ascending and JAS declining. However, the fundamental point of contention was ISWAP's effort to spare and cultivate relations with Muslim civilians, whom JAS sees as "fair game for plunder."[6]

The Shekau faction's raiding operations also alienated it from Muslim communities in northeastern Nigeria, with many Muslims even questioning the faction's Muslim devotion and bona fides. This has created a disjuncture between this faction and the civilian population of that area, an opening that ISWAP sought to fill with what Edward Stoddard argues is a "strategy of population control" in a "competitive ecosystem of violence."[7] ISWAP's approach was to build trust with the local rural civilian population as a way of distinguishing itself from JAS, displacing the latter, and regularizing its precarious control over territories in the Borno–Yobe axis. This approach also signals an attempt on ISWAP's part to transition from a fighting stance to one of bureaucratic state-making, even while maintaining military vigilance and planning new offensive military operations against JAS and state militaries.[8] ISWAP's offer of protection to submissive civilian populations parallels the tactics of the Fodiawa jihadists of old. This parallel does not suggest that Boko Haram is consciously copying the tactical blueprint of the Fodiawa jihad, yet the indiscriminate raiding of JAS recalls a phase in the Fodiawa jihad in which the raiding seemed undisciplined and motivated by predatory pecuniary instincts rather than the strategic or tactical military logic of the war, which caused dismay among the triumvirate leaders of the Sokoto jihad.

If both the old and new jihads degenerated into seemingly unmanageable, chaotic military raiding that purists among their ranks considered off script and in violation of divine prescriptions on jihad, it is because, as Murray Last suggests, the rules governing raiding "are less precise" than those governing jihad in its strict definition of overthrowing and replacing a disbelieving political entity.[9] This meant that in the Boko Haram insurgency, as in the nineteenth-century jihad of Dan Fodio, considerable military improvisation, creativity, and private quotidian initiative on the part of field commanders with daily needs, desires, and predilections overrode commitment to the strict rules of jihad. In both cases, relying on these imprecise rules on raids and separating raiding from jihad proper was a terrain of daily negotiation between fighters, commanders, and ideologues in a fluid and decentralized religious warfare. In such circumstances commanders of small units and even individual fighters imposed their idiosyncrasies on tactical choices.

TACTICAL INNOVATION OR TACTICAL CONVERGENCE

It is important to emphasize that insurgencies do not occur in a historical and ideological lacuna, and that religious rebels in the same region as previous insurgencies or claiming the same ideological inspiration from previous ones often seek, however imperfectly, to model themselves on the previous rebels in ideology, tactics, and strategy. Accordingly, Joseph Smaldone argues that nineteenth-century *mujahidin* tried to "emulate the life of the Prophet Muhammad and classical Islamic customs, and to interpret their mission and fortunes as a repetition of a cycle in Islamic history."[10] Smaldone explores other ways in which the nineteenth-century jihadists of Hausaland also consciously sought to replicate or find tactical inspiration from the Prophet's military campaigns and the military expeditions of subsequent caliphates. Given this, the exploration of similarities between the military tactics of Boko Haram and jihadists of the Sokoto Caliphate should offer clues about the persistence of certain tropes and practices in reformist religious warfare and the novelty of others.

Nineteenth-century jihadists in Hausaland deployed a battle formation that they claimed mirrored that of the early Muslims. The caliphate battle formation had rear, center, and front guards, with the rear guards protecting the supply chain and the center unit composed of the most experienced fighters. The caliphate army had a cavalry unit as well as an infantry, making the front and center guards the critical points in the formation, with the rear guard of reserve units providing cover and protecting the supply line.[11] From eyewitness accounts, we know that Boko Haram's basic battle formation is identical.

The only difference is that in the Boko Haram formation the most seasoned fighters constitute the rear unit while the least experienced and reserve units comprise the vanguard, a strategy of throwing out expendable fighters first to weaken the enemy line and also to deceive enemy forces and resisters about the true strength of the militants' forces.[12] Battlefield deception is another similarity between the nineteenth-century jihadists and today's jihadists. Trickery is a long-established component of warfare in Islamic history. Since the Prophet uttered the famous words "War is trickery," subsequent Muslim warriors have perfected surprise attacks, ambushes, and other battlefield ruses as ways of overcoming disadvantages and turning weakness into strength.[13] In their confrontations with the much larger, better-equipped Nigerian Army and with communities whose populations far outnumber the raiders, Boko Haram militants have often utilized creative deception to attain their battle objectives.

The use of battlefield tricks was a feature of insurgent religious militancy in the nineteenth century and in earlier iterations of Islamic militant warfare. Boko Haram employs familiar battlefield tricks such as false attacks, concealing the main fighting force, and feigning retreat. However, it combines these classical tricks of warfare with new, technologically enabled ones. Its fighters routinely wear Nigerian Army uniforms and ride in painted or captured Nigerian Army gun trucks to disguise themselves as Nigerian soldiers when embarking on offensive missions. They sometimes disguise themselves as itinerant cattle herdsmen and villagers to surprise troops in their camps or undertake critical reconnaissance missions.[14]

Other tactics of the nineteenth-century jihadists bear a striking resemblance to those of Boko Haram. For instance, here is how Smaldone describes the typical battle plan from the nineteenth century: "The main body of the army was preceded by a party of pathfinders . . . whose duty it was to clear the route of obstacles that would impede the progress of the march."[15] Boko Haram similarly sends out scouts, guides, and other forerunners to act as lookouts and to scope out targets of attack. These units are then followed by seasoned, better-armed fighters. Another similarity between the battle tactics of Boko Haram and nineteenth-century jihadists is the establishment of temporary war camps to provide logistical support for operations. War camps proliferated on the frontiers of the nineteenth-century jihad as the caliphate expanded and as commanders initiated new military raids and expeditions. Similarly, prior to attacking Boko Haram fighter units are known to camp outside target communities and institutions for varying lengths of time, depending on the dynamics of a particular operation.

Perhaps the two most glaring parallels between Boko Haram and the old jihadists in terms of military tactics are the common battle chants and the repeated use of the encirclement or enveloping formation. In his *Infakul Maisur* Muhammad Bello narrates how fighters in the Fodiawa jihad would chant "Allahu Akbar" three times before charging at enemy lines during raids.[16] This same tactic is a battlefield staple of Boko Haram fighters. Depending on the intensity of the battle, some chant it from the beginning to the end of a raid.[17] Although separated by two centuries, the old and new jihadists are united by their preference for encirclement sieges. The encirclement technique is deployed to precede "stockade settlement raiding and punitive expeditions." Like nineteenth-century religious militants, Boko Haram fighters also generally prefer surprise attacks, *farmake* in Hausa.[18] These parallels make sense because the patterns of settlement in the Sahel-Savannah zone of Northern Nigeria are such that natural obstacles to flight are few. If killing or capturing people or preventing them from fleeing with valuables is an objective as it was in the nineteenth century and is for Boko Haram today, *farmake* is the most effective strategy. Although the caliphate army fought several pitched battles against the forces of enemy Hausa states, once the major hostile states were defeated and that phase of the jihad was over, raiding became the modus operandi of the emirate armies of the caliphate. In this raiding phase surprise attacks rather than pitched battles proved to be an effective strategy.

In the nineteenth century raiders would surround a target settlement or village. The attack would begin from the rear of the village. The villagers would instinctively run from the rear to the front to escape, whereupon militants stationed at the front of the encirclement would cut them down as they scattered in the ensuing confusion.[19] Survivors of Boko Haram's attacks on villages and settlements have told similar stories about the insurgents' tactics, emphasizing the practice of attacking from the rear to drive unsuspecting inhabitants toward the front units, where they can easily be killed while the rear units plunder and burn the deserted village.[20]

BOKO HARAM'S MILITARY STRUCTURE

Boko Haram's military tactics and strategies are dictated largely by their ties to the plains, hills, and Sahel wilderness of the Nigerian Northeast, the natal home of most of their fighters. The overarching strategy of Boko Haram is to maximize the military advantages of the environmental and human assets of the region. It is no coincidence that two of the most fortified sites of the Boko Haram insurgent fighting force are the Mandara hills of Southern Borno and Northern Adamawa, and the Lake Chad Basin of

Northern and Central Borno. Apart from providing natural defenses, these landscapes enhance the ability of Boko Haram fighters to function, potentially indefinitely, as insurgents living off the land.

The militants' ethnic, religious, and kinship affinity with the populations of the frontline areas of the insurgency provides another advantage to Boko Haram insurgents. In this regard, the war journal of a Nigerian Army soldier who anonymously publishes his battlefield experiences online is an informative document. Its content has been corroborated through interviews with other deployed soldiers and "repentant" Boko Haram fighters—former Boko Haram militants whom the Nigerian military has designated as having been deradicalized. The soldier writes of Boko Haram's extensive rural network of sleeper cells consisting of farmers, fishermen, and rural craftsmen who lead normal lives as villagers but are activated as needed to perform various battlefield tasks. Such tasks include surveillance, sabotage, the planting of Improvised Explosive Devices (IEDs), the supply of critical resources, and sundry roles as combat reservists.[21]

We also know from these testimonials and accounts from the front lines that Boko Haram fighters strategically blur the lines between combatants and noncombatants, keeping the front lines fluid as a way of confusing Nigerian Army troops and maintaining deniability and stealth. Accounts of soldiers and former Boko Haram fighters reveal that Boko Haram combatants disguise themselves as farmers for extended periods, especially during the agriculturally intensive rainy season. These combatants would sometimes live in frontline villages only hundreds of meters away from Nigerian Army camps, growing crops, raising families, and living the lives of normal villagers, but also surveilling the position of Nigerian Army troops.[22]

One soldier recalled in an interview with the author that when the two groups crossed paths on their way to streams and rivers to fetch water for daily use, he and his fellow troops would sometimes exchange "friendly" waves and greetings with villagers they knew were combatants, and who knew they were Nigerian Army troops. He lamented that the military code of war forbade them from shooting or detaining unarmed villagers even if they were sure the villagers were Boko Haram combatants.[23]

For Boko Haram the blurring of the line between "village" and "war camp" (*sansani*; pl. *sansanoni*) on the front lines creates a wide civilian-military zone. This demographic continuum gives Boko Haram militants an advantage in their guerilla tactics against state armies while stifling the operational freedoms of those armies. While the proximity of Nigerian Army camps to those of Boko Haram helps maintain a fairly stable front line in several areas, Boko Haram's tactics of blending their frontline war camps with preexisting villages and settlements enables them to maximize the military utility of such settlements. This is Boko Haram's creative modification of the classic *ribats*, or fortified frontline settlements of Islamic warfare, which the nineteenth-century Sokoto jihadists cultivated extensively and extended to the establishment of temporary war camps. Embedding war camps in villages connects Boko Haram to a rural network of peoples who are sympathetic to, afraid of, and beholden to the insurgents. The value of such communities to an insurgency is immense since they are candidates for spying and surveillance missions and serve as civilian buffers for militants. More crucially, the civilians' mobility between countryside front lines and urban business hubs provides Boko Haram with a means to acquire food, fuel, and other supplies, as interviewed Nigerian Army soldiers and "repentant" Boko Haram fighters attest.[24]

RIBATS AND INSURGENT WARFARE

Whether they consciously intended to do so or not, both factions of Boko Haram have replicated and mimicked an integral part of the Sokoto Caliphate's infrastructure of warfare. In the Sokoto Caliphate *ribats*, or walled, heavily fortified, populated outposts, dotted the frontiers of the Muslim territory. *Ribats* served as reconnaissance centers, spying platforms, and sentry posts. They alerted caliphate forces to enemy activities around the frontier and were the first line of military defense against enemy aggression in a particular area. In some instances, caliphate forces or the armies of specific emirates in the caliphate coordinated offensive operations with *ribat* commanders or relied on resources and intelligence that *ribats* supplied to launch offensive expeditions. In that way, the *ribat* was both a defensive and an offensive military asset.

Historian John Edward Philips demonstrates that the idea of *ribats* as settled frontier defensive fortifications and forts has deep roots in Islamic history, deriving its etymology directly from the Qur'an and then elaborated as a military and administrative concept during the Umayyad and Abbasid caliphates. *Ribat* construction in the ninth and tenth centuries was standardized to align one part of the *ribat* with the direction of Mecca. The classic *ribat* of early Muslim history in the Arabian Peninsula was a large structure with a mosque for preaching, a minaret, a gathering room, and other indoor and outdoor spaces designed to enable the storage of arms for defensive and offensive military operations. This gave *ribats* a religious character, creating a space with a dual military and religious functionality. The construction of *ribats* expanded to all the lands of Islam in North Africa, central Asia, and Muslim Spain. It eventually spread to Hausaland and, during and after the Sokoto jihad, became a central military and administrative strategy of the caliphate, with frontier towns sometimes automatically assuming the role of a *ribat* and then being legally sanctioned, repurposed, and rebuilt to function as an actual *ribat*. When *ribats* were built from scratch, *hadiths* about the necessity for jihad and the place of *ribats* in jihad were invoked to support their construction, and *maliki* jurisprudential treatises on the necessity of protecting the *Ummah* with fortifications were cited as theological justifications.[25]

The dual defensive and offensive function is consistent with classical Islamic military doctrine, which makes little if any distinction between offensive and defensive military assets and operations. In the Sokoto Caliphate *ribats* emerged when Sultan Muhammad Bello sought to defend the burgeoning Muslim federation more robustly against the raids of the Gobir, Kebbi, and Tuareg forces. Settled permanent fortifications were Bello's innovative solution for securing the northern and northwestern frontiers of the empire.[26] With the emerging caliphate struggling to vanquish holdouts and rebels, Bello and his military strategists realized that frontiers needed to be equipped with both defensive and offensive infrastructures.[27]

Like regional military strategists before them, Boko Haram leaders have a robust frontier fortification infrastructure. They have not established *ribats* in the traditional sense, but Boko Haram frontier strongholds, which also serve as thriving population centers, are present in the main war theater of the Nigerian Northeast, especially along Lake Chad and the Mandara Mountains. Such frontier redoubts guard the entrances to Boko Haram's mountain and Lake Chad island hideouts, giving them a relatively stabilized base of operation from which to plan offensive missions and raids designed to resupply their fighting units with food and munitions, and to challenge Nigerian military units. The organization of these frontier defenses is eerily similar to that of the earlier *ribats*. As Muhammad Yusuf declared shortly before the movement launched its jihad phase, "Jihād cannot be done without guarding and watching the borders (*ribats*) and martyrdom operations (*istishhad*)."[28] Once the jihad phase of the reformist project commenced in 2009, Boko Haram prioritized the establishment and reinforcement of their version of *ribats*, in line with Yusuf's declaration. Much like that of the Sokoto Caliphate, in Boko Haram's war manual trusted commanders are usually assigned to these strategic strongholds. To breach these frontier defenses is to gain entrance into the inner military recess of Boko Haram operations and its war room. Thus the insurgent movement entrusts these strongholds to seasoned fighters belonging to the inner nucleus of committed warrior-scholars and members of the secretive *aminiyat* (intelligence) group. For historical perspective, Muhammad Bello appointed his sons and relatives to command the strategic *ribats* of the northern frontiers of the caliphate.

Raids on Boko Haram camps have revealed that the insurgents turn their camps into minisettlements, replete with the instruments of quotidian comforts. In these camps they have wives, children, and crude instruments for treating diseases and war wounds, and engage in scholarship. At the same time, the conditions of the war camps as portrayed in many Boko Haram propaganda videos suggest that they lack the semipermanence of caliphate-era *ribats*, and are only a few steps removed from the ad hoc war encampments that caliphate forces established to house units and troops from various emirates for major military operations. Boko Haram's war camps are not as well organized, cohesive, or stable as the *ribats* of the caliphate, but they are a step above the latter's tent-based war camps. Given the relatively small size of territory that Boko Haram controls, as well as the tenuous nature of that control and the relentless and conventionally superior character of the military opposition to their insurgency, for all practical purposes the war camps are temporary by design and function.

Interestingly, the genealogy of the war camp in the military history of West Africa also has a Borno imprimatur on it, suggesting yet another proximate parallel in the Boko Haram *ribat* repertoire. Relying on the contemporaneous chronicle of Aḥmad Ibn Furṭū, Smaldone traces the institution of West African war camp typology to the Muslim kingdom of Bornu. There Mai Idris Alooma (1570–1603) is recorded to have built the first series of temporary war camps to aid his protracted military operations. Such camps housed warhorses, protected troops against enemy attacks and ambushes, kept troops confined and disciplined, and served as storage for supplies. Precaliphate Hausa states may have borrowed the practice of war camping from Bornu. Smaldone suggests that the Sokoto Caliphate's elaborate and sophisticated war camps, which were strategically established on the front lines to achieve a pincer or encircling effect on the enemy, were borrowed from Borno, citing the similarity between the Borno war camp template popularized by Idris Alooma and those practiced by caliphate war strategists.[29] Philips's analysis suggests a more organically robust and evolving culture of war encampments in the caliphate.[30]

Another parallel between the old and new militancy is the mobilization of fighters. For all its military prowess, the Sokoto Caliphate never built a standing army. Instead, it mobilized fighters from emirates for military operations as needed. This decentralized military structure enabled the caliphate war institution to be flexible and nimble. Similarly, fifteen years into its declared insurgency against the Nigerian state, Boko Haram does not have a standing army of fighters in the traditional sense. It mobilizes fighters from its semiautonomous cells and fighting units for major operations and otherwise trusts commanders in various sectors and frontiers to defend the claimed but unstable territories of its declared *dawla* (theocratic state). The implication of such a decentralized military structure for frontier defense is that, much like the case in nineteenth-century Hausaland, Boko Haram's frontier garrisons are the first line of defense, and sometimes attack, against enemy forces, mainly troops of the Nigerian Army. Frontier garrison commanders, like *ribat* commanders before them, have considerable operational freedom when their services are not needed for major operations. They can both push the frontier limit on their own initiative and establish mini frontier camps and appoint subordinate commanders (*amirs*).

FAMILIAR AND NOVEL TACTICS

Boko Haram insurgents replicate some aspects of the classic religious militancy of the Sahel zone, but in many other respects they reflect the globalized tactics of twenty-first-century jihadists fighting asymmetrical war against more numerous and more powerful state armies. Like all modern religious militants, Boko Haram uses unconventional attacks, surprises, and nimble maneuvers to overcome their military disadvantages. The interviews I conducted with a dozen Nigerian Army soldiers with frontline anti-insurgency combat experience, and with another dozen former Boko Haram fighters, revealed that the insurgents' most recurring tactics were ambushes and surprise attacks. The use of improvised explosive devices (IEDs) and suicide bombing seems dictated more by the desire for short-term battlefield objectives than by a calculated strategy.[31] The interviews overwhelmingly converged on specific tactical choices that Boko Haram fighters employed. In launching surprise attacks on Nigerian Army troops, the militants tended to favor early morning and night attacks as well as attacks when it was raining. In each case, the respondents stated, the aim was to fully exploit stealth and the element of surprise.[32] These tactical choices also clarify the group's dual character as a movement simultaneously embedded in the Sahelian militancy tradition and twenty-first-century globalized jihadi tactics.

Even in the accounts of Nigerian Army troops, Boko Haram fighters are described as motivated professional fighters who are committed to their cause and are not afraid to die in battle, making them a formidable force. However, Nigerian Army soldiers interviewed for this book unanimously stated that Boko Haram soldiers lack discipline. They cited their "unprofessional" treatment of captives but mainly focused on what they described as Boko Haram fighters' tendency to shoot randomly in battle.[33] However, what Nigerian Army soldiers see as random firing, former Boko Haram fighters describe as one aspect of an unconventional battlefield tactic of seemingly random and nonstop firing to communicate a message of indomitable fighting will and abundant ammunition to Nigerian troops. Former Boko Haram fighters stated that they knew they had more ammunition than Nigerian troops and wanted to demoralize their enemies.

Although interviewed Nigerian soldiers unanimously agreed that Boko Haram fighters use sophisticated weapons—RPGs, LMG, GPMGs, gun trucks, antipersonnel mines, and sophisticated rifles—the former militants went further, claiming that they always had superior weapons. For instance, they stated that while Nigerian troops used old rifles, the militants' guns, except those captured from Nigerian troops, were new.[34]

What is the truth about Boko Haram's weaponry? According to a two-part article titled "Resurgent: The Weapons of IS West Africa," which was written by a military blogger and analyst who goes by the pen name Everest65, Boko Haram's main infantry weapon is the Chinese Type 56 AK-47 variant.[35] The rifle is popular with Sahelian jihadists because it is cheaper than the standard Russian-made AK-47. The Type 56 AK is manufactured not just in China but also in multiple factories across the world, making sourcing easy through illicit global weapons pipelines. Some standard issue AK-47s and other kinds of rifles feature in small numbers in the arsenal of Boko Haram, the likely product of capture from regional state armed forces.

The jihadists have become militarily resourceful in the years since they declared war on the Nigerian state. Like jihadists of old in the West African Sahel, what they lack in conventional military assets of a formal state army, they make up for in resourcefulness and improvisations. Their IED-making operations bear out this resourcefulness. As reported by *HumAngle*, relying on a Boko Haram fighter's testimony, Boko Haram fighters routinely repurpose undetonated Nigerian Army ordinances and explosives stolen from Nigerian Army armories and military camps to make IEDs that have had a devastating effect in the battlefield, eroding some of the logistical advantages of the Nigerian Army while also achieving tactical objectives on the battlefield.[36]

The most versatile and consequential weapon in Boko Haram's arsenal is arguably the so-called technical, a pickup truck mounted with a machine gun, an anti-aircraft gun, and even howitzers in some cases. The technical confers mobility and maneuverability without compromising deadly force. Boko Haram's technicals are varied. Some come prefitted with Soviet or Chinese-made heavy machine guns. Others are equipped with models of the American-made Browning heavy machine gun. These heavy machine guns are versatile and adaptable battle weapons because cartridges are transferrable between different models. They are also reliable in battle as they can fire large rounds to accomplish multiple battlefield objectives. The multipurpose utility of technicals makes them the desired tactical weapon of Sahelian militants. The armed vehicles can drive freely in the semiarid terrain of the Sahel. They can be fitted with different light and heavy weapons as desired.

Technicals offer Boko Haram militants various tactical advantages in the rough Sahelian battlefield. They can be used against enemy aircraft, tanks, buildings, and infantry forces. The most important tactical benefit the technical confers on Boko Haram militants is the swiftness of attack that can aid ambushes and surprise enemy forces with speed and deadly force. This is a formidable combination in an asymmetrical warfare in which state armies often require the deployment of airpower at short notice—a difficult task in a vast and remote area—to respond effectively to insurgent attacks. The Nigerian, Chadian, Nigerien, and Cameroonian armed forces all use technicals of various kinds for their own anti–Boko Haram operations in recognition of its battlefield advantages in a terrain such as the Sahel. In many ways, then, airpower aside, the weapons and arsenal of Boko Haram bear an eerie resemblance to those of the regional state armies that constitute the movement's adversaries.

And yet, interviewed former Boko Haram members insisted that they had better equipment than Nigerian Army troops. Even if the claims of former Boko Haram fighters are true, it must be recognized that, given the number of combatants and resources available to the Nigerian Army, Boko Haram's advantages are often ephemeral and confined to aspects of the war. Overall, Boko Haram militants are at a disadvantage. Boko Haram seems to recognize this reality, hence its adoption of guerilla tactics and a variety of battlefield trickery in confronting Nigerian Army forces.

THE HISTORICAL AND THE CONTEMPORARY

The jihadists of Boko Haram diverge from existing protocols of religious insurgent warfare even while replicating some established patterns. For example, interviews with former fighters and Nigerian Army troops as well as internal communication within the group attest to Boko Haram fighters upholding the familiar ethos on handling female captives. Boko Haram takes converted female captives as wives and concubines, and puts unconverted captive women to work as domestic and field slaves, maids, and, at times, in auxiliary combatant roles.[37] This elaborate use of female captives and women in the battlefield mirrors the practice of nineteenth-century Sokoto jihadists, who similarly deployed female captives to support their military operations in a variety of roles, including combat ones.[38]

The most obvious divergence of Boko Haram from the religious insurgency of the nineteenth century is in the realm of weaponry. Nineteenth-century jihadists in Northern Nigeria fought primarily with cavalry, spears, bows, arrows, swords, and daggers. As John Edward Philips notes, while the introduction of firearms into the arsenal of the Sokoto Caliphate in the late nineteenth century catalyzed a tactical shift away from a battle formation led by mounted archers and toward one led by musketeers and armed infantry, the adoption of firearms in the caliphate's warfare was slow, uneven, and limited because of the small number available due to restricted and costly supply.[39] By contrast, Boko Haram's weapons are indistinguishable from the arsenal of a modern state army.

The difference between old and new militants' weaponry is purely a function of time, not a difference of attitude or orientation toward firearms. Even Philips, who argues against the tendency to exaggerate the use of firearms by nineteenth-century Sokoto jihadists, admits that the Sokoto Caliphate eagerly sought firearms and would have adopted and adapted them more extensively in its war economy had the import market for muskets been larger.[40] Unlike the Sokoto jihadists, Boko Haram is awash with the accoutrements of twenty-first-century warfare. Boko Haram's technological divergence from earlier jihadists is further marked by its heavy use of two-way radios and other technological instruments of battlefield communications, including spoofed personal cellphone numbers and the "theft" of telecom signals from neighboring countries when available.[41]

Other noticeable differences between Boko Haram and earlier religious militants include Boko Haram's use of child and teenage soldiers in direct and indirect combat roles, and fighters' widespread reliance on stimulants and hard drugs as a source of battlefield courage, both of which were documented in interviews with former Boko Haram fighters and Nigerian Army troops.[42]

The divergence of Boko Haram from some established practices of religious insurgency in Northern Nigeria should not occlude the ways in which the group, whether self-consciously or otherwise, replicates other aspects of Sahelian insurgent warfare, notably that of the Sokoto Caliphate. Indeed, some of the parallels are worth exploring further, especially the production of material and human spoils of war and the vast apparatuses that religious militants establish to handle them.

THE SPOILS OF WAR

War produces material spoils as well as captives. Boko Haram has been in the news for its enslavement of non-Muslim captives and its harsh treatment of the Muslims it captures in its military campaigns. Much less known is the volatile politics of war booty sharing and distribution that is a significant component of its war economy. Boko Haram is known to raid villages and towns for material goods and foodstuffs, treating the settled communities of northeastern Nigeria as reservoirs or supply depots. The movement also confiscates goods from communities it views as working for or aiding the Nigerian military. In many instances Boko Haram's military raids produce booty when the property of those killed, maimed, and displaced is appropriated by loyal fighters, pooled together, and distributed.

The distribution of war booty has historically tested the commitment of Islamic revolutionaries and leaders to canonical jurisprudential prescriptions on the conduct of war, the treatment of war captives, and the distribution of the material spoils of war. A comparison of war booty acquisition and distribution across time is a complicated exercise. Moreover, each insurgency is animated by a different set of concerns and characterized by different exigencies and pressures. Nonetheless, because the issue of war booty remains central to the self-fashioning of insurgents and retains the potential for strife and discontent among them, it is important to draw on historical precedents and divergence to analyze the behavior of today's insurgents in relation to the material rewards of war.

Both Boko Haram and the old reformers of nineteenth-century Hausaland sustained themselves with, and in certain respects were motivated by, the quest for the material benefits of war. The property of nonbelievers is considered a legitimate target for appropriation by victorious Muslim warriors. In both insurgencies, because of the pressures of the battlefield and the generally chaotic circumstances of war, significant departures from prescribed Islamic principles on war booty management occurred. In the case of Boko Haram such improvisation and pragmatic departure from Islamic war ethos are even more common, given the highly decentralized nature of the war, the multipronged military pressures the movement faces, and the guerilla character of its insurgency.

Practices of war booty acquisition and distribution in the Sokoto Caliphate owed a historical debt to both Islamic and African conceptions of war. Such practices were informed by preexisting traditions of warfare in Hausaland and the broader West African region. As Islamic revolutionaries, the jihad leaders sought to use the canonical texts of the Maliki jurisprudential school of Islam as a guide for their conduct in war and, in particular, for their management of *ghanima* (war booty). War spoils were considered legitimate entitlements of the *mujahidin*. It was both a reward and a motivation for fighters because if the fighter survived the battle and the campaign was victorious, he would emerge materially richer. There were requirements, subject to the specific conditions of the battlefield and the nature of the victory, for how war booty should be shared. However, both the jihad leaders and classical Islamic war theology saw the potential of war booty acquisition as a morale booster for righteous revolutionaries and the actual acquisition as a reward for service in the war effort.

The prescribed requirements were clear, but they allowed for the unpredictability of the battlefield as well as for the distinct character of each military campaign. For instance, although the *mujahidin* were commanded to share the booty on the battlefield and specifically in the territory of the vanquished enemy to serve as both humiliation for the defeated and a motivation for the victorious Muslim fighters, fighters were allowed to deviate from this requirement if the conditions on the battlefield proved too unstable or volatile.[43] Islamic law prescribed elaborate formulas for sharing the booty, defining in specific terms what percentage should go to whom. The same precision also marked prescriptions on the appropriation and treatment of war captives, including females who could be legitimately acquired as concubines.

Islamic prescription was one thing, but conformity to it was another. In both the nineteenth-century jihad and the current one, booty distribution rarely followed the prescribed formula. The fog of war often intersected with self-interest to prevent a strict implementation of prescribed principles, and what latitude and flexibility existed in those prescriptions were stretched to their limits as insurgents struggled over the tempting material by-products of battles. In the Sokoto Caliphate, booty distribution in the early battles was often so rancorous that Dan Fodio regularly appointed special officials to oversee the process. Greed, opportunism, and materialism coalesced into a potent pressure, causing clashes to occur over the sharing of booty. Open, brazen looting was common, as were violent scrambles for defeated enemies' property. Even when Dan Fodio appointed a *ma'aji* (treasurer) to regulate the sharing, the result was still marked with rapacious altercations that caused the triumvirate leaders of the jihad much anguish.[44]

The recurring historical and contemporary problem is the way in which insurgent leaders, whether on the battlefield or as leaders of new emirates or caliphates, assert themselves over war booty, circumventing the prescribed formula for sharing war spoils. This often generates discontent within the rank and file of Islamic revolutionaries, who feel that the established precedents or insurgent leaders shortchange them. The West African Muslim revolutionary leaders of the past were particularly fond of appropriating more than their prescribed share of war booty, partly because they considered such booty too important to their struggle to be put in the hands of regular combatants, and because booty translated to power and status. Smaldone's description of the West African precedent is powerfully accurate: "Although legally entitled to one-fifth of the war spoils, most Muslim states of the Central Sudan claimed considerably more than that. Special weapons and certain 'strategic materials' such as tempered swords, chain mail, quilted armor, and horses were appropriated directly by the emirs. The state also compelled the surrender of about one-half of all war captives taken by the army." Builders of putative Muslim states and leaders of Muslim revolutionary movements routinely appropriated any booty that enslaved soldiers claimed, and took a portion of any booty that free soldiers acquired by asserting their entitlement to patronage obligations from lower-ranked combatants. In a nutshell, precolonial Muslim revolutionary leaders "took the bulk of the spoils of war" and, by doing so, created a schism and disaffection that sometimes erupted into rebellion and infighting.[45]

In the contemporary insurgency of Boko Haram, the politics of war booty is as contentious as in previous Muslim wars in the West African Sahel, pitting Boko Haram commanders and factions against one another. In 2016 Mamman Nur, who would later back Abu Musab al-Barnawi, the son of Boko Haram founder Muhammad Yusuf, as the Islamic State-endorsed leader of its West Africa branch, announced a split from the Abubakar Shekau–led Boko Haram. In a widely publicized statement announcing the separation, Nur accused Shekau and his close lieutenants of appropriating and aggrandizing war spoils for themselves, which deprived many fighting units of supplies and food in the process.[46] Among several other charges, Nur accused Shekau of displaying an "uncaring attitude toward the welfare of Boko Haram soldiers and weak people in his caliphate" and of "withholding the materials of war."[47] Nur and his supporters claimed that Shekau's alleged refusal to supply his fighters and the civilian population of his self-declared caliphate was a result of his greed, an insistence on keeping war booty for himself and close aides.

Other issues exacerbated the fragmentation of Boko Haram, a schism whose many dimensions and causes Abdulbasit Kassim has discussed elsewhere.[48] However, booty distribution loomed large in the dispute since it bordered on the critical issue of the availability of supplies and the centrality of such supplies to Boko Haram's capacity to carry out raids on both military and civilian targets. In his response to Nur, Shekau predictably rejected the accusation of hoarding war booty and undermining the fighting capacity of Boko Haram militants,[49] but the management of war booty had been thrust into the forefront of concerns affecting the morale and capacity of fighters in both factions of Boko Haram.

WAR CAPTIVES AND HUMAN SPOILS

Struggles over war spoils were not restricted to material objects. Covetousness and greed in the distribution and exploitation of war captives have presented historical and contemporary Muslim insurgents with challenges that complicate military operations and undermine morale and solidarity among combatants. Here too, there are both parallels and divergences between Boko Haram and their precolonial Muslim revolutionary predecessors. In the nineteenth-century jihad the struggle over war captives, especially female captives, threatened to ruin the discipline of the fighting force. Fighters would simply appropriate women and girls from defeated enemy groups, disregarding any Islamic requirements regarding their treatment and distribution. Such unlawful concubinage was so widespread and the frenzy for female captives among fighters so fierce that it made a mockery of the pietistic proclamations and claims that underpinned the jihad. In 1809, as a last set of battles raged, Dan Fodio was so disappointed in the conduct of his warriors regarding female war captives that he composed the Fulfulde poem "Tabbat Hakika" (Be Sure of That), in which he expressed his concern at the ongoing desecration of the jihad's moral justifications and restated the boundaries of moral conduct binding fighters of all ranks.[50]

Dan Fodio railed against several cases of abuse by self-proclaimed holy warriors of the jihad, but took particular umbrage at the widespread disregard for Islamic law regarding marrying or entering into concubinage with female war captives. Such abuses included fighters' refusal to observe the mandatory three-month period of abstinence required by Islamic law when wives of defeated enemies were appropriated as wives and concubines. As Mervyn Hiskett observes, "Many of the young and ardent Muslim warriors were impatient of such restrictions and pleasured themselves with their charming booty the moment they had the opportunity to do so." Frustrated by these failures, Dan Fodio berated his warriors for not only flouting Islamic prescriptions but also, in some cases, neglecting their legal wives in favor of their new war-captive concubines.[51] The recurring deviations from declared reformist ideals undermined and fragmented the jihad into multiple, weaker factions and agendas, a process of disillusionment and internal wrangling that foreshadowed what Gilles Kepel describes as "jihad fatigue" in contemporary jihadism.[52] Interestingly, in a rhetorical move that recalled these nineteenth-century jihad disputes, Mamman Nur's allegations against Shekau included the accusation that Shekau was "sleeping with wives and slaves," an accusation that another anti-Shekau Boko Haram commander, Abu Aisha, repeated.[53] If true, this allegation establishes the recurrence of the practice that Dan Fodio lamented. History, it seems, was repeating itself in this regard.

Boko Haram elevated kidnapping and ransom demands to one of the financial mainstays of its insurgency, but whether its capturing, ransoming, and enslavement operations are motivated solely by battlefield needs or are a product of greed is unclear. In its early days between 2009 and 2011, the movement depended on ransom payments for kidnapped expatriates for much of its financing, with several high-profile cases grabbing media headlines.[54] Moreover, its phased releases of most of the kidnapped Chibok schoolgirls were secured with the payment of millions of dollars from the Nigerian government, as has been widely reported.[55] Because of the nature of the current insurgency, which has resulted in the capture of many Boko Haram fighters, the movement has also deftly operationalized the Islamic principle of exchanging enemy prisoners, insisting on and successfully negotiating the release of its captured high-ranking fighters for several groups of Nigerian civilian captives. Since captives thus continue to be valuable assets in the hands of Boko Haram, the practice of capturing and detaining humans remains at the center of the Boko Haram enterprise. The rhetorical, theological, exegetical, and polemical maneuvers and resources that enabled Boko Haram to revive and justify a kind of captivity purportedly associated with an older regional wave of religious warfare require further commentary.

REVIVING AND JUSTIFYING CAPTIVITY

In his Ramadan public lecture on the exegesis of *Sūrat al-'imrān* (Qur'an 3:165–75) delivered on September 9, 2008, Muhammad Yusuf issued a forewarning to his followers to resist the urge to sexually objectify and lust after women when they set out to fight jihad. According to Yusuf, the women captured in the course of fighting jihad should be treated as property and spoils of war, not as objects for fulfilling fighters' sexual desires.[56] At the time Yusuf delivered this lecture, Boko Haram had not declared a total war against the Nigerian government. The leaders of the movement, including Yusuf, Shekau, and Nur, were touring states across Northern

Nigeria to deliver lectures, gain the support of new followers, and debate with the Muslim religious scholars who opposed their creed and methodology of jihad.

While not formally declaring jihad at this time, the three high-profile leaders repeatedly made it clear in their public lectures that the ultimate goal of the movement was the declaration of war against the Nigerian government and the establishment of *dar al-Islam* (abode of Islam). Nearly half a decade after Yusuf's 2008 lecture, Boko Haram had morphed from a dissident religious movement into a movement actively waging war and capturing towns and villages. The transition from a *Da'wa* (preaching) phase to an active phase of jihad saw the revival of captivity, particularly female enslavement, of the type that Yusuf enunciated in his 2008 lecture. The enslavement of women and girls as property and spoils of war, specifically the brazen 2014 kidnapping of schoolgirls, confirmed the prescient 2008 sermon of Yusuf regarding the lawfulness and necessity of female "enemy" enslavement in the context of jihad.

Before Boko Haram's revival of enslavement, scholars had published numerous studies on slavery and the slave trade in the Sokoto Caliphate and its emirates, ransoming practices and policies in West Africa, concubinage, royal slave culture, resistance to slavery, and the course of abolition in Northern Nigeria.[57] None of these works anticipated the twenty-first-century revival of Islamicate slavery in the region because reformist militancy and its attendant endorsement of enslavement were considered historical phenomena to be studied in the present, but not as part of present jihad practice. Boko Haram resuscitated academic interest in what most observers considered an abolished practice and a subject of purely historical inquiry. Shortly after Boko Haram commenced large-scale kidnapping of girls and the raiding of towns and villages, historians began to review the potential parallels, continuities, and variance between Boko Haram slavery and the slavery of the eighteenth and nineteenth centuries.

After explaining the differences between the slave raiding of late nineteenth- and early twentieth-century slaver Hamman Yaji, and that of Abubakar Shekau, scholars Melchisedek Chétima, Scott MacEachern, and Walter van Beek argue that it is no coincidence that non-Muslims living along the border between Cameroon and Nigeria refer to Boko Haram as *hamaji*, a term derived from their memory of Yaji's earlier depredations.[58]

The invocation of the past to make sense of Boko Haram's practices of enslavement is a legitimate field of scholarly inquiry. Not only are folk memories of past slave raids being revived to understand and cope with the slaving practices of today's jihadists, Boko Haram militants themselves have called on past histories of enslavement in their region of operation to justify their practice. However, the analysis below goes beyond drawing historical parallels between the early history of slavery in Northern Nigeria and Boko Haram's slavery. Besides the appropriation of history, Boko Haram grounded its revival of captivity in Islamic legal, intellectual, and moral discourses that have remained relatively stable for two centuries. The availability and situational amenability of these extant discourses, not to mention their transhistorical quality, conduce to a long history in which successive generations of militants have strategically and selectively called on these discourses to legitimize slavery in their time.

According to Paul Lovejoy, the institution of slavery in Northern Nigeria experienced a slow death from 1897 to 1936, partly due to two important factors: abolitionist efforts that found their way into the imperialist rhetoric that the British colonial administration championed, and the protracted series of modifications of the terms of servility that resulted from the interaction between Muslim aristocrats and British colonial administrators.[59] Despite the colonial administration's reliance on the Islamic courts for the promotion of emancipation and self-redemption of the enslaved, the legal corpus of Islamic juristic discourses that Muslim aristocrats and scholars had employed to justify and legitimize the institution of slavery within this setting remained intellectually unchallenged, although it was gradually stripped of its power of enforcement in colonial times. This preexisting, largely undisturbed, ideology of slavery, whose dictates were sometimes neglected in practice, is the same ideology that Boko Haram has attempted to redeem, revive, and enforce in Northern Nigeria through the practice of various forms of enslavement.

TRANSHISTORICAL SCRIPTS OF CAPTIVITY

At the time of the colonial encounter in the first decade of the twentieth century and in the decades that followed, there was no reason to excavate or operationalize the theological authority of the existing orthodoxy regarding enslavement in the context of jihad. No one would have predicted that a reformist movement in the region would move from preaching radical reform to militant jihad in the future. The emergence of Boko Haram in the twenty-first century altered the assumptions of Muslims in the region and took the theological paradigm of holding nonbelievers captive during jihad from the realm of the hypothetical to the domain of reality. In the purview of Boko Haram, this existing ideology of enslavement assumed the status of a multipurpose ideological justification and reference. Boko Haram invokes it to justify kidnapping and enslaving those it deems lawful to enslave on account of their alleged embrace of unbelief. The kidnapping of the Chibok schoolgirls is the most well-known incident, but it is not the only one the group has justified by drawing on the precolonial clerical and aristocratic consensus on slavery.

The Chibok kidnapping incident itself, insofar as it was carefully planned and signaled in Boko Haram's canonical rhetorical pronouncements, represents a brazen practical effort to put to work the theological orthodoxies that were available, but that, for reasons of expediency and the pragmatic reality of life in a multireligious nation, Muslims had all but allowed to recede into abeyance. Boko Haram's point of entry into the Northern Nigerian reformist debate and landscape was the claim that Muslims in the region had abandoned the religious reformist paradigms of old, and had sacrificed these paradigms for secular priorities. If we take this claim seriously, the group's decision to kidnap and enslave the Chibok schoolgirls fits within an expansive reformist rhetorical complex in which Boko Haram sees itself as a restorer of a lost reformist jihad tradition that included the practice of theologically regulated slavery.

A moral economy sacralized by widely accepted theological norms existed and applied discernible pressure and constraints on practitioners of slavery in precolonial times. Thus, a focus on the Islamicate framework of slavery within precolonial Northern Nigeria illuminates how the slave system in the region functioned. This in turn precisely delineates what Boko Haram's ideologues are insisting on reviving in the present. It is not merely the case that Boko Haram invented a new use for an old, long-mutant Islamic ideology; rather, the group disrupted an informal, expedient decision to disregard in practice but leave unchallenged a jurisprudential ideology of enslavement. The origin of that ideology harkens back to the Fodiawa jihad.

The jihad of Dan Fodio institutionalized a continuous military campaign that produced captives from wars and raids on the territories of the caliphate's enemies. Most of these captives could not be sold due to the decline of the Atlantic slave trade, and not all of them embraced conversion to Islam, which would have prevented their servility. To manage these captives, the leaders of the Sokoto Caliphate referred to the theory of slavery written by the famed Timbuktu scholar Ahmad Baba, who was forced into exile after the Moroccan conquest of Songhay in 1591.[60] In his legal treatise on slavery, written in 1614 in response to a request from Saʿīd b. Ibrāhīm al-Jirārī of Tuwāt, Baba addressed the burning question of who could legitimately be enslaved. While citing earlier scholarly works on slavery, Baba concluded that Muslims could not be enslaved but that non-Muslims captured in warfare could be legally enslaved.[61] Baba's treatise provided an ideological legitimization for slave raiding in the lands considered *dar al-kufr* (lands not governed by the *sharia* in West Africa).

Baba's ideological framework became a canonical reference for rulers and clerics across Islamic West Africa seeking to develop their own governing principles on slave raids and slavery, and trying to quiet anxieties and debates among clerics on the parameters of legitimate enslavement within Islam. Baba's text proved both malleable and timeless as a reference. It was also a highly mobile and dynamic document in both spatial and temporal terms. The text remained relevant across centuries and traveled to several parts of West Africa, where Islam had taken root but where there was a dearth of theological manuals to guide the faithful in specific domains of action and devotion. As controversies over enslavement and slave raiding proliferated in correspondence to the inevitable warring and state-building campaigns within and on the borderlands of Islam in West Africa, Baba's treatise became a handy reference to both settle and provoke debate on the subject. In some cases, clerics and political actors used the treatise as a foundational text and a linchpin for their own treatises. The rulers of the Sokoto Caliphate drew on Baba's prescriptive ideas on slavery two centuries later to construct their own ideology when they were confronted with the question of slavery, deploying the text as both an authoritative reference and a basis for further exploration and enunciation.

In his book *Bayān wujūb al-hijra 'alā 'l-'ibād,* Dan Fodio classified the lands of Hausaland into three categories: lands where unbelief predominated and Islam was rarely found; lands where Islam predominated among the masses and unbelief was common among its rulers; and lands where unbelief, either on the part of the rulers or subjects, was rare and Islam predominated or was discernibly ascendant.[62] Based on this classification, Dan Fodio concluded that the first two categories were lands of unbelief while the third category did not exist in the Central Sudan. According to Dan Fodio, the first category of lands in Central Sudan was clearly non-Muslim. Once a people were declared to be outside the realm of Islam, their enslavement was deemed lawful.

A more contentious clause in Dan Fodio's classification concerned the second category of lands, which included Borno, Kano, and Katsina. Ahmad Baba had classified all these lands as the lands of Islam in his "Miʿrāj al-ṣuʿūd."[63] Dan Fodio acknowledged Baba's judgment but argued that, in his era, all these lands were or had become *dar al-kufr*. This was so, he claimed, because the spread of Islam was limited to the masses. Their rulers, he contended, professed Islam but were polytheists in practice. Dan Fodio thus declared *takfir* (excommunication) on them on the basis that they had turned their subjects from the path of God and had raised the banner of the kingdom of this world above the banner of Islam.

What Dan Fodio was doing here was a deft rhetorical maneuver in which he sought to recast the didactic authority of Ahmad Baba's treatise as time- and place-bound, two hundred years after Baba articulated his informed opinions and a long distance away from Baba's physical location at the time that he wrote the treatise. The passage of time and the shift of location allowed Dan Fodio to impose new meanings on Baba's treatise and to expand and constrict the parameters of its application. A great deal was at stake for Dan Fodio and his envisioned militant reform movement. The trajectory of his jihad rested largely on his ability to work around or maneuver his way through the paradigmatic treatise of Baba on the question of who could be lawfully attacked and, if defeated, enslaved. Dan Fodio had to deal with the text's pronouncement on where slavery was lawful and where it was not. Since war captives and their enslavement were integral to jihad practice, embarking on jihad without resolving the question of slavery was impractical, hence Dan Fodio's rigorous theological revisionism within the context of Baba's thesis.

Dan Fodio's classification of polities and peoples in Hausaland influenced how his jihad was fought and who was targeted. His interpretation of Ahmad Baba's theory of slavery informed the process of designating legitimate and illegitimate targets of his jihad. His classification meant that the people in the lands of the first category were legitimate targets of jihad and could therefore be legally enslaved, while those in the second category could not be legally enslaved, but jihad against their rulers was legitimate until they established the Sharia. This classification shaped the ideological framework of slavery in nineteenth-century Northern Nigeria before the European colonial conquest. Dan Fodio advanced a strong criticism against the enslavement of free Muslims, and slaveholders were reprimanded for enslaving Muslims in the lands where Islam predominated among its masses and even in the territories where Islam did not predominate.[64] The overarching principle enabled Dan Fodio to walk a fine line of theological conformity while extending the boundaries of Baba's normative treatise to accommodate the imperatives of his own jihadi project.

Once the jihad against the Hausa rulers had been legally justified, the slavery question was also extended to Muslims who supported the opponents of Dan Fodio and his foot soldiers during the jihad, specifically the Kanem-Bornu empire. Dan Fodio attempted to resolve the conflict between idealism and pragmatism by issuing a verdict that made jihad permissible against Muslims who opposed it, but also made permissible the legitimate enslavement of enemy Muslims whom the caliphate had declared apostates. This verdict offered a departure from the generally accepted view prohibiting the enslavement of apostates, which the majority of scholars advocated. This ruling is Dan Fodio's second major revision on Baba's theory of slavery. To justify this revision, Dan Fodio argued that it was permissible to follow any one of several legal opinions that preceding scholars had formulated unless it was contradictory to the Qur'an, Sunna, or *ijma*. In this sense, even though the lawful enslavement of apostates was a minority jurisprudential position, Dan Fodio argued that it could be applied to enemy Muslims who had been declared apostates by the caliphate.

Under Dan Fodio's nuanced blueprint, the property of Muslim opponents of the jihad could be seized, including their slaves, but their enslavement was declared illegal as long as they remained Muslims and were not declared apostates. Another group of people whose enslavement was made illegal were legally protected non-Muslim populations living under the caliphate (*ahl al-dhimma*, or *dhimmis*). Jihad against the *dhimmis* was outlawed, their property could not be confiscated, and their enslavement was declared illegal. The leaders of the caliphate condemned the sale of slaves to Europeans, both directly and indirectly through African intermediaries, for transportation to the Americas.[65] Dan Fodio succeeded in not only reinscribing Baba's paradigm of lawful and unlawful enslavement in the consciousness of Muslims in the region, but also in deepening and nuancing it into a dynamically novel but robustly usable body of theological proclamations. Along with Baba's existing thesis, Dan Fodio's work became the dominant, binding corpus of texts in matters of enslavement and its permissibility in various scenarios.

From the foregoing, it is evident that the Islamic framework of slavery shaped the institution of slavery in Northern Nigeria from the foundational period of the Dan Fodio jihad. Who could be enslaved, who could not be enslaved, and who possessed the legal right to purchase slaves were all defined within the established Islamic framework of slavery that ossified into a referential ideology of slavery in precolonial Northern Nigeria over several centuries. This ideology lent legitimacy to the enslavement of non-Muslims and to slave raiding in what was designated as zones of unbelief. Throughout the long nineteenth century, these raids led to the capture and enslavement of people who were incorporated into the region's slave structure. When criticized for enslaving kidnapped girls, Boko Haram, through Abubakar Shekau, claimed that it was merely following the example of old Islamic warrior-reformers and reviving an established but long-moribund tradition.

When the British colonial authorities abolished the legal status of slavery in Northern Nigeria in the first decade of the twentieth century, the legally recognized Islamic courts of the caliphate were granted the warrant to operate as "native courts," and their judicial mechanisms were allowed to function in the control of the slave population and not in the enforcement of the official colonial abolitionist ideology. This was a crucial bifurcation that allowed considerable latitude for the Islamic courts to use as their operational legal codes the paradigmatic writings and proclamations of Dan Fodio and the broader caliphate jurisprudential canon. In this way, the legal and deterministic sway of the Fodio treatise on slavery was officially recognized and extended into the colonial period. Other than charges of enslavement and slave raiding, all slavery cases were shifted to the Islamic courts, giving considerable leverage to clerical and political aristocrats to negotiate a less disruptive end to slavery and, more crucially, to reestablish the normative juridical authority of Dan Fodio's treatise on slavery.

Although slavery persisted clandestinely through the first three decades of the twentieth century in Northern Nigeria, it gradually faded away until Boko Haram's spectacular and brazen attempt to resuscitate it through the kidnapping of the schoolgirls. Boko Haram's subsequent public defense of the kidnapping seized on the existing, unchallenged caliphal ideology on slavery. Ideologues of the group later answered Islamic leaders in Northern Nigeria who criticized the kidnapping by accusing them of duplicity. It was hypocritical of the opposing clerics, Boko Haram ideologues argued, to condemn the kidnapping and enslavement of the Chibok girls while venerating a caliphate Islamic tradition that included a powerful ideological precedent of enslaving war captives.

BOKO HARAM AND CAPTIVITY

As global efforts to secure the release of the kidnapped Chibok girls intensified, Abubakar Shekau, in defiance of the global outrage, boasted in released videos about the kidnapping and declared that the girls were lawful slaves of his new caliphate.[66] Clerics in Nigeria and the Arab world, including the sultan of Sokoto, Sa'adu Abubakar III and the grand mufti of Saudi Arabia, 'Abd al-'Aziz Al al-Shaykh, condemned the kidnapping and questioned its Islamic basis. To many, the intervention of Muslim authorities served to proactively discredit the theological case that Boko Haram might make in support of the kidnapping. However, Boko Haram was far from silenced by the pronouncements of these Islamic authorities.

Despite the international outrage, the Islamic State and theologians who shared the group's ideology on the nexus of jihad and slavery lauded Boko Haram's kidnapping and enslavement of the girls. In issues 4 and 5 of its official English-language magazine *Dabiq* (October and December 2014), the Islamic State cited the kidnapping as a justification for its own sexual enslavement of Yazidi women in Iraq, a remarkable validation of the jihadist bona fides of Boko Haram. This boosted the group's belief that it was on the right path theologically, not to mention its visibility in the small world of global jihad. Whereas in several matters Boko Haram, even before the emergence of the ISWAP faction, looked up to the Islamic State and its predecessors for theological clarity and direction, on the matter of slavery in jihad Boko Haram was the group brazenly showing external jihadist groups the way, thus reversing the familiar flow of modern jihadi ideological and tactical ideas. In a Q&A session posted on JustPaste, Musa Cerantonio, an Australian convert to Islam and a supporter of the Islamic State, provided theological justification supporting Boko Haram's actions. Abu Malik Shaybah al-Hamad, the Tunisia-based Anṣar al-Shariʿa member who facilitated the union between Boko Haram and the Islamic State, also cited the kidnapping of the Chibok girls as the major event that strengthened his belief that Boko Haram was a genuine jihadist group, mentioning the "group's revival of the Sunna of taking nonbelievers as captives."[67]

For Boko Haram's ideological sympathizers, the kidnapping of the girls was a seminal moment that announced the group's commitment to the revival of a lost caliphal tradition of enslaving unbelievers, and an indicator of its jihadi authenticity. This was precisely how Boko Haram wanted the kidnapping to be understood, and it basked in the subsequent approval that other jihad movements expressed. Boko Haram also became more emboldened in fleshing out the claim that it was merely returning to a lost caliphate ideology of enslavement, turning the outrage of mainstream Northern Nigerian Muslim clerics against them by accusing them of abandoning the traditions of a caliphate they claimed to revere. The kidnapping and ensuing controversy allowed Boko Haram to strategically declare its commitment to a precolonial Islamic ideology and inaugurate a broader debate on slavery in the Islamic history of Northern Nigeria.

Emboldened by both the inaction of the Nigerian government and these expressions of support, Boko Haram seized the initiative and went on the offensive to justify the enslavement of the Chibok girls and its practice of captivity and enslavement in general. This brazen maneuver put the clerical establishment in Northern Nigeria on the defensive by placing it in the awkward position of disavowing a subsisting body of theological work on Islamic permissions for the enslavement of non-Muslims on which they had been nurtured and to which they still subscribed. The challenge for the mainstream clerics was how to reject Shekau's justification of the modern Islamicate slavery of Boko Haram without disavowing his invocation of the Fodiawa treatise on enslavement that continued to define the exegetical tradition on this topic.

Shekau reopened the debate on slavery in the video "Message to the Ummah," delivered on May 6, 2014.[68] In the video, Shekau cited the theological exegesis that previously defined the official ideology of slavery in Northern Nigeria to justify the girls' kidnapping. While using this exegesis that allowed the enslavement of non-Muslim populations, Shekau supported his proclamation with a rejoinder to clerics who opposed the kidnapping, citing several sources.[69] This was a direct appeal to both the jihad tradition of Dan Fodio and the ensuing dominant theological corpus of the region.

In fact, Shekau had hinted in his video "Raid on Maiduguri," which was released on March 26, 2014, less than a month before the Chibok girls' kidnapping, that his group would embark on the enslavement of women and girls.[70] It was therefore unsurprising when Shekau proudly claimed the kidnapping of the girls in a subsequent series of videos. His interlocutors and critics may have missed his declaration of the permissibility of enslaving women and girls who attended secular schools, especially non-Muslim girls, but it was in plain sight, expressed publicly months before the Chibok incident. In a May 6, 2014, video, Shekau retrospectively defended the kidnapping and threatened to marry off the schoolgirls, stating, "Yes, we will capture slaves. Who told you there are no slaves in Islam? What are human rights? Bastard liars!"[71]

After earlier signaling his intention to revive the ideology of slavery propounded for the nineteenth-century caliphate, Shekau invoked prophetic practice, example, and precedent in his videos to justify it. He preemptively legitimized the kidnapping and enslavement of girls through an appeal to both regional caliphal history and prophetic precedent. This strategy aimed at disarming and silencing his clerical critics.[72] Shekau cited theological exegesis to buttress his position:

Imam Shinqiti said in his *tafsir* none doubt the permissibility of capturing slaves except unbelievers. Please go and check the *tafsir* of Imam Shinqiti. There are also several verses in the Qur'an: "But if you fear that you cannot be equitable, then only one, or what your right hands own" (Q4:3). You should go and check the interpretation of "what your right hands own" [concubines].[73]

The above passage exemplifies Boko Haram's confident belief that by enslaving unbelieving girls or Muslim girls it considered apostates because of their participation in secular schooling, it was upholding and reviving a settled legal ruling governing enslavement in a warring caliphate, a legitimate form of slavery that other Muslims had allegedly abandoned because of secular politics and pursuits. Furthermore, we see in this passage a rather proactive endorsement and justification of concubinage as lawful in the context of jihad and war captivity.

One central element is missing from academic and popular analyses of the Chibok kidnapping—the failure to critically engage the interpretation of Islamic sacred texts that Boko Haram adopted to theologically legitimize its practice of female captivity. The relative preservation and usable malleability of the official caliphate ideology of slavery provided an instrumental possibility for successive Islamic militant movements that could easily appropriate the ideology and call for its resuscitation. That ideology remained a living, breathing, usable manual. As long as this ideology remained theologically unchallenged, even if it had been rendered moribund by the colonial legal eradication of slavery, it persisted in the caliphal canon and was available to reformers, rebels, dissidents, and militants seeking wholesale or piecemeal revival of traditions that the caliphate had established. Boko Haram's claim of reviving that tradition in its kidnapping and enslavement actions should be understood and critiqued in this frame.

THE BOKO HARAM WAR ECONOMY

The modernity of Boko Haram's war arsenal may belie its rhetoric and pronouncements, which regularly invoke the distant past of Islamic state-building in Northern Nigeria, but this is understandable. Insurgents rarely choose the weapons of their rebellion. Instead, they respond in kind to the military tactics and equipment of their state-backed adversaries and adopt the dominant military technologies of their time. Besides, in an interconnected world of mobile and fungible military technologies and illicit weapons flows, a serious insurgency cannot remain closed off from the circulating instruments of warfare. Boko Haram has demonstrated a capacity to remain on the cutting edge of today's infantry warfare and its standard weaponry. The question of how Boko Haram jihadists source and replenish their weapons is a contentious one, but clear evidence and answers are beginning to emerge, pointing to a sophisticated insurgency supplied and sustained by local, regional, and international networks of weapons smuggling and local dynamics. Analyzing Boko Haram's military assets inevitably leads to an analysis of the movement's financing, since it takes a sustainable revenue stream to purchase and replace weapons. Boko Haram's financing is a topic of much speculation, but it does not take much financing for local insurgents who are embedded in local communities and who know the lay of the land to locate and exploit opportunities for revenue generation and profiteering.

Although, as demonstrated by scholars, Boko Haram was initially seed-funded by al-Qaeda in the Islamic Maghreb (AQIM), a regional jihad movement with global affiliations,[74] the insurgency is now sustained in material and financial terms almost wholly by resources derived locally and regionally. Arms purchase represents a significant expenditure for Boko Haram. According to Jacob Zenn, Boko Haram developed an elaborate supply line spanning the length and breadth of the Lake Chad region. This smuggling route arms and resupplies Boko Haram members with weapons sourced from Chad, Sudan, and even Libya through trusted Cameroonian, Nigerien, and Chadian traffickers and their extensive, multinational smuggling networks. Through these pipelines, Boko Haram is able to maintain and restock weapons depots along the volatile borderlands of the Lake Chad region. Here, Boko Haram takes delivery of "replacement parts for sophisticated weaponry like tanks" from traffickers of multiple nationalities operating from and through their respective countries along the Nigeria, Cameroon, Niger, Chad, and Cameroon borders.[75]

Although smuggling provides Boko Haram with a steady stream of weapons, much of the movement's weaponry is captured or stolen from the armies of Nigeria, Cameroon, and Niger, with the bulk coming from Nigerian Army field armories. These are acquisitions that the militants consider licit appropriations and spoils of war or *ghanima*. Boko Haram consistently displays these weapon captures, at times showing the looting of abandoned weapons storage and the capture of equipment in battles. Regardless of where the weapons come from and how they are sourced, there is a financial cost to transporting, storing, and maintaining them, hence it is important to discuss the revenue streams that lubricate the military machinery of the militants.

Kidnap for ransom was the main source of Boko Haram's financing at its inception, with the first major ransom coming in April 2013, when the movement reportedly secured $3 million, in addition to the release of sixteen arrested Boko Haram members, as ransom for a French family kidnapped in Northern Cameroon.[76] This massive take funded Boko Haram's weapons purchase for the next year at least. Over the years, Boko Haram and its subsidiaries, such as Ansaru, have carried out other abductions that were resolved through the payment of large dollar-denominated ransoms.

Boko Haram has built an informal economy on the borderlands of Nigeria, Niger, Cameroon, and Chad, and in the volatile and largely ungoverned Lake Chad region. Boko Haram finances itself through this lucrative war economy and black-market operation. One source of income is the network of illicit businessmen in Cameroon, Nigeria, Niger, and Chad that aids Boko Haram by helping it sell off stolen and captured vehicles. As Zenn demonstrates, this multinational cast of businessmen acts alternately as Boko Haram smugglers, gun suppliers, mediators, negotiators, money couriers, and traffickers, helping the movement launder money or make critical weapons and logistical purchases.[77]

According to a comprehensive report written by the investigative media consortium of the *HumAngle* Media Foundation and the Premium Times Center for Investigative Journalism, this economy, subject to the ebbs and flows of the military conflict, has largely helped Boko Haram meet its financial needs and in turn ensure the availability of military assets even during times of battlefield setbacks.[78] Another important source of the movement's financing is the loose network of Boko Haram exiles, alumni, fugitives, and sympathizers, in several West African and Gulf countries, who continue to fund the movement through their licit and illicit business operations in these countries. Zenn calls this financing stream the diaspora funding mechanism, which is sustained by so-called "non-combatant or inactive members" who continue to support the movement through monetary contributions.[79]

On the ground in the theater of the insurgency, Boko Haram maintains a robust black-market economy focused on revenue generation. The major economic activities in this underground economy include the control of transregional and local trades in smoked fish, fishing in Lake Chad, the farming of red pepper, and livestock production. Boko Haram has exploited a major revenue stream involving these economic endeavors. The militants impose levies on fishermen as well as traders of fish and pepper in designated local markets in Nigeria, Niger, and Cameroon. This system of levies and taxes brings in millions of Naira monthly. The levies are part protection fees guaranteeing safe passage and mobility within the zones controlled by the militants and part permission dues authorizing traders to sell and buy in remote markets controlled by the movement. The *HumAngle* report estimates that fishermen and pepper farmers pay between 400,000 and 500,000 Naira in fees, with some big farmers paying considerably more. The total haul is in the millions of Naira.

Boko Haram also participates in the growing of red pepper, fishing, and the smoking of fish for sale in all regions of Nigeria. During the successful offensive against Boko Haram by Chadian forces in the Lake Chad region in April 2020, the advancing Chadian soldiers uncovered massive underground pits used by the militants for smoking fish for markets across the region. Prior to the emergence of the insurgency in 2009, the World Food Program estimated this pepper and fish economy to be worth about $48 million. With the disruptions, depopulations, and displacements caused by the crisis around the Lake Chad region, the value of this economy has probably declined. Nonetheless, Boko Haram continues to profit directly from what is left of it.

Yet another income stream of the jihadists is a semiannual tax on farmers and herders called *hadaya*, which is paid either in cash or in kind. These taxes sustain the jihadists' operations in Nigeria and neighboring countries where they have camps, cells, networks, and smuggling operations. Smuggling operations run primarily through Chad and Nigeria, which connect to the larger Sahel and ultimately to North African and Mediterranean sources, and ensure that Boko Haram is supplied with medicine, fuel, phones, communication gadgets, and assorted consumer goods. The smuggling routes and the cash and barter economy that sustain them are also crucial for the supply of weaponry and war equipment when stocks need to be replaced and the jihadists cannot steal enough from the forces of the Lake Chad countries to fulfill their battlefield needs.

CONTEMPORARY AND HISTORICAL ADAPTATIONS TO VIOLENCE

The military economy of violence and war-making that enabled Boko Haram to establish and maintain a foothold in the volatile borderlands of the Lake Chad Basin has a long history that is not only about weapons, warfare, and military tactics, but also about socioeconomic, cultural, and political resilience in response to episodic and routine violence. Faced with the nihilistic violence of Boko Haram, both Muslim and non-Muslim communities in the Borno-Yobe-Adamawa axis continued to return to or find ways to survive in the conflict zone, adopting time-honored modalities of self-preservation and maneuvering with knowledge inherited from forebears who adapted to similar upheavals in earlier centuries. This history is not just one of violence, banditry, and displacement, but also one characterized by layers of social and cultural adaptations, survival, and inventive resilience. There is no better scholarly analysis of this nexus of ecology, routinized violence, and adaptive mechanisms in the conflict zone than the work of Scott MacEachern. MacEachern's ethnographic and archaeological research not only helps put Boko Haram's military activities in historical context, it also shows the historical interactions between people, landscape, technologies, and political configurations that have, for centuries, made the Lake Chad shore and Mandara Mountains both a frontier refuge for outlaws and insurgents and an economically lucrative territory for them and their noncombatant auxiliaries and enablers.[80]

MacEachern's illuminating approach contextualizes today's violence in the Sahelian borderlands of Nigeria, Chad, Cameroon, and Niger in centuries-old practices of predation, banditry, and slave raiding. In this ecology of violence nonstate actors were preeminent, but their activities also profited ruling elites in established polities. These rulers permitted and even advanced violence in these zones "in order to obtain the commodity—human bodies—whose possession and sale made elite lifestyles possible."[81] MacEachern explains how, in distant archaeological times and for millennia, commodity flows between nodes and hubs in this region connected mountain peoples to plains peoples, and the two groups to lakeside peoples. The same porous borders and juridical indeterminacy that catalyzed the flow of goods and peoples also normalized banditry as an inevitable aspect of life, while routinizing the violence that accompanied such predation.[82] The result was a sociopolitical and economic condition in which rebels, refugees, and bandits comingled in uneasy tension, conflict, and at times mutually beneficial frontier arrangements that kept state authorities at bay and away from the lucrative activities of the borderland.

This precolonial picture is eerily similar to the quotidian wartime interactions that have taken hold in the Borno-Yobe-Chad-Niger-Northern Cameroon axis in the shadow of the Boko Haram insurgency. Here the lines between insurgents, civilians, and bandits are often blurred, and refugees and civilian holdouts in ravaged communities—captives and prisoners of war, if you will—sometimes come to depend on insurgents as benefactors, and the insurgents in turn depend on the former for revenue and intelligence. Boko Haram's multiple income streams necessitate a certain degree of embeddedness in local life. Kidnapping, a major source of revenue for Boko Haram in its early days, commodity smuggling, protection extortions and informal taxation, and the direct control of certain trades all require elaborate networks of combatants and noncombatants comingling in tense but codependent arrangements. Local actors with profound knowledge of the terrain and perhaps prior experience as bandits, violent outlaws, fugitives, smugglers, and new insurgents find common cause and work together, co-opting some local peoples desperate to survive the new violence. Like its insurgent predecessors and late twentieth-century bandits in the region, Boko Haram has benefited from this history, recruiting some former bandits and smugglers into its ranks and employing others as civilian allies and logistics people.[83]

As MacEachern explains, in the nineteenth century, as the region convulsed with the Fodiawa jihad, the military campaigns of Rabih Fadlalah, the Islamic state builder who in 1893 invaded Bornu from Darfur, in Western Sudan, having fought for and then fallen out with the mahdi, Muhammad Ahmed, further destabilized the region.[84] Several other small state-building insurgencies and quasi-religious rebellions wracked the region. The Sahelian wilderness of the Lake Chad Basin was an attractive terrain for rebels seeking to overcome their military disadvantages against state armies by using the topographical terrain as a platform for effective guerilla warfare and a base from which to overthrow urban-based polities. The Mandara Mountains and the shores of Lake Chad provided refuge for both insurgents retreating strategically from standing state militaries and civilians trying to cope with or escape military confrontations and eke out a living in ungoverned, remote frontier territories with ambiguous jurisdictions and sovereignties, and natural protection against mounted troops. It is not an accident, MacEachern argues, that Boko Haram insurgents, copying the old tactical withdrawals into remote, secluded *tsangaya* enclaves by jihadists and anticaliphate rebels of the past, have made the Mandara Mountains, the Lake Chad shores, and the difficult terrain of the Sambisa Forest Reserve their bases of operation.[85] Nor is it happenstance that when Boko Haram established its short-lived caliphate in 2014, it chose Gwoza, located in the foothills of the Mandara Mountains, as its headquarters. The most profound takeaway from MacEachern's analysis is the intertwinement of profit, warfare, commodity smuggling, and human trafficking in a volatile Sahelian frontier with a history of violence and juridical ambiguity that dates back centuries. In the last several decades in particular, this territory has been transformed into a lawless, ungoverned outpost of multiple nation-states by the proliferation of weapons, illicit commodity flows, and the growth of domestic and transnational networks of jihadism.

In the final analysis, what do this deep history and its contemporary analogue embodied by Boko Haram tell us? One insight from MacEachern's anthrohistorical analysis of the sociocultural contexts of Boko Haram's ongoing insurgency is the *longue durée* development of adaptive techniques in response to turmoil and disorder. MacEachern outlines institutions and practices of resilience, survival, and coping that evolved during past periods of violence. These practices then became part of the social fabric as violence and disorder transitioned from spasmodic occurrences to routine, quotidian realities of life in the contested Lake Chad Basin. These techniques of survival, latent in periods of relative peace but always operational in areas traversed by smuggling routes and lucrative production zones on the border, have carried forward to the twenty-first century.

In precolonial times, as insurgent violence raged alongside opportunistic and criminal predation, communities organized hunters armed with bows and arrows, Dane guns, and protective amulets to confront the threats, police villages, and enforce order in inhabited rural zones. That adaptive cultural institution of self-preservation has now been resurrected, albeit in a modified form. Members of the Civilian Joint Task Force (JTF) work alongside Nigerian troops, supporting operations as lookouts and spies, alerting troops to Boko Haram's offensive military maneuvers, and occasionally holding off Boko Haram attackers in rural outposts before the arrival of troops to the front line. Additionally, in the Adamawa and Southern Borno sectors of the Nigerian Northeast, centuries-old hunters' guilds credited with special knowledge of the terrain, supernatural beliefs, inherited martial courage, and exceptional wilderness navigational skills have been informally recruited by communities, with approval and some funding from local governments, to patrol the outskirts of rural communities as a deterrence against Boko Haram attacks.

Wars that occur in territories suffering from the aftershocks of previous turmoil tend to be particularly devastating since new, improved technologies of war-making and expert local knowledge can produce efficient but deadly military outcomes. One by-product of this is the production of refugees in large numbers. The slave-raiding campaigns of warlord and slave trader Hamman Yaji in the late nineteenth and early twentieth centuries, the religious wars of the mid- to late nineteenth century, and the banditry and social brigandage of the subsequent periods decimated lives, destroyed communities, and created waves of demographic displacement that remade communities, permanently empowered some groups, and marginalized others. Boko Haram's religious warfare has no doubt deepened this demographic rupture and crisis of displacement. Boko Haram's violence has exacerbated the precarity and vulnerability of groups located in the hinterland far from the protective reach of urban authorities. It has also further endangered non-Muslim groups surrounded by Muslim polities. These non-Muslim communities were raided for captives in the past and are now frequently raided in a targeted campaign of religious persecution and slave raiding by the Boko Haram insurgents.

What is not so visible through this gory history, but which MacEachern's work documents, is the quiet persistence of institutions and cultural logics of resilience. In precolonial times populations around the foothills of the Mandara Mountains, most of them non-Muslims unincorporated into any of the centralized Muslim and non-Muslim polities of the region, strategically relocated to the high ground of the mountain to be safe from the cavalry of slave raiders, jihadists, bandits, and state-building warriors. The Marghi, Higgi, Gwoza, Fali, and Matakam ethnic groups, who inhabit and for centuries mastered the art of surviving in the Mandara highlands, not only relied on the natural protection offered by their hilltop residence against the horses of raiding groups affiliated or unaffiliated with urban Muslim polities, they also invented a potent technology of self-defense, a curved throwing sword that they would aim at the tendons of moving raiders' horses to immobilize them.[86]

Today the Mandara Mountains are best known as a Boko Haram stronghold. However, some civilians have also found the mountains to be a natural platform and enclave of survival, even as the mountains have given Boko Haram fighters the topographical vantage point from which to attack several communities in that vicinity. Most of the villages and towns in the Mandara Mountains remain deserted, the aftermath of Boko Haram's scorched-earth slaughter over the past fifteen years. The current marauders of Boko Haram carry out raids on armored vehicles, trucks, and maneuverable motorbikes, against which old weapons such as the throwing sword are ineffective. The current insurgency is also more deadly than precolonial raids, with Boko Haram killing thousands of the autochthonous people of the Mandara Mountains with the help of more sophisticated, long-range weapons.

These differences notwithstanding, some old defensive and self-preservation maneuvers have been revived in the crucible of survivalist resilience. Some Muslim civilians have remained in or around their deserted communities, paying what amounts to protection money to Boko Haram cells and their bandit offshoots.[87] Some surviving civilians have left their destroyed villages and relocated deep into the mountains and other difficult terrains in the Lake Chad Basin, sometimes paying protection, produce, and cattle taxes to Boko Haram in exchange for being spared and being allowed to grow food for subsistence. This is reminiscent of the *al-dhimi* and *amana* populations of old who lived on the fringes of established caliphal states unmolested because they paid tributes. Unlike the protected refugee communities of the past, however, most of today's refugees in remote locations controlled by Boko Haram are Muslim, but the arrangement that allows them and their insurgent protectors to live away from constituted secular authorities in codependence harkens back to the plethora of complex sociopolitical arrangements that enabled populations to survive and cope with violence in the past.

Like many in the violent history of this borderland, other refugees have taken to nomadism and seminomadism as a strategy of survival, hoping to avoid the predation of wrathful insurgents and the indiscriminate violence of counterinsurgency troops. Many refugees have been returning to their villages in the aftermath of repeated Boko Haram attacks, trying to rebuild their lives and their communities against all odds. Some have leaned on kinship networks to restart their lives in safe zones in Maiduguri and in refugee camps located in protected border towns in Niger, Chad, and Cameroon. Many other refugees, relying on their knowledge of the environment and the socioeconomic and arbitrage opportunities that war, insecurity, and precarity create, have started small businesses to meet the wartime needs of refugees and nonrefugees alike.

These survival initiatives are as learned and inherited as they are expedient. Following MacEachern, we argue that they are adaptive techniques grounded in cultural coping resources developed, used, and reused over centuries. The history of insurgent warfare is also a history of survival, resilience, and society's capacity to recover and reproduce itself, especially in a region familiar with violence and brittle order such as the Lake Chad Basin. The deprivations of Boko Haram's war economy and the fearsome arsenal that both Boko Haram and the Nigerian military have brought to bear on the ongoing war have taxed the resilience of local populations to its limit. However, these pressures have also revealed the extent to which old modes of wartime sociability and adaptive survival have been rekindled and, in some cases, repurposed and expanded to help noncombatants and communities in the throes of the current violence survive and find new avenues to thrive despite the war.

CONCLUSION

The history of Boko Haram's warfare, war arsenal, and the religious and material economies that sustain and, however convolutedly, drive the group's war-making repertoire harkens back to the evolution of religious militancy and insurgent warfare in the region. The battlefield challenges facing Boko Haram and the adversarial forces that the group confronts differ from those of earlier militants, but the struggles of managing prolonged war and distributing the material and human spoils of that war unite Boko Haram and older religious insurgencies. Boko Haram militants have wittingly and unwittingly replicated some of the battlefield templates of earlier jihadists in the region, as well as the entwined practices of enslavement and ransoming.

This chapter has analyzed the connections between the military choices and dimensions of the present upheaval represented by Boko Haram and the military strategies and war-management practices of previous Muslim reformers, state builders, and militants in Northern Nigeria. Because it is manifesting in a different time and in different circumstances, Boko Haram's warfare exhibits several features that diverge from earlier traditions of Islamicate warfare in the region. These divergences are as important as the similarities because they point to the ways in which Boko Haram has adapted its military methods and choices to the realities of modern warfare, technology, and war economics, deftly emulating the successful military strategies of earlier reformist insurgents and state builders while avoiding their errors.

It is not only in the realm of military requisitioning and tactics that one finds parallels and divergences in the repertoires of Boko Haram and the resulting social disorder, and those of past insurgencies. Boko Haram has victimized and immiserated on a large scale. Like insurgencies of old, Boko Haram captures and enslaves nonbelieving and apostatized noncombatants and has killed or displaced thousands. However, even with social institutions under strain and kinship networks fraying in response to the conflict, noncombatants, like their counterparts in earlier upheavals in the region, have revived old precolonial, colonial, and postcolonial forms of resilience and self-preservation. Like communities in the region in the past, they have mobilized both to resist Boko Haram, using their asymmetrical military resources, and to support state troops fighting the insurgents. They have also relied on kinship networks, local knowledge, and inherited adaptive resources forged in the region's borderland violence and past insurgencies to invent new, complex ways of coping with adversity. Some have taken economic advantage of wartime needs and hardship to build subsistent economic niches. Some displaced people have pragmatically accepted life in insurgent enclaves as protected tribute payers, while other internally displaced people have used the instrument of mobility to stay ahead of the violence.

Epilogue

HISTORICAL SPECULATIONS ON BOKO HARAM'S FUTURE

As I worked to send this manuscript to press in April 2025, Governor Babagana Zulum of Borno State, the epicenter of the insurgency, shocked Nigerians and rattled the Nigerian federal government by announcing that Boko Haram, which had been dislodged from many of its former strongholds and significantly weakened, was mounting a frightening comeback and had captured and now controlled several communities.[1] Zulum claimed that Boko Haram was reversing some of its earlier losses and urged the government to energize its counterinsurgency efforts. Although the spokesperson of the government, Information and National Orientation Minister Mohammed Idris, later declared that Boko Haram had been weakened and was "on its last legs,"[2] Zulum's alarm, borne out by credible media reports of new, brazen Boko Haram attacks against Nigerian Army camps and positions and of its sacking of communities, jolted Nigerians out of any belief that Boko Haram's insurgency was fizzling out. This illustrates the fundamentally dynamic and unpredictable character of the Boko Haram jihad project.

This was not the first time that Boko Haram's recent history took an unexpected turn. As I prepared the initial draft of this book in 2021, Boko Haram's eccentric factional leader, Abubakar Shekau, was killed by his former jihadist comrades who now run the Islamic State–affiliated faction called ISWAP, or the Islamic State West Africa Province. Shekau's death in May 2021 realigned and further complicated an already fragmented jihadist insurgency. The suddenness of the death, even though the two factions had been locked in bitter, scorched earth fighting for years, threw Boko Haram's different factions into confusion. It also further confounded scholars and observers who had been trying to clearly understand the dominant, enduring tendencies, if any, that define the decade-and-a-half-long insurgency and Boko Haram's future as a jihadist enterprise.

For one thing, Shekau did not die easily. He blew himself up after recording and releasing a twenty-eight-minute audio message to his followers and the world.[3] In this message, he reignited several recurring internal debates and controversies within the group, including the contentious issue of *ghanimah* (war booty), rejecting the accusation that he had misappropriated *ghanimah* and gone against Quranic prescriptions on it. By rekindling an issue that caused a split in the group in 2016 that was yet to be resolved and that portended more disagreements in the future, Shekau kept the *ghanimah* conflict alive, reopened the earlier controversy around it, and ensured that the unresolved questions on it would continue to plague the insurgency, perhaps leading to more divisions as resources and war spoils diminish and competition for them increases.[4] As the group's territory shrinks, along with its capacity to obtain spoils through successful raids, the internal squabble over dwindling resources may escalate. The struggle over *ghanimah* is already deepening the internal fissures in the movement, causing new animosities and feuds to form, and alliances to emerge and fray in a continuous cycle of fragmentation.[5]

To further blur the picture, while many members of the Shekau-led JAS (Jamāʻat Ahl as-Sunnah lid-Daʻwah waʻl-Jihād) faction of Boko Haram performed *bayʻah* or an oath of allegiance to the Islamic State and its West Africa franchise after Shekau's demise,[6] holdouts loyal to the late leader dug in and promised to either avenge Shekau or die fighting ISWAP and defending his honor. At least two JAS garrisons remain loyal to Shekau. One of them is led by Bakura Doro, whose base is located on the border of Chad and Niger. Refusing to pledge allegiance to ISWAP and managing to keep his fighters from joining and being integrated into ISWAP, he has reaffirmed the Shekau faction's radical positions on two key issues: the targeting of Muslim civilians and the use of identity documents issued by a Nigerian government considered un-Islamic. Doro's camp took the initiative of attacking ISWAP positions, resulting in casualties on both sides. Emboldened by Doro's offensive military maneuvers, pro-Shekau holdouts in the Sambisa Forest, under pressure to join ISWAP in the aftermath of Shekau's death, have since fought through ISWAP defense lines to join Doro and form a JAS counterweight to the ascendance of ISWAP.[7] The short-, medium-, and long-term implications of these new fratricidal, intra–Boko Haram attacks are unknown and may yet add another twist to this long-running conflict.

In the immediate post-Shekau landscape of the insurgency, it seemed as though ISWAP had won a decisive victory and had emerged as the sole bearer of the eponymous mantle of Boko Haram. However, history guides us away from concluding that we have seen the last split or twist in the group; after all, ISWAP was considered a vulnerable faction at the time of the split in 2016, with some observers predicting that JAS would maintain its preeminent position in the Lake Chad Basin jihadist landscape. ISWAP's victory has already been successfully challenged not just by Doro's group but also by other breakaway splinters that, according to the international crisis group, have decimated both ISWAP and its rivals and diminished ISWAP's dominance.[8]

We have yet to see the type of clarity that would support a firm conclusion one way or the other regarding the ascendancy of ISWAP on the ashes of JAS, nor have we seen the last of the internal doctrinal, tactical, and personality frictions Boko Haram and its appendages have experienced and managed over the group's existence. The unfolding of the current internal strife may determine or at least affect the success or otherwise of counterinsurgency efforts. To add to the indeterminate outcomes and permutations of the post-Shekau jihadist cartography in the Lake Chad Basin, many members of JAS, in a move that is perhaps suggestive of an ongoing "jihad fatigue" in the insurgents' ranks,[9] have abandoned violent militancy altogether, embracing *Sulhu* (lit. amnesty), a secretive but well-funded amnesty program that the Nigerian government initiated to lure former insurgents away from Boko Haram.[10]

Yet another dimension in the fluidity of the Boko Haram insurgency is the group's determination to groom the children of jihadists in the tenets and practices of violent jihadism to succeed this generation. In January 2022 the ISWAP arm of Boko Haram unveiled its project for training and preparing children in the group's camps to become jihadists. It released a twenty-seven-minute propaganda video that shows instructors taking young boys through a lesson in a classroom equipped with desks, chairs, and a chalkboard.[11] In one particularly revealing footage the teacher tells the boys in Arabic to shun *tawaghit*, idolatrous tyrannical entities, political authorities, and institutions such as legislative and parliamentary bodies that make secular laws the teacher claims not only contradict Allah's laws but also replace Allah's laws as a moral guide for Muslims. The video shows that the school uses the Islamic State–approved school curriculum that, in addition to offering basic Arabic literacy lessons and doctrinal lessons invoking the ideas of prominent jihadi-Salafi scholars, includes graphic lessons on military equipment and weapons and how to use them in the battlefield.

When will these students be ready to enter the battlefield? What kind of insurgents will they be? What doctrinal and ideological currents will underpin and propel their jihad? How resilient and skillful will they be in a changing battlefield in which the state armies of Nigeria and neighboring countries acquire more experience and more effective equipment for prosecuting their counterinsurgency campaign? Being products of an upbringing and socialization processes centered in the harsh, austere Sahelian wilderness, would the next generation of jihadists be emendable to *Sulhu* or other modes of settlement, or pacifist negotiation seeking to integrate them to life in unfamiliar, mainstream urban, and semiurban milieus? These questions elicit multiple conjectures that map onto fast-changing conditions, new events, and complex developments in the political, economic, and social circumstances of the epicenter of the insurgency: the Borno–Yobe axis of Nigeria's Northeast.

These developments illustrate the fundamental fluidity of the Boko Haram insurgency. The jihadi movement is constantly being reinvented by internal and external events and pressures, rendering obsolete previous analyses and projections that appeared sound in the context of familiar realities. It is in fact possible that by the time this book is published some of the scenarios I analyze below, as tentative and provisional as they currently are, will have been overridden by new events.

The death of Shekau and the launch of the Sulhu amnesty program, which has yielded some results by capitalizing on the factional infighting and the many leadership squabbles and turnovers within Boko Haram, have upended many foundational realities of Boko Haram. However, other events have intruded into the picture. The recent breakthrough of the Nigerian government in procuring new weapons from the United States, which previously refused to supply weapons to Nigeria because of human rights concerns, and from China, Pakistan, and Turkey, as well as the injection of money, weaponry, and experienced jihadist advisers from the defunct Middle Eastern core of the Islamic State and its adjacent affiliates in the Sahel, may have seminal effects on the insurgency. These diametrically linked events may prove decisive in the kinetic dimension of the war, or they may simply deepen and prolong the military confrontation. They also have profound implications for how civilians in the Lake Chad Basin experience the war, how they cope with it, and whether they can resettle and resume normal life.

These indeterminate and unpredictable arcs of the conflict point to the impossibility of accurately discerning the future trajectory of an insurgency that is more than a decade old and shows few signs of abating. Violent insurgencies tend to endure well past their peak periods of combat, ebbing and flowing as circumstances change or permit. What is possible is an analytical exercise in which possibilities, pathways, and logical outcomes are explored and highlighted as a way of pointing to future trends. Previous Islamic reformist and jihadi movements similarly proved impervious to prediction. It is easier to prognosticate on insurgencies that succeed and constitute themselves into new governmental, ideological, and theological incumbents than to do so on a militant movement seemingly destined to remain on the margins of existing states.

The Fodiawa jihad and the caliphate that resulted from it fall into the former category, Boko Haram the latter. The Fodiawa jihad was an Islamic reformist militant movement that, upon its military victory, transitioned into a state notionally founded on a set of theological paradigms. Even so, its future was far from certain when the jihad was raging. In the moment of combat and confrontation, multiple possible outcomes and futures looked equally feasible. The Fodiawa jihad eventually succeeded in establishing a fairly cohesive caliphate as early as 1808. However, its reverberations and the smaller, subsidiary military conquests, slave raiding, and state-building efforts it inspired or launched continued well into the second half of the nineteenth century.[12] The jihad continued even after it succeeded in accomplishing the overarching goal that its leaders had envisaged: the overthrow of the Hausa dynasties. From this perspective, the future of that reformist movement was multipronged and not straightforward. The narrative of success, along with the finality that it implies, simplifies and flattens a less linear on-ground reality. Even after the vaunted success of the jihad, the caliphate continued to face rebellions on multiple fronts that were not associated just with its southward expansion but that engulfed geographical areas in the heart of Hausaland, spaces considered already pacified and incorporated into the theocratic federation. Rebellions against the caliphate and caliphate efforts to prosecute a prolonged jihad in Argungu, Kebbi, and Ningi were perhaps the most well-known cases of how the jihad lingered, with sporadic fighting, infighting, and other types of confrontations that spawned spin-off movements.

The jihad spawned several dissident and reformist movements that, while small and geographically contained, mimicked and in some ways sought to replicate and repeat the example of the Fodiawa jihad. Even more instructive is the fact that such movements not only derived their initial ideological fervor from the manual of reform and insurgency that the Fodiawa jihad leaders developed, but that in some cases the new reformers had actually fought with or had been ardent ideologues in the Fodiawa jihad movement. Another important fact about the Fodiawa jihad that invites comparison to the Boko Haram insurgency and may be instructive in the effort to understand Boko Haram's possible futures is the fragmentation of the movement over both doctrinal and material matters. Although this historical reality has been elided by the paradigmatic but simplistic popular and academic narrative of cohesion and common ideological purpose in the Fodiawa jihad, it is a significant factor in the way the jihad unfolded and "ended." All insurgencies face internal doctrinal and tactical divisions and disagreements. Such schisms sometimes metastasize into bigger factional infighting and even fratricidal conflicts, which could imperil the cause and gift victory to the enemy. Other times the internal factions are well managed, and implacably recalcitrant actors are isolated and dealt with. This is what seems to have happened in the case of the Fodiawa jihad.

It is not a given that the same scenario will unfold in the Boko Haram insurgency. The Fodiawa jihad's military successes helped to mitigate internal conflict since victory can help bitter rivals paper over internal disagreements. With a clear victory and sustainable battlefield successes eluding Boko Haram insurgents, a similar process of overcoming internal conflicts within its ranks seems less feasible. Boko Haram's current trajectory is a mixed one, replete with minor victories, defeats, and setbacks. If such outcomes proliferate across the theater of the insurgency in the coming years, it is likely that the existing internal divisions will intensify, chasms will widen, and tensions, frustrations, mutual suspicions, and distrust will grow, leading to more factions emerging or at least the existing ones digging in to pursue nihilistic goals.

For an Islamist rebellion already plagued by internal problems, the margin of error appears thin, and future disagreements over ideology, tactics, strategy, and the spoils of war may threaten the entire jihadi enterprise of Boko Haram. The Fodiawa jihad was able to project and exhibit tangible and sustainable territorial and ideological victories and momentum over several years to establish itself as a viable replacement for the existing Hausa states and as a state in waiting. This minimized the appeal of dissent from the core mission. Boko Haram lacks similar advantages.

Yet for all its victories, the Fodiawa jihad did not conclude with a neat, victorious defeat of the old order and its replacement with a new one, as its intellectual guides would have wished. Instead, flashpoints remained, grew, and expanded, and the emergent state faced many rebellions in and outside Hausaland. In fact, it became a victim of its own military victories once it transformed from an insurgent movement into a caliphate. New insurgents who had earlier allied with and fought for the caliphate quickly emerged as foes and rebels, and several pieces of unfinished military business continued to occupy the frontier emirates as restive populations resisted new jihadist endeavors, and new reformers launched critiques and military attacks against a theocratic state they accused of abandoning its religious identity.

The Sokoto Caliphate remained in this state of self-making and self-remaking and continued to wage both internal and external jihads throughout the nineteenth century. From this perspective, the jihad never really ended, it morphed. This is consistent with the character of religious insurgencies. The nineteenth century was not a period of perpetual jihad but was marked by a fluctuating upheaval that vitiates the narrative of success, triumph, and finality that often defines how the jihad's outcomes and futures are discussed in both popular discourse and scholarship.

To what extent does this history point to what lies ahead for Boko Haram? Will Boko Haram endure in multiple, unpredictable forms regardless of the fate of the ongoing insurgency? We return to our original point: insurgencies, especially those driven by theological and ideological constructs, are intractable and fluid, and have the capacity to persist and mutate in several forms years or decades after the most significant combat encounters are over. Like the Fodiawa jihad, the current rebellion is unlikely to have an abrupt, clean conclusion. Instead, the hostility and violence are likely to decrease in intensity, ushering in a period of continued low-intensity conflict between multiple groups, and between waves of Boko Haram holdouts on one side and the Nigerian state and people on the other.

Thus, the likely endgame scenario is not one in which the ideology and combat experiences and infrastructures of Boko Haram fizzle out or are decimated at some future date. Rather, it is one in which, due to attrition, atrophy, fatigue, and changing socioeconomic and political dynamics in the Nigerian Northeast and the larger southern Sahel region, the insurgency goes into remission but does not disappear, making cameo appearances as new generations of insurgents and ideologues with various ideological and military connections to Boko Haram continue to fight for the original cause and other causes allied to it. Along with this scenario, the ideological and physical apparatuses of Boko Haram are likely to be repurposed and channeled into newly emerging Islamist reformist causes and agendas, which may be superintended by some of the same actors that are active in Boko Haram or by their ideological heirs. The degree to which Boko Haram's ideological and combat assets will be appropriated for such future reformist projects remains unclear.

In peering into the future, it is important to account for contingencies—unpredictable events on the local, regional, and global levels—that may impact the state of the insurgency, transforming, intensifying, or calming it. It is also important to note that an insurgency that is a decade and a half old has already in all likelihood undergone significant transformations in personnel and ideology and is in a perpetual state of self-reinvention. These facts make the Boko Haram insurgency difficult for historians to read. Further evidence of the movement's defiance of conventional prognosis is the fact that several previous permutations have predicted either Boko Haram's self-destruction or its decimation by the combined armed forces of Nigeria, Chad, Cameroon, and Niger. Such predictions have mostly been confounded by unfolding realities in the theater of the insurgency.

Boko Haram is a highly adaptable and nimble insurgency. Its actors are able to absorb setbacks, endure adversity and internal problems, and restrategize. They also routinely confound logical prognostications by exploiting changes in the Nigerian army and political responses to the crisis. The future of Boko Haram is thus difficult to clearly discern because of this history. This is an important overarching caveat for the analysis and speculative assertions that follow.

A GENERATIONAL SHIFT

One aspect of Boko Haram's adaptive repertoire that will become more evident in the coming years is a transformation in the ranks of its fighters. As older fighters die in battle, abandon the cause, or fall victim to the infighting that has wracked the group, younger fighters, some of whom came of age in the group's bush camps, will take up the mantle of the insurgency. Another element of this shift is the fact that there is now a cohort of children who were born or raised in these camps and who have been profoundly socialized in the ways of surviving and adapting to warfare scenarios and the vagaries of a harsh Sahel ecology. These children already have experience as both combatants and battlefield auxiliaries. This socialization in the mechanics of insurgent religious warfare will produce a new generation of militants with no memory of any other life, purpose, or vocation.

The Boko Haram insurgency had early success in recruitment because of poverty and the appealing novelty of its ideology in the Nigerian Northeast. Recruitment was critical to replenishing the ranks of fighters.

The promise of stipends, prevalent grievances against the Nigerian secular state, and the seemingly inexorable momentum of the movement in those early days helped attract young men to the group. However, this early success in recruitment became imperiled when Boko Haram acquired a deserved reputation for targeting Muslim communities. As these atrocities came to light and as communities were sacked and their inhabitants killed, maimed, or rendered refugees, recruitment began to lag. The fall in recruitment led to more direct involvement of the older, experienced fighters in the group's military operations. This was unsustainable because of the inevitable mental and physical exhaustion of combat and the emergence of squabbles within the group as military pressures from regional armies made bush life and survival challenging. Furthermore, more experienced, older fighters were more likely to covet and fight over titles, leadership positions, and resources. This resulted in the many internal crises that have erupted in the movement, weakening it from within.

As the insurgency expanded, many first-generation jihadists were killed in battle. Others tired of the endless leadership arguments that contradicted the vaunted ideas of jihadi brotherhood that drew them to the cause. Some members lost their fervor for the reformist project after facing prolonged existential vagaries in Sambisa and other forested zones in the Northeast, deciding to return to a life of relative stability and earthly piety in Nigeria's urban and rural areas rather than remain in an unpredictable life of wilderness survival. Other fighters ran afoul of strict camp regulations and, fearing deadly retribution and punishment, left the movement to try to establish new lives outside. In some cases, family members and family obligations helped convince fighters to abandon jihad to reintegrate with their families. In other cases, the failure of the promised and hoped-for overthrow of Nigeria's secular state and the delayed arrival of a theocratic state (*dawla*) caused disillusionment and desertion. Some Boko Haram members left the fight after reaching a mental breaking point as they struggled with the propriety of participating in violence against fellow Muslims.

The net result of these developments was a gradual but steady depletion of the ranks of the fighters, which created a vacuum that Boko Haram commanders, out of necessity, began to fill with teenage and child soldiers. This trend of younger fighters replacing older ones may have started as early as 2015, when the group faced what appeared to be a fatal onslaught from the Nigerian Army. Today, according to *HumAngle*, Boko Haram's fighting cadres are predominantly comprised of what the publication calls "a new demographic of teenagers."[13] Our own interviews with former Boko Haram members and Nigerian army troops unanimously corroborate this, as discussed in chapter 4. One interviewee for *HumAngle* puts the percentage of teenage and child fighters aged between ten and twenty at 80 percent,[14] a figure that is consistent with the testimonies of our own interviewees. It is not just children born or raised in the insurgency who have become soldiers; Boko Haram is reported to have intensified its recruitment of child soldiers from northeastern Nigerian communities and in camps for internally displaced persons, believing that teenagers and children are more amenable than adult recruits. In many cases, the word *recruitment* misrepresents the process that led the teenagers into Boko Haram, since many of them were abducted and forcefully conscripted under the threat of death.

This generational shift will continue to define Boko Haram's immediate future because the conditions that caused it to happen have persisted. As is discussed in greater detail below, desertion has continued even as the insurgency faces more military and socioeconomic pressures. Child fighters are far less likely to question departures from jihadi doctrinal orthodoxies or seek to upend hierarchies. As older fighters abandon the group, children and teenagers emerge as the most loyal demographic. This abiding loyalty is also a product of one fact: the younger members have little to no foothold outside of the Boko Haram bush camps, have rarely lived in Nigeria's urban and rural communities, and have only known the jihad-based filial and familial networks of Boko Haram fighters and their bush camp ethos. Moreover, teenage fighters have proved capable of sustaining and prosecuting Boko Haram's operations in the rural areas of the Northeast. The appeal and instrumentality of teenage fighters remain strong within Boko Haram, and the trend points to their growing involvement in the insurgency in the near future. Unquestioning loyalty to Boko Haram flows from necessity and the absence of outside options. There is no indication that this dynamic will change in any fundamental way over the next few years, regardless of what happens with and to the insurgency itself.

A TACTICAL SHIFT

The demographic shift toward a younger, less inhibited but less experienced and unurbanized group of fighters has occasioned a corresponding tactical shift in Boko Haram's operations that is likely to continue into the immediate future. The nexus of demography and tactics has already emerged as the latest feature of an evolving insurgency. Boko Haram has shifted discernibly from a tactic of large-scale field operations to one of carefully laid ambushes against troops and civilian vehicular convoys, although it continues to attack military targets of opportunity wherever and whenever such opportunities arise. Boko Haram had earlier moved from launching spectacular urban suicide and vehicular bombings, a shift that was also partly the result of the demographic transformation of the group. In 2024, some instances of the spectacular suicide bombing tactic of earlier years resurfaced, but they appear to have been one-offs, perhaps designed to send a message or spread fear for a finite purpose rather than to signal a major tactical shift.

In the last six years, Boko Haram has taken to laying ambushes along highways in the Northeast, attacking, robbing, killing, and abducting passengers while opportunistically destroying property and institutions affiliated with the government and with Western education, as well as institutions capable of providing logistical support to Nigerian troops. Civilian personnel affiliated with humanitarian agencies have been targeted regularly, with the most spectacular example occurring in September 2020 when the ISWAP faction of Boko Haram abducted five Borno State humanitarian workers at a roadblock that the group had set up. A week earlier, the group had ambushed an army patrol unit, leading to the death of a colonel. Several other such attacks and ambushes have occurred almost daily along the Damaturu–Maiduguri, Monguno–Maiduguri, Maiduguri–Damboa–Biu, and Maiduguri–Ngala highways, with hundreds of civilians and security personnel abducted or executed.[15]

As of the end of 2023, such opportunistic attacks and ambushes had replaced raids on communities and military camps as the dominant mode of operation of Boko Haram insurgents. Some of this shift occurred because rural communities had already been raided repeatedly and stripped of any valuable resources. Many of them had been deserted.

Raids were thus beginning to produce diminishing returns. As for raids on Nigerian army camps, improvements in air power and the abandonment of a failed policy of sheltering sentry troops in so-called supercamps diminished the success rates of such raids. The battlefield has thus changed and is still evolving.

The biggest factor that catalyzed the shift to ambushes, abductions, and highway attacks was the demographic shift analyzed earlier. As a *HumAngle* report concluded, "the [demographic transformation] is seriously impacting the terror group's strategies and effectiveness." The loss of older, experienced fighters has meant the loss of personnel who were raised in Nigeria's cities and towns and were thus familiar with them. Such fighters maintained ties and connections to cities. When this generation of fighters was preeminent in Boko Haram's fighting cadres they could establish, reestablish, or command urban cells that exploded improvised ordnance, recruit urban suicide bombers, and use their knowledge of cities to acquire logistical support for urban-based cells. Since these experienced fighters have been killed or left the battlefield, Boko Haram has lost this crucial urban asset.

Moreover, older fighters in urban spaces have been hampered by increased surveillance and by a new policy in Borno State that mandates the reporting of new tenants to the authorities. The teenagers who now dominate the ranks of the Boko Haram do not have the urban background of their predecessors and cannot survive, let alone coordinate terrorist attacks, in cities and towns. This has constrained Boko Haram's choices, leading to the transition in tactics.[16] Attacks on highways and traveling convoys serve immediate needs for the insurgents such as replenishing supplies, instilling fear in the civilian population, discouraging them from cooperating with the Nigerian military, disrupting military and humanitarian supply chains of the Nigerian government, and diverting military assets from critical field operations. Strategically, however, such attacks have little value.

This tactical evolution is likely to define the movement's immediate operational future. Even though the ISWAP faction of Boko Haram has made deliberate efforts to woo the local population and win their support, there is no evidence that the group is expanding or replenishing its membership significantly outside the natural cycle of reproduction. The implication is that the movement is likely to continue to rely on young fighters who put their youthful energies at the disposal of commanders but cannot support more complex military operations or the type of coordinated urban bombing campaigns that launched Boko Haram as an Islamist insurgency.

URBAN SLEEPER CELLS

The previous discussion is an instructive segue to a related ongoing phenomenon that will likely continue into the next few years and help shape the future of the insurgency. On September 27, 2020, the investigative journalistic consortium led by *Premium Times* and *HumAngle* published a story by Ahmad Salkida, a journalist respected for his knowledge of Boko Haram's inner workings and his access to the group's leaders and members. The story, the result of a three-month-long investigation, tracks former members of Boko Haram to major Nigerian cities where they have clandestinely reinvented themselves as artisans, laborers, and family men while retaining their allegiance to Boko Haram's core ideologies and remain embedded in the loose networks connecting active and dormant members. The former fighters are careful to reveal no hints about their prior or ongoing involvement with Boko Haram, but maintain their connections to members of the group who are still active combatants in the movement or are similarly seeking a fresh start in Nigeria's cities and towns. The reasons given for such members' desertion from Boko Haram include escape from the injustice in the group's bush camps, military operations, mental and physical fatigue, disillusionment, and family pressure. The former fighters, estimated to number more than three thousand, live in cities such as Kano, Abuja, Kaduna, Suleija, and as far south as Lagos and Ibadan. They have taken up new trades or adapted the crafts they learned in Boko Haram camps, such as welding, car repair, and metal fabrication, to civilian use in order to earn a living.[17] These former fighters continue to circulate in Nigeria outside any official surveillance and are unknown to those in charge of tracking threats. The *Premium Times'* investigation revealed a sophisticated network of former Boko Haram fighters who stay in touch, help one another evade scrutiny, and assist those leaving the group to find housing and work. Even more revealing is a critical finding in the report: The former Boko Haram fighters interviewed have not abandoned armed jihad and expressed a desire to help the cause if called upon.

Working with nongovernmental organizations, the Nigerian government has established rehabilitation and deradicalization programs for Boko Haram fighters who voluntarily surrender under its amnesty program called Operation Safe Corridor.[18] Boko Haram fighters who renounce violence under the rehabilitation program, learn a trade, and graduate are released and monitored as they integrate back into society. So far, fighters rehabilitated under this program number in the hundreds, far below the number of those who, out of distrust for the government-run program and its surveillance and out of a desire to retain allegiance to jihadist ideology, prefer to leave the group and seek a new life on their own terms in Nigerian cities and in neighboring Sahelian countries.[19] Defectors and deserters who rejected the government-sanctioned rehabilitation programs told investigators they wanted to avoid state surveillance and, more crucially, keep open the option of returning to the bush or engaging in assigned urban combat or logistical missions on behalf of Boko Haram.

In the immediate future, the defections from Boko Haram will increase and will, in turn, swell the number of unmonitored former fighters in Nigeria's cities. This heightens the risk that as Boko Haram faces more setbacks and longer odds in its struggle against the Nigerian state, it could call on and activate these cells of urban-based former fighters to carry out attacks in cities to both rattle the Nigerian state and achieve spectacular visibility for its cause. Alternatively, this cohort of former fighters could become an informal reserve unit that could rejoin former comrades in the Sahelian bush. It is impossible to determine how significant a role the increasing population of these former Boko Haram fighters will play in the future of the insurgency, but it is almost certain that those who remain fervently committed to the cause of overthrowing secular institutions and replacing them with a theocratic state will respond favorably if the Boko Haram leadership calls on them. The question is whether their response could reenergize a waning movement, let alone turn the tide in its favor.

Even if such urban cells become active and succeed in carrying out attacks in the future, such attacks may tell us more about the dwindling battlefield capabilities of Boko Haram than about their operational dexterity and reach. Thus, even as the threat of urban sleeper cells of former fighters endures into the near future, these cells' strategic value to the insurgents remains in question, and may even reveal moments of weakness in which a reliance on inactive cells as a last-gasp gambit of self-preservation becomes an unintended indicator of a diminishing insurgency. As Gilles Kepel and other scholars have observed, spectacular attacks with devastating human tolls are not necessarily indicative of a peaking Islamist insurgency and could in fact signal desperation on the part of beleaguered jihadists.[20]

JIHAD FATIGUE

One of the most debated theses regarding the global jihadist movement is Gilles Kepel's popular but controversial argument that gory atrocities that global jihadist movements commit over a period of time have the effect of turning Muslims away from the former's cause, but more crucially of creating disillusionment among the militants' own ranks. Because nihilistic violence undermines an already elusive promise of a caliphate, it causes jihad movements to atrophy even when their acts suggest that their strength is increasing.[21] Kepel argues that since violent jihadism is inherently nihilist, a jihadi movement tends to exhaust itself under the weight of its own violent contradictions—such as professing the protection of Muslim civilian lives while killing Muslim civilians deemed apostates.

Over time, the argument goes, both mental and physical fatigue and disillusionment grip the rank and file as well as potential recruits, who see no strategic profits from the unbridled violence and instead see significant theological trade-offs that cannot justify the bloodshed. Violent acts do not win more recruits to jihadism and in fact disillusion Muslim youth over the long term. Fatigue thus sets in after the initial sentimental allure of armed dissidence wears off, and atrocities that do not produce strategic successes begin to take a toll on jihadism's appeal. In the end, Kepel suggests, violent jihadist movements sink themselves and gradually lose their appeal among those whose support and membership they need in order to survive. Scholars and analysts who have critiqued Kepel's thesis point out that new jihadist frontiers emerge as old ones are closed off, and that as "new terrains and individuals emerge to incubate and cause havoc" attention has to be paid to the psychological and individual motivations of violent radicals.[22]

WILL BOKO HARAM WITHER AWAY?

In reflecting on the future of Boko Haram, it is important to do so in relation to the influential thesis of jihad fatigue. The questions that frame this reflection are: Will Boko Haram's jihad atrophy and peter out? Will the insurgency collapse as its contradictions become apparent, and with a growing rejection of its ideology and tactic by the vast majority of Muslims in Nigeria? Will the collapse of the Islamic State in the Middle East, and with it the appeal of the territorial theocratic state model, doom Boko Haram's quest for a state ruled by Sharia and a theocratic constitution? Religious insurgencies rarely have finite endpoints, whether or not they result in the establishment of a territorially defined state. In many respects, the quest for an ideal Islamic society through the instrumentality of armed or unarmed reform is a continuous process, a journey without a clear-cut destination. It is a generational struggle that fluctuates discernibly, has inflection points, and tends to recede and reemerge as new reformist impulses and ideologies emerge and coalesce. The thesis of jihad fatigue assumes a definite, linear trajectory of jihadism, one that either succeeds or atrophies because its ideological foundations lose their appeal.

Our own thesis regarding the future of Boko Haram takes off from a less-linear premise and is grounded in the idea of contingency as a critical element of historical change—the idea that the convoluted and unpredictable pursuit of change is a permanent feature of society. To this end, applying the logic of fatigue to Boko Haram imposes a rather arbitrary expectation of finality on a movement with deep historical antecedents, an insurgency that I argue is part of a long history of Muslim reform and dissidence in the region and is an escalation of a continuum of long-incubating religious upheavals. Of course, history is marked by uncertainty and unpredictability, and history-making social movements are particularly intractable, remarkable for their ability to endure, mutate, and morph over decades and centuries, all the while appearing to atrophy or attain a predetermined end goal. While useful as an analytic, the notion of jihad fatigue imposes a consistent pattern on reformist militancy that is not borne out by the history of Islamist dissidence and jihad in Northern Nigeria.

We argue that Boko Haram may in fact recede over the next few years or decades. It may exhibit signs of fatigue and lose much of its appeal and ability to generate organic local support. We are already seeing that occur, and there is no reason to assume that this trend will not continue into the remaining years of this decade. However, historical change often manifests in cyclical and dialectical forms, so that what appears to be a trend in the Boko Haram insurgency could actually be merely a phase in a longer convoluted process that may repeat itself over a long period of time, or abruptly take on a radically different character. Additionally, while we believe that the inevitable waning that plagues an insurgency that loses local support and is besieged by multiple state adversaries has set in for Boko Haram, our historical sensibility guides us toward a more somber analytical conclusion. Specifically, instead of exploring finality and endgames, we are more interested in mapping the ways in which a religious insurgency can and does reinvent itself by changing tactics and recalibrating its ideological repertoire. More crucially, we are keenly attuned to how failed social movements set the stage for future, successive, and ideologically entwined movements to emerge and thrive.

The last point about how waning movements birth new ones, even if the process is not apparent and may occur over a long period of time, bears restating in relation to Boko Haram. Boko Haram did not emerge on a historical blank slate. As I have argued in this book, it connects to and in some respects was enabled by a long, centuries-old history of armed and unarmed reform efforts. In the same way that Boko Haram emerged from and inherited the ideological assets and burdens of previous generations of reformers, it is quite possible, perhaps inevitable, that Boko Haram's demise, were it to occur from fatigue and military pressure, would prepare the ground for successor movements. This would not be an end but a mutation. Indeed, the fragmentation of Boko Haram and the emergence of splinter movements or independent jihadist movements that are self-consciously imitating the Boko Haram template bear out the prognosis of continuity. Here we pose continuity not necessarily as a counter to suggestions of finality, or what some scholars critique in another context as endism,[23] but rather to underline our conviction that an insurgency with such deep historical roots is just as likely to illustrate continuity as change and rupture. Relatedly, in this context continuity can be read literally since it is unlikely that Boko Haram will simply fizzle out along with the ideas, nostalgia, anxieties, and disillusionments that drive it. What is more likely to happen is consistent with what this book demonstrates—that once insinuated and released into the Islamic public sphere in Northern Nigeria, reformist ideas and methods tend to percolate and continue in multiple forms long after the original reform movement is believed to have ended.

Given our argument that the seminal reformist movement of the Fodiawa jihad never really ended and spawned a long history of violent and nonviolent reformist projects, we do not believe in the analytical utility of speculating on when and how the Boko Haram insurgency will end. If Boko Haram is connected to a long history of reform and dissidence in Northern Nigeria, however tenuous such a connection may be, it is logical to recognize that it too is more likely to extend this history than to end it. In this sense, we see Boko Haram as a highly disruptive interlude in a long history of armed and unarmed reformist struggle in this part of Africa.

Notes

INTRODUCTION

1. Zacharias P. Pieri and Jacob Zenn, "The Boko Haram Paradox," *African Security* 9, no. 1 (2016): 66–88, esp. 68.
2. Pieri and Zenn, "Boko Haram Paradox," 68.
3. Abdulbasit Kassim, "Old Reformers, New Dissidents: Continuity and Change in the Intellectual History of Islamic Thought, Reform and Jihad in Nigeria from the Late 18th to Early 21st Centuries" (PhD diss., Rice University, 2022).
4. Kassim, "Old Reformers, New Dissidents."
5. Muhammad Yusuf, "History of the Muslims," transcription of video lecture, trans. Abdulbasit Kassim, in *The Boko Haram Reader: From Nigerian Preachers to the Islamic State*, ed. Abdulbasit Kassim and Michael Nwankpa (Oxford University Press, 2018), 85–101.
6. For recent histories of the Sokoto Caliphate, see Paul Naylor, *From Rebels to Rulers: Writing Legitimacy in the Early Sokoto State* (James Currey, 2021); see also Stephanie Zehnle, *A Geography of Jihad: Sokoto Jihadism and the Islamic Frontier in West Africa* (De Gruyter, 2020); Kota Kariya, "ʿUthmān b. Fūdī's Sirāj al-Ikhwān: An Aspect of the Reorganization of Knowledge in Muslim West Africa," *Journal of Asian and African Studies* 107 (2024): 51–124; Kariya, "Reconsidering the Intellectual Relationship Between Muḥammad al-Maghīlī and ʿUthmān b. Fūdī: A Comparative Examination of Ajwiba and

Sirāj al-Ikhwān," *Islamic Africa* 13, no. 2 (2022): 251–82; Kariya, "*Muwālāt* and Apostasy in the Early Sokoto Caliphate," *Islamic Africa* 9, no. 2 (2018): 179–208; and Kariya, "A Revolt in the Early Sokoto Caliphate: Muḥammad Bello's *Sard al-Kalām*," *Journal of Asian and African Studies* 95 (2018): 221–303.

7. Anonymous, "The Popular Discourses of Salafi Radicalism and Salafi Counter-Radicalism in Nigeria: A Case Study of Boko Haram," *Journal of Religion in Africa* 42 (2012): 127.

8. *Fodiawa* refers to the triumvirate leaders of the Sokoto jihad, comprised of Usman Dan Fodio, his son Muhammad Bello, and his brother Abdullahi.

9. As a unit of historical study, Central Bilād al-Sūdān comprises the geographical boundaries and areas that correspond more or less to present-day Northern Nigeria, southern Niger, northern Cameroon, and western Chad. The protracted insurgency of Boko Haram that started in Northern Nigeria has since spread into other regions of Central Bilād al-Sūdān. For a definition of Central Bilād al-Sūdān in terms of geography, history, culture, language, and religion, see Muhammad A. Al-Hajj, "The Character of the Central Bilād al-Sūdān in Historical Perspective," in *The Central Bilād Al-Sūdān: Tradition and Adaptation; Essays on the Geography and Economic and Political History of the Sudanic Belt*, ed. Yūsuf Fadl Hassan and Paul Doornbos (Institute of African and Asian Studies, University of Khartoum, 1977), 14–21; and John O. Hunwick, *The Arabic Literature of Africa II: The Writings of Central Sudanic Africa* (Brill, 1995), 1–15.

10. "Osama Baby Craze Hits Nigeria," BBC, January 3, 2002, http://news.bbc.co.uk/2/hi/africa/1741171.stm.

11. Musa Umar Kazaure, "Price of bin Laden's Portraits Hikes in Kano," *Weekly Trust*, October 19–25, 2001, 6.

12. Take, for instance, the case of Muhammed Auwal Ibrahim Gombe. Gombe was a member of the Salafi establishment, preached in mainline Salafi mosques, and was associated with and mentored by Sheikh Isa Pantami. Alongside other Salafi preachers, Gombe regularly monitored Al-Jazeera and mined materials from there to craft explicitly projihad *da'awa* (preaching). He later joined the ranks of Muhamad Yusuf in Boko Haram, and after 2009 he became a founding member of Boko Haram's jihadist rival Ansaru. See Jacob Zenn, *Unmasking Boko Haram: Exploring Global Jihad in Nigeria* (Lynne Rienner, 2020), 136.

13. The most notable example is Salafi cleric Sheikh Albani Zaria, who went public with his opposition to Boko Haram and was assassinated by people believed to be members of Boko Haram.

14. *Quietist Salafism* has emerged as a term to describe the creed of Muslims who subscribe to the Salafist sectarian corpus and to its canon but shun political activism and the use of violence to accomplish political ends. They instead devote their time and energy to the pursuit of learning and piety, and to propagating the creed. Alexander Thurston's *Salafism in Nigeria: Preaching and Politics* (Cam-

bridge University Press, 2016) is an illuminating study of the emergence and evolution of quietist Salafism in Nigeria.

15. 'Uthmān b. Fūdī, *Tamyīz ahl al-Sunna*, manuscript, Melville J. Herskovits Library of African Studies, Northwestern University, NU/Hunwick/151.2/ME.

16. The most notable cases are those of the Yandoto and Kurmin Dan Ranko in Katsina. Upon Dan Fodio's bestowal of *takfīr* status on them, they were dismissed by Muhammad Bello. See Murray Last, "From Dissent to Dissidence: The Genesis & Development of Reformist Islamic Groups in Northern Nigeria," in *Sects & Social Disorder: Muslim Identities & Conflicts in Northern Nigeria*, ed. Abdul Raufu Mustapha (James Curry, imprint of Boydell and Brewer, 2014), 28–29.

17. For studies on the Fodiawa jihad and the Sokoto Caliphate, see Marilyn Robinson Waldman, "The Fulani Jihad: A Reassessment," *Journal of African History* 6, no. 3 (1965): 333–55; Murray Last, *The Sokoto Caliphate* (Longman, 1967); H. A. S. (Hugh Anthony Stephen) Johnston, *The Fulani Empire of Sokoto* (Oxford University Press, 1967); R. A. Adeleye, *Power and Diplomacy in Northern Nigeria, 1804–1906: The Sokoto Caliphate and Its Enemies* (Humanities Press, 1971); and Mervyn Hiskett, *The Sword of Truth: The Life and Times of the Shehu Usuman dan Fodio* (Northwestern University Press, 1994).

18. A. D. H. Bivar, "The Wathiqat Ahl Al-Sudan: A Manifesto of the Fulani Jihad," *Journal of African History* 2, no. 2 (1961): 235–43.

19. 'Uthmān Ibn Fūdī, *Bayān wujūb al-hijra 'alā 'l-'ibād*, trans. Fatḥī Ḥasan El-Maṣrī (Oxford University Press, 1978).

20. Jamā'at Ahl Al-Sunna Li-L-Da'Wa Wa-L-Jihād, "Application of the Rulings of Islam in the Islamic State in Africa," in Kassim and Nwankpa, *Boko Haram Reader*, 383–84.

21. Abdulbasit Kassim, "A Sermon on Colonialism," in Kassim and Nwankpa, *Boko Haram Reader*, 174. For another of Boko Haram's strategic invocations of caliphal history, see Yusuf, "History of the Muslims."

22. Ahmed Ibn Fartua. *History of the First Twelve Years of the Reign of Mai Idris Alooma of Bornu: Together with the "Diwan of the Sultans of Bornu" and "Girgam" of the Magumi*, translated from the Arabic with an introduction and notes by H. R. Palmer (Government Printer, Lagos, 1926; repr., Cass, 1970).

23. Yusuf, "History of the Muslims."

24. Pier and Zenn, "Boko Haram Paradox," 78.

25. Kyari Tijjani, "George Bush Before Al-Kanemi's Court: A Reflection on the Anglo-American Invasion of Iraq," *Daily Trust*, April 11, 2003; Sanusi Lamido Sanusi, "Al-Kanemi Before Danfodio's Court: Sultan Bello's Response to Kyari," *Daily Trust*, April 18, 2003. The second part of Sanusi's essay was published on page 6 of the newspaper's April 21 edition.

26. Scott MacEachern, *Seaching for Boko Haram: A History of Violence in Central Africa* (Oxford University Press, 2018).

27. Caitriona Dowd and Clionadh Raleigh, "The Myth of Global Islamic Terrorism and Local Conflict in Mali and the Sahel," *African Affairs* 112, no. 448 (July 2013): 504; Kyari Mohammed, "The Message and Methods of Boko Haram," in *Boko Haram: Islamism, Politics, Security and the State in Nigeria*, ed. Marc-Antoine Perouse de Montclos (IFRA-Nigeria, 2014), 9–32; Adam Higazi, "Mobilisation Into and Against Boko Haram in North-East Nigeria," in *Collective Mobilisation in Africa*, ed. Kadya Tall, Marie-Emmanuelle Pommerolle, and Michel Cahen (Brill, 2015), 305–58; Christian Seignobos, "Boko Haram and Lake Chad: An Extension or a Sanctuary?" *Afrique Contemporaine* 255, no. 3 (2015): 89–114; Kyari Mohammed, "Origins of Boko Haram," in *The Oxford Handbook of Nigerian Politics*, ed. Carl Levan and Patrick Ukata (Oxford University Press, 2018), 584–604; Brandon Kendhammer and Carmen McCain, *Boko Haram* (Ohio University Press, 2018), 25–57; Virginia Comolli, *Boko Haram: Nigeria's Islamist Insurgency* (Hurst & Company, 2017); Caroline Varin, *Boko Haram and the War on Terror* (Praeger, 2016); Hilary Matfess, *Women and the War on Boko Haram: Wives, Weapons, Witnesses* (Zed Books, 2017); James J. Hentz and Hussein Solomon, eds., *Understanding Boko Haram: Terrorism and Insurgency in Africa* (Routledge, 2018); Mike Smith, *Boko Haram: Inside Nigeria's Unholy War* (I. B. Tauris, 2016); Alexander Thurston, *Boko Haram: The History of an African Jihadist Movement* (Princeton University Press, 2017).

28. Last, "From Dissent to Dissidence," 20.

29. Last, "From Dissent to Dissidence," 20.

30. Last, "From Dissent to Dissidence," 21.

31. Last, "From Dissent to Dissidence," 30–34.

32. Marc Antoine Perouse de Montclos, "Boko Haram and 'Sahelistan' Terrorism Narratives: A Historical Perspective," *Afrique Contemporaine* 255, no. 3 (2015): 21–39; Jennifer Lofkrantz, "Intellectual Tradition, Education, and Jihad: The (Non)Parallels Between the Sokoto and Boko Haram Jihads," *Journal of West African History* 44, no. 1 (2018): 75–98; Scott MacEachern, *Searching for Boko Haram: A History of Violence in Central Africa* (Oxford University Press, 2018). Perouse de Montclos uses the careers of rebellion and conquest of nineteenth-century insurgents Rabih Fadlallah (1838–1900) and Sa'id b. Hayat (1887–1978) to critique scholars' tendency to ignore the history of religious and quasi-religious upheaval in the region and to instead exclusively connect current insurgencies to more recent and external continental and global jihadism. Lofkrantz argues that although their reformist ambitions unite the Sokoto jihad and Boko Haram's jihadi endeavor, they differ in ideology, geographical concentration, tactics, and leadership because the two movements have different ideological and intellectual inspirations. My analysis acknowledges the important differences in time, space, and ideology that Lofkrantz emphasizes, but I see both ideological and tactical parallels and convergences between the two reform-

ist movements. More importantly, my analysis recognizes the ways in which the Sokoto jihad has, more than a century later, established an ideational baseline in the popular Muslim imagination in Northern Nigeria, shaping contemporary debates on piety and how to engineer the ideal Islamic society. Instead of simply looking at Boko Haram on its own twenty-first-century terms, Scott MacEachern's work digs into five hundred years of history in the southern Lake Chad region. Relying primarily on an archaeological and anthropological investigation as well as some historical texts, MacEachern explores how Boko Haram maps onto a history of lawlessness, criminality, and sociopolitical precarity in that volatile borderland. Analyzing landscape, culture, and natural phenomena and the way they condition and constrain practices of enslavement, banditry, smuggling, warfare, and violence, MacEachern argues that understanding these deep environmental, cultural, and sociopolitical forces over the longue durée is critical to making sense of the activities of Boko Haram.

33. A notable event in this model of Islamic reform in Northern Nigeria was a conference organized by the MSSN at Bayero University, Kano, in 1980. The "International Islamic Seminar," as the conference was officially called, was convened to "discuss . . . Muslim [reformist and revolutionary] movements past and present with a view to finding common methods of formation, mobilization and strategy so that the Muslims can utilize this vast experience in their struggle to realise an Islamic change in their midst." "Kano Conference," *Radiance*, December 1980, 9.

34. "Kano Conference," 9.

35. On the value of speculative history, see John Lewis Gaddis, *The Landscape of History: How Historians Map the Past* (Oxford University Press, 2004); Paul E. Bolin, "Imagination and Speculation as Historical Impulses: Engaging Uncertainties Within Art Education History and Historiography," *Studies in Art Education* 50, no. 2 (2009): 110–123; and Frank Palmeri, "In Praise of Speculative History," *Chronicle of Higher Education—The Review*, July 10, 2016, 1–2.

36. Palmeri, "In Praise of Speculative History," 2.

CHAPTER 1. BEFORE BOKO HARAM

1. Paul Naylor, *From Rebels to Rulers: Writing Legitimacy in the Early Sokoto Caliphate* (James Currey, 2021), 6–7.

2. Naylor, *From Rebels to Rulers*, ch. 2.

3. Naylor, *From Rebels to Rulers*, 26.

4. Usman Bin Fodio, *Al-Amr bi-muwalat al-mu minin wa-al-naha an muwalat al-kafirin* [Commanding friendship with the faithful and prohibiting friendship with infidels], 1805.

5. Louis Brenner, "The Jihad Debate Between Sokoto and Borno: An Historical Analysis of Islamic Political Discourse in Nigeria," in *People and Empires in*

African History: Essays in Memory of Michael Crowder, ed. J. F. Ade Ajayi and J. D. Y. Peel (Longman, 1992), 21–43; Brenner, "Religion and Politics in Bornu: The Case of Muhammadu Al-Amin Al-Kanemi," in *Studies in West African Islamic History*, ed. J. R. Willis (Taylor and Francis, 1979), 160–76.

6. Al-Hajj Said, *Taqayid Mimma wasala ilayna*, Paris (BNF) Arabe 5422, f. 2a, cited in Naylor, *From Rebels to Rulers*, 62.

7. Usman bin Fodio, *Masa il Muhimma, f. 155a; Nasihat ahl al-zaman*.

8. Usman bin Fodio, *Nasihat ahl al-zaman*.

9. Usman bin Fodio, *Tanbih al-ikhwan*, in H. R. (Herbert Robert) Palmer, "An Early Fulani Conception of Islam (Continued)," *Journal of the Royal African Society* 14, no. 53 (1914): 53–59, esp. 53.

10. Naylor, *From Rebels to Rulers*, 65.

11. Naylor, *From Rebels to Rulers*, 79–80.

12. Naylor, *From Rebels to Rulers*, 80.

13. See Usman bin Fodio, *Siraj al-ikhwan* [The guiding light of the brethren], trans. Shaykh Muhammad Shareef bin Farid, ch. 3, https://siiasi.org/wp-content/uploads/2014/12/Siraajl-Ikhwaan-2.pdf, accessed June 2, 2025.

14. Abdullahi bin Fodio, *Diya al-sultan*.

15. Abdullahi bin Fodio, *Diya al-sultan*.

16. Abdullahi bin Fodio, *Diya al-sultan*.

17. Abdullahi bin Fodio, *Sabil al-salama fi-l-imama*, NU/Paden 244, 2, quoted in Naylor, *From Rebels to Rulers*, 97.

18. Muhammad Bello, *al-Insaf fi dhikr ma-fi masa il al-khilafa min wifaq wa-khilaf* [Fair judgment of conflicting views on questions concerning the caliphate], MSParis (BI) 206 (1817): 4–5.

19. Abdulbasit Kassim and Michael Nwankpa, "Exposé: An Open Letter to Abubakar Shekau," in *The Boko Haram Reader: From Nigerian Preachers to the Islamic State* (Oxford University Press, 2018).

20. ʿUthmān Ibn Fūdī, *Bayān wujūb al-hijra ʿalā ʾl-ʿibād*, trans. Fatḥī Ḥasan El-Maṣrī (Oxford University Press, 1978), 86–87.

21. ʿUthmān Ibn Fūdī, *Bayān wujūb al-hijra*, 117–18.

22. A. D. H. Bivar, "The Wathiqat Ahl Al-Sudan: A Manifesto of the Fulani Jihad," *Journal of African History* 2, no. 2 (1961): 240.

23. Examples of this type of rhetorical maneuver to the nineteenth-century jihad include Boko Haram leaders' references to that jihad tradition. For example, Mamman Nur describes how he and Muhammad Yusuf visited Sokoto and saw in the museum the flag that Usman Dan Fodio hoisted during his jihad. Nur stated that "our forefathers waged jihad," and lamented that the flag is now folded instead of raised (Kassim and Nwankpa, *Boko Haram Reader*, 152–53). Another instance of this nostalgic invocation of the Fodiawa jihad was the 2013 Ansaru message in which the movement, a Boko Haram offshoot and now subsidiary, called on "grandsons of ʿUthman Dan Fodio and al-Hajj ʿUmar Tall

al-Futi to 'arise'" (Kassim and Nwankpa, *Boko Haram Reader*, 277). Ansaru particularly anchored its mission on the Fodiawa legacy: "We are not killing innocent civilians. Our mission is to return the law of Allah on the earth and to reform the empire of Uthmān Dan Fodio, which was conquered by the colonialists. For this reason, jihād will not cease until the day of judgment. We will not stop until we return the law of Allah in the land and everywhere on the face of the earth by Allah's will. This is our call, and this is what we call upon the Muslims to know" (Kassim and Nwankpa, *Boko Haram Reader*, 376).

24. Abiodun Alao, *Rage and Carnage in the Name of God: Religious Violence in Nigeria* (Duke University Press, 2022); Abdul Raufu Mustapha, *Sects and Social Disorder: Muslim Identities and Conflict in Northern Nigeria* (James Currey, 2014).

25. Andrew Barnes, *Making Headway: The Introduction of Western Civilization in Colonial Northern Nigeria* (University of Rochester Press, 2009); Barnes, "Administrators and Missionaries in Northern Nigeria During the First Third of the Twentieth Century," *Journal of Religion in Africa* 25, no. 4 (1995): 412–41.

26. Barnes, "Administrators and Missionaries"; Barnes, "The Great Prohibition: The Expansion of Christianity in Colonial Northern Nigeria," *History Compass* 8, no. 6 (2010): 440–54; Emmanuel Ayandele, "The Missionary Factor in Northern Nigeria, 1870–1918," *Journal of the Historical Society of Nigeria* 3, no. 3 (1966): 503–22.

27. Niels Kastfelt, *Religion and Politics in Nigeria: A Study of Middle Belt Christianity* (I. B. Tauris, 1994); Chunun Logams, "The Middle Belt Movement in Nigerian Political Development: A Study in Political Identity, 1949–1967" (PhD diss., University of Keele, 1985); Yusufu Turaki, *Tainted Legacy: Islam, Colonialism, and Slavery in Northern Nigeria* (Isaac Publishing, 2010).

28. Alexander Thurston, "Interactions Between Northern Nigeria and the Arab World in the Twentieth Century" (MA thesis, Georgetown University, 2009), 23–36; Lynn Schlar, "The Sardauna's Middle East: Regionalism and Backstage Politics in Nigeria's Postcolonial Diplomacy," *Journal of African History* 63, no. 2 (2022): 197–213.

29. Ruth Marshall, *Political Spiritualities: The Pentecostal Revolution in Nigeria* (University of Chicago Press, 2009); Abimbola Adelakun, *Performing Power in Nigeria: Identity, Politics, and Pentecostalism* (Cambridge University Press, 2021).

30. Jibrin Ibrahim, "The Politics of Religion in Nigeria: The Parameters of the 1987 Crisis in Kaduna State," *Review of African Political Economy* 45, no. 46 (1989): 65–82, esp. 66.

31. A. H. Yadudu, "Constitution-Making and the Politicization of Sharia in Nigeria," *Journal of Islamic and Comparative Law* 18 (1991): 19–37; Philip Ostein, "An Opportunity Missed by Nigeria's Christians: The 1976–78 Sharia

Debate Revisited," in *Muslim-Christian Encounters in Africa*, ed. Benjamin F. Soares (Brill, 2006), 221–55.

32. *Report of the Constitution Drafting Committee* (Government Printer, Lagos, 1976); David D. Laitin, "The Sharia Debate and the Origins of Nigeria's Second Republic," *Journal of Modern African Studies* 20, no. 3 (1982): 411–30; Matthew Hassan Kukah, *Religion, Politics, and Power in Northern Nigeria* (Spectrum Books, 1993).

33. See, for instance, Ishaq Olanrewaju Oloyede, *Sharia Versus Secularism in Nigeria* (Islamic Publications Bureau, Lagos, 1986).

34. Philip Ostein, "Opportunity Missed."

35. Suleiman Ibrahim and Siraj Abdukarim, eds., *On the Political Future of Nigeria* (Hudahuda, 1988).

36. Ibrahim and Abdukarim, *On the Political Future of Nigeria*, 65.

37. See "History of the Muslims," a sermon by Muhammad Yusuf, and Yusuf, "Open Letter to the Nigerian Government, or Declaration of War," both in Kassim and Nwankpa, *Boko Haram Reader*, 85–102, 179–98.

38. Vincent O. Nmehielle, "Sharia Law in the Northern States of Nigeria: To Implement or Not to Implement, the Constitutionality Is the Question," *Human Rights Quarterly* 26, no. 3 (2004): 730–59; Brandon Kendhammer, "The Sharia Controversy in Northern Nigeria and the Politics of Islamic Law in New and Uncertain Democracies," *Comparative Politics* 45, no. 3 (2013): 291–311.

39. Personal communication with Mallam Ibrahim Ado Kurawa, prominent Northern Nigerian scholar of the Sokoto jihad, author, and intellectual.

40. The authors featured in the previously cited volume *On the Political Future of Nigeria* represented this MSSN alumni wing of reformist intellectuals. Dr. Ibrahim Datti Ahmed, the chairman of the Supreme Council for Sharia in Nigeria, a Sharia advocacy organization campaigning for the "full implementation" of Sharia in Nigeria, suggested that the struggle for Sharia began before independence, that the British colonizers had deceived Ahmadu Bello and other Northern Nigerian political leaders into accepting a Sharia penal code without the criminal and punitive core, and that the implementation of Sharia criminal codes by many Northern Nigerian states was a good start but that Sharia needed to be consolidated and extended to Southern Nigeria. Isyaku Dikko and Tanimu Usman, "Sardauna Was Deceived—Dr. Datti Ahmed," *Weekly Trust*, September 15–21, 2000, 1–4.

41. Abdullahi Doki, "Islamic State of Zamfara," *Weekly Trust*, October 8–14, 1999, 2.

42. Anonymous, "The Popular Discourses of Salafi Radicalism and Salafi Counter-Radicalism in Nigeria: A Case Study of Boko Haram," *Journal of Religion in Africa* 42, no. 2 (2012): 118–44.

43. A survey of the *Weekly Trust* between 2001 and 2004 shows that many letters to the editor, op-eds, and stories touched on the topic of a lost opportunity

and an incomplete reform. See, for instance, Abdullahi Doki, "Muslim North, The Caliphate and Sharia States: Re-Islamisation Uncompleted," *Weekly Trust*, August 9–15, 2003.

44. Doki, "Muslim North."
45. Alao, *Rage and Carnage*, ch. 3.
46. Alao, *Rage and Carnage*, 79.
47. Ben Adaji, "Five Killed, Houses Razed as Christians, Muslims Clash in Taraba," *P.M. News*, July 13, 2010, 9.
48. "Nigeria Unrest: Suicide Bomb Targets Church in Jos," *BBC*, February 26, 2012, www.bbc.com/news/world-africa-17169935.
49. Alao, *Rage and Carnage*, 83–87.
50. Emeka Mamah, "Boko Haram: Christian Extremist Group, Akhwat Akwop Threatens Retaliation," *Vanguard*, September 29, 2011; Emeka Umejei, Tunde Opeseitan, and Abdulkareem Haruna, "Jang, Yakowa, Nyako Back Christian Militants, Says Boko Haram," *Daily Independent*, July 28, 2011.
51. See, for instance, Yusuf, "History of the Muslims," and Yusuf, "Open Letter to the Nigerian Government," both in Kassim and Nwankpa, *Boko Haram Reader*, 85–101, 179–98.
52. "Nigeria's ThisDay Newspaper Hit by Abuja and Kaduna Blasts," *BBC*, April 26, 2012, www.bbc.com/news/world-africa-17856362.

CHAPTER 2. REFORM AND REJECTION

1. Khalifa Aliyu Ahmad Abulfathi, *The Metamorphosis of Boko Haram: A Local's Perspective* (Sheikh Aliyu Ahmad Abulfathi Foundation, 2016). For an extensive discussion of Abdulfathi's treatise, see Andrea Brigaglia, "The 'Popular Discourses of Salafi Counter-Radicalism in Nigeria' Revisited: A Response to Abdullahi Lamido's Review of Alexander Thurston, *Boko Haram*," CCI Occasional Papers 2 (March 2019): 10–23.
2. Brigaglia, "'Popular Discourses,'" 11.
3. Jonathan N. C. Hill, *Sufism in Northern Nigeria: Force for Counter-Radicalization* (Strategic Studies Institute, 2010), 1–56; Hill, "Religious Extremism in Northern Nigeria Past and Present: Parallels Between the Pseudo-Tijanis and Boko Haram," *The Round Table: The Commonwealth Journal of International Affairs* 102, no. 3 (2013): 235–44; Mark Sedgwick, "The Support of Sufism as a Counterweight to Radicalization: An Assessment," in *Countering Radicalization and Violent Extremism Among Youth to Prevent Terrorism*, ed. Marco Lombardi et al. (IOS Press, 2015), 113–19; Mark Sedgwick, "Sufis as 'Good Muslims': Sufism in the Battle Against Jihadi Salafism," in *Sufis and Salafis in the Contemporary Age*, ed. Lloyd Ridgeon (Bloomsbury Academic, 2015), 105–17; Fait Muedini, *Sponsoring Sufism: How Governments Promote*

"Mystical Islam" in Their Domestic and Foreign Policies (Palgrave Macmillan, 2015), 43–174.

4. For a parallel analysis of the different schools of thought for understanding the Boko Haram phenomenon, see Musa Ibrahim, "In Search of a Plausible Theory to Explain the Boko Haram Phenomenon: Analysis of Intellectual Discourses on Insurgency and Violent Extremism in Nigeria," *CCI Occasional Papers* 2 (March 2019): 24–35.

5. Ibrahim Zakzaky is the leader of the Shiite-oriented Islamic Movement of Nigeria. He has been in detention since the aftermath of the 2015 Zaria massacre in which hundreds of his followers were extrajudicially killed for allegedly planning an assassination attempt of Nigeria's former chief of army staff, Tukur Buratai. For studies on Shiism and the Islamic movement in Nigeria, see Muhammad Dahiru Suleiman, "Shiaism and the Islamic Movement in Nigeria, 1979–1991," in *Islam et islamismes au sud du Sahara*, ed. Ousmane Kane and Jean-Louis Triaud (Karthala, 1998), 183–95; Mukhtar U. Bunza, "The Iranian Model of Political Islamic Movement in Nigeria (1979–2002)," in *L'islam politique au sud du Sahara: Identités, discours et enjeux*, ed. Muriel Gomez-Perez (Karthala, 2005), 227–41; Kabiru Haruna Isa and Sani Y. Adam, "A History of Shia and Its Development in Nigeria: The Case-Study of Kano," *Journal for Islamic Studies* 36 (2017): 226–56; Abdullahi Lamido, "From Zakzakiya Movement to Boko Haram: The History of Muhammad Yusuf's Journey to Violent Extremism," and Salisu Shehu, "Islam, Education and Politics: A Critical Engagement with the Ideological Framings of Boko Haram," papers presented at the International Conference on the Boko Haram Phenomenon, Kano Grand Central Hotel, November 13–15, 2018.

6. Andrea Brigaglia traces the shift from endorsement, to avoidance, to rejection of the global jihad movements by the so-called "quietist Salafi" clerics, to the mix of external pressures that accompanied the War on Terror, internal politics, and gradual disavowal of the mass violence perpetrated by the global jihadi movements. Brigaglia, "'Popular Discourses,'" 13.

7. Jennifer Lofkrantz, "Intellectual Tradition, Education, and Jihad: The (Non)Parallels Between the Sokoto and Boko Haram Jihads," *Journal of West African History* 44, no. 1 (2018): 75–98.

8. Aliyu Dahiru, "Muslim Clerics Condemned Boko Haram While Praising Al-Qaeda Post 9/11 Attacks," *Humangle*, April 15, 2021, https://humanglemedia.com/muslim-clerics-condemned-boko-haram-while-praising-al-qaeda-post-9-11-attacks/.

9. "Suwaye Yan Taliban, Imam Isa Ali Ibrahim Pantami," Dawah Nigeria, https://dawahnigeria.com/dawahcast/a/34152, accessed February 6, 2019. See also Brigaglia, "'Popular Discourses.'"

10. Brigaglia, "'Popular Discourses.'"

11. For an explication of Albani's "gradualist-pragmatism," see Thomas Hegghammer, "Jihadi-Salafis or Revolutionaries?" in *Global Salafism: Islam's New*

Religious Movements, ed. Roel Meijer (Oxford University Press, 2014), 245–74, esp. 258.

12. Brigaglia, "'Popular Discourses,'" 19.

13. See a video excerpt from the debate titled "Muqabalar Dr Isa Ali Pantami da Shugaban Kungiyar Boko Haram Muhammad Yusuf" at www.youtube.com/watch?v=QuGXdE-09eg. Only one hour of the six-hour debate has survived in audiovisual form online. Recordings of the rest of the debate seem to have been lost.

14. Brigaglia, "'Popular Discourses,'" 19.

15. Brigaglia, "'Popular Discourses," 19.

16. "Osama Baby Craze Hits Nigeria," *BBC*, January 3, 2002, http://news.bbc.co.uk/2/hi/africa/1741171.stm.

17. Aliyu Dahiru, "Muslim Clerics Condemned Boko Haram."

18. Aliyu Dahiru, "Muslim Clerics Condemned Boko Haram."

19. "Sauka akan Fatawa Kukar Bakin Wake by Sheikh Aminu I Daurawa," YouTube video, www.youtube.com/watch?v=lkWUFGM_EOQ, accessed April 20, 2021.

20. "Muqabalar Dr Isa Ali Pantami da Shugaban Kungiyar Boko Haram Muhammad Yusuf." A few videos of other clerics' debates with Boko Haram founder Muhammad Yusuf are also available on YouTube.

21. Idris Ibrahim, "Boko Haram Terrorists Are Our Muslim Brothers, Shouldn't Be Killed Like Pigs: Minister Pantami," *Peoples Gazette*, April 16, 2021, www.gazettengr.com/boko-haram-terrorists-are-our-muslim-brothers-shouldnt-be-killed-like-pigs-minister-pantami/. The newspaper obtained the audio of the preaching session through an anonymous contact on April 15.

22. Thomas Hegghammer, "Jihadi-Salafis or Revolutionaries? On Religion and Politics in the Study of Militant Islamism," in *Global Salafism: Islam's New Religious Movement*, ed. Roel Meijer (Columbia University Press, 2009), 245–66.

23. Alexander Thurston, *Boko Haram: The History of an African Jihadist Movement* (Princeton University Press, 2018).

24. For an overview of the Mahdist rebellions of the early twentieth century in Northern Nigeria, see Paul E. Lovejoy and J. S. Hogendorn, "Revolutionary Mahdism and Resistance to Colonial Rule in the Sokoto Caliphate 1905–1906," *Journal of African History* 31, no. 2 (1990): 217–44.

25. Murray Last, "From Dissent to Dissidence: The Genesis and Development of Reformist Islamic Groups in Northern Nigeria," paper presented at the African History Seminar, School of Oriental and African Studies (SOAS), University of London, March 6, 2013, 2.

26. Last, "From Dissent to Dissidence," 32.

27. Ian Linden, "The Isawa Mallams c. 1850–1919: Some Problems in the Religious History of Northern Nigeria," occasional paper (Ahmadu Bello University, Zaria), 1971.

28. See Linden, "Isawa Mallams," 6, for an outline of the group's beliefs.
29. Linden, "Isawa Mallams," 6.
30. Linden, "Isawa Mallams," 12.
31. Linden, "Isawa Mallams," 7.
32. Testimony of Mallam Idi of Kano, reproduced in Linden, "Isawa Mallams," 13-14.
33. Linden, "Isawa Mallams," 8. See also National Archives Kaduna (NAK)/SNP Confidential Memo 106/1914 to Zaria resident, February 3, 1914.
34. Linden, "Isawa Mallams," 11.
35. Ibrahim A. Sambo, *Tarikh 'Umara Bauchi* [History of the emirs of Bauchi] (self-published, 1902, 1957), 161-63. This is an Arabic chronicle narrating the postjihad history of Bauchi Emirate, its relations within the Sokoto Caliphate, and its military campaigns (the text calls them jihad) in several non-Muslim areas around its vicinity. The text has been translated into English by Adell Patton Jr. in his article "Tarikh 'Umara Bauchi and Its Contribution to Pre-Colonial Ningi Resistance to Sokoto Caliphate: Exegesis and Methodology in African Oral History, ca. 1846-1902," *A Current Bibliography on African Affairs* 18, no. 2 (1986): 105-16.
36. Linden, "Isawa Mallams," 18.
37. Sambo, *Tarikh 'Umara Bauchi*, Arabic version, 2-3.
38. Patton, "Tarikh 'Umara Bauchi," 110.
39. NAK/SNP 10/2 431p/1914, J. F. J. Fitzpatrick, "Assessment Report on Ningi District," August 15, 1914.
40. Sambo, *Tarikh 'Umara Bauchi*, Arabic version, 168.
41. Much of the *Tarikh 'Umara Bauchi* tradition narrates the decades-long military confrontations between the Isawa/Ningawa rebels and the Bauchi Emirate.
42. Linden, "Isawa Mallams," 21.
43. *Tarikh 'Umara Bauchi*, 172.
44. Mervyn Hiskett, *The Sword of Truth: The Life and Times of Shehu Usuman Dan Fodio* (Oxford University Press, 1973), 163-64.
45. Beverly B. Mack and Jean Boyd, *One Woman's Jihad: Nana Asma'u, Scholar and Scribe* (Indiana University Press, 2000); Mack and Boyd, *Educating Muslim Women: The West African Legacy of Nana Asma'u, 1793-1864* (Kube Publishing, 2013); Mack, *Equals in Learning and Piety: Muslim Women Scholars in Nigeria and North America* (University of Wisconsin Press, 2023).
46. "The 'Impulse of Curiosity': Hugh Clapperton's Explorations into the African Interior," Devon & Exeter Institution, https://devonandexeterinstitution.org/the-impulse-of-curiosity-hugh-claperttons-explorations-into-the-african-interior/, accessed June 5, 2024.
47. Hugh Clapperton, *Journal of Second Expedition into the Interior of Africa, from the Bight of Benin to Soccatoo* (John Murray, 1829), 294.

48. Paul E. Lovejoy, *The Bello-Clapperton Exchange: The Sokoto Jihad and the Transatlantic Slave Trade* (Lynne Rienner, 2001), 212–14.

49. Last, "From Dissent to Dissidence," 18. See also the poem "Nūniyya," which urged Muslims to return to the true faith of "our Prophet and His Book" and stand firm so that Allah "will support us against oppression." The poem is published in Muhammad S. Umar, *Islam and Colonialism: Intellectual Responses of Muslims of Northern Nigeria to British Colonial Rule* (Brill, 2006), 174.

50. Last, "From Dissent to Dissidence," 19.

51. Sheikh Abubakar Gumi and Ismaila Abubakar Tsiga, *Where I Stand* (Spectrum Books, 1992).

52. Gumi and Tsiga, *Where I Stand*, 136.

53. Gumi and Tsiga, *Where I Stand*, 90.

54. Gumi and Tsiga, *Where I Stand*, 93–96.

55. Gumi and Tsiga, *Where I Stand*, 104.

56. Gumi and Tsiga, *Where I Stand*, 107.

57. For an exploration of this value imperative across multiple Islamic ages and contexts, see Michael Cook, *Commanding Right and Forbidding Wrong in Islamic Thought* (Cambridge University Press, 2000). The book explores the didactic Islamic injunction and value system that enjoins Muslims to chastise those violating Allah's laws through their acts or negligence, and to forbid wrongdoing.

58. Farooq Adamu, "The Sarkin Karuwai Controversy in Kano," *Weekly Trust*, October 23–29, 1998, 8.

59. Adamu, "Sarkin Karuwai Controversy."

60. Zainab Taiwo Musa, "Death Threat on Filmmaker," *Weekly Trust*, November 5–11, 1999, 40.

61. Musa, "Death Threat on Filmmaker."

62. Naziru Suleiman, "Hausa Films and Moral Degeneration," *Weekly Trust*, January 14–20, 2000, 16.

63. Suleiman, "Hausa Films."

64. Hassan A. Karofi, "Sharia Protesters Clash with Performing Artistes in Katsina," *Weekly Trust*, July 27–August 2, 2001, 7.

65. For a brief biography and career of Shaykh Yakubu Musa, including how he earned his moniker "Yakubu Musa Kafanchan" and hosted Hassan Allane of the Algerian GIA in 1994, see Jacob Zenn, *Unmasking Boko Haram: Exploring Global Jihad in Nigeria* (Lynne Rienner, 2020), 32–34.

66. Karofi, "Sharia Protesters Clash."

67. Novian Whitsitt, "Hausa Women Writers Confronting the Traditional Status of Women in Modern Islamic Society: Feminist Thought in Nigerian Popular Fiction," *Tulsa Studies in Women's Literature* 22, no. 2 (2003): 387–408.

68. Whitsitt, "Hausa Women Writers," 388.

69. Danjuma Katsina, "Death to the Soyayya Novel," *New Nigerian Weekly*, September 5, 1998, 5.

70. Ahmed Mansur, "Re: The 'Best' Hausa Books 1998," *New Nigerian Weekly*, December 19, 1998, 15.

71. Abadalla Uba Adamu, "Hausa Literary Expression in the Decade of the 1990s: A Further Contribution to the Soyayya Genre Debate, Part I," *New Nigerian Weekly*, April 24, 1999; Adamu, "Hausa Literary Expression in the Decade of the 1990s: A Further Contribution to the Soyayya Genre Debate, Part II," *New Nigerian Weekly*, May 1, 1999.

72. In 2001 the Kano State government set up a censorship board to scrutinize stories for content that breached existing and emergent moral taboos. In 2007 the government intensified the censorship regime, tightening the rules and making a public spectacle of burning some banned titles. Laura Mallonee, "The Subversive Women Who Self-Publish Novels Amidst Jihadist War," *Wired*, February 17, 2016, www.wired.com/2016/02/glenna-gordon-diagram-heart/; Thomas Page, "Beyond Heartache and Boko Haram: Nigerian Women Prove Love Is Universal," *CNN*, February 9, 2018, www.cnn.com/2016/02/15/africa/nigeria-love-literature.

73. Adamu, "Hausa Literary Expression," parts 1 and 2.

74. Sheikh Abubakar Mahmud Gumi, *Al-Akudatus Sahihat Bi Muwafakatus Shariah*, trans. Imam Ahmad Adam Kutubi and Ahmad Garba (self-published, n.d.), 33.

75. Gumi, *Al-Akudatus Sahihat*, 34.

76. Michael Watts, *Silent Violence: Food, Famine, and Peasantry in Northern Nigeria* (1983; University of Georgia Press, 2013).

77. Paul Lubeck, "Protest Under Semi-Industrial Capitalism: 'Yan Tatsine Explained," *Africa: Journal of the International African Institute* 55, no. 4, Special Issue on Popular Islam (1985): 369–89.

78. Paul Lubeck, *Islam and Urban Labor in Northern Nigeria* (Cambridge University Press, 1987).

79. Lubeck, "Protest Under Semi-Industrial Capitalism," 372.

80. Lubeck, "Protest Under Semi-Industrial Capitalism," 371.

81. Murray Last, "The Search for Muslim Security in Northern Nigeria," *Africa: Journal of the International African Institute* 78, no. 1 (2008): 41–63.

82. Last, "Search for Muslim Security."

83. Last, "Search for Muslim Security," 46.

84. Last, "Search for Muslim Security," 41.

CHAPTER 3. BOKO HARAM'S ANTIMODERNISM HISTORICIZED

1. Ishaku Aliyu, "Aspects of Political Administration in Sokoto Caliphate with Special Reference to Diya Al-Sultan of Abdullahi Ibn Fodiyo," in *State and Soci-*

ety in the Sokoto Caliphate, ed. Ahmad Muhammad Kani and Kabir Ahmed Gandi (Usmanu Danfodio University, 1990), 63–75.

2. Aliyu, "Aspects of Political Administration," 72.

3. 'Abd Allāh b. Fūdī, *Maṣaliḥ al-insān al-muta'alliqa bi-l-adyan wa-l-'abdan*, MS Folio 34, Waziri Junaidu History and Culture Bureau.

4. Muḥammad Bello, *Talkhīs aṭ-ṭibb al-nabawī*, MS Folio 4, Waziri Junaidu History and Culture Bureau.

5. Mercedes Garcia-Arenal, "Imam et Mahdi: Ibn Abî Mahallî," in *Revue des mondes musulmans et de la Méditerranée*, 2000, 157–80, translation in English, in Mercedes Garcia-Arenal, *Messianism and Puritanical Reform: Mahdīs of the Muslim West* (Brill, 2006). Abî Mahallî is known for his seventeenth-century rebellion against the Sa'adian rulers of Morocco due to his accusation that they had fallen into innovations and had not sufficiently resisted the influences of Europeans.

6. Muhammad Ahmad Al-Hajj, "The Mahdist Tradition in Northern Nigeria" (PhD diss., Ahmadu Bello University Zaria, 1973); Paul E. Lovejoy and J. S. Hogendorn, "Revolutionary Mahdism and Resistance to Colonial Rule in the Sokoto Caliphate, 1905–1906," *Journal of African History* 31, no. 2 (1990): 217–44.

7. R. A. Adeleye, "Mahdist Triumph and British Revenge in Northern Nigeria: Satiru 1906," *Journal of the Historical Society of Nigeria* 6, no. 2 (June 1972): 193–214.

8. Muhammad S. Umar, *Islam and Colonialism: Intellectual Responses of Muslims of Northern Nigeria to British Colonial Rule* (Brill, 2006), 6.

9. Umar, *Islam and Colonialism*, 67.

10. Scholarly accounts of the military conquest of the British Sokoto Caliphate include D. J. M. Muffett, *Concerning Brave Captains: Being a History of the British Occupation of Kano and Sokoto and of the Last Stand of the Fulani Forces* (Andre Deutsch, 1964); R. A. Adeleye, *Power and Diplomacy in Northern Nigeria, 1804–1906: The Sokoto Caliphate and Its Enemies* (Humanities Press, 1971), 288–313; and Obaro Ikime, *Fall of Nigeria: The British Conquest* (Heinemann, 1977). A detailed account of the events and months following the British conquest of Sokoto and terminating with the final showdown at Burmi is chronicled in H. A. S. Johnston, *The Fulani Empire of Sokoto* (Oxford University Press, 1967); see the epilogue in particular.

11. Umar, *Islam and Colonialism*, 80–88.

12. Umar, *Islam and Colonialism*, 89–96.

13. Umar, *Islam and Colonialism*, 96–102.

14. James P. Hubbard, *Education Under Colonial Rule: A History of Katsina College, 1921–1942* (University Press of America, 2000).

15. For the history of colonial education policy in Northern Nigeria, see Sonia F. Graham, *Government and Mission Education in Northern Nigeria*,

1900–1919: With Special Reference to the Work of Hanns Vischer (Ibadan University Press, 1966); Albert F. Ogunsola, *Legislation and Education in Northern Nigeria* (Oxford University Press, 1974); Albert Ozigi and Lawrence Ocho, *Education in Northern Nigeria* (Allen and Unwin, 1981); Peter Kazenga Tibenderana, "The Emirs and the Spread of Western Education in Northern Nigeria, 1910–1946," *Journal of African History* 24, no. 4 (1983): 517–34; and Tibenderana, "The Beginnings of Girls' Education in the Native Administration Schools in Northern Nigeria, 1930–1945," *Journal of African History* 26, no. 1 (1985): 93–109.

16. "Miller, Walter Richard Samuel," *Dictionary of African Christian Biography*, Classic Collection, https://dacb.org/stories/nigeria/miller-wr-samuel/.

17. NNAK/SNP, Kadmineduc, August 10, 1937, from Kaduna to residents. While the sultan, the shehu of Borno, and the emirs of Kano and Gwandu supported the proposal, those of Adamawa, Katsina, and Ilorin opposed the idea of a new, exclusive middle school for princes and children of the nobility and instead wanted an inclusive school open to children from all strata of society.

18. Aliyu Tilde, "We Are Boko Haram: A Search into the Cultural Origins of Boko Haram in Nigeria," *Discourse with Dr. Tilde*, August 11, 2009, https://aliyuutilde.wordpress.com/2010/05/13/discourse-261-we-are-boko-haram/.

19. CMS/ACC/237: *Papers of Walter Richard Samuel Miller*, University of Birmingham Cadbury Research Library, Church Mission Society Unofficial Papers 1290–2017; Walter S. Miller, *Walter Miller 1872–1952, An Autobiography* (Gaskiya Corporation, Zaria, 1953); *Walter Miller, Yesterday and Tomorrow in Northern Nigeria* (Student Christian Movement Press, London, 1938); Graham, *Government and Mission Education*.

20. Tibenderana, "Emirs and the Spread of Western Education," 525–28.

21. The most famous of these emir–missionary spats occurred between Rev. Walter Miller and Emir Abbas.

22. Tibenderana, "Emirs and the Spread of Western Education," 526.

23. Tibenderana, "Emirs and the Spread of Western Education," 532. Emirs in Northern Nigeria protested the ten-year educational development proposals of 1943 when they did not include the teaching of English in elementary schools, essentially retaining the status quo of vernacular instruction.

24. For a discussion of the British colonial obsession with Hausa (written in Romanized script) as both a language of educational instruction and colonial administration, see John Edward Philips, *Spurious Arabic: Hausa and Colonial Nigeria* (University of Wisconsin Press, 2000).

25. The most famous example was Shaykh Abubakar Gumi who, at the beginning of his clerical career and along with his fellow reformist clerics, was frequently derided by established Sufi clerics for being associated with *zamani* and *boko*.

26. Tilde, "We Are Boko Haram."

27. Tilde, "We Are Boko Haram."

28. For a discussion of the work, see Holger Weiss, *Between Accommodation and Revivalism: Muslims, the State, and Society in Ghana from Precolonial to the Postcolonial Era* (Finnish Oriental Society, Studia Orientalia 105, 2008), 161–62. See also B. W. Andrzejewski, S. Pitoszewicz, and W. Tyloch, eds., *Literatures in African Languages: Theoretical Issues and Sample Surveys* (Cambridge University Press, 2010), 207–8.

29. For a discussion of the poem, see Umar, *Islam and Colonialism*, 74–80. The poem was first published in Bello Sa'id, "Gundummahwar Masu Jihadi Kan Adabin Hausa" (MA thesis, Bayero University, Kano, 1978), 443–47. The poem was also published in Mervyn Hiskett, *The Development of Islam in West Africa* (Longman, 1984), 269–71, and appears in Isa A. Abba and P. J. Shea, "Decision to Flee at the Time of the British Conquest of the Sakkwato Caliphate," paper presented at the International Seminar on the Impact of Colonialism on Islamic Education in the Sokoto Caliphate and Other Institutions During the Period 1903–1960 (University of Sokoto, June 1988), 22–27.

30. Umar, *Islam and Colonialism*, 175–76.

31. For more antimodern, anticolonial Hausa poetry and songs, see Sambo Junaidu, "Resistance to Western Culture in the Sakwato Caliphate: A Lesson to Generations Yet Unborn," in *State and Society in the Sokoto Caliphate*, ed. Ahmad Muhammad Kani and Kabir Ahmed Gandi (Usmanu Danfodio University, 1990), 238–52.

32. Mervyn Hiskett, *The Sword of Truth: The Life and Times of Shehu Usuman Dan Fodio* (Oxford University Press, 1973), 164–65.

33. For these allusions in Yusuf's recorded sermons, see Abdulbasit Kassim and Michael Nwankpa, *The Boko Haram Reader: From Nigerian Preachers to the Islamic State* (Oxford University Press, 2018), 85–102.

34. Junaidu, "Resistance to Western Culture," 245.

35. Junaidu, "Resistance to Western Culture," 246.

36. Junaidu, "Resistance to Western Culture," 246.

37. Junaidu, "Resistance to Western Culture," 247.

38. Junaidu, "Resistance to Western Culture," 247.

39. Northern Nigerian Muslims were not the only ones debating the appropriate relationship between Muslims and modern technologies and goods. Such debates were occurring all over the Islamic world including in North Africa, where Muslims were writing to clerics and asking for guidance and fatwas on specific engagements with a variety of modern goods and institutions. Leor Halevi, *Modern Things on Trial: Islam's Global and Material Reformation in the Age of Rida, 1865–1935* (Columbia University Press, 2019).

40. John N. Paden, *Religion and Political Culture in Kano* (University of California Press, 1973), 132–33.

41. Quoted in Paden, *Religion and Political Culture*, 133.

42. Paden, *Religion and Political Culture*, 162.
43. Paden, *Religion and Political Culture*, 163.
44. Anonymous, "The Popular Discourses of Salafi Radicalism and Counter-Radicalism in Nigeria: A Case Study of Boko Haram," *Journal of Religion in Africa* 42, no. 2 (2012): 121.
45. Jacob Zenn, *Unmasking Boko Haram: Exploring Global Jihad in Nigeria* (Lynne Rienner, 2020), 214.
46. Shekau, for instance, famously declared that Muslims could lawfully adopt the use of guns, communication technologies, and other inventions emanating from modern science and Western education in furtherance of both jihad and *da'wa*. Kassim and Nwankpa, *Boko Haram Reader*, 128.
47. The name Maitatsine came from a phrase Marwa used frequently in his preaching. In his Fula-accented Hausa, he would say "Allah *tatsine*" (Allah curses). *Maitatsine* means the one who says or is known for *tatsine*. The correct Hausa expression is *Allah ya tsine*. He said this often to condemn people, practices, or objects he considered impure. The name was both a theological and linguistic mockery of Marwa.
48. Tilde, "We Are Boko Haram."
49. Paul Lubeck, "Islamic Protest Under Semi-Industrial Capitalism: 'Yan Tatsine Explained," *Africa: Journal of the International Africa Institute* 55, no. 4, Special Issue on Popular Islam (1985): 369–89; I. L. Bashir, "Classism Conflict and Socio-Economic Transition in a Changing Society: A Case Study of Kano's Oligarchy," University of Sokoto History Seminar, April 1983.
50. Mervyn Hiskett, "The Maitatsine Riots in Kano, 1980: An Assessment," *Journal of Religion in Africa* 17, no. 3 (October 1987): 209–23. This is Hiskett's argument. He contends that the nonmembership of this unlettered population of urban poor in the religious orthodoxy of the times—indeed, their distance from it—made them receptive to Maitatsine's heterodox theology.
51. Hiskett, "Maitatsine Riots," 218.
52. Hiskett, "Maitatsine Riots," 219.
53. Hiskett, "Maitatsine Riots," 219.
54. Hiskett, "Maitatsine Riots," 219.
55. See Kassim and Nwankpa, *Boko Haram Reader*, 12–18.
56. Kassim and Nwankpa, *Boko Haram Reader*, 12–18.
57. See Kassim and Nwankpa, *Boko Haram Reader*, 117–29.
58. See Kassim and Nwankpa, *Boko Haram Reader*, 215–19.
59. Kassim and Nwankpa, *Boko Haram Reader*, 118.
60. The translations are mine.
61. See Pierre Bourdieu, *Outline of a Theory of Practice* (Cambridge University Press, 1977).
62. Tibenderana, "Emirs and the Spread of Western Education," 523–28. Several emirs had non-Muslim areas in their domains and saw no reason to prevent

missionary and government educational institutions from being established among such non-Muslim people. Others eagerly courted the establishment of government schools in their emirates. In the case of the emir of Zaria, Kwasau, after initially opposing the establishment of a Church Missionary Society (CMS) Anglican mission in Zaria at the turn of the century, he relented in 1901 after British troops sent to extend British rule to Hausaland helped him defeat the emir of Kontagora, Nagwamatse, and helped him secure his throne, although subsuming his sovereignty in the process. Kwasau rewarded the British officers, some of whom were connected to Rev. Walter Miller, leader of the CMS mission, by allowing CMS to establish a mission station, a school, and a dispensary in Zaria. See "Miller, Walter Richard Samuel," *Dictionary of African Christian Biographies*, https://dacb.org/stories/nigeria/miller-wr-samuel/.

63. See Shobana Shankar, *Who Shall Enter Paradise? Christian Origins in Muslim Northern Nigeria, 1890–1975* (Ohio University Press, 2014), for a comprehensive discussion of missionary activities in the emirates, especially their work with marginal groups in Hausa Muslim society.

64. Nuhu Muhammadu Bayero, *My Life* (University of Lagos Press, 1990).

65. Bayero, *My Life*, 7.

66. Kassim and Nwankpa, *Boko Haram Reader*, 119, 121.

67. Kassim and Nwankpa, *Boko Haram Reader*, 217.

68. Kassim and Nwankpa, *Boko Haram Reader*, 127.

69. Kassim and Nwankpa, *Boko Haram Reader*, 127.

70. Kassim and Nwankpa, *Boko Haram Reader*, 128.

71. See chapter 1 of this book.

72. Halilu Musa, "Conventional Insurance Is Haram in Islam," *Weekly Trust* April 7, 2001.

73. "Insurance Is Not Against Islam—NCRIB President," *Weekly Trust*, April 7, 2001.

CHAPTER 4. COMBAT, CAPTIVES, AND COPING

1. Murray Last, "Slavery or Death in Sokoto and Borno: Tactics, Legalities and Sources," in *Landscape, Sources, and Intellectual Projects: Politics, History, and the West African Past*, ed. Toby Green and Benedetta Rossi (Brill, 2018), 422–42.

2. Last, "Slavery or Death," 422.

3. Last, "Slavery or Death," 428.

4. Mervyn Hiskett, *The Sword of Truth: The Life and Times of Shehu Usuman Dan Fodio* (Oxford University Press, 1973), 87.

5. "Jas vs. ISWAP: The War of the Boko Haram Splinters," Crisis Group Africa Briefing no. 196 (March 28, 2024), 2.

6. "Jas vs. ISWAP," 3. For a comprehensive discussion of the extent and impact of JAS's predatory raids on farming and pastoral communities in northeastern Nigeria, see Adam Higazi, "Boko Haram: The Impact of Insurgency on Pastorialists and Farmers," *Afrique Comtemporaine* 22, no. 274 (2022): 163–69.

7. Edward Stoddard, "Competitive Control? 'Hearts and Minds' and the Population Control Strategy of the Islamic State West Africa Province," *African Security* 16, no. 1 (2023): 32–60.

8. ISWAP's ongoing outreach to the civilian population of the Nigerian Northeast now involves preaching and persuasion sessions, and the distribution of foodstuffs. "ISWAP Terror Group Holds Public Meetings with Borno Residents to Recruit New Members, Stresses Plan to Have Separate Islamic Country," *Sahara Reporters*, June 9, 2024, https://saharareporters.com/2024/06/09/iswap-terror-group-holds-public-meetings-borno-residents-recruit-new-members-stresses#google_vignette.

9. Last, "Slavery or Death," 425.

10. Joseph Smaldone, *Warfare in the Sokoto Caliphate: Historical and Sociological Perspectives* (Cambridge University Press, 1977), 24.

11. Smaldone, *Warfare*, 77–78.

12. Voice of America, "Boko Haram Part 2: Anatomy of an Attack," www.youtube.com/watch?v=yI1Bu9PhaUA&t=300s, accessed February 10, 2020.

13. Smaldone, *Warfare*, 83.

14. Adamu (pseudonym), a soldier, interview by the author, May 20, 2024.

15. Smaldone, *Warfare*, 78.

16. Muhammad Bello, *The Rise of the Sokoto Fulani: Being a Paraphrase and in Some Parts a Translation of the Infaku'l Maisuri of Sultan Mohammed Bello*, trans. Edward John Arnett (Emirate Printing, Kano, 1922), 56–57.

17. Battlefield videos disseminated by Boko Haram as part of their propaganda bear out this phenomenon.

18. Smaldone, *Warfare*, 84–85.

19. Smalldone, *Warfare*, 82–89; Murray Last, personal communication.

20. Last, personal communication.

21. As per this soldier's preference, the author has chosen to identify this soldier with the pseudonym Adamu.

22. Adamu interview.

23. Adamu interview.

24. Interviews with deployed soldiers and "repentant" Boko Haram fighters. The term "repentant Boko Haram" is a coinage of the Nigerian military, which uses it to designate Boko Haram fighters who surrender to the military and undergo its deradicalization program.

25. John Edward Philips, "Ribats in the Sokoto Caliphate, 1804–1903" (PhD diss., University of California–Los Angeles, 1992), 223–26. All members of the

Fodiawa triumvirate wrote treatises on the importance of *ribats*, as documented by Philips.

26. Philips, "Ribats in the Sokoto Caliphate," 225.
27. Philips, "Ribats in the Sokoto Caliphate," 412.
28. Abdulbasit Kassim and Michael Nwankpa, *The Boko Haram Reader: From Nigerian Preachers to the Islamic State* (Oxford University Press, 2018), 169.
29. Smaldone, *Warfare*, 79.
30. Philips, "Ribats in the Sokoto Caliphate," 418.
31. The present author conducted these interviews in May 2024 in Maiduguri, Bama, Konduga, and Monguno, and other parts of the Borno–Yobe axis of the Nigerian Northeast.
32. Interviews with Nigerian soldiers and former Boko Haram fighters.
33. Interviews with deployed Nigerian Army soldiers.
34. Interviews with "repentant Boko Haram fighters."
35. Everest65, "Resurgent: The Weapons of IS West Africa," *Calibre Obscura*, January 20, 2019, www.calibreobscura.com/the-weaponary-of-is-west-africa-boko-haram/.
36. Ahmad Salkida, "Inside the War Front: Nigerian Military Take Out Boko Haram Bases," *HumAngle*, May 11, 2020, https://humanglemedia.com/inside-the-war-front-nigerian-military-take-out-major-boko-haram-bases/. Also see Salkida, "Boko Haram Sustains Operations Through International Trade in Smoked Fish," *Premium Times*, April 26, 2020, www.premiumtimesng.com/news/headlines/389916-how-boko-haram-sustain-operations-through-international-trade-in-smoked-fish.html.
37. Interviews with "repentant Boko Haram fighters."
38. John Edward Philips, relying on accounts by Heinrich Barth and Hugh Clapperton and other sources, notes the mobilization of women as part of a large auxiliary army that accompanied the main fighting force to battle, and remained on the front lines to perform a variety of logistical and even combat tasks. Philips, "Ribats in the Sokoto Caliphate," 418.
39. Philips, "Ribats in the Sokoto Caliphate," 422.
40. Philips, "Ribats in the Sokoto Caliphate," 422–23.
41. These are revealed in my interviews with Nigerian Army soldiers and "repentant Boko Haram fighters."
42. Interviews with Nigerian Army soldiers and "repentant Boko Haram fighters."
43. Smaldone, *Warfare*, 91–93.
44. Smaldone, *Warfare*, 91–93.
45. Smaldone, *Warfare*, 92.
46. "Exposé: Open Letter to Abubakar Shekau by Mamman Nur," in Kassim and Nwankpa, *Boko Haram Reader*, 445–66, esp. 457–58.
47. "Exposé."

48. Abdulbasit Kassim, "Boko Haram's Internal Civil War: Stealth Takfir and Jihad as Recipes for Schism," in *Boko Haram Beyond the Headlines: Analyses of Africa's Enduring Insurgency*, ed. Jacob Zenn (Combating Terrorism Center, West Point, NY, 2018), 3–32.

49. "Shekau Responds to His Critics," in Kassim and Nwankpa, *Boko Haram Reader*, 471–80.

50. Hiskett, *Sword of Truth*, 106.

51. Hiskett, *Sword of Truth*, 106.

52. Gilles Kepel, "'There Is Jihad Fatigue,' Says Islamist Terrorism Expert," *BBC*, May 25, 2017, www.bbc.com/news/av/world-middle-east-40043212. Kepel argues that contemporary jihadism tends to fragment under the weight of internal ideological disputes, accusations and counteraccusations, and mutual recriminations over moral conduct. According to him, when jihadists fail to accomplish their ambitious external objectives they increasingly turn their rejectionist ire inward within their groups, which leads to internal schisms, rebellions, and disillusionment.

53. "Exposé," 463.

54. Ngala Killian Chimtom, Jason Hanna, and Michael Martinez, "Freed German Hostage Calls Boko Haram Captivity Total Darkness," *CNN*, January 21, 2015, www.cnn.com/2015/01/21/world/cameroon-boko-haram-german-hostage/index.html.

55. Joe Parkinson and Drew Hinshaw, "Freedom for the World's Most Famous Hostages Came at a Heavy Price," *Wall Street Journal*, May 6, 2017, www.wsj.com/articles/two-bags-of-cash-for-boko-haram-the-untold-story-of-how-nigeria-freed-its-kidnapped-girls-1513957354. The newspaper reports that some of the Chibok schoolgirls were released in exchange for a three million Euro ransom.

56. In his lecture, Muhammad Yusuf said, "When you set out to fight jihād, you should treat each and every one in the theater of war as enemies of Allah. The way you loathe the sight of a pig is the same way you should loathe the sight of their women. If you hold back and sexually admire their women, then you should be prepared for a catastrophe. I hope it is understood. How would you set out to fight jihād and sexually admire their women at the same time? Their women should be treated as properties and spoils of war." This is a revised translation of Muhammad Yusuf's exegesis of *Sūrat al-'imrān* (Qur'an 3: 165–75); see Kassim and Nwankpa, *Boko Haram Reader*, 66.

57. David Tambo, "The Sokoto Caliphate Slave Trade in the Nineteenth Century," *International Journal of African Historical Studies* 9, no. 2 (1976): 187–217; Ann O'Hear, *Power Relations in Nigeria: Ilorin Slaves and Their Successors* (University of Rochester Press, 1997); John E. Philips, "The Persistence of Slave Officials in Sokoto Caliphate," in *Slave Elites in the Middle East and Africa: A Comparative Study*, ed. Miura Toru and John Edward Philips (Kegan Paul Inter-

national, 2000), 215–34; Philips, "Slavery on Two Ribats in Kano and Sokoto," in *Slavery on the Frontiers of Islam*, ed. Paul E. Lovejoy (Markus Wiener Publishers, 2003), 111–24; Paul E. Lovejoy, *Slavery, Commerce and Production in the Sokoto Caliphate of West Africa* (Africa World Press, 2005); Ojo Olatunji, "Islam, Ethnicity and Slave Agitation: Hausa 'Mamluks' in Nineteenth Century Yorubaland," in *Slavery, Islam and Diaspora*, ed. Behnaz A. Mizrai, Ismael Montana, and Paul E. Lovejoy (Africa World Press, 2009), 103–24; Mohammed Bashir Salau, *The West African Slave Plantation: A Case Study* (Palgrave Macmillan, 2011); Jennifer Lofkrantz, "Ransoming of Captives in the Sokoto Caliphate in the Nineteenth Century," in Mizrai et al., *Slavery, Islam and Diaspora*, 125–37; Lofkrantz, "Protecting Freeborn Muslims: The Sokoto Caliphate's Attempts to Prevent Illegal Enslavement and Its Acceptance of the Strategy of Ransoming," *Slavery and Abolition* 32, no. 1 (2011): 109–27; Lofkrantz, "Intellectual Discourse in the Early Sokoto Caliphate: The Triumvirate's Opinions on the Issue of Ransoming, c. 1810," *International Journal of African Historical Studies* 45, no. 3 (2012): 385–401; Lovejoy, "Concubinage in the Sokoto Caliphate (1804–1903)," *Slavery and Abolition* 11 (1990): 159–89; Heidi J. Nast, *Concubines and Power: Five Hundred Years in a Northern Nigerian Palace* (University of Minnesota Press, 2005); Sean Stilwell, "'Amana' and 'Asiri': Royal Slave Culture and the Colonial Regime in Kano, 1903–1926," *Slavery and Abolition* 19, no. 2 (1998): 167–88; Stilwell, "Power, Honour and Shame: The Ideology of Royal Slavery in the Sokoto Caliphate," *Africa* 70, no. 3 (2000): 394–421; Stilwell, "The Power of Knowledge and the Knowledge of Power: Kinship, Community and Royal Slavery in Pre-Colonial Kano, 1807–1903," in Toru and Philips, *Slave Elites in the Middle East and Africa*, 81–98; Stilwell, *Paradoxes of Power: The Kano "Mamluks" and Male Royal Slavery in the Sokoto Caliphate, 1804–1903* (Heinemann, 2004); Lovejoy, "Fugitive Slaves: Resistance to Slavery in the Sokoto Caliphate," in *In Resistance: Studies in African, Afro-American, and Caribbean History*, ed. Gary Okihiro (University of Massachusetts Press, 1986), 71–95; Paul E. Lovejoy and Jan S. Hogendorn, *Slow Death for Slavery: The Course of Abolition in Northern Nigeria, 1897–1936* (Cambridge University Press, 1993).

58. Melchisedek Chétima, Scott MacEachern, and Walter van Beek, "The Slave Holders on the Border," *Africa Is a Country*, December 17, 2018, https://africasacountry.com/2018/12/the-slave-holders-on-the-border.

59. Lovejoy and Hogendorn, *Slow Death for Slavery*, 27–30.

60. Aḥmad Bābā, *Miʿrāj al-ṣuʿūd: Ajwibat Aḥmad Bābā ḥawla al-istirqāq: Nuṣūṣ wa-wathāʾiq*, ed. John Hunwick and Fatima Harrak (Maʿhad al-Dirāsāt al-Ifrīqīyah, al-Rabāṭ, 2000); Lovejoy, *Slavery, Commerce and Production*, 20, 209; John Hunwick, "The Religious Practices of Black Slaves in the Mediterranean Islamic World," in Lovejoy, *Slavery on the Frontiers of Islam*, 149–53; Paul E. Lovejoy, *Transformations in Slavery: A History of Slavery in Africa* (Cambridge University Press, 2012), 31.

61. Baba, *Miʿrāj al-ṣuʿūd*, 22–40.
62. Uthmān Ibn Fūdī, *Bayān wujūb al-hijra ʿalā ʾl-ʿibād*, trans. Fatḥī Ḥasan El-Maṣrī (Oxford University Press, 1978), 49–51.
63. Baba, *Miʿrāj al-ṣuʿūd*, 22.
64. Paul E. Lovejoy, "Slavery, the Bilād al-Sūdān and the Frontiers of the African Diaspora," in Lovejoy, *Slavery on the Frontiers of Islam*, 15.
65. Paul E. Lovejoy, *Slavery, Commerce and Production*, 19–25, 213. See also Lovejoy, "Problems of Slave Control in the Sokoto Caliphate," in *Africans in Bondage: Studies in Slavery and the Slave Trade*, ed. Paul E. Lovejoy (University of Wisconsin, 1986), 238–40.
66. "Message About the Chibok Girls by Abubakar Shekau," in Kassim and Nwankpa, *Boko Haram Reader*, 311–17.
67. Kassim and Nwankpa, *Boko Haram Reader*, 403–5.
68. Abubakar Shekau, "Message to the *Umma*," in Kassim and Nwankpa, *Boko Haram Reader*, 301–9.
69. Kassim and Nwankpa, *Boko Haram Reader*, 63–69.
70. Abubakar Shekau, "Raid on Maiduguri," in Kassim and Nwankpa, *Boko Haram Reader*, 289–95.
71. Kassim and Nwankpa, *Boko Haram Reader*, 301–9.
72. Kassim and Nwankpa, *Boko Haram Reader*, 301–9.
73. Kassim and Nwankpa, *Boko Haram Reader*, 301–9.
74. See Jacob Zenn, *Unmasking Boko Haram Exploring Global Jihad in Nigeria* (Lynne Rienner, 2020), 159. Zenn describes the process that saw AQIM transfer the 200,000 Euros to Boko Haram after the latter's operatives helped carry out the kidnap of a Spanish couple in Mauritania, with the ransom reportedly running into millions of Euros. This €200,000 transfer represented major seed money that enabled Boko Haram to organize and finance its initial logistics.
75. Zenn, *Unmasking Boko Haram*, 221–22.
76. Zenn, *Unmasking Boko Haram*, 214.
77. Zenn, *Unmasking Boko Haram*, 19–20.
78. Salkida, "Boko Haram Sustains Operations."
79. Zenn, *Unmasking Boko Haram*, 220.
80. Scott MacEachern, *Searching for Boko Haram: A History of Violence in Central Africa* (Oxford University Press, 2018).
81. MacEachern, *Searching for Boko Haram*, 136–37.
82. MacEachern, *Searching for Boko Haram*, 139–41.
83. MacEachern, *Searching for Boko Haram*, 197.
84. John Neville Hare, "How Northern Nigeria's Violent History Explains Boko Haram," *National Geographic*, March 14, 2015. Fadlallah had been an ally of the Mahdi but upon their falling out set out to carve out his own Islamic fiefdom to the south. Notorious for beheadings, enslavement of his enemies, and his

ruthlessness and bloodlust, his predation in the late nineteenth century prefigured and in many ways is similar to the current carnage.

85. MacEachern, *Searching for Boko Haram*, 174.

86. Hare, "How Northern Nigeria's History Explains Boko Haram."

87. Several communities in the Nigerian Northeast have been attacked so repeatedly that some locals have reached a truce with insurgents, paying protection levies in exchange for being allowed to remain and work their land. One recent evidence of this is in a story on the sacking of several communities in Hong Local Government of Adamawa State by Boko Haram and bandits. "Terrorists, Bandits Take Over Hometown of Secretary to Nigerian Government, Boss Mustapha, Residents Flee Homes over Impending Attacks," *Sahara Reporters*, December 27, 2021, http://saharareporters.com/2021/12/27/exclusive-terrorists-bandits-take-over-hometown-secretary-nigerian-government-boss.

EPILOGUE

1. Mansur Abubakar and Chris Ewokor, "Nigerian Governor Warns of Boko Haram Comeback," *BBC*, April 9, 2025, www.bbc.com/news/articles/c0kxxg5jy0ro.

2. Mayowa Oladeji, "Boko Haram 'On Its Last Legs,' Says Minister Mohammed Idris," *RipplesNigeria*, April 15, 2025, www.ripplesnigeria.com/boko-haram-on-its-last-legs-says-information-minister-mohammed-idris.

3. Several publications have published transcripts of excerpts from the audio, but the full message can be found on the companion website of Jacob Zenn's book *Unmasking Boko Haram* (https://unmaskingbokoharam.com/2021/05/23/boko-haram-abubakar-shekau-final-audio-sermon-may-22-2021/). Vincent Foucher has published the most comprehensive commentary on Shekau's final sermon to date to accompany a transcribed translation that may be the most accurate so far. Foucher, "Last Words of Abubakar Shekau: A Testament in the Politics of Jihadi Extraversion," *Sources: Materials and Fieldwork in African Studies* 3 (2021): 1–27, www.sources-journal.org/684#.

4. Foucher, "Last Words," 8.

5. "JAS vs. ISWAP: The War of the Boko Haram Splinters," Crisis Group Africa Briefing no. 196 (March 28, 2024), 6.

6. ISWAP and the Islamic State propaganda units have since released several videos to celebrate what they present as the reunification of Boko Haram and a reenergized jihadi insurgency. Some of these videos are curated on https://unmaskingbokoharam.com/2021/05/23/boko-haram-abubakar-shekau-final-audio-sermon-may-22-2021/.

7. Foucher, "Last Words," 7.

8. "JAS vs. ISWAP."

9. Gilles Kepel, "'There Is Jihad Fatigue,' Says Islamist Terrorism Expert," *BBC*, May 25, 2017, www.bbc.com/news/av/world-middle-east-40043212.

10. Obi Anyadike, "Nigeria's Secret Program to Lure Top Boko Haram Defectors," *The New Humanitarian*, August 19, 2021, www.thenewhumanitarian.org/news/2021/8/19/nigerias-secret-programme-to-lure-top-boko-haram-defectors.

11. Aliyu Dahiru, "Terrorism for Children: The Corrosive Doctrine Jihadists Pass to Next Generation," *HumAngle*, January 23, 2022, https://humanglemedia.com/terrorism-for-children-the-corrosive-doctrine-jihadists-pass-to-next-generation/.

12. Adell Patton, *The Ningi Chiefdom and the African Frontier: Mountaineers and Resistance to the Sokoto Caliphate, 1800–1908* (University of Wisconsin Press, 1975); Patton, "Ningi Raids and Slavery in Nineteenth Century Sokoto Caliphate," *Slavery and Abolition* 2 (1981): 114–45; Moses Ochonu, "Caliphate Expansion and Sociopolitical Change in Nineteenth-Century Lower Benue Hinterlands," *Journal of West African History* 1, no. 1 (2015): 133–78.

13. Kunle Adebajo, "Boko Haram's Heavily Juvenile Militia Confines Them to the Fringes," *HumAngle*, September 1, 2020, https://humanglemedia.com/boko-harams-heavily-juvenile-fighters-confines-them-to-the-fringes/

14. Adebajo, "Boko Haram's Heavily Juvenile Militia."

15. Ahmad Salkida, "#Boko Haram Roadblocks, Ambushes in Borno Claiming Prime Targets," *HumAngle*, September 22, 2020, https://humanglemedia.com/bokoharam-roadblocks-ambushes-in-borno-claiming-prime-targets/.

16. Adebajo, "Boko Haram's Heavily Juvenile Militia."

17. Ahmad Salkida, "Ex-Boko Haram Fighters, Eluding Detection, Start New Lives in Kaduna, Kano, Abuja," *Premium Times*, September 27, 2020, www.premiumtimesng.com/news/headlines/417056-ex-boko-haram-fighters-eluding-detection-start-new-lives-in-kaduna-kano-and-abuja.html.

18. Sakia Brechenmacher, "Achieving Peace in Northeast Nigeria: The Reintegration Challenge," *National Endowment for Peace*, September 5, 2018, https://carnegieendowment.org/2018/09/05/achieving-peace-in-northeast-nigeria-reintegration-challenge-pub-77177; Fonteh Akum and Malik Samuel, "Understanding the Dangerous Journey from Boko Haram to Rehabilitation," *ISS Today*, May 4, 2020, https://issafrica.org/iss-today/understanding-the-dangerous-journey-from-boko-haram-to-rehabilitation.

19. Akum and Samuel, "Understanding the Dangerous Journey."

20. Of particular relevance here is Gilles Kepel's argument about how the Islamic State's escalating atrocities coincided with its moment of weakness and its waning appeal to Muslim youth. His idea of "jihadi fatigue" is also important since it is similarly anchored on the notion that moments of increased violence against civilians by jihadis can offer clues about their struggle to appeal to Muslim youth and their adversity. Kepel, "'There Is Jihad Fatigue.'"

21. Kepel, "'There Is Jihad Fatigue.'"

22. Samantha May, "Are We Really Seeing the Rise of a 'New Jihad'?" *The Conversation*, May 26, 2017, https://theconversation.com/are-we-really-seeing-the-rise-of-a-new-jihad-78422; Olivier Roy, *Les Illusions du 11 septembre. Le débat stratégique face au terrorisme* (Seuil, 2002). Roy argues that the culturalist understanding of jihadists as acting out a central script of Islamist extremism is wrong and dangerously misinterprets the radicals' individuated motives.

23. Endism characterizes the ideological penchant of some scholars and commentators to pronounce the end or final stage of an evolutionary process, or of history itself. The most prominent work associated with this way of thinking is Francis Fukuyama's *End of History and the Last Man* (Free Press, 2006). For a prominent critique of endism, see Samuel P. Huttington, "No Exit: The Errors of Endism," *The National Interest* 17 (Fall 1989): 3–11.

Bibliography

BOOKS AND JOURNAL ARTICLES

Adamu, Dorugu Kwage. *Magana Hausa*. Society for Promoting Christian Knowledge, London, 1888.

Adelakun, Abimbola. *Performing Power in Nigeria: Identity, Politics, and Pentecostalism*. Cambridge University Press, 2021.

Adeleye, R. A. "Mahdist Triumph and British Revenge in Northern Nigeria: Satiru 1906." *Journal of the Historical Society of Nigeria* 6, no. 2 (June 1972): 193–214.

———. *Power and Diplomacy in Northern Nigeria, 1804–1906: The Sokoto Caliphate and Its Enemies*. Humanities Press, 1971.

Alao, Abiodun. *Rage and Carnage in the Name of God: Religious Violence in Nigeria*. Duke University Press, 2022.

Al-Hajj, Muhammad A. "The Character of the Central Bilād al-Sūdān in Historical Perspective." In *The Central Bilād Al-Sūdān: Tradition and Adaptation; Essays on the Geography and Economic and Political History of the Sudanic Belt*, edited by Yūsuf Fadl Hassan and Paul Doornbos, 14–19. Institute of African and Asian Studies, University of Khartoum, 1977.

Ali, Mohamed Bin. *The Roots of Religious Extremism: Understanding the Salafi Doctrine of al-Walā'wal Barā'*. Imperial College Press, 2016.

Aliyu, Ishaku. "Aspects of Political Administration in Sokoto Caliphate with Special Reference to Diya Al-Sultan of Abdullahi Ibn Fodiyo." In *State and

Society in the Sokoto Caliphate, edited by Ahmad Muhammad Kani and Kabir Ahmed Gandi, 63–75. Usmanu Danfodio University Press, 1990.

Amara, Ramzi Ben. *The Izala Movement: Genesis, Fragmentation and Revival*. Göttingen University Press, 2020.

Andrzejewski, B. W., S. Pitoszewicz, and W. Tyloch, eds. *Literatures in African Languages: Theoretical Issues and Sample Surveys*. Cambridge University Press, 2010.

Anonymous. "The Popular Discourses of Salafi Radicalism and Salafi Counter-Radicalism in Nigeria: A Case Study of Boko Haram." *Journal of Religion in Africa* 42, no. 2 (2012): 118–44.

Ayandele, Emmanuel. "The Missionary Factor in Northern Nigeria, 1870–1918." *Journal of the Historical Society of Nigeria* 3, no. 3 (1966): 503–22.

Bala, Mubarak. "My Journey from Islamist to Free Thinker." *Feminist Dissent* 1 (2016): 119–30.

Balogun, Ismail A. B. *The Life and Works of 'Uthmān Dan Fodio: The Muslim Reformer of West Africa*. Islamic Publications Bureau, Lagos, 1975.

Barnes, Andrew. "Administrators and Missionaries in Northern Nigeria During the First Third of the Twentieth Century." *Journal of Religion in Africa* 2, no. 4 (1995): 412–41.

———. "The Great Prohibition: The Expansion of Christianity in Colonial Northern Nigeria." *History Compass* 8, no. 6 (2010): 440–54.

———. *Making Headway: The Introduction of Western Civilization in Colonial Northern Nigeria*. University of Rochester Press, 2009.

Bayero, Nuhu Muhammadu. *My Life*. University of Lagos Press, 1990.

Bivar, A. D. H. "The Wathiqat Ahl Al-Sudan: A Manifesto of the Fulani Jihad." *Journal of African History* 2, no. 2 (1961): 235–43.

Boahen, Adu. *Britain, the Sahara, and the Western Sudan, 1788–1861*. Oxford University Press, 1964.

Bobboyi, Hamid, and A. M. Yakubu, eds. *The Sokoto Caliphate: History and Legacies, 1804–2004*. Arewa House Publishing, 2006.

Bolin, Paul E. "Imagination and Speculation as Historical Impulses: Engaging Uncertainties Within Art Education History and Historiography." *Studies in Art Education* 50 (2009): 110–23.

Bourdieu, Pierre. *Outline of a Theory of Practice*. Cambridge University Press, 1977.

Brenner, Louis. "The Jihad Debate Between Sokoto and Borno: An Historical Analysis of Islamic Political Discourse in Nigeria." In *People and Empires in African History: Essays in Memory of Michael Crowder*, edited by J. F. Ade Ajayi and J. D. Y. Peel, 21–43. Longman, 1992.

———. "Religion and Politics in Bornu: The Case of Muhammadu Al-Amin Al-Kanemi." In *Studies in West African Islamic History*, edited by J. R. Willis, 160–76. Routledge, 1979.

———. *The Shehus of Kukawa: A History of the Al-Kanemi Dynasty of Bornu.* Oxford University Press, 1973.

Brigaglia, Andrea. "A Contribution to the History of the Wahhabi Daʿwa in West Africa: The Career and the Murder of Shaykh Jaʿfar Mahmoud Adam (Daura, ca. 1961/1962–Kano 2007)." *Islamic Africa* 3, no. 1 (2012): 1–23.

———. "Jaʿfar Mahmoud Adam, Mohammed Yusuf and Al-Muntada Islamic Trust: Reflections on the Genesis of the Boko Haram Phenomenon in Nigeria." *Annual Review of Islam in Africa* 11 (2012): 33–44.

———. "The 'Popular Discourses of Salafi Counter-Radicalism in Nigeria' Revisited: A Response to Abdullahi Lamido's Review of Alexander Thurston, *Boko Haram*." *CCI Occasional Papers* 2 (March 2019): 10–23.

———. "The Volatility of Salafi Political Theology, the War on Terror and the Genesis of Boko Haram." *Diritto e Questioni Pubbliche* 15, no. 2 (2015): 193–98.

Brigaglia, Andrea, and Alessio Iocchi. "Entangled Incidents: Nigeria in the Global War on Terror (1994–2009)." *African Conflict and Peacebuilding Review* 10, no. 2 (2020): 10–42.

Bunza, Mukhtar U. "The Iranian Model of Political Islamic Movement in Nigeria (1979–2002)." In *L'islam politique au sud du Sahara: Identités, discours et enjeux*, edited by Muriel Gomez-Perez, 227–41. Karthala, 2005.

Clapperton, Hugh. *Journal of a Second Expedition into the Interior of Africa, from the Bight of Benin to Soccatoo.* John Murray, 1829.

Comolli, Virginia. *Boko Haram: Nigeria's Islamist Insurgency.* Hurst & Company, 2017.

Cook, Michael. *Commanding Right and Forbidding Wrong in Islamic Thought.* Cambridge University Press, 2000.

Dalen, Dorrit van. *Doubt, Scholarship and Society in 17th-Century Central Sudanic Africa.* Brill, 2016.

Decorse, Gaston Jules, and Maurice Gaudefroy-Demombynes. *Rabah et les Arabes du Chari: Documents arabes et vocabulaire.* E. Guilmoto, 1905.

Dowd, Caitriona, and Clionadh Raleigh. "The Myth of Global Islamic Terrorism and Local Conflict in Mali and the Sahel." *African Affairs* 112, no. 448 (July 2013): 498–509.

Eddins, Barkley B. "Speculative Philosophy of History: A Critical Analysis." *Southern Journal of History* (Spring 1968): 52–58.

Foucher, Vincent. "Last Words of Abubakar Shekau: A Testament in the Politics of Jihadi Extraversion." *Sources: Materials and Fieldwork in African Studies* 3 (2021): 1–27. www.sources-journal.org/684#.

Fukuyama, Francis. *The End of History and the Last Man.* Free Press, 2006.

Gaddis, John Lewis. *The Landscape of History: How Historians Map the Past.* Oxford University Press, 2004.

Garcia-Arenal, Mercedes. *Messianism and Puritanical Reform: Mahdīs of the Muslim West.* Brill, 2006.

Gentil, Émile. *La chute de l'empire de Rabah.* Hachette, 1902.

Graham, Sonia F. *Government and Mission Education in Northern Nigeria, 1900–1919: With Special Reference to the Work of Hanns Vischer.* Ibadan University Press, 1966.

Gumi, Sheikh Abubakar, and Ismaila Abubakar Tsiga. *Where I Stand.* Spectrum Books, 1992.

Halevi, Leor. *Modern Things on Trial: Islam's Global and Material Reformation in the Age of Rida, 1865–1935.* Columbia University Press, 2019.

Hamani, Djibo. *L'Islam au Soudan central: Histoire de l'Islam au Niger du VIIe au XIXe siècle.* L'Harmattan, 2007.

Hare, John Neville. "How Northern Nigeria's Violent History Explains Boko Haram." *National Geographic*, March 14, 2015. http://news.nationalgeographic.com/2015/03/150314-boko-haram-nigeria-borno-rabih-abubakar-shekau/.

Hayatu, Bi Sa'idu Sultan, Wilfried Günther, Herrmann Jungraithmayr, and August Klingenheben. *Sultan Sa'idu Bi Hayatu Tells the Story of His and His Father's Life.* W. Fink, 1978

Hegghammer, Thomas. "Jihadi-Salafis or Revolutionaries? On Religion and Politics in the Study of Militant Islamism." In *Global Salafism: Islam's New Religious Movements*, edited by Roel Meijer, 245–74. Oxford University Press, 2009.

Hentz, James J., and Hussein Solomon, eds. *Understanding Boko Haram: Terrorism and Insurgency in Africa.* Routledge, 2018.

Higazi, Adam. "Boko Haram: The Impact of Insurgency on Pastorialists and Farmers." *Afrique Comtemporaine* 22, no. 274 (2022): 163–69.

———. "Mobilisation Into and Against Boko Haram in North-East Nigeria." In *Collective Mobilisation in Africa*, edited by Kadya Tall, Marie-Emmanuelle Pommerolle, and Michel Cahen, 305–58. Brill, 2015.

Hill, Jonathan N. C. "Religious Extremism in Northern Nigeria Past and Present: Parallels Between the Pseudo-Tijanis and Boko Haram." *The Round Table: The Commonwealth Journal of International Affairs* 102, no. 3 (2013): 235–44.

———. *Sufism in Northern Nigeria: Force for Counter-Radicalization.* Strategic Studies Institute, 2010.

Hiskett, M. "*Kitāb Al-farq*: A Work on the Habe Kingdoms Attributed to 'Uthmān Dan Fodio." *Bulletin of the School of Oriental and African Studies* 23, no. 3 (1960): 558–79.

Hiskett, Mervyn. *The Development of Islam in West Africa.* Longman, 1984.

———. "The Maitatsine Riots in Kano, 1980: An Assessment." *Journal of Religion in Africa* 17, no. 3 (October 1987): 209–23.

——. *The Sword of Truth: The Life and Times of Shehu Usuman Dan Fodio.* Oxford University Press, 1973.
Hubbard, James P. *Education Under Colonial Rule: A History of Katsina College, 1921–1942.* University Press of America, 2000.
Huntington, Samuel P. "No Exit: The Errors of Endism." *The National Interest* 17 (Fall 1989): 3–11.
Hunwick, John O. *The Arabic Literature of Africa II: The Writings of Central Sudanic Africa.* Brill, 1995.
——. "The Religious Practices of Black Slaves in the Mediterranean Islamic World." In *Slavery on the Frontiers of Islam*, edited by Paul E. Lovejoy, 149–53. Markus Wiener, 2004.
——. *Shari'a in Songhay: The Replies of al-Maghili to the Questions of Askia al-Hajj Muhammad.* Oxford University Press, 1985.
——. *Timbuktu and the Songhay Empire: Al-Saadi's Taarīkh Al-Sūdān Down to 1613 and Other Contemporary Documents.* Brill, 1999.
Ibrahim, Jibrin. "The Politics of Religion in Nigeria: The Parameters of the 1987 Crisis in Kaduna State." *Review of African Political Economy* 45, no. 46 (1989): 65–82.
Ibrahim, Musa. "In Search of a Plausible Theory to Explain the Boko Haram Phenomenon: Analysis of Intellectual Discourses on Insurgency and Violent Extremism in Nigeria." *CCI Occasional Papers* 2 (March 2019): 24–35.
Ibrahim, Suleiman, and Siraj Abdukarim, eds. *On the Political Future of Nigeria.* Hudahuda, 1988.
Ikime, Obaro. *Fall of Nigeria: The British Conquest.* Heinemann, 1977.
Imam, Alhaji Ibrahim. *A Short History of Rabeh Ibn Fadel Allah (1838–1900).* Academy Press, 1974.
Isa, Kabiru Haruna, and Sani Y. Adam. "A History of Shia and Its Development in Nigeria: The Case-Study of Kano." *Journal for Islamic Studies* 36 (2017): 226–56.
Johnston, H. A. S. *The Fulani Empire of Sokoto.* Oxford University Press, 1967.
Junaidu, Sambo. "Resistance to Western Culture in the Sakwato Caliphate: A Lesson to Generations Yet Unborn." In *State and Society in the Sokoto Caliphate*, edited by Ahmad Muhammad Kani and Kabir Ahmed Gandi, 238–52. Usmanu Danfodio University, 1990.
Kane, Ousmane. *Muslim Modernity in Postcolonial Nigeria: A Study of the Society for the Removal of Innovation and Reinstatement of Tradition.* E. J. Brill, 2003.
Kani, Ahmad Muhammad. *The Intellectual Origin of Sokoto Jihad.* Iman Publications, 1984.
Kassim, Abdulbasit. "Boko Haram's Internal Civil War: Stealth Takfir and Jihad as Recipes for Schism." In *Boko Haram Beyond the Headlines:*

Analyses of Africa's Enduring Insurgency, edited by Jacob Zenn, 3–32. Combating Terrorism Center, West Point, NY, 2018.

Kassim, Abdulbasit, and Michael Nwankpa. *The Boko Haram Reader: From Nigerian Preachers to the Islamic State.* Oxford University Press, 2018.

Kastfelt, Niels. *Religion and Politics in Nigeria: A Study of Middle Belt Christianity.* I. B. Tauris, 1994.

Kendhammer, Brandon. "The Sharia Controversy in Northern Nigeria and the Politics of Islamic Law in New and Uncertain Democracies." *Comparative Politics* 45, no. 3 (2013): 291–311.

Kendhammer, Brandon, and Carmen McCain. *Boko Haram.* Ohio University Press, 2018.

Khadduri, Majid. *War and Peace in the Law of Islam.* Johns Hopkins University Press, 1955.

Kota, Kariya. "*Muwālāt* and Apostasy in the Early Sokoto Caliphate." *Islamic Africa* 9, no. 2 (2018): 179–208.

———. "Reconsidering the Intellectual Relationship Between Muḥammad al-Maghīlī and ʿUthmān b. Fūdī: A Comparative Examination of Ajwiba and Sirāj al-Ikhwān." *Islamic Africa* 13, no. 2 (2022): 251–82.

———. "A Revolt in the Early Sokoto Caliphate: Muhammad Bello's *Sard al-Kalām*." *Journal of Asian and African Studies* 95 (2018): 221–303.

———. "ʿUthmān b. Fūdī's Sirāj al-Ikhwān: An Aspect of the Reorganization of Knowledge in Muslim West Africa." *Journal of Asian and African Studies* 10 (2024): 51–124.

Kukah, Hassan Matthew. *Religion, Politics, and Power in Northern Nigeria.* Spectrum Books, 1993.

Laitin, David D. "The Sharia Debate and the Origins of Nigeria's Second Republic." *Journal of Modern African Studies* 20, no. 3 (1982): 411–30.

Last, Murray. "An Aspect of the Caliph Muhammad Bello's Social Policy." *Kano Studies* 2 (1966): 56–59.

———. "From Dissent to Dissidence: The Genesis and Development of Reformist Islamic Groups in Northern Nigeria." In *Sects & Social Disorder: Muslim Identities & Conflict in Northern Nigeria*, edited by Abdul Raufu Mustapha, 18–53. James Curry, imprint of Boydell and Brewer, 2014.

———. "The Search for Muslim Security in Northern Nigeria." *Africa: Journal of the International African Institute* 78, no. 1 (2008): 41–63.

———. "Slavery or Death in Sokoto and Borno: Tactics, Legalities and Sources." In *Landscape, Sources, and Intellectual Projects: Politics, History, and the West African Past*, edited by Toby Green and Benedetta Rossi, 422–42. Brill, 2018.

———. *The Sokoto Caliphate.* Longman, 1967.

Last, Murray, and Muhammad A. al-Hajj. "Attempts at Defining a Muslim in 19th Century Hausaland and Bornu." *Journal of Historical Society of Nigeria* 2 (1965): 231–40.

Lofkrantz, Jennifer. "Idealism and Pragmatism: The Related West African Discourses on Identity, Captivity, and Ransoming." In *Ransoming, Captivity, and Piracy in Africa and the Mediterranean*, edited by Jennifer Lofkrantz and Olatunji Ojo, 133–54. Africa World Press, 2016.

———. "Intellectual Discourse in the Early Sokoto Caliphate: The Triumvirate's Opinions on the Issue of Ransoming, c. 1810." *International Journal of African Historical Studies* 45, no. 3 (2012): 385–401.

———. "Intellectual Tradition, Education, and Jihad: The (Non)Parallels Between the Sokoto and Boko Haram Jihads." *Journal of West African History* 44, no. 1 (2018): 75–98.

———. "Protecting Freeborn Muslims: The Sokoto Caliphate's Attempts to Prevent Illegal Enslavement and Its Acceptance of the Strategy of Ransoming." *Slavery and Abolition* 32, no. 1 (2011): 109–27.

———. "Ransoming of Captives in the Sokoto Caliphate in the Nineteenth Century." In *Slavery, Islam and Diaspora*, edited by Behnaz A. Mizrai, Ismael Musah Montana, and Paul E. Lovejoy, 125–37. Africa World Press, 2009.

Loimeier, Roman. *Islamic Reform and Political Change in Northern Nigeria*. Northwestern University Press, 1997.

Lovejoy, Paul E. *The Bello-Clapperton Exchange: The Sokoto Jihad and the Transatlantic Slave Trade*. Lynne Rienner, 2001.

———. "Concubinage in the Sokoto Caliphate (1804–1903)." *Slavery and Abolition* 11 (1990): 159–89.

———. "Fugitive Slaves: Resistance to Slavery in the Sokoto Caliphate." In *In Resistance: Studies in African, Afro-American, and Caribbean History*, edited by Gary Okihiro, 71–95. University of Massachusetts Press, 1986.

———. "Jihad and the Era of the Second Slavery." *Journal of Global Slavery* 1, no. 1 (2016): 28–43.

———. *Jihad in West Africa During the Age of Revolutions*. Ohio University Press, 2016.

———. "Problems of Slave Control in the Sokoto Caliphate." In *Africans in Bondage: Studies in Slavery and the Slave Trade*, edited by Paul E. Lovejoy, 238–40. University of Wisconsin, 1986.

———. *Slavery, Commerce and Production in the Sokoto Caliphate of West Africa*. Africa World Press, 2005.

———. "Slavery in the Context of Ideology." In *The Ideology of Slavery in Africa*, edited by Paul E. Lovejoy, 11–38. Sage Publications, 1981.

———, ed. *Slavery on the Frontiers of Islam*. Markus Wiener, 2004.

———. "Slavery, the Bilād al-Sūdān and the Frontiers of the African Diaspora." In *Slavery on the Frontiers of Islam*, edited by Paul Lovejoy, 1–30. Markus Wiener, 2004.

———. *Transformations in Slavery: A History of Slavery in Africa*. Cambridge University Press, 2012.

Lovejoy, Paul E., and J. S. Hogendorn. "Revolutionary Mahdism and Resistance to Colonial Rule in the Sokoto Caliphate 1905–1906." *Journal of African History* 31, no. 2 (1990): 217–44.

Lovejoy, Paul E., and Jan S. Hogendorn. *Slow Death for Slavery: The Course of Abolition in Northern Nigeria, 1897–1936*. Cambridge University Press, 1993.

Lubeck, Paul. *Islam and Urban Labor in Northern Nigeria*. Cambridge University Press, 1987.

———. "Islamic Protest Under Semi-Industrial Capitalism: 'Yan Tatsine Explained." *Africa: Journal of the International Africa Institute* 55, no. 4, Special Issue on Popular Islam (1985): 369–89.

MacEachern, Scott. *Searching for Boko Haram: A History of Violence in Central Africa*. Oxford University Press, 2018.

Mack, Beverly. *Equals in Learning and Piety: Muslim Women Scholars in Nigeria and North America*. University of Wisconsin Press, 2023.

Mack, Beverly B., and Jean Boyd. *Educating Muslim Women: The West African Legacy of Nana Asma'u, 1793–1864*. Kube Publishing, 2013.

———. *One Woman's Jihad: Nana Asma'u, Scholar and Scribe*. Indiana University Press, 2000.

Marshall, Ruth. *Political Spiritualities: The Pentecostal Revolution in Nigeria*. University of Chicago Press, 2009.

Matfess, Hilary. *Women and the War on Boko Haram: Wives, Weapons, Witnesses*. Zed Books, 2017.

Miller, Walter R. S. *Walter Miller, 1872–1952: An Autobiography*. Gaskiya Corporation, 1953.

———. *Yesterday and To-morrow in Northern Nigeria*. Student Christian Movement Press, London, 1938.

Mohammed, Kyari. "The Message and Methods of Boko Haram." In *Boko Haram: Islamism, Politics, Security and the State in Nigeria*, edited by Marc-Antoine Perouse de Montclos, 9–32. IFRA-Nigeria, 2014.

———. "Origins of Boko Haram." In *The Oxford Handbook of Nigerian Politics*, edited by Carl Levan and Patrick Ukata, 584–604. Oxford University Press, 2018.

Muedini, Fait. *Sponsoring Sufism: How Governments Promote "Mystical Islam" in Their Domestic and Foreign Policies*. Palgrave Macmillan, 2015.

Muffett, D. J. M. *Concerning Brave Captains: Being a History of the British Occupation of Kano and Sokoto and of the Last Stand of the Fulani Forces*. Andre Deutsch, 1964.

Mustapha, Abdul Raufu, ed. *Sects and Social Disorder: Muslim Identities and Conflict in Northern Nigeria*. James Currey, 2017.

Nast, Heidi J. *Concubines and Power: Five Hundred Years in a Northern Nigerian Palace.* University of Minnesota Press, 2005.

Naylor, Paul. *From Rebels to Rulers: Writing Legitimacy in the Early Sokoto State.* James Currey, 2021.

Nmehielle, Vincent O. "Sharia Law in the Northern States of Nigeria: To Implement or Not to Implement, the Constitutionality Is the Question." *Human Rights Quarterly* 26, no. 3 (2004): 730–59.

Ochonu, Moses. "Caliphate Expansion and Sociopolitical Change in Nineteenth-Century Lower Benue Hinterlands." *Journal of West African History* 1, no. 1 (2015): 133–78.

Ogunsola, Albert F. *Legislation and Education in Northern Nigeria.* Oxford University Press, 1974.

O'Hear, Ann. *Power Relations in Nigeria: Ilorin Slaves and Their Successors.* University of Rochester Press, 1997.

Olatunji, Ojo. "Islam, Ethnicity and Slave Agitation: Hausa 'Mamluks' in Nineteenth Century Yorubaland." In *Slavery, Islam and Diaspora*, edited by Behnaz A. Mizrai, Ismael Montana, and Paul E. Lovejoy, 103–24. Africa World Press, 2009.

Oloyede, Ishaq Olanrewaju. *Sharia Versus Secularism in Nigeria.* Islamic Publications Bureau, Lagos, 1986.

Oppenheim, Max Freiherrn von. *Rabeh Und Das Tschadseegebiet.* D. Reimer (E. Vohsen), 1902.

Ostein, Philip. "An Opportunity Missed by Nigeria's Christians: The 1976–78 Sharia Debate Revisited." In *Muslim-Christian Encounters in Africa*, edited by Benjamin F. Soares, 221–55. Brill, 2006.

Ozigi, Albert, and Lawrence Ocho. *Education in Northern Nigeria.* Allen and Unwin, 1981.

Paden, John N. *Religion and Political Culture in Kano.* University of California Press, 1973.

Palmer, H. R. (Herbert Robert). "An Early Fulani Conception of Islam (Continued)." *Journal of the Royal African Society* 14, no. 53 (1914): 53–59.

Palmeri, Frank. "In Praise of Speculative History." *Chronicle of Higher Education—The Review*, July 10, 2016, 1–2.

Patton, Adell, Jr. *The Ningi Chiefdom and the African Frontier: Mountaineers and Resistance to the Sokoto Caliphate, 1800–1908.* University of Wisconsin Press, 1975.

———. "Ningi Raids and Slavery in Nineteenth Century Sokoto Caliphate." *Slavery and Abolition* 2 (1981): 114–45.

———. "Tarikh Umara Bauchi and Its Contribution to Pre-Colonial Ningi Resistance to Sokoto Caliphate: Exegesis and Methodology in African Oral History, ca. 1846–1902." *A Current Bibliography on African Affairs* 18, no. 2 (1986): 105–16.

Perouse de Montclos, Marc Antoine. "Boko Haram and 'Sahelistan' Terrorism Narratives: A Historical Perspective." *Afrique Contemporaine* 255, no. 3 (2015): 21–39.

Philips, John E. "The Persistence of Slave Officials in Sokoto Caliphate." In *Slave Elites in the Middle East and Africa: A Comparative Study*, edited by Miura Toru and John Edward Philips, 215–34. Kegan Paul International, 2000.

———. "Slavery on Two Ribats in Kano and Sokoto." In *Slavery on the Frontiers of Islam*, edited by Paul E. Lovejoy, 111–24. Markus Wiener, 2003.

———. *Spurious Arabic: Hausa and Colonial Nigeria*. University of Wisconsin Press, 2000.

Pieri, Zacharia P., and Jacob Zenn. "The Boko Haram Paradox." *African Security* 9, no. 1 (2016): 66–88.

Plumb, J. H. *The Death of the Past*. MacMillan, 1969.

Roy, Olivier. *Les Illusions du 11 septembre. Le débat stratégique face au terrorisme*. Seuil, 2002.

Salau, Mohammed Bashir. *The West African Slave Plantation: A Case Study*. Palgrave Macmillan, 2011.

Schlar, Lynn. "The Sardauna's Middle East: Regionalism and Backstage Politics in Nigeria's Postcolonial Diplomacy." *Journal of African History* 63, no. 2 (2022): 197–213.

Sedgwick, Mark. "Sufis as 'Good Muslims': Sufism in the Battle Against Jihadi Salafism." In *Sufis and Salafis in the Contemporary Age*, edited by Lloyd Ridgeon, 105–17. Bloomsbury Academic, 2015.

———. "The Support of Sufism as a Counterweight to Radicalization: An Assessment." In *Countering Radicalization and Violent Extremism Among Youth to Prevent Terrorism*, edited by Marco Lombardi et al., 113–19. IoS Press, 2015.

Seesemann, Rüdiger. "The Takfīr Debate: Sources for the Study of a Contemporary Dispute Among African Sufis, Part I: The Nigerian Arena." *Sudanic Africa* 9 (1998): 39–70.

Seignobos, Christian. "Boko Haram and Lake Chad: An Extension or a Sanctuary?" *Afrique Contemporaine* 255, no. 3 (2015): 89–114.

Shankar, Shobana. *Who Shall Enter Paradise? Christian Origins in Muslim Northern Nigeria, 1890–1975*. Ohio University Press, 2014.

Smaldone, Joseph. *Warfare in the Sokoto Caliphate: Historical and Sociological Perspectives*. Cambridge University Press, 1977.

Smith, Mike. *Boko Haram: Inside Nigeria's Unholy War*. I. B. Tauris, 2016.

Stilwell, Sean. "'Amana' and 'Asiri': Royal Slave Culture and the Colonial Regime in Kano, 1903–1926." *Slavery and Abolition* 19, no. 2 (1998): 167–88.

———. *Paradoxes of Power: The Kano "Mamluks" and Male Royal Slavery in the Sokoto Caliphate, 1804–1903*. Heinemann, 2004.

———. "Power, Honour and Shame: The Ideology of Royal Slavery in the Sokoto Caliphate." *Africa* 70, no. 3 (2000): 394–421.

———. "The Power of Knowledge and the Knowledge of Power: Kinship, Community and Royal Slavery in Pre-Colonial Kano, 1807–1903." In *Slave Elites in the Middle East and Africa: A Comparative Study*, edited by Miura Toru and John Edward Philips, 81–98. Kegan Paul International, 2000.

Stoddard, Edward. "Competitive Control? 'Hearts and Minds' and the Population Control Strategy of the Islamic State West Africa Province." *African Security* 16, no. 1 (2023): 32–60.

Sulaiman, Ibraheem. *The African Caliphate: The Life Work & Teachings of Shaykh Usman Dan Fodio*. Diwan, 2009.

———. *The Islamic State and the Challenge of History: Ideals, Policies, and Operation of the Sokoto Caliphate*. Mansell Publishers, 1987.

———. *A Revolution in History: The Jihad of Usman Dan Fodio*. Mansell, 1986.

Suleiman, Muhammad Dahiru. "Shiaism and the Islamic Movement in Nigeria, 1979–1991." In *Islam et islamismes au sud du Sahara*, edited by Ousmane Kane and Jean-Louis Triaud, 183–95. Karthala, 1998.

Tambo, David. "The Sokoto Caliphate Slave Trade in the Nineteenth Century." *International Journal of African Historical Studies* 9, no. 2 (1976): 187–217.

Thurston, Alexander. "Abubakar Gumi's al-ʿAqīda al-Ṣaḥīḥa bi-Muwāfaqat al-Sharīʿa: Global Salafism and Locally Oriented Polemics in a Northern Nigerian Text." *Islamic Africa* 2, no. 2 (2011): 9–21.

———. "Algeria's GIA: The First Major Armed Group to Fully Subordinate Jihadism to Salafism." *Islamic Law and Society* 24 (2017): 412–36.

———. *Boko Haram: The History of an African Jihadist Movement*. Princeton University Press, 2018.

———. *Salafism in Nigeria: Islam, Preaching and Politics*. Cambridge University Press, 2016.

Tibenderana, Peter Kazenga. "The Beginnings of Girls' Education in the Native Administration Schools in Northern Nigeria, 1930–1945." *Journal of African History* 26, no. 1 (1985): 93–109.

———. "The Emirs and the Spread of Western Education in Northern Nigeria, 1910–1946." *Journal of African History* 24, no. 4 (1983): 517–34.

Turaki, Yusufu. *Tainted Legacy: Islam, Colonialism, and Slavery in Northern Nigeria*. Isaac Publishing, 2010.

Umar, Muhammad S. *Islam and Colonialism: Intellectual Responses of Muslims of Northern Nigeria to British Colonial Rule*. Brill, 2006.

Varin, Caroline. *Boko Haram and the War on Terror*. Praeger, 2016.

Wagemakers, Joas. "A Purist Jihadi-Salafi: The Ideology of Abu Muhammad al-Maqdisi." *British Journal of Middle Eastern Studies* 36, no. 2 (2009): 286–89.

Waldman, Marilyn Robinson. "The Fulani Jihad: A Reassessment." *Journal of African History* 6, no. 3 (1965): 333–55.

Watt, Montgomery. *Islamic Creeds: A Selection*. University of Edinburgh Press, 1994.

Watts, Michael. *Silent Violence: Food, Famine, and Peasantry in Northern Nigeria*. 1983; repr. University of Georgia Press, 2013.

Weiss, Holger. *Between Accommodation and Revivalism: Muslims, the State, and Society in Ghana from Precolonial to the Postcolonial Era*. Finnish Oriental Society, Studia Orientalia 105, 2008.

Whitsitt, Novian. "Hausa Women Writers Confronting the Traditional Status of Women in Modern Islamic Society: Feminist Thought in Nigerian Popular Fiction." *Tulsa Studies in Women's Literature* 22, no. 2 (2003): 387–408.

Yadudu, A. H. "Constitution-Making and the Politicization of Sharia in Nigeria." *Journal of Islamic and Comparative Law* 18 (1991): 19–37.

Zakari, Maïkorema. *Rabih Au Bornou (1893–1900): Une étape de la colonisation française*. Institut de recherche en sciences humaines, Université de Niamey, 1979.

Zehnle, Stephanie. *A Geography of Jihad: Sokoto Jihadism and the Islamic Frontier in West Africa*. De Gruyter, 2020.

Zenn, Jacob. *Unmasking Boko Haram: Exploring Global Jihad in Nigeria*. Lynne Rienner, 2020.

CONFERENCE PROCEEDINGS AND DISSERTATIONS

Abba, Isa A., and P. J. Shea. "Decision to Flee at the Time of the British Conquest of the Sakkwato Caliphate." Paper presented at the International Seminar on the Impact of Colonialism on Islamic Education in the Sokoto Caliphate and Other Institutions During the Period 1903–1960, Sokoto, June 1988.

Al-Hajj, Muhammad Ahmad. "The Mahdist Tradition in Northern Nigeria." PhD diss., Ahmadu Bello University Zaria, 1973.

Bashir, I. L. "Classism Conflict and Socio-Economic Transition in a Changing Society: A Case Study of Kano's Oligarchy." University of Sokoto History Seminar, April 1983.

Kassim, Abdulbasit. "Old Reformers, New Dissidents: Continuity and Change in the Intellectual History of Islamic Thought, Reform and Jihad in Nigeria from the Late 18th to Early 21st Centuries." PhD diss., Rice University, 2022.

Lamido, Abdullahi. "From Zakzakiya Movement to Boko Haram: The History of Muhammad Yusuf's Journey to Violent Extremism." Paper presented at the International Conference on the Boko Haram Phenomenon, Kano, November 13–15, 2018.

Last, Murray. "From Dissent to Dissidence: The Genesis and Development of Reformist Islamic Groups in Northern Nigeria." Paper presented at the African History Seminar, School of Oriental and African Studies (SOAS), University of London, March 6, 2013.

Linden, Ian. "The Isawa Mallams c. 1850–1919: Some Problems in the Religious History of Northern Nigeria." Occasional paper, Ahmadu Bello University, Zaria, 1971.

Logams, Chunun. "The Middle Belt Movement in Nigerian Political Development: A Study in Political Identity, 1949–1967." PhD diss., University of Keele, 1985.

Philips, John Edward. "Ribats in the Sokoto Caliphate: Selected Studies, 1804–1903." PhD diss., University of California–Los Angeles, 1992.

Saeed, Asma'u Garba. "A Biographical Study of Shaykh Sa'id b. Hayat (1887 to 1978) and the British Policy Towards the Mahdiyya in Northern Nigeria (1900–1960)." PhD diss., Bayero University Kano, 1992.

Sa'id, Bello. "Gundummawar Masu Jihadi Kan Adabin Hausa." MA thesis, Bayero University Kano, 1978.

Shehu, Salisu. "Islam, Education and Politics: A Critical Engagement with the Ideological Framings of Boko Haram." Paper presented at the International Conference on the Boko Haram Phenomenon, Kano, November 13–15, 2018.

Thurston, Alexander. "Interactions Between Northern Nigeria and the Arab World in the Twentieth Century." MA thesis, Georgetown University, 2009.

Yamusa, Shehu. 1975. "The Political Ideas of the Jihad Leaders: Being a Translation, Edition and Analysis of (1) Usul al-siyasa by Mohammed Bello and (2) Diya al-hukkam by Abdallah B. Fodio." MA thesis, Bayero University Kano.

Yandaki, Aminu Isyaku. "A History of the Izalah Movement in Northern Nigeria Up to 1989." MA thesis, Usman Dan Fodio University, 1990.

Zahradeen, Muhammad Sani. "Abd Allāh Ibn Fodio's Contributions to the Fulani Jihad in Nineteenth Century Hausaland." PhD diss., McGill University, 1977.

MANUSCRIPTS AND TRANSLATIONS OF ARABIC WORKS

Al-Badawī, Aḥmad Muḥammad. "Kitāb Shifā' al-ghalīl wa'l- 'alāqa bayn 'Uthmān wa-Jibrīl." *al-Muntaka* 2, no. 1 (1987): 1–20.

Bābā, Aḥmad. *Mi'rāj al-ṣu'ūd: Ajwibat Aḥmad Bābā ḥawla al-istirqāq: Nuṣūs wa-wathā'iq.* Translated by John Hunwick and Fatima Harrak. Ma'had al-Dirāsāt al-Ifrīqīyah, al-Rabāṭ, 2000.

Bello, Muhammad. *al-Insaf fi dhikr ma-fi masa il al-khilafa min wifaq wa-khilaf* 1817 [Fair judgment of conflicting views on questions concerning the caliphate]. *MSParis* (BI) 206: 4–5.

———. *The Rise of the Sokoto Fulani: Being a Paraphrase and in Some Parts a Translation of the Infaku'l Maisuri of Sultan Mohammed Bello.* Translated by Edward John Arnett. Emirate Printing, Kano, 1922.

———. *Talkhīs aṭ-ṭibb al-nabawī.* MS Folio 4, Waziri Junaidu History and Culture Bureau.

Fartua, Aḥmad Ibn. *History of the First Twelve Years of the Reign of Mai Idris Alooma of Bornu (1571–1583) by His Imam: Ahmed Ibn Fartua; Together with the "Diwan of the Sultans of Bornu" and "Girgam" of the Magumi.* Translated by Herbert Richmond Palmer. Government Printer, Lagos, 1926; repr., Cass, 1970.

Fodio, Usman. *Al-Amr bi-muwalat al-mu minin wa-al-naha an muwalat al-kafirin* [Commanding friendship with the faithful and prohibiting friendship with infidels], 1805.

Fodio, Usman. *Lamma balaghtu.* Gaskiya Corp., Zaria, n.d.

Fodio, Usman. *Masa il Muhimma, f.* 155a; *Nasihat ahl al-zaman.*

Fodio, Usman. *Siraj al-ikhwan* [The guiding light of the brethren]. Translated by Shaykh Muhammad Shareef bin Farid. https://siiasi.org/wp-content/uploads/2014/12/Siraajl-Ikhwaan-2.pdf.

Fūdī, 'Abd Allāh b. *Maṣaliḥ al-insān al-muta'alliqa bi-l-adyan wa-l-'abdan.* MS Folio 34, Waziri Junaidu History and Culture Bureau.

Fūdī, 'Uthmān b. *Sirāj al-ikhwān fī ahamm mā yuḥtāju ilayhi fī hadhā 'l-zamān.* Manuscript Arabe 5528, ff. 230a–231b, Bibliothèque nationale de France.

———. *Tamyīz ahl al-Sunna.* Manuscript, Melville J. Herskovits Library of African Studies, Northwestern University, NU/Hunwick/151.2/ME.

Fūdī, 'Uthmān Ibn. *Bayān wujūb al-hijra 'alā 'l-'ibād.* Translated by Fatḥī Ḥasan El-Maṣrī. Oxford University Press, 1978.

Gumi, Abubakar. *Al-'aqīda al-ṣaḥīḥa bi-muwāfaqat al-sharī'a.* Dar al-'Arabiyya, 1972.

———. *Sheikh Abubakar Mahmoud Gumi's Selected Fatwas, Book Two.* Compiled by Musa Lawal Funtuwa. Hudahuda, 1984.

———. *Al-Akudatus Sahihat Bi Muwafakatus Shariah.* Translated by Imam Ahmad Adam Kutubi and Ahmad Garba. Self-published, n.d.

Muḥammad, 'Abdullāh ibn. *Tazyīn Al-waraqāt.* Translated by M. Hiskett. University of Ibadan Press, 1963.

Ruxton, F. H., ed. *Mâliki Law: Being a Summary from French Translations of the Mukhtaṣar of Sîdî Khalîl: With Notes and Bibliography.* Hyperion Press, 1980.

Sambo, Ibrahim A. *Tarikh 'Umara' Bauchi* [History of the emirs of Bauchi]. Self-published, 1902, 1957.

NEWSPAPER/MAGAZINE ARTICLES AND
WEBSITE CONTENT

Abubakar, Mansur, and Chris Ewokor. "Nigerian Governor Warns of Boko Haram Comeback." *BBC*, April 9, 2025. www.bbc.com/news/articles/c0kxxg5jy0ro.

Adaji, Ben. "Five Killed, Houses Razed as Christians, Muslims Clash in Taraba." *P.M. News*, July 13, 2010, 9.

Adamu, Abadalla Uba. "Eunuchs in the Harem of Hausa Cultural Epistemology." *Weekly Trust*, December 20, 2002.

———. "Hausa Literary Expression in the Decade of the 1990s: A Further Contribution to the Soyayya Genre Debate, Part I." *New Nigerian Weekly*, April 24, 1999.

———. "Hausa Literary Expression in the Decade of the 1990s: A Further Contribution to the Soyayya Genre Debate, Part II." *New Nigerian Weekly*, May 1, 1999.

Adamu, Farooq. "The Sarkin Karuwai Controversy in Kano." *Weekly Trust*, October 23–29, 1998, 8.

Adaoyichie, Goodness. "Female Suicide Bomber Attacks Mosque in Yobe." *Pulse*, March 2, 2018. www.pulse.ng/news/local/boko-haram-female-suicide-bomber-attacks-mosque-in-yobe/p6x2yp1.

Adebajo, Kunle. "Boko Haram's Heavily Juvenile Militia Confines Them to the Fringes." *HumAngle*, September 1, 2020. https://humanglemedia.com/boko-harams-heavily-juvenile-fighters-confines-them-to-the-fringes/.

Akinwotu, Emmanuel. "UN Condemns One Year Detention of Nigerian Humanist Mubarak Bala." *The Guardian*, April 28, 2021. www.theguardian.com/world/2021/apr/28/un-condemns-one-year-detention-of-nigerian-humanist-mubarak-bala.

Al-Bishak. "The Soyayya Debate: A Redirection." *New Nigerian*, December 22, 2001.

Alhassan, Amina. "AKTH Denies Holding Kano Patient 'Captive.'" *Weekly Trust*, June 28, 2014.

Anyadike, Obi. "Nigeria's Secret Program to Lure Top Boko Haram Defectors." *The New Humanitarian*, August 19, 2021. www.thenewhumanitarian.org

/news/2021/8/19/nigerias-secret-programme-to-lure-top-boko-haram-defectors.

Asim, Imam Qari. "The Nigeria Mosque Attack Should Remind Us That the People Most Likely to Be Victims of Terrorism Are Muslims." *Independent*, November 21, 2017. www.independent.co.uk/voices/nigeria-mosque-bombing-killed-dead-prayers-islam-boko-haram-muslim-victims-a8067846.html.

Bala, Mubarak (@MubarakBala). "Sheikh Ja'far started the ideology that led to Boko Haram." Twitter, April 12, 2017, 4:18 a.m. https://mobile.twitter.com/MubarakBala/status/852088591819968512.

Barnett, James H. "Understanding Boko Haram." *Washington Examiner*, February 14, 2018. www.washingtonexaminer.com/weekly-standard/understanding-boko-haram.

Bunzel, Cole. "Caliphate in Disarray: Theological Turmoil in the Islamic State." *Jihadica*, October 3, 2017. www.jihadica.com/caliphate-in-disarray/.

Chétima, Melchisedek, Scott MacEachern, and Walter van Beek. "The Slave Holders on the Border." *Africa Is a Country*, December 17, 2018. https://africasacountry.com/2018/12/the-slave-holders-on-the-border.

Chimtom, Ngala Killian, Jason Hanna, and Michael Martinez. "Freed German Hostage Calls Boko Haram Captivity Total Darkness." *CNN*, January 21, 2015. www.cnn.com/2015/01/21/world/cameroon-boko-haram-german-hostage/index.html.

Dahiru, Aliyu. "Muslim Clerics Condemned Boko Haram While Praising Al-Qaeda Post 9/11 Attacks." *Humangle*, April 15, 2021. https://humanglemedia.com/muslim-clerics-condemned-boko-haram-while-praising-al-qaeda-post-9-11-attacks/.

———. "Terrorism for Children: The Corrosive Doctrine Jihadists Pass to Next Generation." *Humangle*, January 23, 2022. https://humanglemedia.com/terrorism-for-children-the-corrosive-doctrine-jihadists-pass-to-next-generation/.

Dikko, Isyaku, and Tanimu Usman. "Sardauna Was Deceived—Dr. Datti Ahmed." *Weekly Trust*, September 15–21, 2000, 1–4.

Dogarawa, Ahmad Bello. "Tilde Was Wrong on Hausa Music." *Weekly Trust*, October 12–18, 2001.

Doki, Abdullahi. "Islamic State of Zamfara." *Weekly Trust*, October 8–14, 1999, 2.

———. "Muslim North, The Caliphate and Sharia States: Re-Islamisation Uncompleted." *Weekly Trust*, August 9–15, 2003.

Everest65. "Resurgent: The Weapons of IS West Africa." *Calibre Obscura*, January 20, 2019. www.calibreobscura.com/the-weaponry-of-is-west-africa-boko-haram/.

Hamming, Tore. "The Extremist Wing of the Islamic State." *Jihadica*, June 9, 2016. www.jihadica.com/the-extremist-wing-of-the-islamic-state/.

---. "The Increasing Extremism Within the Islamic State." *Jihadica*, November 19, 2016. www.jihadica.com/the-increasing-extremism-within-the-islamic-state/.

Ibrahim, Idris. "Boko Haram Terrorists Are Our Muslim Brothers, Shouldn't Be Killed Like Pigs: Minister Pantami." *Peoples Gazette*, April 16, 2021. www.gazettengr.com/boko-haram-terrorists-are-our-muslim-brothers-shouldnt-be-killed-like-pigs-minister-pantami/.

"The 'Impulse of Curiosity': Hugh Clapperton's Explorations into the African Interior." *Devon & Exeter Institution*. https://devonandexeterinstitution.org/the-impulse-of-curiosity-hugh-claperttons-explorations-into-the-african-interior/, accessed June 5, 2024.

"ISWAP Terror Group Holds Public Meetings with Borno Residents to Recruit New Members, Stresses Plan to Have Separate Islamic Country." *Sahara Reporters*, June 9, 2024. https://saharareporters.com/2024/06/09/iswap-terror-group-holds-public-meetings-borno-residents-recruit-new-members-stresses#google_vignette.

"Kano Conference." *Radiance* (magazine published by the Muslim Students Society of Nigeria), December 1980.

Karofi, Hassan A. "Sharia Protesters Clash with Performing Artistes in Katsina." *Weekly Trust*, July 27–August 2, 2001, 7.

Katsina, Danjuma. "Death to the Soyayya Novel." *New Nigerian Weekly*, September 5, 1998, 5.

Kazaure, Musa Umar. "Price of bin Laden's Portraits Hikes in Kano." *Weekly Trust*, October 19–25, 2001, 6.

Kepel, Gilles. "'There Is Jihad Fatigue,' Says Islamist Terrorism Expert." *BBC*, May 25, 2017. www.bbc.com/news/av/world-middle-east-40043212.

Maclean, Ruth. "Nigeria Mosque Attack: Suicide Bomber Kills Dozens." *The Guardian*, November 21, 2017. www.theguardian.com/world/2017/nov/21/nigeria-mosque-attack-teenage-suicide-bomber-kills-at-least-50.

---. "Outspoken Atheist, Arrested in Nigeria for Blasphemy, Hasn't Been Seen Since." *New York Times*, August 25, 2020. www.nytimes.com/2020/08/25/world/africa/nigeria-blasphemy-atheist-islam.html?searchResultPosition=1.

Mallonee, Laura. "The Subversive Women Who Self-Publish Novels Amidst Jihadist War." *Wired*, February 17, 2016. www.wired.com/2016/02/glenna-gordon-diagram-heart/.

Malumfashi, Ibrahim. "Beyond Market Criticism." *New Nigerian Weekly Literary Supplement*, May 15, 1999.

Mamah, Emeka. "Boko Haram: Christian Extremist Group, Akhwat Akwop Threatens Retaliation." *Vanguard*, September 29, 2011.

Mansur, Ahmed. "Re: The 'Best' Hausa Books 1998." *New Nigerian Weekly*, December 19, 1998, 15.

May, Samantha. "Are We Really Seeing the Rise of a 'New Jihad'?" *The Conversation*, May 26, 2017. https://theconversation.com/are-we-really-seeing-the-rise-of-a-new-jihad-78422.

"Miller, Walter Richard Samuel." *Dictionary of African Christian Biography*, Classic Collection. https://dacb.org/stories/nigeria/miller-wr-samuel/.

Muhammad, Bala. "Top 10 Reasons to Turn Off Your TV." *Weekly Trust*, January 11, 2014.

Musa, Zainab Taiwo. "Death Threat on Filmmaker." *Weekly Trust*, November 5–11, 1999, 40.

"Nigeria Unrest: Kano Mosque Attack Kills Dozens." *BBC*, November 28, 2014. www.bbc.com/news/world-africa-30250950.

"Nigeria Unrest: Suicide Bomb Targets Church in Jos." *BBC*, February 26, 2012. www.bbc.com/news/world-africa-17169935.

"Nigeria's ThisDay Newspaper Hit by Abuja and Kaduna Blasts." *BBC*, April 26, 2012. www.bbc.com/news/world-africa-17856362#:~:text=The%20Kaduna%20explosion%20happened%20outside,AFP%20quoted%20police%20as%20saying.

Oladeji, Mayowa. "Boko Haram 'On Its Last Legs,' Says Minister Mohammed Idris." *RipplesNigeria*, April 15, 2025. www.ripplesnigeria.com/boko-haram-on-its-last-legs-says-information-minister-mohammed-idris/.

"Osama Baby Craze Hits Nigeria." *BBC*, January 3, 2002. http://news.bbc.co.uk/2/hi/africa/1741171.stm.

Page, Thomas. "Beyond Heartache and Boko Haram: Nigerian Women Prove Love Is Universal." *CNN*, February 9, 2018. www.cnn.com/2016/02/15/africa/nigeria-love-literature.

Parkinson, Joe, and Drew Hinshaw. "Freedom for the World's Most Famous Hostages Came at a Heavy Price." *Wall Street Journal*, May 6, 2017. www.wsj.com/articles/two-bags-of-cash-for-boko-haram-the-untold-story-of-how-nigeria-freed-its-kidnapped-girls-1513957354.

Salkida, Ahmad. "#Boko Haram Roadblocks, Ambushes in Borno Claiming Prime Targets." *HumAngle*, September 22, 2020. https://humanglemedia.com/bokoharam-roadblocks-ambushes-in-borno-claiming-prime-targets/.

———. "Boko Haram Sustains Operations Through International Trade in Smoked Fish." *Premium Times*, April 26, 2020. www.premiumtimesng.com/news/headlines/389916-how-boko-haram-sustain-operations-through-international-trade-in-smoked-fish.html.

———. "Ex-Boko Haram Fighters, Eluding Detection, Start New Lives in Kaduna, Kano, Abuja." *Premium Times*, September 27, 2020. www.premiumtimesng.com/news/headlines/417056-ex-boko-haram-fighters-eluding-detection-start-new-lives-in-kaduna-kano-and-abuja.html.

———. "Inside the War Front: Nigerian Military Take Out Boko Haram Bases." *HumAngle*, May 11, 2020. https://humanglemedia.com/inside-the-war-front-nigerian-military-take-out-major-boko-haram-bases/.

Sanusi, Sanusi Lamido. "Al-Kanemi Before Danfodio's Court: Sultan Bello's Response to Kyari." *Daily Trust*, April 18, 2003.

Shinkafi, Abubakar Liman. "Dr. Tilde Got It Wrong." *Weekly Trust*, November 9–15, 2001.

Smith, David. "Nigerian Man Is Locked Up After Saying He Is an Atheist." *The Guardian*, June 24, 2014. www.theguardian.com/world/2014/jun/25/nigerian-man-locked-up-atheist.

"Suicide Attack on Nigeria Mosque Causes Multiple Deaths." *Aljazeera*, January 3, 2018. www.aljazeera.com/news/2018/1/3/suicide-attack-on-nigeria-mosque-causes-multiple-deaths.

Suleiman, Naziru. "Hausa Films and Moral Degeneration." *Weekly Trust*, January 14–20, 2000, 16.

"Terrorists, Bandits Take Over Hometown of Secretary to Nigerian Government, Boss Mustapha, Residents Flee Homes over Impending Attacks." *Sahara Reporters*, December 27, 2021. http://saharareporters.com/2021/12/27/exclusive-terrorists-bandits-take-over-hometown-secretary-nigerian-government-boss.

"13 Dead as Boko Haram Terrorists Attack Mosque, Others in Borno—Police Confirm." *Vanguard*, June 8, 2017. www.vanguardngr.com/2017/06/13-dead-boko-haram-terrorists-attack-mosque-others-borno-police-confirm/.

Tijjani, Kyari. "George Bush Before Al-Kanemi's Court: A Reflection on the Anglo-American Invasion of Iraq." *Daily Trust*, April 11, 2003.

Tilde, Aliyu. "No to 'Mullah Dictatorship.'" *Weekly Trust*. September 7–13, 2001.

———. "*We Are Boko Haram:* A Search into the Cultural Origins of Boko Haram in Nigeria." *Discourse #261*, August 11, 2009. https://aliyuutilde.wordpress.com/2010/05/13/discourse-261-we-are-boko-haram/.

Townsend, Mark. "Rape and Sexual Slavery Was Lure for UK ISIS Recruits with History of Sexual Violence." *The Guardian*, October 7, 2017. www.theguardian.com/world/2017/oct/07/isis-rape-slavery-british-recruits-islamic-state.

Umejei, Emeka, Tunde Opeseitan, and Abdulkareem Haruna. "Jang, Yakowa, Nyako Back Christian Militants, Says Boko Haram." *Daily Independent*, July 28, 2011.

COLONIAL RECORDS

Church Missionary Society (CMS)/ACC/237. *Papers of Walter Richard Samuel Miller*, University of Birmingham Cadbury Research Library, Church Mission Society Unofficial Papers, 1290–2017.

National Archives Kaduna (NAK)/SNP. Kadmineduc, August 10, 1937, from Kaduna to Residents.
National Archives Kaduna (NAK)/SNP. Confidential Memo 106/1914.

AUDIO-VISUAL SOURCES

"Muqabalar Dr Isa Ali Pantami da Shugaban Kungiyar Boko Haram Muhammad Yusuf." www.youtube.com/watch?v=QuGXdE-09eg.
"Sauka akan Fatawa Kukar Bakin Wake by Sheikh Aminu I Daurawa." www.youtube.com/watch?v=lkWUFGM_EOQ.
"Suwaye Yan Taliban, Imam Isa Ali Ibrahim Pantami." Dawah Nigeria. https://dawahnigeria.com/dawahcast/a/34152.
Voice of America. "Boko Haram Part 2: Anatomy of an Attack." www.youtube.com/watch?v=yI1Bu9PhaUA&t=300s, accessed February 10, 2020.

INTERVIEWS

Interviews with a dozen Nigerian Army Soldiers with combat experience on the frontlines of the antiinsurgency campaign.
Interviews with half a dozen former Boko Haram fighters in the Maiduguri axis.

THINK-TANK REPORTS AND DOCUMENTS FROM GOVERNMENTS AND MULTILATERAL ORGANIZATIONS

Abulfathi, Khalifa Aliyu Ahmed. *The Metamorphosis of Boko Haram: A Local's Perspective*. Sheikh Aliyu Ahmad Abulfathi Foundation, 2016.
Akum, Fonteh, and Malik Samuel. "Understanding the Dangerous Journey from Boko Haram to Rehabilitation." *ISS Today*, May 4, 2020. https://issafrica.org/iss-today/understanding-the-dangerous-journey-from-boko-haram-to-rehabilitation.
Braunschweiger, Amy. "Interview: Life After Boko Haram's Clutches." *Human Rights Watch*. https://features.hrw.org/features/Interview_2014/Life_After_Escaping_Boko_Harams_Clutches/index.html, accessed February 20, 2020.
Brechenmacher, Sakia. "Achieving Peace in Northeast Nigeria: The Reintegration Challenge." *National Endowment for Peace*, September 5, 2018. https://carnegieendowment.org/2018/09/05/achieving-peace-in-northeast-nigeria-reintegration-challenge-pub-77177.

"Jas vs. ISWAP: The War of the Boko Haram Splinters." Crisis Group Africa Briefing no. 196, March 26, 2024.

Report of the Constitution Drafting Committee. Government Printer, Lagos, 1976.

Soyinka, Wole. "Letter to Mubarak Bala on His 100th Day in Detention." *Humanists International*, August 6, 2020. https://humanists.international/2020/08/wole-soyinka-sends-message-of-solidarity-to-mubarak-bala/.

United Nations Human Rights Office of the High Commissioner. "UN Rights Experts Urge Nigeria to Immediately Release Humanist Accused of Blasphemy." www.ohchr.org/EN/NewsEvents/Pages/DisplayNews.aspx?NewsID=26123&LangID=E, accessed August 20, 2020.

Index

9/11 attacks, 7, 63, 79-80. *See also* Nigeria, Northern

Abdulfathi, Shaykh, 72-73; Sufism of, 73
Abduljalil b. Kadai, Abdullahi b., 14
Abubakar, Sa'adu, 4, 184; criticism of, by Muhammad Yusuf, 4
Abuja, 212
Adamawa State, 85, 161, 191, 194; churches/Christian communities, attacks on by Boko Haram, 67
Adamu, Abdallah Uba, 103
Adamu, Mahdi, 120
Afghanistan, US military action in, 7, 63
Ahmadu Bello University, 26
Aisha, Abu, 176
Akhwat Akwop, 67
Alao, Abiodun: *Rage and Carnage in the Name of God: Religious Violence in Nigeria*, 65-68
al-Baghdādī, 'Alī b. Muḥammad b. Ibrāhīm b. Khāzin: *Lubāb al-ta'wīl fī ma'ānī 'l-tanzīl*, 49
Albani, Sheikh Nasiruddin, 77
al-Banna, Hassan, 25
al-Barnawi, Abu Musab, 174
al-Barnawi, Khalid, 157

al-Hajj Dunama, Muhammad Yanbu b. Ali b., 14
al-Hajj Umar, Mai Ali b., 14
al-Hudaybi, Hassan, 25
al-Kanemi, Muhammad al-Amin, 15, 37; piety of, 15. *See also* Boko Haram; Yusuf, Muhammad
Allah, 3-4, 8, 77, 84, 87, 125-27, 147, 149, 202
al-Mawdūdī, Abū al-A'lā, 25
Alooma, Mai Idris, 166. *See also* Boko Haram; Bornu
al-Qaeda, 76, 78; Nigerian Salafis, support for, 76, 78-79. *See also* al-Qaeda in Iraq (AQI); al-Qaeda in the Islamic Maghreb (AQIM); Islamic State
al-Qaeda in Iraq (AQI), 76
al-Qaeda in the Islamic Maghreb (AQIM), 188, 242n74
al-Uthayimin, Ibn, 77
Alzarqawi, Abu Musab, 76
Ansaru, 189, 220n12; Fodiawa jihad and, 224n23
Asmau, Nana, 93; Yan Taru movement of, 93. *See also* modernity, Western
Association of Nigerian Authors, 103

269

Babangida, Ibrahim (Gen.), 56
Bauchi, 76; interreligious violence in (2001), 66
Bauchi Emirate, 90–91, 230n35
Bayero University, 103, 152
Bello, Ahmadu, 52. *See also* Nigeria, Northern, interreligious conflict in
Bello, Muhammad, 35, 37, 39, 45, 157, 164; Abdullahi Dan Fodio, disagreements with, 42; *al-Insaf*, 42; Hugh Clapperton and, 93; *Infakul Maisur* and, 160; *Infaq al-Maysur fi ta rich bilad al-Takrur*, 38; Jewish physicians, opposition to, 111–12; *ribats* and, 165; succession to sultanate and, 42; *Talkhīs aṭṭ-ṭibb al-nabawī*, 111–12; Usman Dan Fodio's rulings and, 37–39; Yandoto scholars, attack on, 38. *See also* Bornu; modernity, Western
bin Laden, Osama, 78; popularity of, in Northern Nigeria, 79. *See also* Kano; Pantami, Sheikh Dr. Isa Ali; Zaria, Auwal Albanin
Boko Haram: Bornu's history, rejection of and, 14–18; caliphate of (2014), 193; children of fighters and, 207; colonization, blame on and, 4; condemnation of by Islamic authorities, 2, 8; conventional views of, 21–23; creed of, 81; *dar al-Islam*, establishment of, as goal, 177; *dawla* (theocratic state) and, 45, 166, 208; as defenders of Islam, 34, 56, 67; demographic shifts, impact on, 208–11; history of Islamic reform and, 2, 5, 10, 13, 20–24, 29–31, 82, 215–17; internal ideological conflict and, 20, 35, 157–58, 174, 200–201, 205, 208; Islamic State, links with, 28, 185; Kanem-Bornu, history of and, 15–17; Kanuri community and, 34, 72; kidnap for ransom and, 189, 192; lack of Western education, exploitation of, 117–18; Mai Idris Alooma, praise for, 15; moral rejectionism and, 3, 5; motivations of, 3–4; Muhammad al-Amin al-Kanemi, condemnation of, 15; multimedia archive of, 22, 28–29; Muslim injustice/grievances, exploitation of, 56–58; Nigerian democracy, opposition to, 58, 68, 70; Nigerian Salafism, relationship with, 27–28, 80–81; Nigerian secular state, relationship with, 20, 22, 65, 82, 124; piety and ideal state, search for, 71–72, 83; preaching and, 5, 21–22, 82; propaganda of, 13, 22, 28, 50, 165; protection money/tribute and, 190, 192, 196–98, 243n87; radicalization and, 72; reformism, justification of, 44; "repentant" fighters and, 162–63, 238n24; rhetoric of, 18, 21–22; Salafi clerics, links with, 73, 80–82; Salafi clerics, opposition to, 81; Salafi clerics (quietist), relationship with, 80–82; Salafi-jihadism of, 1, 9, 27, 47, 72; sermons of, 28, 57, 62, 123, 176–77; smuggling/black market, as financing method, 189–92; sources for, 28–30; *Sulhu* (amnesty) and, 201, 203; Wahhabism and, 72. *See also* Boko Haram, antimodernism of; Boko Haram, jihad of (2009-); Boko Haram, warfare and; captivity and enslavement; Fodiawa tradition; Islamic State in West African Province (ISWAP); Jamāʿat Ahl al-Sunna li-Daʿwa wa-l-Jihād (JAS); Nigeria, Northern, Islamic reform in; politics, Islamic; Shekau, Abubakar; Yusuf, Muhammad

Boko Haram, antimodernism of, 3, 5, 10, 31, 46, 62, 70, 92–95, 103, 106, 117, 122, 152; *boko*, pronouncements and views on, 142–48; Christians and, 95; earlier Nigerian antimodernism, links with, 129, 131, 142–53; modern technology, use of, 137, 148–49; Muslims and, 95; Northern Nigerian public sphere, receptivity to, 95, 105–6; Sokoto jihad and, 92; suspicion/ambivalence and, 95; Western education, opposition to, 4–5, 31, 70, 73–74, 117–18, 122, 129, 141–48; "Western education is forbidden," mantra of, 117; Y'antatsine/Maitatsine, comparisons with, 110, 138–39

Boko Haram, jihad of (2009-), 2–3, 6, 17–18, 34–35, 37, 43–44, 80, 82, 148, 165, 177, 203–7; apostasy and, 46, 49, 187; Christian violence and, 67; death of Muhammad Yusuf (2009) and, 67; dissent/fragmentation and, 44, 46, 157, 200–201; excommunication *(takfīr)* and, 43, 48, 50; Fodiawa tradition and, 3, 12–14, 16–20, 30–31, 43, 47–50, 70, 92, 175–79, 224n23; interreligious violence in Northern Nigeria, relationship with, 60, 63–70; jihad, rules of and, 157; lack of governance and, 45; Muslims, attacks on, 37, 43–44, 48, 81, 201, 208, 214; national militaries, pressure from, 44–45; neocolonialism and, 70; open-ended nature of, 45; Salafism and, 1, 9, 27, 47–49, 71–78, 80; Sokoto jihad, differences from, 44–47, 49–50, 222n32; Sokoto jihad, similarities with, 43–44, 50; target groups of, 48. *See also* Adamawa State; Boko Haram, warfare and; Borno State; Islamic State in West African Province (ISWAP); Jamāʿat Ahl al-Sunna li-Daʿwa wa-l-Jihād (JAS); Shekau, Abubakar; Yobe State

Boko Haram, warfare and, 31–32; battlefield chanting and, 160–61; battlefield deception and, 159–60; battle formation of, as imitation of early Islamic warriors, 159; Cameroonian army and, 45, 169, 207; Chadian army and, 45, 169, 190, 207; child/teen soldiers and, 170, 208–11; desertions from, 208–9, 212; destruction/death, scale of, 156; drugs/stimulants and, 171; encirclement tactics and, 160–61; ethnic/religious links to local areas and, 155, 162–63, 192; *farmake* (surprise attacks) and, 161; Fodiawa jihad/Sokoto Caliphate, divergences from, 155–56, 170–71, 197; Fodiawa jihad/Sokoto Caliphate, similarities with, 156, 159–63, 171, 175–76, 197; improvised explosive devices (IEDs), use of, 162, 167–68; logistics and, 155, 163, 188; Muslim communities, raids on, 156; Nigerian Army and, 45, 156, 160, 162, 165–70, 189, 196, 199, 207, 209–11; Nigerien army and, 45, 169, 207; non-Muslim communities, raids on, 156; novel tactics of, 167; poor discipline and, 167; raiding of, 156, 171; recruitment and, 207–9; refugees, recruitment of, 209; *ribats*/war camps and, 162–63, 165–66; sleeper cells and, 162, 212–14; standing army, lack of and, 166; suicide bombing and, 167, 210–11; tactics, shift of towards ambushes and, 210–11; tactics of, as links to 19th c., 159–60, 197; technicals and, 168–69; terrain, mastery of, 155, 161–62; war booty *(ghanimah)* and, 171–74, 200; war economy and financing of, 155, 187–92, 196, 242n74; weaponry and technology of, 156, 160, 168–70, 187–88, 195–96. *See also* al-Qaeda in the Islamic Maghreb (AQIM); captivity and enslavement; Islamic State in West African Province (ISWAP); Jamāʿat Ahl al-Sunna li-Daʿwa wa-l-Jihād (JAS)

Borno State, 1, 33–34, 161–62, 191–92, 194, 199, 202, 210; churches/Christian communities, attacks on by Boko Haram, 67; Sharia, implementation in, 64; surveillance policies in, 211

Bornu, 33, 193; Islamic inauthenticity, concerns about, 17; Mai Idris Alooma, wars of, 14; Muhammad Bello and, 37; Rabih az-Zubayr ibn Fadl Allah, invasion of, 14–15; reformism in, 14, 17; war camps and, 166; ʿ*ulamā* of, 14. *See also* Abduljalil b. Kadai, Abdullahi b.; al-Hajj Dunama, Muhammad Yanbu b. Ali b.; al-Hajj Umar, Mai Ali b.; Ibn Furtuwa, Ahmad; Kanem-Bornu; Salih b. Ishaq, Muhammad; Sokoto Caliphate

Bourdieu, Pierre, 145

Brigaglia, Andrea, 72, 76, 79

Buhari, Muhammad, 110. *See also* modernity, Western

Burum Burum, 89

Cameroon, 32, 45, 177, 188–89, 191–92, 196

captivity and enslavement, 6, 10, 32, 154, 173–82; abolition of, in colonial Nigeria, 177–79, 183, 187; Ahmad Baba, theory of slavery and, 180–83; apostates, enslavement of, 180, 182–83, 187, 197; Boko Haram, *hamaji*, nickname for, 177–78; Boko Haram, revival and justification of, 49, 176–80, 183–87; Boko Haram, treatment of Muslims and, 171; Boko Haram and, 156, 167, 170–71, 175–78, 195, 197; colonial-era Islamic courts and, 183–84; concubinage and, 40, 49, 170, 173, 175–76, 187; conversion to Islam and, 66, 156, 170, 180; *dhimmis* and, 183; female slaves and, 156, 170, 176–77, 183, 187; Fodiawa jihad and, 156–57, 175, 177–84, 204; Hamman Yaji and, 177, 194; ideological fragmentation and, 175; Islamic State, enslavement of Yazidis and, 185; Islamic warfare and, 32; "Message to the Ummah" (Shekau, 2014) and, 186; non-Muslim girls/women and, 49, 156, 170–71, 187; non-Muslims and, 177, 180, 183, 197; Northern Nigerian ideology of enslavement and, 177–87; prisoner exchange and, 176; "Raid on Maiduguri" (Shekau, 2014) and, 186; ransom and, 2, 156, 176, 189, 192; Sokoto Caliphate and,

captivity and enslavement *(continued)*
    177, 180; Sokoto jihad and, 170; Sunna
    and, 185; Usman Dan Fodio, views of, 36,
    40, 49, 175–76, 181–84, 186–87. *See
    also* Chibok, abduction of girls from
    (2014); Sokoto jihad; Yusuf, Muhammad
Chad, 32, 45, 188–91, 196, 200
Chétima, Melchisedek, 177
Chibok, abduction of girls from (2014), 1–2,
    32, 49, 177, 179, 184; Boko Haram, jus-
    tification of, 2, 179, 185–86; #Bring-
    BackOurGirls movement and, 2; criticism
    of, by Muslim clerics, 184; Islamic State,
    use of as justification for enslavement,
    185; ransom and, 176, 240n55; Shekau,
    boasting/justification of and, 184, 186–
    87; support for, by Muslim clerics, 185
Christian Association of Nigeria (CAN), 67
Church Mission Society (CMS), 87, 146,
    236n62
Cohen, Ronald, 16

Daba, 89
Daily Independent (newspaper), 75
Daily Trust (newspaper): Malam Usman
    Muhammad Zunnaurain and, 151–52;
    Tijanni Sanusi debate and (2003), 17;
    Tilde/Dogorawa debate (2001) and, 151
Dan Fodio, Abdullahi, 35, 39, 41, 157; disa-
    greement with Usman over *takfir* and, 41,
    46; *Diyā' al-sulṭān wa-ghayrihi min
    al-ikhwān fī ahamm mā yuṭlabu
    'ilmuhu fī umūr al-zamān*, 111; leader-
    ship/succession, views on, 42; literalism/
    orthodoxy of, 41, 45; music/alcohol, con-
    demnation of, 111. *See also* Bello,
    Muhammad; modernity, Western; poli-
    tics, Islamic
Dan Fodio, Usman, 3, 19, 35, 45, 83, 92,
    156–58, 180; Ahmad Baba's theory of
    slavery and, 180–83; apostate Muslims'
    property, seizure of and, 49, 172, 182–
    83; *Bayān wujūb al-hijra 'alā 'l-'ibād*
    and, 12–13, 48–49, 181; *bid'a* (sinful
    innovations), criticism of, 11, 112; colo-
    nization, motivation for, 4; *Dar al-Islam*,
    absolutist position on, 37, 40; death of
    (1817), 42; excommunication *(takfīr)*
    rulings and, 11, 36–38, 40–41, 50, 181,
    221n16; flag of, 224n23; *Ihya 'us Sun-
    nah Wa Ikhamadul Bid'ah*, 104–5; jihad,
    rulings and pronouncements on, 36–41,
    47–49, 175–76, 180–82; jihadi-Salafism,

influence on, 47–49; *kufr* (unbelievers),
    view of, 39; moderation of, 39–41, 44;
    moral rejectionism and, 3, 5; non-Islamic
    practices, condemnation of, 36, 41;
    pledges of political loyalty, insistence on,
    38–39; postjihad views of, 36, 39, 83;
    pre-jihad legitimacy of, 35; prophetic tra-
    dition *(Sunna)* and, 11; relations with
    unbelievers *(muwalat/tawalli)*, views on,
    36, 39; Sharia law and, 3, 39, 182; syn-
    cretism *(takhlit)*, condemnation of, 11,
    36; "Tabbat Hakika" (Be Sure of That)
    and, 175; war booty, imposition of rules
    on and, 173; *Wathīqa (ila jamī') ahl
    al-Sūdān* and, 12. *See also* Asmau, Nana;
    Bello, Muhammad; Boko Haram; captiv-
    ity and enslavement; Dan Fodio, Abdul-
    lahi; Fodiawa jihad (19th c.); Gumi,
    Sheikh Mahmud Abubakar; Hausaland;
    jihad; modernity, Western; Nigeria,
    Northern, Islamic reform in; Shekau,
    Abubakar; Sokoto Caliphate
dan Mariya, Mallam Labbo, 130
Daurawa, Aminu, 79; suicide bombing, sup-
    port for, 79–80
DawahNigeria.com, 76
Doro, Bakura, 200–201
Dutse, 85

education, Western: access to and restriction
    of, in Northern Nigeria, 117–25, 234n17,
    234n23; *boko*, etymology and understand-
    ing of, 120–22, 141–43; *boko akida/boko
    sana'a* duality and, 123–24; conflation
    with Christianity and, 62, 121; corruption,
    association with, 117, 146; Islam, per-
    ceived threat to, 123–24, 143–47; lack of,
    correlation with extremism and, 118; mal-
    administration, association with, 117;
    missionaries and, 117–19, 121; moder-
    nity, association with, 113, 117, 145–49;
    Northern Nigerian folk wisdom/songs and,
    144–45; Nuhu Bayero *(My Life)*, account
    of, 146; Salafists, debates over and, 74, 80,
    147; Shekau, views of, 143–44, 146–47;
    Sunna and, 143; Yusuf, views of, 74, 80,
    142–43, 146, 148. *See also* Boko Haram,
    antimodernism of; Izala; Nigeria, North-
    ern; Nigeria, Northern, antimodernism in;
    Nigeria, Southern

Fadlalah, Rabih, 193, 222n32, 242n84. *See
    also* Sahel

INDEX 273

Fellowship of Christian Students (FCS), 59
Fodiawa jihad (19th c.), 3-5, 10-16, 19, 34-39, 82-84; afterlife of, 203-6, 217; *ahl al-sunna* and, 19-20; *aman* communities, raids on, 156-57; antimodernist legacy of, 94; apostasy and, 35, 40-41, 46, 83, 112; Ashari theology and, 83; battlefield chanting and, 160; battlefield deception and, 159-60; circular conditions of disappointment/disillusionment and, 83-84; clerical decrees and, 12; creed of, 13, 17; Dan Fodio's *Bayān wujūb al-hijra 'alā 'l-'ibād* and, 12-13; encirclement tactics and, 160-61; *farmake* (surprise attacks) and, 161; Fodiawa corpus and, 12-13, 47; Fulani nomads and, 11; governance, transition to, 45, 83-84; Hausa-Fulani and, 11-12, 16; Hausaland, non-Islamic practices in, 16, 36, 41; Hausa rulers and, 20, 36-38, 83, 182, 204-5; internal conflict and, 204-5; jihad, rules of and, 156-57; jihadi-Salafism, influence on, 47-48; Mahdi, links with and, 83; millenarianism and, 83; political radicalism and, 83; Prophet Muhammad, imitation of and, 159; purism/piety and, 12, 50, 82-84, 94; Qadiriyya Sufi brotherhood and, 12; raiding and, 156, 158, 161; secondary/postjihad phase of, 19-20, 83; Sharia law and, 12, 45; Sufi Islam and, 47, 71, 75, 95-96, 104, 136; *takfir*, debates over, 36-38, 40-41, 45; target groups of, 48; unbelievers, views on, 36, 45; war against Muslims, position on, 12, 48; war booty and, 172; war camps and, 160. *See also* Ansaru; Boko Haram, warfare and; captivity and enslavement; Fodiawa tradition; jihad; modernity, Western; Nigeria, Northern, Islamic reform in; politics, Islamic; Sokoto Caliphate; Sokoto jihad
Fodiawa tradition, 30, 34, 42-47; endurance of, as guide for reform, 92. *See also* Boko Haram; Gumi, Sheikh Mahmud Abubakar; Izala
Foi, Buji, 64

Ghazali, Zainab, 25
Gumi, Sheikh Mahmud Abubakar, 81, 234n25; Ahmadu Bello and, 97; *Al-Akidatus Sahihat Bi Muwafakatus Shariah*, 104; anti-Sufism of, 96-97, 104-5, 110, 135; exegesis of, 135; Fodiawa tradition and, 104-5; *hajj*, impact on, 97-98; Islamic modernity of simplicity and, 135-37; Jama'atu Nasril Islam (JNI), establishment of, 98; Kaduna, time in and, as deputy grand khadi, 96-97; Salafi followers of, 136, 151; Saudi Arabia, visits to, 97; secularism, view of, 97, 135-37; Sharia, view of, 96-97, 135; Sudan, time in and, 96; syncretism, attacks on, 135; theological teachings of, 135; Usman Dan Fodio and, 104-5; Wahhabi-Salafism, impact on, 97-98; *Where I Stand* (autobiography) and, 96; World Muslim League and, 97. *See also* Izala; modernity, Western; Nigeria, Northern, Islam in
Gwandu, 85

Hamza, Mallam, 89-91; *Tarikh 'Umara Bauchi* and, 90-91. *See also* Isawa; Kano Emirate
Hausaland, 12, 16, 33, 38, 40-41, 120, 159, 164, 166, 172; Islam, spread of in (15th-16th c.), 38; postjihad society in, 16, 204-5; traditions of warfare in, 172; tripartite classification of (Usman Dan Fodio), 181-82. *See also* Fodiawa jihad (19th c.)
Hawa, Saeed, 25
Hayat, Sa'id b., 222n32
Hegghammer, Thomas, 81
Hiskett, Mervyn, 92, 140, 175
HumAngle Media Foundation/Premium Times Center for Investigative Journalism, 189-90, 209, 211-12

Ibn Furtuwa, Ahmad, 14; *Ta'rīkh Mai Idris wa-Ghazāwatihī*, 14
Ibrahim, Abdullahi Lamido Musa, 79
Idris, Mohammed, 199
Ikara, 61
Ikhwan (Egypt), 25
Indimi, Alhaji Mohammed, 72
International Crisis Group, 157
Iranian revolution (1979), 25-26. *See also* Nigeria, Northern, Islamic reform in
Iraq, US invasion of, 7, 63
Isawa: Christian missionaries and, 87; Isawa-Ningi rebellion and, 86-92; Jesus and, 86-88; Kharijites, similarities with, 91; Mallam Hamza and, 90; Mallam Ibrahim and, 87-89; Mallam Yahaya and, 89; persecution of, 86, 88-89; Prophet Muhammad, view of, 87-88; syncretism and, 86, 91; theology of, 87

Ishaq, Ja'afaru, 133
Islamic Movement of Nigeria (IMN), 26, 64, 73; criticism of the Zamfara declaration and, 64; Ibraheem El Zakzaky and, 26, 64, 73–74, 228n5
Islamic State, 28, 184–85, 200, 203, 243n6, 244n20; collapse of, 215; school curriculum of, 202. *See also* Boko Haram; captivity and enslavement
Islamic State in West African Province (ISWAP), 157, 185, 200–201, 238n8; ambushes and, 210; children, training of and, 201–2, 212; Fodiawa jihad, similarities with, 158; idolatry/secularism, opposition to, 202; local populations, relationship with, 157, 211; propaganda of, 202, 243n6; statecraft and, 158
Islamophobia, 63, 68
Izala, 24–25, 27, 96, 101–2, 134–37; anti-Sufism and, 134–36; Boko Haram's view of, 137; Fodiawa tradition, links with, 101; Islamic modernity of simplicity and, 98, 134–36; literalist piety, vision of, 135–36; music, opposition to, 101; Northern Nigerian antimodernism, alignment with, 136; Saudi financial support for, 98; Western education, opposition to, 104; Western modernity, opposition to, 97, 102, 104–5, 134–36. *See also* Musa, Shaykh Yakubu; Nigeria, Northern, Islam in

Jamaat-e-Islami, 25
Jamā'at Ahl al-Sunna li-Da'wa wa-l-Jihād (JAS), 157–58, 200–201, 238n6; Muslims, raids on, 157–58; oath of allegiance *(bay'ah)* to Islamic State and, 200
Jedo, Ali, 156
jihad, 2–6, 73–74, 154; Dan Fodio's *Bayān wujūb al-hijra 'alā 'l-'ibād*, as literary basis for, 12–13; deviation from ideals of, 38–39; dhimmis and, 183; *fardh ayn* (obligation) and, 75; global jihad and, 74–79, 222n32; *hadiths* and, 164; ideological fragmentation and, 175, 240n52; injustice and, 8; internal disruptors *('yan tawaye)* and, 20; jihad fatigue and, 175, 201, 214–16, 244n20; jihadi gradualism and, 77; Muslims, killing of, Sharia and, 78; Nigerian secularism and, 27–28; Northern Nigeria and, 2, 11–14, 18, 31; purification and, 50; quietist Salafi clerics and, 228n6; Qur'an and, 157; rules of, 157–58; secondary jihads and, 20; state repressions of, 20; Sunna and, 77, 157; Taliban/al-Qaeda and, 76; target groups of, 48; theological/political dissonance and, 37; variegated discourse of, 8; war booty, acquisition and sharing of, 171–74. *See also* Boko Haram, jihad of (2009-); Boko Haram, warfare and; captivity and enslavement; neojihad; Pantami, Sheikh Dr. Isa Ali; politics, Islamic; Salafism

Kaduna, 59, 61, 135, 139, 212; interreligious violence in (2000), 66
Kaduna State, 54, 61
Kafanchan, 59. *See also* Nigeria, Northern, interreligious conflict in; Qur'an
Kanama, 77
Kanem, 14. *See also* Kanem-Bornu
Kanem-Bornu, 3, 14; Dan Fodio's jihad on, 37, 182; Mais (rulers) of, 15–16; political unrest in, 17; religious unrest in, 14; "Waqu'i al-Rābih" (Ali Arkwayami) and, 14–15; *'ulamā'* of, 15. *See also* Boko Haram; Hausaland
Kankanri, 89
Kano, 86, 88, 96, 99, 100, 102, 139, 181, 212
Kano Emirate, 87–91, 148; Emir Aliyu and, 119; Mallam Hamza and, 89–91; peasant anti-tax revolt in (1840s-), 89–90; persecution in, 89–90. *See also* Isawa
Kano State, 7, 103; censorship in, 232n72; Osama bin Laden, popularity in, 7–8, 79
Kassim, Abdulbasit, 28, 62, 174; *The Boko Haram Reader* (with Michael Nwankpa), 28–29
Kastfelt, Niels, 52
Katsina, 38, 181
Katsina State: Sharia law in (2000-)., 101
Kawuri, 89
Kebbi, 164, 204
Kepel, Gilles, 175, 214
Khomeini, Ruhollah, 25

Lagos, 121, 212
Lake Chad, region of, 15, 17, 44, 157, 191–94, 201; Boko Haram presence/strongholds in, 161, 164, 188–89; civilians in, 203; Islam in, 15; raiding/nonstate violence in, 17, 193, 222n32; refugees/internally displaced peoples in, 190, 196, 198;

ribats in, 164; self-preservation/defense in, 196; state armies and, 157, 190
Last, Murray, 18–20, 106–7, 155, 158. *See also* jihad; politics, Islamic
Lemo, Sani Rijiyar, 79
Libya, 188
Linden, Ian, 87–88, 91
Logams, Chunun, 52
Lovejoy, Paul, 178
Lubeck, Paul, 106
Lugard, Frederick, 121

MacEachern, Scott, 17, 177, 191–96, 222n32. *See also* Sahel
Mahalli, Ibn Abi, 112, 233n5
Mahmud, Ja'far Adam, 72–73, 79; assassination of, by Boko Haram, 81; Boko Haram leadership, links with, 72–73; Wahhabism/Salafism and, 73
Maiduguri, 73, 138, 148, 210; Boko Haram's base, raid on (2009), 138; safe zones in, 196; Y'antatsine base, raid on (1982), 138–39
Maikaratu, Abubakar, 130–31
Maitatsine: antimodernism of, 138–42; armed conflict and, 138–39; folk Islam of, 139; *haram* prohibitions of, 140–41, 236n47; heterodox theology of, 138–40; preaching style of, 142; Qur'anic exegesis and, 139–41; Sunni establishment, attacks on, 138; Western technology and, 138–42; Y'antatsine movement and, 138–40. *See also* Maiduguri
Makarfi, Ahmad, 66
Mandara Mountains, region of, 17, 44, 191; Boko Haram presence/strongholds in, 161, 164, 193; ethnic groups in, 195; Gwoza and, 193; raiding/nonstate violence in, 17, 191, 193, 195; *ribats* and, 164; self-preservation/defense in, 195
Marshall, Ruth, 53
Marwa, Muhammadu. *See* Maitatsine
Mecca, 87
millenarianism, 86, 107; Digawa and, 86; Liman Yamusa (Sufi) and, 85; Salihawa and, 86. *See also* Fodiawa jihad (19th c.); Isawa; Sokoto Caliphate
Miller, Rev. Walter, 87, 146, 236n62
modernity, Western, 6, 43; Abdullahi Dan Fodio and, 93–94, 111; apostasy, association with, 128–29, 145; *bid'a* (innovation) and, 94, 101–2, 130; British rule/Christianity, conflation with, 114, 125–30; colonial modernity *(zamani)* and, 95, 113; community, disruptions to and, 105–7; Fodiawa and, 31, 93–95, 111–12; globalization and, 151; Gumi and, 96–97, 135–37; injustice, association with, 4; insularity *vs.* cosmopolitanism and, 104–5, 107; Islam, as perceived threat to, 125–28; millenarianism and, 107; moral panic, Northern Nigeria and, 106–7; Muhammad Bello and, 93–94; Muhammad Buhari and, 110; Nana Asmau and, 93; quasi-theological critiques of, 31; Shekau and, 147, 236n46; Sokoto jihad and, 92; Usman Dan Fodio and, 93–94, 111. *See also* Boko Haram, antimodernism of; education, Western; Izala; Maitatsine; Nigeria, Northern, antimodernism in; Nigeria, Northern, interreligious conflict in; Nigeria, Northern, Islamic reform in; Waziri Buhari, Muhammadu
Morocco, Alouite, 94
Musa, Shaykh Yakubu, 101
Muslim Student Organization (MSO), 25
Muslim Students' Society of Nigeria (MSSN), 7, 25, 63; anthem of, 8; Kano conference of (1980), 25, 223n33; *Radiance*, official magazine of, 24

neojihad, 8–9, 78
New Nigerian, The (newspaper), 24, 102
New Nigerian Weekly (newspaper), 102
Niasse, Ibrahim, 133; fatwa on use of the radio (1954), 133–34, 148
Niger, 32, 45, 188–89, 191, 196, 200
Nigeria, Central, 76
Nigeria, Northern, 1–2, 4; 9/11 attacks, impact of in, 7; 1948 Education Ordinance and, 122; anti-Christian feeling in, 113, 120–21; anticolonialism in, 110–15; *boko*, etymology of, 120; British ban on missionary activities in, 118, 121–22; British colonization of, 31, 51, 63–64, 113–15; British Protectorate in (1900-), 113, 118; Burmi, showdown at, 114–15; caliphate, aspiration for in, 7; Educationally Less Developed States (ELDS), designations of, 122; English teaching in, 122; Hausa Muslims and, 120; Imam Musa and, 114–15; Iraq/Afghanistan/War on Terror, impact of US involvement in, 7, 63, 73–74, 79–80; Katsina College and, 118–19; Mahdist rebellions and,

Nigeria, Northern *(continued)*
113–15; Malam Jibrilla Gaini and, 114; missionary propaganda against Fulani and, 121; precolonial religious politics in, 33; religious public sphere in, 7–9, 79; Satiru revolt (1906) and, 113; secularity in, 4; Sokoto Caliphate, resonance for population of, 4–5; Sultan Muhammadu Attahiru I and, 113–15; Sultan Muhammadu Attahiru II and, 113, 115; Western education, access to in, 117–25; Western education, suspicion of in, 119–20; Western education, two-tiered system in, 118–19, 145. *See also* captivity and enslavement; Nigeria, Northern, Islamic reform in; Nigeria, Northern, Islam in; Nigeria, Southern; warfare, Islamic

Nigeria, Northern, antimodernism in: accommodation/strategic engagement with colonial modernity and, 115–16; anti-British uprisings and, 110, 114–15; anticolonialism and, 31, 110, 112–16, 125–29; anxiety and, 110; artistic and Hausa literary expressions of, 110, 125–31, 134, 150; *bid'a* (innovations) and, 112, 130; *boko*, rhetoric of and, 142–43, 145–46; British rule and Christianity, reaction against, 114–17, 125–32; debates/treatises and, 111; financial insurance and, 152; Fodiawa jihad, importance for, 109; folk traditions and, 110, 124–25, 129, 132, 150; globalization and, 151; Gumi religious revolution and, 110; Imam Umar and, 125; Islam, as perceived threat to, 125–28, 132, Malam Shi'itu and, 125; music/entertainment and, 151; piety and, 94, 116, 152; radio technology, debate over (1954), 132–34; romanticized/ideal past, yearning for and, 132; Sokoto Caliphate writings and, 112; Western colonial-era education and, 109, 117–25, 144; Western technology and culture, suspicion of, 125–34, 138, 148–53, 235n39; Yantatsine/Maitasine sect and, 110. *See also* Boko Haram, antimodernism of; Gumi, Sheikh Mahmud Abubakar; Izala; Nigeria, Northern, Islamic reform in; Qur'an; Waziri Buhari, Muhammadu

Nigeria, Northern, interreligious conflict in, 30, 50–54; Ahmadu Bello, promotion of Islam and, 52–53; Christian Atyap and, 60–61; Christian identity, perceived threats to and, 53, 58, 66; Christian-Muslim competition and, 52–54, 60–61; Christian violence/radicalism, 33–34, 50–54, 58–62, 65–68, 70; Civilian Joint Task Force (JTF) and, 67, 194; colonial Christianity and, 51–52; Evangelical/ Pentecostal organizations and, 53–54; expansionist Islam and, 51; forced conversions, claims of, 66; Fulani herdsmen and, 66–67; Hausa-Fulani Muslims and, 59–61; Judeo-Christian culture, fear of and, 51; Kafanchan crisis (1987) and, 54, 58–61; mission schools and, 51–52; modernity and, 50–51; mosques/ churches, violence against and, 66; Muslim identity, perceived threats to and, 52, 59, 62; Muslim violence/radicalism, 59–61, 66–67, 70; political Christianity and, 34, 52; postcolonial period and, 51, 53–56, 62, 65–70; radicalism, growth of (2000s), 62–63; religion, as source of identity and, 53; Sharia constitutional debate (1979) and, 55–56, 58; Sharia implementation (1999-2001) and, 64–68, 70; *shirk* (polytheism and idolatry), criticism of, 102; Sobon Gari (Kano) crisis (1982) and, 54; Southern Nigeria, contrast with, 53; Zangon Kataf conflict (1992) and, 60–61. *See also* Akhwat Akwop; Bauchi; Boko Haram, jihad of (2009-); Kaduna; Wukari

Nigeria, Northern, Islamic reform in, 5–7, 9, 63–64, 84–92, 179, 206; *Ahl al-Sunna wa'l-Jama'a* and, 85; alternative Islamic communities, creation of, 95; anti-Sufism and, 96; betrayal, criticism of and, 11, 85; *bid'a* (innovation), opposition to, 101–2; Boko Haram, deviation from, 10; Boko Haram, links with, 9–11, 15, 21, 23, 57, 74, 82, 215–17; circular conditions of disappointment/disillusionment and, 83–84, 95; Fodiawa jihad, importance for, 12, 85, 92–96, 104; Gumi-Izala revolution and, 95–98, 110; Hausa musical performances, backlash against, 101–2; Hausa *soyayya* literature, backlash against, 102–3; history of, 10–18, 23–28; insecurity/precarity, feelings of and, 50, 105–6; Iranian revolution, importance for, 25; Islamic conservatism and, 92–93; Izala reformism and, 104–5; Kannywood (Hausa cinema), viewed as impious and, 100–101; literalist creed and, 75; migration, impact on, 106–7; moral vigilantism and, 99–104; Nigerian democratic transition and, 54–57; piety in, as response to modernity, 94–95, 99, 107–8, 146; political Islam and, 75; pre-Islamic practices and, 16; Prophet, emulation of and, 85; quietist Salafi clerics and, 10, 73; Qur'an, adherence to and, 85; religious public sphere and, 7–9; romanticized/ideal past, yearning for and, 82–84, 107, 132; Salafism, ascendence of, 96, 99–102; Sarkin Karuwai controversy (Kano), 99–100; scholars of, 11; Sharia constitutional debate (1979) and, 56; Sharia law, criminal codes and (1999–2001)., 63–64, 108; Sharia law and, 44, 69, 81, 100; *shirk* (polytheism and idolatry), criticism of, 11; social/economic networks, dislocation of and, 105–7. *See also* Boko Haram, jihad of (2009-); Bornu; Gumi, Sheikh Mahmud Abubakar; Kanem; Kanem-Bornu; Kano; Sokoto Caliphate

Nigeria, Northern, Islam in, 10, 21; anti-Sufism and, 24, 96; *bid'a* (sinful innovations), condemnation of, 24; disillusionment and, 25; excommunication *(takfīr)* and, 11; Fodiawa jihad, legacy of in, 17, 26; four phases of, in postcolonial Nigeria, 23–28; global jihad, popularity of in, 79; Hausa Muslim dynasties in, 12, 16; international influences on, 25–26; intolerant Muslim, stereotype of, 58; Islamic orthodoxy, maintenance of and, 92–93; Islamic revivalism in, 7–8, 25; "Islam Only" campaign and, 24, 26; Izala movement, impact on, 98; jihad, aspiration for in, 7, 79; jihadist militancy in, 2, 11–14, 18; Mallam Ibraheem Suleiman and, 24; Muslim majority in, 4, 6; political Islam in, 7, 9–10, 75; reformist youth and, 25–26; Salafism and, 26–28, 71, 75–79, 96–98; Saudi Islamic practice, different from, 97–98; secular politics and democracy, participation in/rejection of, 24–27, 73; Sharia and, 27, 31, 34, 79, 96–97; Shia Islam in, 26; Sufi Islam in, 71–72, 79; *ummah* and, 24; westernization, clerical suspicions about, 92–93. *See also* bin Laden, Osama; Fodiawa jihad (19th c.); Fodiawa tradition; Gumi, Sheikh Mahmud Abubakar; Nigeria, Northern, Islamic reform in; Sokoto Caliphate; Taliban

Nigeria, Southern, 54, 56, 61, 122; education gap vis-a-vis Northern Nigeria, 122; Western education in, 118

Nigeria, state of: Corporate Affairs Commission of, 136; corruption in, 117; democracy, transition to, 55–58; liberal democracy and, 57; Muslim reform and, 56–58; Operation Safe Corridor and, 213; *On the Political Future of Nigeria* (reformist manifesto) and, 57; secularism and, 2, 7, 20, 22, 46, 63–64, 208; Sharia, place of in, 57; Sharia constitutional debate (1979) and, 55–56; United States, weapons supplies from, 203

Nigerian Council of Registered Insurance Brokers (NCRIB), 152

Ningi, 90, 204

Nur, Mamman, 46, 174, 176, 224n23; Abubakar Shekau, disagreements with, 46, 174–75

Nwankpa, Michael, 62. *See also* Kassim, Abdulbasit

Oloyede, Ishaq, 56
Omar, Mullah, 76–77
Oritsejafor, Pastor Ayo, 67
Ostein, Philip, 55
Ottoman Caliphate, 94
Oyedepo, David, 67

Pantami, Sheikh Dr. Isa Ali, 75–79, 220n12; Bin Laden, view of, 78; Boko Haram as misguided, view of, 81; jihad, view of, 75–77; Sunnah, support for, 76–77; "Su waye Yan Taliban" sermon of (2006), 76; Taliban, as model for Northern Nigerians, 76–77; Taliban/al-Qaeda, support for, 76. *See also* Yusuf, Muhammad

Philips, John Edward, 163–64, 166, 170
Pieri, Zacharia, 16
politics, Islamic, 18–19; 7th c. Islam, relevance of to, 18–19; *ahl al-sunna* and, 19; Boko Haram, relationship with, 19; electoral council *(shura)* and, 42; internal rebels *('yan tawaye)* and, 19–20; rebellion, susceptibility to, 18–19; secondary jihad/counteroffensives and, 19–20; secular/theocratic governments, counterinsurgency and, 19–20; succession and, 42; Sunna, interpretation/application of and, 18–20; technology, acceptance/rejection of, 18–19

poverty, 3–4, 72, 117, 146, 207

INDEX

Qadiriyya Sufi brotherhood, 12, 85, 134
Qur'an, 8, 49, 85, 87, 119, 135, 157, 164, 182, 187, 200; interpretive elasticity of, 140–41; Kafanchan crisis (1987) and, 59; radio recitation of, debate over (1954), 132–34. *See also* jihad; Maitatsine; Yusuf, Muhammad
Qutb, Sayyid, 25

Rano, 89
refugees, 194–96; nomadism/seminomadism and, 196, 198; refugee camps and, 196; tribute and, 196, 198, 243n87. *See also* Boko Haram, warfare and; Lake Chad, region of

Sahel, 112, 161, 191, 203, 206, 213; ecology of, 207; Fodiawa jihad and, 193; kinship networks and, 196–98; militancy and violence in, 167–69, 171, 191–98; political economy in, 32, 191–93; precolonial *vs.* modern situation in, 192–98; Rabih Fadlalah and, 193; self-preservation, history of in, 191, 194–98
Salafism: Boko Haram, demarcation from, 27; jihad, belief in and, 82; jihad, timing of and, 77–78, 81; jihadi-Salafism and, 1, 9–10, 12–13, 47–49, 75, 80, 96, 152; pietism and, 81; quietist Salafism and, 10, 73–74, 80, 220n14; reformism and, 9, 26–27, 80–81; Saudi Arabia and, 26–27, 151; secular politics and democracy, as *Kufr al-Akbar*, 26–27; Sheikh Muqbil bin Hādī and, 26; *A shiga a gyara* (Hausa slogan) and, 81; Sudan and, 151; Sunnah, adherence to, 77, 80; violent jihad, support for, 75–78; Western technology and, 134. *See also* Nigeria, Northern, Islamic reform in; Nigeria, Northern, Islam in
Salih b. Ishaq, Muhammad, 14; *Ta'rīkh Birni Gazargamu*, 14
Salkida, Ahmad, 212
Sambisa Forest Reserve, 193, 201, 208
Sani Umar, Muhammad, 127
Sanusi, Muhammadu, 133
Sharia, 3, 96; Christians, fear of, 55; colonization, impact on, 4, 55, 226n40; Da'wa group and, 101; federal Sharia Court of Appeal, proposal for in 1979 constitution and, 55–56; Supreme Council for Sharia in Nigeria and, 226n40; use of for criminal cases, 63. *See also* Boko Haram; Borno State; Dan Fodio, Usman; Gumi, Sheikh Mahmud Abubakar; Nigeria, Northern, interreligious conflict in; Nigeria, Northern, Islamic reform in; Yusuf, Muhammad; Zamfara State
Shekau, Abubakar, 2, 13, 15, 43, 45, 157, 174, 176; death of (2021), 22, 47, 157, 199–200, 203; Hamman Yaji and, 177; idolatry, condemnation of, 147; jihad rules, violation of, 157; Niasse's fatwa of (1954), links with, 148–49; secularism/polytheism, conflation of, 147; Sokoto Caliphate and, 13; *takfir* on Chibok/Baga, 46; Usman Dan Fodio, comparison with, 45. *See also* Chibok, abduction of girls from (2014); education, Western; modernity, Western; Nur, Mamman
Sheriff, Ali Modu, 64
Smaldone, Joseph, 159–60, 173
Sokoto Caliphate, 3–4, 12, 16, 31, 33–34, 71, 83, 113, 159; battlefield deception and, 159; battle formation of, as imitation of early Islamic warriors, 159; Bornu, *takfir* declaration/jihad against, 17, 37, 40; creation of (19th c.), 12–13; destruction of, by colonial forces, 4, 13, 113–14, 233n10; emirs/aristocracy, criticisms of, 84, 86; internal cohesion of, 35; Isawa-Ningawa rebellion and, 86–92; Islamic heterodoxy, as challenge to, 84–92; Maliki jurisprudential tradition and, 92, 172; millenarianism Sufism and, 85; rebellions and, 85–92, 204–6; *ribats* and, 163–66; standing army, lack of and, 166; taxation, opposition to, 86, 89; Tijaniyya opposition to Qadiriyya *tariqa* and, 85; war booty and, 172; weapons of, 170. *See also* Abubakar, Sa'adu; Boko Haram; captivity and enslavement; Isawa; Kano Emirate; millenarianism; Nigeria, Northern; Yusuf, Muhammad
Sokoto jihad, 3–5, 31, 33–43, 82, 204–6, 222n32; disagreement/fragmentation and, 35–36, 39–42, 157–58; enslavement and, 36, 39; finite nature of, 45; *jama'a* (army) and, 38–39; moderation of, 39–41, 44; preaching phase of, 41, 43; *From Rebels to Rulers* (Naylor) and, 35–36; *ribats* and, 163–64; *shirk* (idolatry) and, 41; *takfir* discourse and, 36–41, 43; theological improvisation and, 37; triumviral leadership of, 35–36, 111, 157–58, 173, 220n8, 238n25; violence

against Muslims and, 37–41; war camps and, 163; Yandoto clerical community and, 37–38. *See also* Boko Haram; Sokoto Caliphate
Sokoto jihad tradition. *See* Fodiawa tradition
Stoddard, Edward, 158
Sudan, 83, 96, 115, 151, 173, 181, 188; Western Darfur and, 193. *See also* Gumi, Sheikh Mahmud Abubakar; Salafism
Suleiman, Apostle Johnson, 67
Sunna, 11, 18, 48, 76, 85, 182; *Ahl al-sunna* and, 19–20; dress code and, 76; piety and, 135. *See also* captivity and enslavement; education, Western; Taliban; Yusuf, Muhammad
syncretism, 3, 16, 86; folk Islam and, 91; Sufism and, 135. *See also* Dan Fodio, Usman; Gumi, Sheikh Mahmud Abubakar; Isawa

Tafawa Balewa Local Government, 66
Taliban, 76–78; Nigerian Salafis, support for, 76–79; Nigerian Taliban and, 77; popularity of, in Northern Nigeria, 79; Sunna and, 77. *See also* Pantami, Sheikh Dr. Isa Ali
Thurston, Alexander, 82
Tibenderana, Peter, 121
Tijaniyya Sufi brotherhood, 85, 133–34
Tilde, Aliyu, 120, 124, 138
Triumph, The (newspaper), 24
Tsakuwa, 89–90
Turaki, Yusufu, 52
Turawa, 89

Umar, Muhammad Sani, 113; *Islam and Colonialism*, 115
Umbuta, 90

van Beek, Walter, 177

warfare, Islamic, 6, 10; Northern Nigeria and, 14; *ribats* and, 163–64. *See also* Boko Haram, jihad of (2009–); Boko Haram, warfare and; captivity and enslavement
Watts, Michael, 105–6
Waziri Buhari, Muhammadu, 115; colonial modernity, position on, 115–16; "Risālat al-wazīr ilā ahl al-'ilm wa al-tadabbur" (1903), 115–16, 134

Weekly Trust (newspaper), 24, 99, 101, 226n43
Whitsitt, Novian, 102
World Food Program, 190
Wukari: interreligious violence in (2010), 66

Yelwan Shendam, 76
Yemen, 26
Yobe State, 77, 191–92, 202; churches/Christian communities, attacks on by Boko Haram, 67
Yusuf, Muhammad, 3, 15, 27, 43, 64, 220n12, 224n23; captive women, sermons on, 176–77, 240n56; death of (2009), 67, 72; Hausa antimodernist poetry and, 129; heterodox theology of, 129, 140; implementation of Sharia, reaction to, 64–65; "Islam-only" activism and, 74; Kanem-Bornu Mais, criticisms of, 16; Muhammad al-Amin al-Kanemi, criticism of, 15–16; Muslim persecution, view of, 68; Nigerian secularism, view of, 27–28, 68–69, 80; Pantami, debate with, 77, 80; preaching style of, 139, 142; Qur'anic exegesis and, 129, 140, 142–43, 176, 240n56; rejectionism/jihad and, 68, 77; *ribats* and, 165; Salafi clerics, relationship with, 27–28, 69, 73, 80, 84; Salafi clerics (quietist), relationship with, 80, 84; sermons of, 57, 68; Sokoto Caliphate, view of, 3–5; Sunna and, 80; "Tarihin Muslumai" (2007 sermon) and, 15. *See also* Abubakar, Sa'adu; al-Barnawi, Abu Musab; captivity and enslavement; education, Western; Foi, Buji

Zamfara State, 63–64; Sharia penal code, implementation in (1999), 63–64. *See also* Islamic Movement of Nigeria (IMN)
Zaria, 59
Zaria, Auwal Albanin, 79; assassination of, by Boko Haram, 81, 220n13; Bin Laden, association with, 79
Zaria Emirate, 61, 89, 146
Zaria massacre (2015), 228n5
Zazzau Emirate, 133, 146, 148
Zenn, Jacob, 16, 188–90
Zulum, Babagana, 199

Founded in 1893,
UNIVERSITY OF CALIFORNIA PRESS
publishes bold, progressive books and journals
on topics in the arts, humanities, social sciences,
and natural sciences—with a focus on social
justice issues—that inspire thought and action
among readers worldwide.

The UC PRESS FOUNDATION
raises funds to uphold the press's vital role
as an independent, nonprofit publisher, and
receives philanthropic support from a wide
range of individuals and institutions—and from
committed readers like you. To learn more, visit
ucpress.edu/supportus.

www.ingramcontent.com/pod-product-compliance
Lightning Source LLC
Chambersburg PA
CBHW021340230426
43666CB00006B/355